Theorizing Sound Writing

Edited by Deborah Kapchan

THEORIZING SOUND WRITING

Wesleyan University Press Middletown, Connecticut

Wesleyan University Press
Middletown CT 06459
www.wesleyan.edu/wespress

Manufactured in the United States of America
Designed by Mindy Basinger Hill
Typeset in Minion Pro

Library of Congress Cataloging-in-Publication Data

NAMES: Kapchan, Deborah A. (Deborah Anne)
TITLE: Theorizing sound writing / edited by Deborah Kapchan.
DESCRIPTION: Middletown, Connecticut : Wesleyan University Press, [2017] |
Series: Music/culture | Includes bibliographical references and index.
IDENTIFIERS: LCCN 2016030957 (print) | LCCN 2016038984 (ebook) |
ISBN 9780819576644 (cloth : alk. paper) | ISBN 9780819576651 (pbk. : alk. paper) |
ISBN 9780819576668 (ebook)
SUBJECTS: LCSH: Musicology. | Ethnomusicology. | Sound (Philosophy)
CLASSIFICATION: LCC ML3797 .T46 2017 (print) | LCC ML3797 (ebook) |
DDC 780.72—dc23
LC record available at https://lccn.loc.gov/2016030957

5 4 3 2 1

CONTENTS

Acknowledgments

The original idea for this volume was inspired by my reading of a special issue of the journal *Anthropology and Humanism*, entitled "The Art of Ethnography: Narrative Style as a Research Method." Edited by Russell Sharman, the writers in this issue (who included Paul Stoller, Kirin Narayan, Ruth Behar, and Edith Turner, among others) began from a simple premise: style creates knowledge. They didn't put it that simply; however, their volume brought attention to the fact that the way we write—the genres and styles we employ—is in fact a mode of world making. Of course, Bakhtin said as much, as have others. The authors in this volume, however, sought to raise the bar for academic, and in particular, ethnographic writing, while at the same time questioning the relation of style to method. Most of the authors were relating the method of embodied ethnography to styles of writing, making analogies between the two orders of mediation. However, this inspired me to think of the implications of writing style as a method itself. And to take it further, to reconsider the relation and limits of sound and writing, sound method and sound theory. What's more, I was interested in how sonic forms of knowledge might transform pedagogies in the academy.

Before it was a volume, *Theorizing Sound Writing* was a double roundtable event at the Society for Ethnomusicology meetings in Mexico City in 2009. The response was enthusiastic, and in the spring of 2010, my then colleague Jason Stanyek and I applied for funding from the New York University Humanities Center, which subsequently provided support for two years of fructuous meetings with colleagues and advanced graduate students from New York University, Columbia University, University of Pennsylvania and the City University of New York Graduate Center. I thank Jane Tylus, the director of the center, and Aysa Berger, for providing the forum for such rich discussions during two years. Jason Stanyek, my colleague in the Music Department, co-directed this working group.

His mark in the volume is indelible as are the ideas spawned by the collective. He has been an ideal colleague, friend and collaborator, and we sorely miss him now that he has taken his new position at Oxford University. I feel privileged to have had the chance to work with him. My colleague Martin Daughtry and I subsequently collaborated on a graduate seminar called *The Politics of Listening* in the spring of 2013. The energy and ideas generated in that class (and in hours of discussion as Martin and I walked to and from our respective sons' elementary school) enriched my life beyond what words can describe and continue to do so.

I also extend my thanks to all the participants in the Theorizing Sound working group, composed of colleagues and advanced graduate students from across disciplines and universities. I am not exaggerating when I say that our meetings have been some of the most stimulating experiences of my career. Thinking with, rather than against, such brilliant minds around the table has been a tremendous honor. In particular, I give heartfelt thanks to my inspiring students (many now colleagues), Ana Chavez, Serap Erincin, Ana Pais, Alex Waterman and Charmy Wells for volunteering their time and energy with such care and enthusiasm.

Theorizing Sound Writing

DEBORAH KAPCHAN

The Splash of Icarus

Theorizing Sound Writing / Writing Sound Theory

The zendo is on the eleventh floor of a loft on south Broadway, in a long rectangular room fitted with black meditation pads and cushions on polished wood floors. Gongs, metallic bowls, and wooden blocks sound periodically as we sit, listening. The back windows look over the lower East Side of Manhattan. In May they are open to the sounds of New York: trucks accelerating, car horns, sirens, objects being lifted and released onto loading docks—the clangs and reverberations of mechanical urban life. And with them, birds sing, perched precariously on roof garden trees on their way back north.

Sitting here, I taste my body the way a baby tastes itself, before it is encumbered with awareness of its skin ego and its image. I swallow the saliva as it gathers in my mouth. I hear the sound of the muscles in my throat, in my jaw and ears, as the saliva passes from my head, down my trachea to my stomach. I hear through myself, through bone and liquid being.

This taste, this sound, moves in and out of my lungs, as oxygen and water mix, releasing recessive thoughts, images, and desires into the present moment, where they only ever live.

But what hears? Not just my ears. For sounds touch and resonate throughout my body. And why "my" body, "my" ears? Bone and liquid claim no ownership. Yet the site where sound touches flesh—the body—becomes a magnet for memories, an assembly of cells, of selves imagining themselves a unity, an author, a faithful student of sound knowledge.[1]

Sound knowledge—a nondiscursive form of affective transmission resulting from acts of listening.

Sound writing—a performance in word-sound of such knowledge. Not a representation. Not just an intersemiotic translation. Sound writing is a gong resonating through bodies, sentient and non.

WRITING SOUND THEORY

The essays in this volume respond to one simple but essential question: how theorize sound writing? In order to answer that question, we review basic definitions—of theory, method, listening, and genre—returning ultimately to the technology of writing sound as a method that employs "sound knowledge" in speculative inquiry. Sound knowledge—defined here as a nondiscursive form of affective transmission resulting from acts of listening—is a subtext in this volume. What promise does sound knowledge hold for cultural analysis? How might we not only write sound but sound theory differently?

Jacques Attali set the stage for these questions in 1977, when he presciently noted that "no theorizing accomplished through language or mathematics can suffice any longer; it is incapable of accounting for what is essential in time—the qualitative and the fluid, threats and violence. . . . It is thus necessary to imagine radically new theoretical forms, in order to speak to new realities." Almost thirty years later, social theorist Lauren Berlant reiterates this call, attending to the persistent need "to invent new genres for the kind of speculative work we call 'theory'" (2006, 21).

"Speculative" comes from the Latin root, *speculatio,* meaning "observation, contemplation," and like the word "theory" itself (from the Greek, *theria,* to see),[2] is rooted in a visual and thus objectifying relation of self to world, subject to object.[3] The call for new theoretical forms arises from the knowledge that subject and object can no longer be held apart, even conceptually. The myth of the detached analyst, in both the sciences and the humanities, is untenable not only because it assumes a hierarchy from which objective ("true") observations can be made "from outside," but also because a theory rooted only in the intellective is of necessity incomplete. At any given moment we know the world in a myriad of ways—through the sounds we hear, through the odors we smell, through the weight and temperature of the air on our skins, through the density of our body in the space that surrounds it. As soon as we reflect on these forms of knowledge, however—tactile, fragrant, pulsing—we remove them from the flow of time, the "ever-present now" of their becoming to render them objects of memory. On the other hand, to raise these nonintellective modes of sensory knowledge to consciousness (as when the hand feels itself touching) is to employ intuition.[4] And intuition is inseparable from the speculative—what is predictive because prescient, known through the senses.

In this volume we turn the "speculative work" of theory in a sonorous direction, recognizing that turns are movements and that sound is experienced in the touch—of sound wave to eardrum, of vibration to emotion. We gesture toward the creation of new genres of theorizing by pushing into what is usually withdrawn but always present in theory: namely, method. Indeed, just as ways of knowing and ways of being are inseparable, so theory and method are likewise entangled (Barad 2007).

Sounding a Speculative Method

Historically, method has been the ox pulling the shiny carriage of theory, rarely acknowledged, a means toward an end. Yet more than fifty years ago, Sartre noted the inextricable relation of method and theory in his work *Search for a Method* (1960):

> The only theory of knowledge which can be valid today is one which is founded on that truth of microphysics: the experimenter is a part of the experimental system. This is the only position which allows us to get rid of all idealist illusion, the only one which shows the real man in the midst of the real world [*sic*]. But this realism necessarily implies a reflective point of departure; that is, the *revelation* of a situation is effected in and through the *praxis* which changes it. We do not hold that this first act of becoming conscious of the situation is the originating source of an action; we see in it a necessary moment of the action itself—the action, *in the course of its accomplishment,* provides its own clarification.[5]

For Sartre, theory and method give rise to one another, like consciousness and practice, in intra-action.[6]

Think of the word *method* as a synaesthete might, as a word with a particular taste; imagine it like a piece of bread—consistent, hearty, with a bit of sweetness lingering on the tongue after it is swallowed, though with just enough salt that the salt is an imperceptible presence.

Method is usually equated with a system for doing, steps in a procedure, a plan. This kind of method belongs in a scientific lab. It is about numbers, facts. In this usage it has a more metallic and much saltier taste. It is a "how-to" mode, decidedly unyeasty. But there is another use of method, and that is method as a mode of practice. There are musical methods—ways of moving, breathing, reading, listening—that take us along the path not only to playing an instrument, but to becoming one with that instrument. Here method *involves* practice. And there is yet another way to think about method, and that is as a technique of the body. As in method acting, the actors draw on their own memories and affective experiences in order to enter into another character. Here method *is* practice, one that skews subject and object, much like spirit possession does (Kapchan 2007).

Listening is also a method that skews subject and object. This is why ethnographies of listening (ethnographies that employ ways of listening to understand not only how others listen but also the political import of social listening writ large) are difficult yet imperative to enact: the ethnographer is necessarily confounded in the paradox of being with and being apart from the social field of listening. Such paradoxes require that we release our hold on intellective knowledge (with its drives to categorize, objectify, and subjugate) in order to activate intuition—conscious sentience.[7] Listening itself is a speculative method.

How listen to our own listening with others? How practice the translation of listening, as well as listening-as-translation? And how write sound knowledge into being?

LISTENING ACTS

There are acoustic limits to what humans can hear, yet much of our sound environment remains mute to our ears simply because we have not been trained to listen to more than a limited range of sonorous events. Music appreciation is learned, of course, and enlarges our sonic sensibility. Listening attentively to sonic environments, while no different, is nonetheless a skill rarely cultivated since its relevance is not always immediately evident. There are no practical and capitalist reasons to use this kind of listening. Rather, the cosmopolitan subject is entrained in what Kassabian calls "ubiquitous listening," a kind of diffuse and unintentional hearing that nonetheless structures the acoustic unconscious much like Muzak, the genre of music played in shopping malls and thought to encourage consumption (Kassabian 2013). Yet just as sensing one's hand relies on the interactions of the hand with its instruments (opening a door, cutting a tomato, caressing a child), so the limits of our hearing depend on the instrumentality of acts of listening: *what we hear depends on how we listen and what we listen for.*

Genres of Listening

While listening is usually oriented toward an object (listening to music, listening for the cry of a baby waking from sleep, listening for an approaching car), methods of aural attention—the "how" of listening—usually remain outside the purview of consciousness. There is, however, a growing literature on listening in which scholars have provided a veritable taxonomy of listening practices to consider. Film music scholar and composer Michel Chion defines three: *semantic listening* (listening for meaning), *causal listening* (listening for the source of a sound), and *reduced listening* (listening to sound qua sound) (Chion 1994). The concept of "Deep Listening," coined by composer Pauline Oliveros (2005), delineates listening that leads to trance and states of profound absorption and transformation across cultures (Oliveros 2005; cf. Becker 2004).[8] To these add:

(1) Transitive versus intransitive listening[9] (listening in relation to an object vs. nonrelational or "ubiquitous listening")[10]
(2) Empathic listening (the *techné* of auditory empathy)
(3) Layered listening (Daughtry, this volume)
(4) Tactical listening—listening to effect pedagogical and political change (Cusick, this volume; Kapchan, this volume; Wong, this volume)[11]
(5) Listening as witness (Kapchan, this volume; Wong, this volume)

While these genres of listening overlap (as all genres do), they also distinguish themselves by orienting the listener in particular *affective* directions. They thus perform different aesthetic and political work.[12] Like musical genres, genres of listening have their own tempos and temporalities. (Just as Mahler is not hip-hop, concerted listening is not ubiquitous listening.) Listening genres are embodied tuning systems, vibrating at their own frequencies, interacting and transforming the sounds they transduce. Indeed, just as there are styles, registers, and ways of speaking (Hymes 1974), we may think about listening in similarly elaborate ways. J. L. Austin's "illocutionary speech acts" find equivalency in "listening acts" insofar as both are performative. Listening acts do not simply re-present sound, as waves reach the ears and are relayed to the brain, but they *transduce* these sound waves, changing them in the process. Employing the mechanical metaphor of *transduction* insists on the process whereby one kind of energy (water) meets another (generator) to transform into a third thing (energy) (Silverstein 2003, 83–84; cf. Helmreich 2015). Likewise a listening body interacts with sound, conducting but also transforming it in the process.[13]

Such listening-as-transduction resonates with what Roman Jakobson called intersemiotic translation, wherein a sound (like a text) is defracted—passed through the prism of the ear and transformed with new colors and meanings that extend and "transmute" it in another medium, such as writing (Jakobson 1959).[14] As with intersemiotic translation, listening changes one form of affective materiality into another. Pais (this volume) details the way an audience listening attentively qualitatively changes the materiality of an actor's performance. And indeed, we can apply the notion of translation as transmutation to other forms of semiosis as well: the translation of wind by trees, for example, or the thickly patterned sounds of a rainforest translated into the synthesized compositions of David Monacchi.[15] "There is . . . only a series of mediations, each of them translating a more complicated reality into something whose forces can more easily be passed down the line," notes philosopher Graham Harman in his discussion of the work of Bruno Latour. Just as "truth is nothing but a chain of translation without resemblance from one actor to the next,"[16] so listening is a method whereby these transformations and translations take place. Birds, waterfalls, ancestors, songs—all are involved in the translation of sensation, vibration, and the refrains of memory.[17]

Writing of the late South African jazz singer Sathima Bea Benjamin, Carol Muller (this volume) notes, " 'Sathima' translates as the one who listens, and it is the name that was given to then 'Bea Benjamin' by her compatriot bass player Johnny Dyani while both were in exile, traveling between Europe and the United States in the 1970s. The name pays tribute to the woman's compassion, care, and willingness to listen to the struggles of the young Dyani, but it also speaks of the manner in which Sathima engaged with popular song, and ultimately moved into the improvisational language of jazz. Listening to the sounds around her, remembering and transforming them have long been the means by which Benjamin incorporated remembered sounds from home as personal inscription once she left South Africa." Sathima Bea Benjamin listened to remember, she listened to improvise, she listened to *translate* an African American genre into a South African one—and to create a new genre thereby. Indeed, translation is always a new creation that begins in listening. How "translate into words the experience of learning through hearing?" (Rasmussen, this volume). How translate and transmit sound knowledge?

Such intersemiotic translations often rely on metaphor. And indeed, the most enduring aspects of theory are also its metaphors, particularly its synecdoches: Foucault's analysis of the *panopticon* (Jeremy Bentham's circular architecture wherein inmates of an institution may be surveyed at any time, but never know if and when they are being seen) expresses more about how modern hegemonic power is inculcated and embodied than any abstract philosophy. Merleau-Ponty evokes the *phantom limb* (the sense an amputee has of the missing limb) to talk about the habit body–how perception and memory arise from an embodied engagement with the world (such that the hand continues to exist as a "phantom" even after it has been amputated). In discussing globalization and violence, Appadurai relates the nation to a vertebrate society, one that is defenseless when conflict occurs on the cellular level (Appadurai 2005). Deleuze's rhizome, as the root that proliferates in all directions, constantly connecting and morphing according to its environment, provides not only a model for culture, but also aptly captures the cosmopolitan subject (as well as musical form).[18] And what Morton calls the hyperobject—"things that are massively distributed in time and space relative to humans" (Morton 2013, 1)—is a metaphor that inaugurates a nonanthropocentric paradigm in the true afterward of modernity.

If metaphors are the keys of theory (salty, metallic, like blood, molecular, magnetic), it is not surprising that the terms *vibration,*[19] *resonance,*[20] *rhythm,*[21] as well as *affect* and *energy,*[22] are at the fore of theoretical thought (words that would have been eschewed a few decades ago for their esotericism). Indeed, these concepts have one thing in common: they all mediate material and immaterial worlds and problematize the difference between them, often forcing an encounter with paradox in the process: visible and invisible, harmonious and cacophonous, together and separate.[23] Music (and sound more broadly) has a particular status in this regard. Music colonizes, creating place through the channeling of vibration and the appropriation of space. But music also blows place apart, dissipating energy, unraveling lines of tension and force, and traveling faster than any other medium.[24]

Metaphor is not just good to think, however; it actually performs affective and aesthetic understanding, transmitting sound knowledge. As Kisliuk notes, "When we ourselves engage in metaphoric communication, we are both conceptualizing emotion and constituting aspects of our experience in the process—piecing together little metaphor dwellings in which to tuck and shape affective experiences that would otherwise remain abstract" (Kisliuk, this volume). Building on the work of Ramachandran as well as Lakoff and Johnson, Kisliuk reminds us of what anthropologists Steven Feld as well as James Fernandez and Michael Jackson elaborated quite some time ago: metaphor is not just descriptive, but performative.[25] It creates cognitive abodes in which humans dwell, both singularly and together, but it also is a *method* by which that cognitive construction takes place. Metaphor is basic to human development at early stages of life, creating semantic domains that humans continue to inhabit, but it is also a way of transforming the habitus through aesthetic, cognitive, and emotional means throughout the life cycle.[26]

The metaphors in this volume demonstrate the intimate relation between listening, sound, and inscription. "If we translate 'sound writing' into Greek," notes Waterman (this volume), "we render *phonography.* Phonography [*phōnē* 'sound, voice' and *graphē* 'writing'] . . . first brings to mind the *phonograph*—the mechanical instrument that could both record (*inscribe)* and playback (*re-sound*). The phonograph is an instrumental model and metaphor for how sound writing might be both an *inscriptive/prescriptive* and a *descriptive/resonant* practice." Waterman's use of the metaphor of phonography insists upon the inseparability of theory and method.

Daughtry (this volume) uses the metaphor of the *palimpsest* to understand what he calls "layered listening" (a kind of listening through the "scrim" of ambient sounds to the sound object). He tells the story of how underground musical recordings in the postwar Soviet Union were printed on used and discarded X-rays. The "palimpsest metaphor," he notes, "draws our attention to the ways in which playing and listening to music always involves a type of inscription, a writing-over of other sounds that seldom perfectly erases them" (Daughtry, this volume; cf. Eidsheim, Muller 2011). Daughtry's piece also insists on the continuity of sound across different densities of materiality. "In the end," Daughtry notes, "how could those who made or purchased these records not take delight in the fact that the music of the nascent Soviet 'underground' was written on images of the human skeleton, denizens of the *literal* Soviet underground? How could they not smile at the notion that the songs of artists who were actively censored in the Soviet Union were circulating upon official images of Soviet bodies?" In Daughtry's example, the metaphor of the palimpsest resounds through multisensorial worlds that bear the mark of sound encounters.

Such events are, in the words of Michelle Kisliuk (this volume) "moments that crystallize . . . aesthetic and interpersonal sentiment fused with cultural and existential affect." These "magnified musicking moments," as Kisliuk calls them, are rarely the subject of ethnographic inquiry, perhaps because they are by definition intersensorial and ephemeral, always in excess of their description in words.

Yet "despite our passion for experience, we continue to transmit textual supremacy as a means of measuring academic merit," Hahn reminds us (this volume). There is a hierarchy of genres that is very difficult to unsettle, a hierarchy of styles that demands our submission. Unless of course we imagine and propose an alternative such as sound writing:[27]

> Like a great blue heron facing you in stillness, the lush expanse of experience appears narrowed, flattened in text, virtually disappearing into typographic symbols. But when she flies, how extraordinary!
>
> *Hahn, this volume*

THEORIZING SOUND WRITING

"Why would we wish to theorize and experiment with the print medium in the digital age? Why write, rather than do something else?" asks Henderson (this volume).

Writing about sound has historically fallen into just a few categories: music criticism (including journalism) and music scholarship (concerning both Western and non-Western music in history and the present). Yet another strand of writing about sound is found in the history of ethnopoetics—the school of poetry whose focus on orality attempts not just to describe and analyze poetry, but to decidedly evoke its SOUND on the page. These histories have been charted (Hymes 1975; Tedlock 1983; Rothenberg 1983; see Henderson, this volume; Jackson, this volume). Since the advent of sound studies as an interdisciplinary field, however, writings on sound have further proliferated in the direction of soundscapes, sound ecologies, sound art criticism, and what Feld presciently defined as "acoustemology," ways of knowing through sound and sounding (Feld 2015, 1996; cf. Feld 1994; Feld and Brenneis 2004; Sterne 2003; Schafer 1977).

Why then open up the (theoretical) possibilities of writing (and) sound anew? The answer lies in the potential of both listening and writing to transform experiences of temporality.

Before literacy was widespread, writing was a sacrosanct and embodied activity. Scribes spent their days laboring over calligraphic inscriptions of sacred texts. And even when the texts were not sacred, the act of writing *was*, insofar as it was set apart. Today as I write these words, I momentarily close my eyes. I gather my thoughts, summoning them up from the core of my belly, pulling them down from a place behind my temples, through my arms and down into my fingers. As if by magic, I see them materialize on the screen. Writing is an act of keystroke speed in which the labor value all but disappears. Yet there is a materiality to the writing act that often gets lost, a part of *listening* as inaudible yet essential as the breath of a violinist playing a concerto.

Despite the very embodied act of writing, however, it has been equated with an archive that has suppressed the oral, the feminine, and the queer (Phelan 1993; cf. Taylor 2003). In his exploration of reggae sound systems in Jamaica, for example, Henriques refers to writing as a prison to which technology has provided the key: "Having been imprisoned in writing for the past two and a half millennia," he notes, "in little over a hundred years of phonographic recording, sound and music are being liberated from music's transcription and sound's circumstances of embodied production" (Henriques 2011, xvi). While Henriques rightly celebrates the acceleration that (new) technology has afforded human experience, it is important to note that in the *longue durée,* writing (whether words or music) is a rather recent technology, and mass literacy *much* more recent than that. And while writing has been instrumental in Enlightenment philosophies that split mind work from bodywork as well as imagination from sensation, it is also true that this alliance is not the only one imaginable, nor the only one enacted. It is not writing that is a prison house per se, but our modes of perception, of listening and translation, that must be broken through.

As a tool that extends the faculties of the human being in other and immanently human directions, writing is a technology that can be instrumentalized in various ways. It is not necessarily a cognitive evolutionary shift as Ong thought, but a technique of the body that employs a tool of human invention to create a vibration, a territory, a story that exceeds the merely human. What's more, writing is what Foucault called a "technology of the self," an act whereby individuals "effect by their own means or with the help of others a certain number of operations on their own bodies and souls, thoughts, conduct, and way of being, so as to transform themselves in order to attain a certain state of happiness, purity, wisdom, perfection, or immortality."[28] For Foucault a technology of the self is always allied with other technologies—of production, signification, and power. Nonetheless, such a technology rewires the circuits so that energy flows in unexpected ways, creating new connections. As Jackson notes (this volume), "Sound writing echoes the events, encounters and conversations that make up our everyday life in another society, bringing them back to life on the printed page while at the same time offering our reflections on them." Such ways of knowing through feeling require not just new theories, but new *methods*—ways of holding intuition and consciousness in dynamic tension.

In writing themselves and others into being have humans exhausted the technology of writing? In his article in this volume, Henderson questions the meaning of a format (to paraphrase Sterne 2012) and how different genres of inscription/transmission orient us differently in time and space. Sound writing itself is a kind of format, a method of data arrangement, "an attempt to engrave the sound itself into the page, the effort to make the page vibrate with the acoustic presence of the sounding body" (Henderson, this volume).

Of course, there are many ways of inscribing. For Emerson writing in 1850, inscription was ubiquitous and not only a human endeavor. "All things are engaged in writing their history," he noted.

> The planet, the pebble, goes attended by its shadow. The rolling rock leaves its scratches on the mountain; the river its channel in the soil; the animal its bones in the stratum; the fern and leaf their modest epitaph in the coal. The falling drop makes its sculpture in the sand or the stone. Not a foot steps into the snow or along the ground, but prints, in characters more or less lasting, a map of its march. Every act of the man inscribes itself in the memories of his fellows and in his own manners and face. The air is full of sounds; the sky, of tokens; the round is all memoranda and signatures, and every object covered over with hints which speak to the intelligent. (Emerson 1850)[29]

For Emerson, the sounds in the air were themselves inscriptions of other phenomena.

In this volume we advance sound writing as a genre in which sound is not (just) an object of analysis but a vibration that infuses the word with its own materiality to produce a third thing. As such, *sound writing is the inscriptive dimension of listening.* Much like the river leaving behind its channel in the soil, listening as well as sound writing are acts of translation with the potential to "vibrate our very skin and bones" (Cusick, this volume).

The authors in *Theorizing Sound Writing* make an intervention into the ethics of academic knowledge, one in which *listening* is the first step not only in translating sound into words, but in compassionate scholarship (Kapchan, this volume; Wong, this volume). As a method of inquiry, both listening and sound writing expand not only what is known but also how we come to know (and be) as public intellectuals and artisans of the sounded world. Taking our cues from politics (Cusick; Wong), popular culture (Daughtry; Henderson), ritual performances (Hagedorn; Kapchan; Rasmussen), as well as memoir and autobiography (Kisliuk; Muller; Waterman), the sound writing on these pages examines the relation of (1) theory to method, (2) listening to translation, and (3) sound to inscription. In the process, we attend to the power of metaphor to perform knowledge often analyzed in academic writing but seldom consciously instructed (Kisliuk, this volume).

Writing *about* sound and writing *sound* are two different processes. The first maintains the positivist position of subject (writer) and object (sound). The second breaks out of duality to inhabit a multidimensional position as translator between worlds—the writer listening to and translating sound through embodied experience, the body translating the encounter between word and sound, sound translating and transforming both word and author. This is sound writing. When she flies, how extraordinary!

THE SPLASH OF ICARUS

In one of William Carlos Williams's poems, he describes the landscape of a Breughal painting, *The Fall of Icarus,* to make a sound intervention:

LANDSCAPE WITH THE FALL OF ICARUS
William Carlos Williams

According to Breughel
when Icarus fell
it was spring

a farmer was ploughing
his field
the whole pageantry

of the year was
awake tingling
near

the edge of the sea
concerned
with itself

sweating in the sun
that melted
the wings' wax

unsignificantly
off the coast
there was

a splash quite unnoticed
this was
Icarus drowning

Williams is translating the visual medium of the painting (already a translation of the verbal medium of the myth) into the written medium of the poem. But it is also a commentary on human inattention to listening. The farmer plows. He uses the tools at hand. The whole "pageantry of the world"—the public spectacle[30]—is "concerned with [only] itself" and not with the boy falling from the sky. No one hears the splash. And while the farmer continues to plow, a boy drowns. The farmer remains unaware of his suffering, unaware of the gods, and unaware of how his own universe will shift because of this event (the waters that soak his fields polluted with death, the disposition of the heavens transformed in grief). An opportunity for empathy has been lost because the world did not listen.

What might be done so that we hear the splash of Icarus?

Theoretical speculations have rarely been "predictive." Weber's disenchanted secular world did not come to pass, rationality has not been a defense against violence, socialism did not fulfill its promise, and Foucault was wrong about the Iranian revolution. Yet perhaps we can do more than simply follow in the wake of experience that runs ever before us in order to know where we have been (Stewart 1988). Attending to sound knowledge—the transmission of affect through listening—while employing the technology of sound writing (a conscious application of intuition in poiesis, or meaning making) may poise us toward the future in ways that make the splash of Icarus not only visible, but audible.

Coda: Echoes Resounding, Sound without End

Describing the performance of a spirit, Katherine Hagedorn (this volume) says, "This is how Cuban folkloric dancer Jesús Ortíz portrays Babalú Ayé, *oricha* of smallpox and healing . . . as a diseased body dancing toward death":

> The helpless imposition of the body's angles: bent knees, sharp elbow, hunched shoulders, jutting chin. Eyes bulging and head rolling, the figure lurches from side to side, just about to topple: he is the picture of disease. Oddly, he is also smiling.

Without knowing it, or perhaps knowing but not saying it, Katherine Hagedorn was writing sound as she herself was dancing toward death. Her contribution here as well as her life work in general is a kind of sound writing—one that evokes sound and spiritual worlds without reducing them to analytical categories. Her chapter in this volume is unfinished, like her life work when she passed. And yet sound writing is never quite finished. It continues to resound. Oddly, we are all smiling . . .

NOTES

1. Speaking of A. N. Whitehead's process philosophy, Harmon notes, "Not only is there no personal immortality after death, there is not even personal endurance before death, since every actual entity perishes immediately after its birth. The unusual ethical conclusion Whitehead draws from this is that the egoistic basis of morality is a falsehood. The Other is Other, certainly, but the I of five minutes ago is also the Other, since it was not at all the same entity as the I of right now. What is primary is eros: the love of self is only a special case of a general enthusiasm for all of the objects surrounding us" (Harman 2010, 41).

2. From the Latin word *theria,* it means "a looking at, viewing, contemplation, speculation . . . also a sight, a spectacle." [*Oxford English Dictionary:* abstr. n. f. (:*) spectator, looker on, f. stem—of to look on, view, contemplate. In mod. use prob. from med. L. transl. of Aristotle. Cf. It. *teoria* (Florio 1598 *theoría*), F. *théorie* (15. in Godef. *Compl.*). 1. A sight, a spectacle. *Obs. rare.*]

3. There is an irony in the very notion of theorizing sound, having to do with the etymology of the word *theory* itself. Implicit in the history of the word, that is, is a relation to the senses that privileges sight over audition—a classic formation in the historical construction of modern sensibilities. Indeed, the "lower" senses of olfaction, tactility, and taste are often neglected and explicitly disparaged in relation to it (Howes 2003). Audition, while

not defining modernity like sight, does have an intimate relation to it insofar as the sonic can be reproduced, circulated, and if not controlled, then manipulated to control (Erlmann 2004; Hirschkind 2006). Discussing the relation of audition to modernity, Erlmann notes, "If the auditory is deeply caught up in the modern project—rather than standing apart from it—and if therefore the ear joins the eye in consolidating the fragile modern self, we must nevertheless ask the reverse question: How are these modern identities constantly being sonically haunted and—perhaps confirming McLuhan's greatest fear—troubled by a return of the repressed? What do we really know about vocal knowledges that are being forced underground, silenced, or ridiculed as superstitious?" (Erlmann 2004, 5).

4. Bergson 2004.

5. Jean-Paul Sartre, "Search for a Method," part 1, "Introduction" to *Critique of Dialectical Reason*, in *Existentialism from Dostoyevsky to Sartre*, ed. Walter Kaufmann and trans. Hazel Barnes (New York: Vintage Books, 1960), accessed on April 17, 2012, http://www.marxists.org/reference/archive/sartre/works/critic/sartre1.htm.

6. Of course, Sartre was not alone in his philosophical preoccupations. Neo-Marxists such as Bourdieu, Foucault, and De Certeau have been more cited in the academy and have all grappled with this. For Bourdieu, however, practice and theory were intertwined, but analytically and experientially separate. Indeed, a close reading of the *Logic of Practice* reveals that Bourdieu made a stinging critique of scholars who "went native," that is, those who embraced the practices of difference so much as to lose their objectivity. On "intraactivity," see Barad 2003.

7. This is what Morton, like others before him, has called "attunement" (Morton 2013; cf. Schafer 1977; Langer 1941).

8. "To hear a siren, a bird, or a drum is already each time to understand at least the rough outline of the situation, a context if not a text" (Nancy 2007, 6).

9. Transitive listening must take an object, so to speak (from Late Latin *transitivus* (Priscian) "transitive," literally "that may pass over (to another person)," from *transire* "go or cross over," accessed January 24, 2013, http://www.etymonline.com/index.php. Intransitive listening is like Chion's "reduced listening," with the nuance that the intransitive takes place in the phenomenological "eidetic moment"—that is, in a time and space free of associations and relationalities. It is a listening as if for the first time.

10. See Kassabian 2013.

11. De Certeau wants to know how subjects and collectivities use tactics in the everyday to create, and be creative in the midst of "nets" of discipline. Users (of culture) make "innumerable and infinitesimal transformations of and with the dominant culture economy to adapt it to their own interests and their own rules" (De Certeau 2011, xiv).

12. Bakhtin coined the term *chronotope* to draw attention to the time and space orientations in genre. He neglected to note, however, that orientations configure and transmit affect as well, whether wonder, competition, anger, boredom, or inspiration (cf. Ahmed

2006). Genres—sermons, lectures, fairytales, ethnography, gossip, playing the dozens, pillow talk—are affective orientations. This is clear in musical and dance genres as well: hip-hop draws on a different emotional vocabulary than Mahler; salsa inhabits the body differently than tango.

13. Thinking of listening with the mechanical metaphor of *transduction* insists on the process whereby one kind of energy (water) meets another (generator) to transform into a third thing (energy) (Silverstein 2003, 83–84; cf. Helmreich 2015). Likewise, a listening body interacts with sound, conducting but also transforming it in the process. Silverstein notes that: "One form of organized energy . . . is asymmetrically converted into another kind of energy at an energetic conduction site . . . , harnessing at least some of it across energetic frameworks. In this transducer, the two modes of mechanical energy are converted in a functionally regular way into another kind of energy altogether, . . . of course with some slippage between the two systems of energy organization" (Silverstein 2003, 83–84; see also Kapchan, this volume; cf. Austin 1960; Helmreich 2015; Szendy 2007).

14. Like Martha Graham's danced interpretations of Greek tragedies, intersemiotic translation is an "interpretation of verbal signs by means of signs of nonverbal sign systems" and is synonymous with "transmutation" (Jakobson 1959).

15. David Monacchi, "Fragments of Extinction," accessed on March 1, 2016, http://www.davidmonacchi.it.

16. Harman 2010, 76.

17. Latour 2005, 245; cf. Feld 1982. What's more, the listening body is not necessarily only human. Plants also receive and respond to sensory date in a measurable way, emitting their own sounds (inaudible to humans without technology). Indeed, "most of the genome may be involved with signal transduction of one sort or another," notes plant biologist Trewasvas (2002). Insofar as plants convert sounds into other forms of energy, they may be said to "listen." The cochlea even *produces* sound in response to acoustic stimulation. Called *evoked otoacoustic emissions,* EOAEs are detectable with sensitive microphones but are otherwise inaudible.

This is not to anthropomorphize the world, but only to recognize that, following process philosophers such as A. N. Whitehead, the entire environment is one of "prehensions," a place of minute and invisible interactions. "For modern philosophy, all the problems of translation occur at a single critical point where human meets the world. But for Latour, translation is ubiquitous: any relation is a mediation, never some pristine transmission of data across a noiseless vacuum" (Harman 2009, 77).

All these movements are acts of translation—events that move through the world by touch, apprehending, transforming, and translating in the *always-mediated* encounter with other things or events (Latour 2005; cf. Whitehead 1929). "Hermeneutics is not a privilege of humans," Latour reminds us, "but . . . a property of the world itself" (Latour

2005, 245). For Latour, as well as for the purposes of this volume, "Translation is ubiquitous" (Harman 2009, 77).

How we listen determines what we hear. Indeed, we listen the way we read, "according to certain codes" (Barthes 1985, 245). Listening is both a socially overdetermined and generic act, as well as a deeply personal one (Kapchan, this volume).

18. "Music has always sent out lines of flight, like so many transformational multiplicities, even overturning the very codes that structure or arborify it, that is why musical form, right down to its ruptures and proliferations, is comparable to a weed, to a rhizome" (Gilles Deleuze and Felix Guattari, *A Thousand Plateaus* (Minneapolis: University of Minnesota Press, 1987); cited in Frances Dyson, *Sounding New Media* (Berkeley: University of California Press, 2009), 184).

19. Deleuze and Guattari 1987.

20. Nancy 2007; cf. Erlmann 2010.

21. Lefebvre 1992.

22. Brennan 2004.

23. Bennett 2010.

24. We find echoes of this affective "force" of music in speech act theory, which focuses not on the referential meaning of the utterance, but on its effects in the world.

25. Feld 1982, as well as Fernandez 1974; 1991.

26. Lakoff and Johnson 1980; Johnson 1987.

27. In Merleau-Ponty's 1960 meditation on "indirect language and the voices of silence," he notes that style is not separable from perception, but is in fact "an exigency that has issued *from* . . . perception" (Merleau-Ponty, 1964, 54, emphasis mine). For Merleau-Ponty, style is a method by which the artist breaks through accepted forms and meanings (genres) in order to express a particular relation to being and history. It is, he says, a "way of shaking the linguistic or narrative apparatus in order to tear a new sound from it" (Merleau-Ponty, 1964, 46). For Deuleuze and Guattari, this "shaking loose" helps create a new "territory," which they say also transpires through "style"—in motifs, rhythms, and counterpoints within territories (or genres) and across them (Deleuze and Guattari, 1987, 318).

Scholars of music have long studied style as something that creates and performs identity and community, whether individual, local, or global. We have theories about the elements of style (participatory discrepancies, Keil 1995), the role of synesthesia and the parallelism between musical and other semiotic forms of style (Feld 1982, 1990), the way style creates identity and community (endotropic style, Erlmann 2003; iconicity, Feld 1990, 1996), to say nothing about theories for acquiring style (bimusicality, Hood 1960). We also have numerous ethnographies that document the emergence, improvisation, and performance of style in various cultural traditions. But while scholars have been scrupulous in their contextualization of musical style in the realms of class (Fox 2004), gender

(Muller 1999), race (Radano and Bohlman 2000; Monson 1996, 2004), and culture (Averill 1997; Wong 2001), we have been less than attentive to the ways that styles of writing create the very knowledge we portend to convey. What's more, we have not acknowledged that just as our senses determine our perceptions of the world (as humans we can only hear a certain range of sounds, for example), so our methods and tools of analysis determine our theoretical apparatuses, which in effect carve out particular affective territories. Stone, metal, lenses, laser: our tools determine our discoveries. Dialogic editing, writing performatively, writing against culture, listening to subjects listening, and ourselves remembering—these are all techniques as well as theories. Indeed, they are methods.

28. Says Foucault: "As a context, we must understand that there are four major types of these 'technologies,' each a matrix of practical reason: (1) technologies of production, which permit us to produce, transform, or manipulate things; (2) technologies of sign systems, which permit us to use signs, meanings, symbols, or signification; (3) technologies of power, which determine the conduct of individuals and submit them to certain ends or domination, an objectivizing of the subject; (4) technologies of the self, which permit individuals to effect by their own means or with the help of others a certain number of operations on their own bodies and souls, thoughts, conduct, and way of being, so as to transform themselves in order to attain a certain state of happiness, purity, wisdom, perfection, or immortality.

These four types of technologies hardly ever function separately, although each one of them is associated with a certain type of domination. Each implies certain modes of training and modification of individuals, not only in the obvious sense of acquiring certain skills but also in the sense of acquiring certain attitudes. I wanted to show both their specific nature and their constant interaction. For instance, one sees the relation between manipulating things and domination in Karl Marx's *Capital,* where every technique of production requires modification of individual conduct—not only skills but also attitudes." Michel Foucault, "Technologies of the Self," accessed on March 1, 2016, http://cognitiveenhancement.weebly.com/uploads/1/8/5/1/18518906/technologies_of_self_michel_foucault.pdf.

29. Ralph Waldo Emerson, "Goethe; or, the Writer," Literature Network, accessed on September 5, 2015, http://www.online-literature.com/emerson/3774/. Thanks to Sam Wilson for bringing this quote to my attention.

30. From the Medieval Latin *pagina,* late fourteenth century, "play in a cycle of mystery plays," perhaps from Latin *pagina* ("page of a book"). "Pageant," Wictionary, accessed on June 25, 2014, http://en.wiktionary.org/wiki/pageant.

WORKS CITED

Ahmed, Sarah. *Queer Phenomenology: Orientations, Objects, Others*. Durham, NC: Duke University Press, 2006.

———. *The Cultural Politics of Emotion*. New York: Routledge, 2004.

Appadurai, Arjun. *Fear of Small Numbers*. Durham, NC: Duke University Press, 2005.

Attali, Jacques. *Noise: The Political Economy of Music*. Foreword by Frederic Jameson. Translated by Brian Massumi. Minneapolis: University of Minnesota Press, 1977.

Austin, John Langshaw. *How to Do Things with Words*. 2nd ed. Edited by J. O. Urmson and Marina Sbisà. Cambridge: Harvard University Press, 1975.

Averill, Gage. *A Day for the Hunter, a Day for the Prey: Popular Music and Power in Haiti*. Chicago Studies in Ethnomusicology. Chicago: Chicago University Press, 1997.

Bakhtin, M. M. *The Dialogic Imagination: Four Essays*. Translated by Michael Holquist and Caryl Emerson. University of Texas Press Slavic Series, bk. 1. Austin: University of Texas Press, 1981.

Barad, Karen. *Meeting the Universe Halfway: Quantum Physics and the Entanglement of Matter and Meaning*. Durham, NC: Duke University Press, 2007.

———. "Posthumanist Performativity: Toward an Understanding of How Matter Comes to Matter." *Signs: Journal of Women in Culture and Society* 28, no. 3 (2003): 801–31.

Becker, Judith. *Deep Listeners: Music, Emotion, and Trancing*. Indianapolis: Indiana University Press, 2004.

Bergson, Henri. *Matter and Memory*. Unabridged republication of the 1912 MacMillan edition. Translated by N. Margaret Paul and W. Scott Palmer. Mineola, NY: Dover Publications, 2004.

Bennett, Jane. *Vibrant Matter: A Political Economy of Things*. Durham, NC: Duke University Press, 2010.

Berlant, Lauren. *Cruel Optimism*. Durham, NC: Duke University Press, 2006.

Brennan, Teresa. *The Transmission of Affect*. Ithaca, NY: Cornell University Press, 2004.

Chion, Michel. *Audio-Vision: Sound on Screen*. Edited and translated by Claudia Gorbman. Foreword by Walter Murch. New York: Columbia University Press, 1994.

De Certeau, Michel. *The Practice of Everyday Life*. Translated by Steven F. Rendall. 3rd ed. Berkeley: University of California Press, 2011.

Deleuze, Gilles, and Felix Guattari. *A Thousand Plateaus*. Minneapolis: University of Minnesota Press, 1987.

Erlmann, Veit. *Reason and Resonance: A History of Modern Aurality*. New York: Zone Books, 2010.

Erlmann, Veit, ed. *Hearing Cultures: Essays on Sound, Listening, and Modernity*. New York: Berg, 2004.

Feld, Steven. 2015. "Acoustemology." In *Keywords in Sound Studies.* Edited by David Novak and Matt Sakakeeny. Durham, NC: Duke University Press.

———. *Sound and Sentiment: Birds, Weeping, Poetics, and Song in Kaluli Expression.* 3rd ed., with a new introduction by the author. Durham, NC: Duke University Press, 2012a. Companion CDs issued by Smithsonian Folkways.

———. *Jazz Cosmopolitanism in Accra: Five Musical Years in Ghana.* Durham, NC: Duke University Press, 2012b. Companion DVDs and CDs issued by VoxLox.

———. "Waterfalls of Songs: An Acoustemology of Place Resounding in Bosavi, Papua New Guinea." In *Senses of Place.* Edited by Steven Feld and Keith H. Basso. Santa Fe, NM: SAR Press, 1996.

———, with Charles Keil. *Music Grooves.* Chicago: University of Chicago Press, 1994. Accessed on September 5, 2015. http://www.acousticecology.org/writings/echomuseecology.html.

Feld, Steven, and Donald Brenneis. "Doing Anthropology in Sound." *American Ethnologist* 31, no. 4 (2004): 461–74.

Fernandez, James, ed. *Beyond Metaphor: The Theory of Tropes in Anthropology.* Stanford: Stanford University Press, 1991.

———. *Persuasions and Performances: The Play of Tropes in Culture.* Bloomington: Indiana University Press, 1986.

Foucault, Michel. *Technologies of the Self: A Seminar with Michel Foucault,* edited by Luther H. Martin, Huck Gutman, and Patrick H. Hutton, 16–49. Amherst: University of Massachusetts Press, 1988.

———. *Discipline and Punish: The Birth of the Prison.* Translated By Alan Sheridan. New York: Vintage Books, 1977.

Fox, Aaron. *Real Country: Music and Language in Working-Class Culture.* Durham, NC: Duke University Press, 2004.

Harman, Graham. *Towards a Speculative Realism: Essays.* Winchester, UK: Zero Books, 2010.

———. *Prince of Networks: Bruno Latour and Metaphysics.* Anamnesis Series. Prahran, AU: re.press, 2009.

Helmreich, Stefan. "Transduction." In *Keywords in Sound Studies.* Edited by David Novak and Matt Sakakeeny. Durham, NC: Duke University Press, 2015.

Henriques, Julian. *Sonic Bodies: Reggae Sound Systems, Performance Techniques and Ways of Knowing.* New York: Continuum International, 2011.

Hood, Mantel. "The Challenge of Bi-Musicality." *Ethnomusicology* 4, no. 2 (1960): 55–59.

Howes, David. *Sensual Relations: Engaging the Senses in Culture and Social Theory.* Ann Arbor: University of Michigan Press, 2003.

Hymes, D. H. "Breakthrough into Performance." In *Folklore: Performance and Communication,* edited by D. Ben-Amos and K. Goldstein, 11–74. The Hague: Mouton, 1975.

———. "Ways of Speaking." In *Explorations in the Ethnography of Speaking,* edited by R. Bauman and J. Sherzer, 433–52. Cambridge: Cambridge University Press, 1974.

Jackson, Michael. *Paths Toward a Clearing: Radical Empiricism and Ethnographic Inquiry.* Bloomington: Indiana University Press, 1989.

———. "Thinking through the Body: An Essay on Understanding Metaphor." *Social Analysis* 14 (1983): 127–48.

Jakobson, Roman. "The Poetry of Grammar and the Grammar of Poetry." In *Selected Writings.* Edited by Stephen Rudy. 6 vols. (1971–1985). The Hague: Mouton, 1980.

———. "Closing Statement: Linguistics and Poetics," In *Style in Language.* Edited by Thomas Albert Sebeok. Cambridge, MA: MIT. Press, 1960.

Keil, Charlie. "Participatory Discrepancies." In *Music Grooves.* Edited by Steven Feld and Charlie Keil. Tucson, AZ: Fenestra Books, 2005.

Kapchan, Deborah. *Traveling Spirit Masters: Moroccan Gnawa Trance and Music in the Global Marketplace.* Middletown, CT: Wesleyan University Press, 2007.

Kassabian, Anahid. *Ubiquitous Listening: Affect, Attention and Distributed Subjectivity.* Berkeley: University of California Press, 2013.

Lakoff, George, and Mark Johnson. *Metaphors We Live by.* Chicago: University of Chicago Press, 1980.

Langer, Susanne, and Katherina Knauth. *Philosophy in a New Key; a Study in the Symbolism of Reason, Rite, and Art.* Cambridge: Harvard University Press, 1957.

Latour, Bruno. *Reassembling the Social: an Introduction to Actor-Network-Theory.* Oxford New York: Oxford University Press, 2005.

Lefevbre, Henri. *Rhythmanalysis: Space, Time and Everyday Life.* London: Continuum, 2004.

Merleau-Ponty, Maurice. *Phenomenology of Perception.* Translated by Colin Smith. New York: Humanities Press, and London: Routledge and Kegan Paul, 1962. Translation revised by Forrest Williams 1981; reprinted, 2002. New translation by Donald A. Landes. New York: Routledge, 2012.

———. "Indirect Language and the Voices of Silence." In *Signs.* Translated by R. McCleary. Evanston, IL: Northwestern University Press, 1964.

Monson, Ingrid. *Saying Something: Jazz Improvisation and Interaction.* Chicago Studies in Ethnomusicology. Chicago: University of Chicago Press, 1996.

Monson, Ingrid, ed. *The African Diaspora: A Musical Perspective.* Shrewsbury, MA: Garland Press, 2000.

Morton, Timothy. *Hyperobjects: Philosophy and Ecology after the End of the World.* Minneapolis: University of Minnesota Press, 2013.

Muller, Carol. *Rituals of Fertility and the Sacrifice of Desire: Nazarite Women's Performance in South Africa.* Chicago: University of Chicago Press, 1999.

Nancy, Jean-Luc. *Listening.* Translated by Charlotte Mandell. New York: Fordham University Press, 2007. First published in French in 2002.

Oliveros, Pauline. *Deep Listening: A Composer's Sound Practice.* Deep Listening Publication. Lincoln, NE: iUniverse Books, 2005.

Phelan, Peggy. *Unmarked: the Politics of Performance.* New York: Routledge, 1993.

Radano, Ronald M., and Philip V. Bohlman, eds. *Music and the Racial Imagination.* Chicago: University of Chicago Press, 2000.

Ramachandran, V. S. *The Tell-Tale Brain: A Neuroscientist's Quest for What Makes Us Human.* New York: W. W. Norton, 2011.

———. *A Brief Tour of Human Consciousness: From Impostor Poodles to Purple Numbers.* New York: Pi Press, 2004.

———. *The Emerging Mind: The BBC Reith Lectures 2003.* London: BBC/Profile Books, 2003.

Sartre, Jean-Paul. *Search for a Method.* Foreword by Fredric Jameson. 1960. Reprint, London: Verso, 2004.

Schafer, J. Murray. *The Soundscape: Our Sonic Environment and the Tuning of the World.* 1977. Republished, Douro-Dummer, Ontario: Arcana Editions, 1994.

———. *A Sound Education: 100 Exercises in Listening and Soundmaking.* Douro-Dummer, Ontario: Arcana Editions, 1992.

Silverstein, Michael. *Translation, Transduction, Transformation: Skating Glossando on Thin Semiotic Ice.* In *Translating Cultures: Perspectives on Translation and Anthropology,* edited by P. Rubel and A. Rosman, 75–105. Oxford: Berg, 2003.

Sterne, Jonathan. *MP3: The Meaning of a Format.* Durham, NC: Duke University Press, 2012.

———. *The Audible Past.* Durham, NC: Duke University Press, 2003.

Stewart, Kathleen. "Nostalgia—a Polemic." In *Rereading Cultural Anthropology,* edited by George E. Marcus, 252–66. Durham, NC: Duke University Press, 1992.

Szendy, Peter. *Listen: A History of Our Ears.* Translated by Charlotte Mandell. New York: Fordham University Press, 2009.

Taylor, Diana. *The Archive and the Repertoire: Performing Cultural Memory in the Americas.* Durham, NC: Duke University Press, 2003.

Trewasvas, Anthony. *Plant Behaviour and Intelligence.* Oxford: Oxford University Press, 2014.

Williams, William Carlos. "Landscape with the Fall of Icarus." In *Collected Poems of William Carlos Williams,* vol. 2: 1939–1962. Edited by Christopher MacGowan. New York: New Directions, 1991.

Whitehead, Alfred North. *Process and Reality: An Essay in Cosmology.* Gifford Lectures. New York: Macmillan, 1929.

Wong, Deborah. *Sounding the Center: History and Aesthetics in Thai Buddhist Ritual.* Chicago: University of Chicago Press, 2001.

PART ONE

Writing Sound Theory

SUZANNE G. CUSICK

1. Musicology, Performativity, Acoustemology

In the 1990s, in North America, the nexus of ideas associated with performativity and performance studies were all the rage in musicology, indeed in music studies across the subdisciplines. Performativity promised to invigorate academic, professional, and public thought about music (and in music), and to enable critics, practitioners, and ordinary listeners to understand music's myriad imbrications in the always tense power relations of race, gender, sexuality, and class. Moreover, it promised to release music studies from the parochialism encouraged by our practice and rehearsal regimens into fully reciprocal engagement with other humanistic disciplines, and ultimately with the intersecting economic, political, and social worlds that we were still inclined, in the 1990s, to describe as "real."

Sometime in the new century, however, the musicological fashion for performativity began (like the fashion for hermeneutics) to fade, gradually replaced by insistent and pervasive calls to refocus on music as heard sound, and by the rise to near-disciplinary status of something variously called "sound studies," "auditory" or "aural" culture, or "acoustemology." Whatever musicology's new "Other" might be called, by its attention to the whole spectrum of acoustic experience in which musical behaviors nestle, the new field promises to be intellectually exciting because, unlike the musicologies, it tries to theorize the myriad relationships among acoustical energy, human agency, technologies, and power that characterize contemporary acoustical experience—whether that experience be called musical or not. Yet until quite recently "sound studies"/ acoustemology has also proven to be a problematic interdiscipline. Curiously detached from critical thinking about race, gender, sexuality, or class, it is more celebratory than critical about the new regimes of listening enabled by twenty-first-century technology. Almost exclusively a practice of white men, too, it is often oblivious to questions of performance and performativity, even when, as in the case of hip-hop deejaying, the performance of relationships to technology, commerce, history, and power are obviously inseparable from the production of a characteristic set of sounds.

Because "sound studies"/acoustemology could well prove to be the interdiscipline that serves our century's needs for a way to talk about acoustical experience (parallel to the way that the musicologies served the last century's needs), it seems important to think through the possible relationships of musicology, performativity, and acoustemology. This essay is my first effort to think about these relationships: it is therefore an avowedly speculative text, the thoughts of someone with long experience in the musicology of early modern Italy who awoke, as if from a long dream made of music, to discover that her country used music as a tool of psychological and physical torture—and that she needed to know what sound studies taught if she was to understand that practice.

Still, I dare to hope that the effort to think the relationship of these interdisciplines to each other might prompt others to have productive thoughts, perhaps on new ways of engaging the acoustical practices and regimes that characterize twenty-first-century lives.

PERFORMATIVITY AND THE "NEW MUSICOLOGY"

Theories of performativity entered musicology from two directions in the 1990s—from gender-and-sexuality studies and from performance studies.[1] Both, of course, were relatively new interdisciplines that had emerged slowly from the intellectual and social ferment of the 1960s and 1970s, and that offered intentionally eclectic intellectual tools by which to think, rethink, and destabilize categories of human experience that traditional academic disciplines had rendered both unthinkable and fixed. In both, performativity theory's emphasis on human action and interaction as what constituted reality promised to have enormous liberatory power.

Indeed, theories of performativity did wonders for North American musicology in the 1990s and early 2000s. First, they validated the artistic labor and artistic contributions of performers, after several generations of musicological thought that had treated performance as merely the realization of a composer's intentions and performers as if they (we) were ideally transparent media through which a composer's thoughts moved, as if we were living playback systems. Theories of performativity spurred some of us to think long and hard about the physicality of music making, about the myriad strange ways that we humans discipline our bodies so that we can produce sounds and sonic-social interactions with each other that our fellows will hear as meaningful, or beautiful, or both. Furthermore, theories of performativity facilitated interpretations of musical works that included the social relations enacted by music in performance—including the many levels of paraperformance social relations about which Christopher Small wrote so eloquently for so long, and the social relations of production that Marxist theory associated with the "base."[2] Theories of performativity allowed musicians and music scholars intellectual access to an understanding of gender, sexuality, ethnicity, and race as produced by constantly repeated "performance" (actions), rather than as fixed categories of being (or of analysis); and therefore they allowed us to decipher some of the ways that our self-disciplined bodies and musical performances were also performances of gender, ethnicity, or race—both when our performances were transparent to a composer's intentions (or audience desires) and when they resisted those intentions and desires. Finally, performativity theory encouraged writing about music that aspired to the performative (as well as the constative)—that is, it encouraged us to write in ways that might intervene in the very relations of power our writing also described.[3]

Despite these rich contributions, however, in musicology (if not so much in ethnomusicology) the turn to performativity was part of a larger turn to scholarly immersion in critical and cultural theory that led to the emergence of a new kind of musicology-without-music. Too often, this so-called "new musicology" proved every bit as hermetic as the old musicology, focused more on source studies, style analysis and archive-based history, that it had sought to supplant. As Carolyn Abbate pointed out mordantly in a 2004 essay, even critical musicology that claimed allegiance to performers' perspectives, performance studies, or performativity theory often got so wrapped up in some form of hermeneutics as to ignore the physical fact of music's sound.[4] Consequently, she argued, this "new musicology" tended to ignore the ways in which musical sound linked physical beings in profoundly physical ways—in physical joys or physical anguish that defied written description. Abbate did not note that the same entanglement in hermeneutical practices which ignored the physical reality of music-as-sound was combined with critical musicology's renewed focus on canons of masterworks and musical cultures that correlated closely with variants of the "Western art music tradition," to which the commercial descendant of that tradition, Western popular music, was increasingly joined. Thus the "new musicology without music" was neither all that new nor all that liberated: by remaining hermetically and hermeneutically focused on the canonic musics of Western elites, it had largely retreated from musicology's once-strong commitment to creating audiences for new music in the Western concert tradition, and it had retreated both from its fleeting commitment to performers as knowers and creators of knowledge and from intense engagement with music as sound. An unfortunate side effect, then, of musicology's assimilation of performativity theory to hermeneutics and the study of music's embodied practices was the unintentional distancing of performativity from sound.

OUT OF THE SILENCE, SOUND STUDIES

At the turn of the present century, musicologists who were troubled by the gradual return of a "silent musicology" began increasingly to notice that scholars in a variety of nonmusical disciplines seemed to be writing not just about music, but about sound. About sound as sound. About film sound as contributing to the illusions of realism and human subjectivity projected as images on a screen. And especially, about recorded sound, as an innovation of the late nineteenth and twentieth centuries that had surely revolutionized what it meant to be musical, and about the new listening practices facilitated by portable audio devices. It was not until I turned my attention to my country's weaponizations of music in the so-called "global war on terror" that I, personally, realized how solidly a new, sound-centered interdiscipline had coalesced. It was an interdiscipline I would need to know if I were to understand the full implications of something a psychological operations officer said to a journalist after the sonic bombardment of Fallujah in November 2004, "It's not the music, it's the sound."[5]

Sound studies had been emerging gradually over the course of the twentieth century, as a field in which inventors, engineers, architects, physicists of sound, military planners, businessmen, and eventually, anthropologists, linguists, musicians, philosophers, computer scientists, and new media artists would find common interest in the phenomena and phenomenology of sound. One way to trace the genealogy of the interdiscipline goes back to Edison's invention of phonography and Bell's invention of telephony (in the same generation, of course, that saw the invention of musicology) and leads forward to Jonathan Sterne's historicist theorizing of audio technologies, Michael Bull and Les Back's studies of auditory culture, and Jason Stanyek and Sumanth Gopinath's collection of essays studying such phenomena as iPhone orchestras and ringtones.[6] Another path can include General Charles Squier's invention and management of various devices that used the physical properties of sound, mathematics, and multiplex telephony to locate artillery placements on the battlefield in World War I and communicate the coordinates to bomber pilots, and then move directly to Squier's best-known civilian application of multiplex telephony, the technology that led to Muzak, mother of all "piped music."[7] Still another leads through Varese's involvement with Western Electric's labs in lower Manhattan; Pierre Schaeffer's theory and practice of *musique concrete* in post–World War II Paris; John Cage's many experimental efforts to reconfigure the relationships linking sound, silence, listening practices, and the increasingly problematized concept "music"; and Pauline Oliveros's recordings of "deep caves," to the various sound-centered rather than music-centered rewritings of modernist and postmodernist acoustical practice produced by Friedrich Kittler.[8] And still another derives from Canadian composer R. Murray Schafer's theorization of "the soundscape"—a term that he meant, I think, to encompass the entire range of sounds and acoustical practices in a given place.[9] Schafer's work generated a significant swath of contemporary "sound studies" work that ranges from "sound walks" to electroacousmatic "soundscape" compositions to both ethnographic studies of specific acoustical ecologies and scientific studies commissioned in the service of local, national, and international noise abatement policies.

The intellectual influence of Schafer's work on current "sound studies" scholarship is matched only by the influence of anthropologist Steven Feld, who coined the word "acoustemology" to mean "a union of acoustics and epistemology" that could "investigate the primacy of sound as a modality of knowing and being in the world."[10] Feld went on to articulate what has become the foundational premise of most "sound studies" writing in the last decade—foundational because it is so broad:

> Sound both emanates from and penetrates bodies; this reciprocity of reflection and absorption is a creative means of orientation—one that tunes bodies to places and times through their sounding potential. Hearing and producing sound are thus embodied competencies that situate actors and their agency in particular historical worlds. These competencies contribute to their distinct and shared ways of being human: they contribute to possibilities for and realizations of authority, understanding, reflexivity, compassion and identity.

If Feld's statement can be said to be the foundational premise of "sound studies," it can also be said to have inspired many scholars in the humanities who had been writing about music—mostly popular music—for years, but who persisted in feeling intimidated by the expert knowledges to which scholars trained in music departments laid claim, especially the technical knowledges necessary to analyze musical style. By widening the field to include all sound, Feld made intellectual room for these scholars, many of whom had highly developed expert knowledges of their own, especially the technical knowledges about microphone placement, mixing of recorded tracks, and so forth that are necessary to analyze recorded sounds. Because these were scholars who had long been driven by their sheer, passionate love for an entity called "music" that they knew almost exclusively through electronic technologies of sound production and reproduction—through media, that is—they have been able both to acknowledge and to think critically about the fact that the listening practices of almost every human being now alive were formed in a media-saturated world. These scholars—people such as Josh Kun, Jayna Brown, and Daphne Brooks—have written some of the most accurate and compelling critical studies of contemporary musical life, especially as contemporary musical practices interact with practices of power, but they have written them more as studies of contemporary acoustical life.[11] Overwhelmingly, however, they have written as extremely attentive listeners. To the limited extent that they have applied performativity theory to the recordings they discuss, it has mostly been in the way that literary critics apply performativity theory to written texts. In that privileging of specific recorded texts, some of these writers have inadvertently erased both the performative acts of musical and acoustical labor that produced those texts and the economic interests served by the proliferation of new acoustical technologies.

Feld's statement can also be said to have produced subsidiary, often unspoken premises about sound that echo across the different strands of the interdiscipline. One (to which I will return at the end of this essay) is the radical decentering of music from the field of study. The other is the provocative notion that, in Jennifer Stoever-Ackerman's words, "sound is not merely a scientific phenomenon—vibrations passing through matter at particular frequencies—it is also a set of social relations."[12] This statement might be read as implying that because sound is vibration passing through matter at particular frequencies, it automatically creates social relations among all the people present, which would make sound always performative.

That is not, however, the way the idea is generally used. Instead, particularly in the rapidly growing literature on phonographies, sound is taken to condense the social relations that produced it—rather in the way that a phonograph record could once be said to have condensed into the grooves carved in wax or molded in vinyl both the somatic labor of performers and the acoustical energy their efforts produced. This belief seems (even in the recent, very sophisticated special issues of *American Quarterly, differences,* and *Social Text* devoted to sound studies) to go along with a kind of utopian fantasy that recordings in whatever format allow us to know by hearing the social relations of either past cultures (early twentieth-century North America) or distant ones (twenty-first-century Brazil), and to know those social relations in ways that neither writing nor the performative acts required to turn written music into sound allow.[13] Present in another foundational text of the field that is very widely cited, Josh Kun's *Audiotopia,* that fantasy has an extremely familiar ring, for it resembles the fantasy attributing something like transcendent knowledge to music in nineteenth-century European culture. (It even resembles the old Neoplatonic fantasy of early modern Italy, which proclaimed the world to be made of geometric relations that music made audible—and that music could then change—or the even older fantasy of the pre-Socratics, for whom the world was made of vibrations.) Still, fantastical and perhaps hopelessly Western though it might seem to be, the idea that sound might both condense social relations and constitute them through its inherent performativity seems extremely promising: it promises to illuminate, for example, both efforts to understand the cultural factors that produce the particular ways music has been used to torture people recently and any broader effort to understand how musicology, performativity and sound studies might yield insights about how we live now.

Occupella

I had been contemplating several thought experiments that I hoped might help me imagine how a braiding of these three interdisciplines might work when a student walked into my classroom with the example I had sought.

The night before, Trevor had been rehearsing the a cappella group he led, in one of the dorms, but it was noisy there.[14] Because it was still warm in the evenings, the group moved their rehearsal outside, to Washington Square Park. They went to a spot under the neoclassical arch built in 1892 to commemorate George Washington's inauguration; they formed a circle; and they began to rehearse one of their signature numbers, an a cappella arrangement of Led Zeppelin's "Ramble On" (complete with vocal imitations of percussion, electronics, and wailing guitars).[15]

Before they were finished with one run-through of the number, Trevor and his group of nine singers found themselves surrounded by police cars, and more ominously, by about fifty policemen wielding the helmets, shields, and batons of full riot gear. They were told to stop singing and leave the park. When one student protested that it was only 9:15 at night, that the park didn't close until midnight, that there were no residential buildings facing that part of the park, and that, after all, they were only singing, she was threatened with arrest. Indeed, they were all threatened—poked with nightsticks, yelled at to go away, threatened with immediate arrest. So they dispersed.

Back in his room, Trevor finished his homework, reading these words at the end of Rachel Beckles Willson's "The Parallax Worlds of the West-Eastern Divan Orchestra":

> [Music] . . . creates "moments of intensity" that may come suddenly and without warning, obstruct conceptual faculties, and have the potential to occupy and block the route on which we were set. This is essentially an emotional violence, rather than a life-threatening one, but it is extremely powerful.[16]

What about his group's rehearsal, Trevor wondered, could have created such a moment of intensity for the New York police that they would have perceived it as having the potential to occupy and block, or to be emotionally violent? What could have provoked those same police to threaten violence of their own? In class, we focused our discussion on three elements of the performance—the circle, the arch, and Led Zeppelin—and so I will here.

The Circle

Like many singing groups, especially ones practicing outdoors, Trevor's group had formed a circle so as to hear each other, tune to each other. Above all, it was a sound-centered choice—a choice to focus on sound, and on the intimate mutual hearing of each other and mutual exchange of riffs that produces well-tuned, well-timed a cappella performance. But however they sounded to others, and however comprehensibly sound-centered their circle would have seemed to musicians, my students thought that the group must have somehow seemed to the police reminiscent of the so-called "drum circle" that characterized daily life at lower Manhattan's Zuccotti Park during the nearly two months it was "occupied" by a largely youthful group of anticapitalist protesters called "Occupy

Wall Street." Therefore, we thought, the singers might have inadvertently evoked the association of Zuccotti Park's occupiers with noise.

Likened by sound studies blogger Gina Arnold to the highly political drum circles of Harlem in the 1960s, and to the vaguely countercultural drum circles of so-called "hippie" festivals ever since, the drum circle at Zuccotti Park seems to have varied in size from day to day, sometimes including professional and semi-professional players and sometimes reduced to people banging on the bottoms of overturned plastic buckets.[17] It probably never played in a literal circle, although I don't know that for sure: all the descriptions and videos I have consulted refer to concrete steps at the western end of the park as the location for drumming, which often prompted free-form dancing by other participants. Several regular drummers commented to the press that they felt the drumming was important to the occupation, in the words of one, "to give a pulse to keep something alive." By far the drum circle's most annoying practice was the percussion-band march in front of the New York Stock Exchange every day at 3 p.m., but some of the encampment's neighbors found the twelve-hour drumming sessions of the occupation's early days to be a close second. From September 17 to November 9, 2011, 115 complaints about noise from Occupy Wall Street were lodged by people living within a quarter mile, as compared to 175 complaints from the same neighborhood about the nighttime construction, featuring jackhammers drilling into bedrock, just down the street at the Word Trade Center site.[18] According to the *New York Times,* most of the complaints about the drumming came from a single high-rise that faces directly onto Zuccotti Park, which includes many multimillion-dollar condos. On October 26, the general assembly at Zuccotti Park reached an agreement with the community board that restricted the drumming to four hours a day, between noon and 2 p.m., and then again between 4 and 6 p.m.

"Noise" is, of course, a highly charged word, one that sound studies scholars are quick to define as also politicized, a way of characterizing as unwanted the sounds and sound-making practices of Others—people who are different, out of place, dangerous, incomprehensible, and unintelligible.[19] Not surprisingly, New York's lengthy noise abatement code defines "noise" more abstractly, as "an erratic, intermittent, or statistically random oscillation."[20] The code also defines in detail the decibel levels that are permitted in neighborhoods of various residential density, specifying maximum decibel levels for indoor readings of sixty-five by day and fifty-five at night for high-density areas such as lower Manhattan, and fines ranging from $350 to $875 for a first offense of "causing or permitting unreasonable noise." Arrest is not an option for any violation of the city's noise code, however; this was a cappella singing, not drumming, in an area of the park far from residential buildings, at 9:15 at night; and it was a literal, not a metaphorical, circle without a dancing "hippie"—or an African American—in sight. So even if the idea of "unreasonable noise" might have been evoked by what was apparently quite loud singing for an unamplified group, could that really have been what brought the police in such numbers, with such threats?

In class, we thought again about the configuration of the singing bodies, and about the social relations that they could be seen (and assumed by nonmusicians) to bring into being. Unlike most people who make music in Washington Square Park, Trevor's group was not performing, not making music for others (mainly tourists at that time of night), and not performing to solicit their listeners' spare change. Their music making was a matter of shared labor, of bodies and pleasures, of musically intimate relations in a public space. Moreover, they were kids, apparently leaderless kids sharing labor and pleasure, listening hard to each other while trying to tune everything else out, showing no interest in using the occasion for commerce. They looked just like the dominant demographic of Occupy Wall Street; and apparently leaderless, as they listened closely to each other while ostentatiously turning their physical backs on the possibility of exchanging their musical labor for other people's money, they must have looked like they instantiated both the "horizontal" organization of the Occupy movement that drives the media mad and the movement's articulated critique of late capitalism's reduction of all sociality to economic relations. Furthermore, on the night after the police had rousted hundreds of protestors from their makeshift beds at the Occupy Wall Street protest in Zuccotti Park, which was also the night before a citywide student strike was to rally in nearby Union Square, they must have looked like an advance guard sent to use music to occupy Washington Square Park.

The Arch

The students were gathered under the arch of Washington Square to use it as a resonator. Trevor reported that they were "really loud" for nine voices unamplified, but they couldn't have been much louder than any of the buskers who regularly set up on a nice night in Washington Square. I wasn't there, but it is hard to imagine nine people singing the arrangement they used as making "unreasonable noise." But it does seem possible that their use of a natural amplifier rather than an electronic one was more reminiscent of Occupy Wall Street than their circle was: it could have seemed like a new twist on Occupy's best-known acoustical practice, known variously as the "mic check" or the "human microphone."

Like most cities, New York requires a permit for amplified sound in public spaces. Not surprisingly, Occupy Wall Street did not seek such a permit, so they had no access to microphones, speakers, or even battery-powered bullhorns. Instead, all public speaking was amplified by humans, who repeated what was said in the center of the circle, outward in concentric circles. Approval was signaled silently by wiggling the fingers of upraised hands; disapproval was signaled silently by wiggling the fingers of downturned hands; the desire to block or veto a proposal in a general assembly or other meeting was signaled silently by crossing one's arms in front of one's chest:

Mic check!
    MIC CHECK!
It seems important
    IT SEEMS IMPORTANT
to demonstrate
    TO DEMONSTRATE
this phenomenon live
    THIS PHENOMENON LIVE
rather than to play
    RATHER THAN TO PLAY
a video or recording.
    A VIDEO OR RECORDING.
As you can tell,
    AS YOU CAN TELL,
this is not a method
    THIS IS NOT A METHOD
that is well suited
    THAT IS WELL SUITED
to the communication
    TO THE COMMUNICATION
of nuanced or complex ideas.
    OF NUANCED OR COMPLEX IDEAS.
But Richard Kim has pointed out
    BUT RICHARD KIM HAS POINTED OUT
that it is also not suited

THAT IT IS ALSO NOT SUITED
to demagoguery.
TO DEMAGOGUERY.
It requires speaker and microphones
IT REQUIRES SPEAKER AND MICROPHONES
to speak clearly,
TO SPEAK CLEARLY,
to think about phrasing,
TO THINK ABOUT PHRASING,
and to listen very, very well.
AND TO LISTEN VERY, VERY WELL.[21]

The first time I participated in the human microphone, I laughed with pleasure, for it seemed to me brilliant as a tactic that combines the performative with the acoustic to make everyone at an Occupy rally understand exactly how one voice, raised in protest or critique, can echo through a community. That alone seemed tremendously empowering—and dangerous to the 1 percent. But the more I thought about it, the more brilliant and dangerous it seemed to me: always, regardless of its semantic content, it is a performative of very specific relationships to the power regime the Occupy movement means to critique.

Overall, it seemed to me to enact a collective renunciation of the complex economy and power system that depends on limited ownership of energy and technology. It renounced, that is, nearly a century of dependence on PA systems for public protest to be heard, and therefore cut one important link that has ensured the dependence of anticapitalist protest movements on the technologies and theories of ownership they mean to protest. At the same time, it seemed to enact the substitution for that economy (which I call the economy of broadcast) of an economy of literally free speech—literally free because no one had to pay for it. Instead, when the things that individuals in the center of the group said were repeated—or not—by successively larger circles echoing the sounds of a single center, the resounding of speech and exchange of ideas happened without any exchange of wealth, and without any observable regard for the wealth of any body present. This seemed to be an extremely dramatic performance both of what a nonplutocratic community might feel like and of resistance to the then-recent decision by the United States Supreme Court that equated the financial contributions of corporations with the political speech of embodied human beings.[22]

If the human microphone responded to the city's prohibition by dramatically renouncing the several ways that public "free speech" has become entangled with a capitalist system that has made wealth a prerequisite (and equivalent) of speech, it harnessed the power of that renunciation to the power of iterative performance. As the ideas of the speaker resounded through the park, everyone within earshot heard them multiple times. For those of us who chose to repeat the ideas—to participate in the human microphone, that is—the iterative, unison performance of a speaker's cadence and phrasing inscribed in our own performances of self: (a) the ideas present in the semiotic level of her speech, (b) the actions of his body, and (c) our togetherness with the other participants in the microphone. Taken together, the renunciation of capital's effort to make money the prerequisite (or substitute) for speech and the embodiment of solidarity with like-minded strangers could actually produce a new, genuinely radical affect in the human microphone, what Kapchan calls "sound knowledge" (2015, this volume). And so, I think, to the extent that Trevor's group evoked the human microphone, they evoked a very real danger to the system that the city's police are paid to protect.

Led Zeppelin

Still, the music these students were singing would seem to have been a fairly innocent choice—or at least, so my students thought. Led Zeppelin is, after all, one of the classic bands of classic rock, known for blues-based songs and for innovative microphone and production effects that pointed the way to heavy metal. Because Americans from twenty to sixty-five know their songs and like them (albeit often for different reasons), the sound of Led Zeppelin songs in the night would seem, on the face of it, likely to appeal as much to passersby as to the police, a multiracial mix of mostly men in their thirties and early forties. Possibly some of the police would have known that Led Zeppelin had once been notorious for singing among the most misogynist lyrics of classic rock, and as the band most associated with trashing entire hotel suites on their tours. Maybe they would even have known the song "Ramble On" (from *Led Zeppelin II*, 1969), best known for its vaguely psychedelic lyrics based on Tolkien poems, for Jimmy Page's characteristic mic technique to produce the illusion of depth and ambient sound, for the band's combination of simultaneous riffs for electric and acoustic guitar, and for the fact that the engineering was so important to the track's sonorous effect that the band never performed it during a live concert.[23] But really, what role could any of this have played in these students' inadvertent performance of Occupy's dangers?

Performed a cappella, this music's sounds take on different meanings—because they are different sounds from the ones we all know. For the sounds of electrically amplified instruments to be produced by unamplified human bodies changes the acoustical energy that circulates in the space—it is less loud (and more), its resonating harmonics are differently produced, and its sonorous effect lacks both the depth of Page's mic and engineering tricks and the meticulously detailed hierarchies that make each line of the texture distinct because it does not blend but stays in its place. In almost every way, therefore, the sound of "Ramble On" performed live by only human voices literally brings into being different social relations than the recording covered would ever have done—just as it would literally bring into being different social relations than those it brought into being if the readers of this essay were to play the YouTube video of this song recorded by Trevor's group in 2010. It is not just that liveness matters; it is not just that the sight and presence of laboring bodies matter; it is that the sound is a different thing, produced by a different thing and therefore producing a different thing.

What could those social relations in the sound have been, and why might they have, so to speak, amplified the echoes of Occupy Wall Street I have already tried to hear in this incident?

The most immediate response I can give begins with the fact that the sounds were a transduction, through the medium of late adolescent human bodies alone, of sounds conceived and usually heard through the medium of electronic amplification. Led Zeppelin's characteristic sounds, as we know them, were always the sounds of cyborgs—music-making entities made of harmoniously interacting human bodies and both mechanically and electrically powered machines (acoustic and electric guitars, microphones, mixing boards, electromagnetized particles on tape that have since been sampled and sampled again by digitizing devices). All those devices that produced the version of this song which most of us would know were, in effect, also transducers—transducing the acoustical energy put in circulation by agential human bodies into various forms of electrical energy and then transducing it back again into the acoustical energy of the cyborg sound we know.

In Trevor's a cappella performance, the transduction ran the opposite way—from the acoustical energy of the cyborg sound produced by playback machines to his imagination as the song's arranger, to the acoustical energy of the noncyborg humans imitating cyborg sounds. Leaving aside the noncyborg imitation of cyborg sounds for just a second, I first want to point out that the social relations which are embedded in the a cappella performances run in a particular direction:

they transduce toward the noncyborg human, whereas even Led Zeppelin's live performance of this song, had it ever happened, would have embedded in the sounds a transduction away from the noncyborg human. I want, further, to posit that if one thinks about the direction of the transduction—away from the cyborg and toward the human—and one knows the principle and the practice of the human microphone, it would be easy to hear in the a cappella performance an echo of the human microphone's repudiation of the system, the whole way of life, in which electrically powered transductions and amplifications are enmeshed.

That repudiation, a performative that is the acoustical signature of Occupy Wall Street, is completely consistent with the movement's stated intention of working toward the creation of alternative social relations that do not depend so helplessly on the commercial exchanges that constitute the nexus of nonrenewable energy, corporate profiteering, and global capitalism. Many of the Occupy movement's spokespeople in New York are perfectly willing to admit that they and most of the rest of the so-called 99 percent in North America have enjoyed relatively easy lives thanks to the very system they hope to change. But in their acoustical practice they, like Trevor and his a cappella singers, mean to run the transduction of that system in reverse—away from the social relations embedded in the multiple transductions of the cyborg sound—while themselves transducing its benefits into what might almost be called postcyborg sounds, because they contrast with the human microphone's noncyborg sounds, or with the noncyborg sounds they would have made if they had been singing Palestrina, or barbershop, or doo-wop. From an analytical perspective that melds some aspects of performativity theory to some aspects of sound studies, the postcyborg sounds of the students covering Led Zeppelin (of all bands) would have to be considered absolutely central to the group's rousting—for, however inadvertently, they performed in sound (as well as in a social body) the most threatening aspect of the Occupy movement's politics, a transduction away from the cyborg's dependence on purchased electricity to a postcyborg, rather than a posthuman, space. And because the sound was acoustical energy, resonating off the marble of the Washington Square Arch, it occupied the space. Indeed, it occupied—literally moved—the arch's expensively restored stones; and in the same sense of literally moving molecules, it occupied the very bodies of the police. To paraphrase Feld's definition of *acoustemology,* musical sound that emanated from and penetrated bodies tuned those bodies to a place and a time; hearing and producing sound situated these actors and their agency in a particular historical world.

How, exactly, did I come to this interpretation? Critical musicology (what was once called "new musicology") authorized me to focus on context, and particularly to identify the general context that led the rousted students, their leader Trevor, and probably the police to receive the performance in relation to the acoustic practices and political challenge of Occupy Wall Street. Performativity theory informed my analysis of the human microphone as a literal embodiment of OWS's critique that is more eloquent than any of the movement's public statements—and that, if the practice is sustained, is more likely to effect change than any statement the group might make via established or social media. "Sound studies" authorized me to hear a musical practice in relationship to a nonmusical acoustical practice. Traditional musicological knowledge about the specific repertoire performed that night—the meanings available to anyone who recognized it as that song, associated with that group, with that performance history—was necessary to understand how this particular a cappella performance could be logically, musically connected to the concept of the human mic. Sound studies' focus on technology gave me the concept of transduction (the basic process of a microphone). Performativity allowed me to think about transduction as a process that, if performed by human bodies, could go in either direction, and thus could produce as sound (but not exactly condense into sound) an idea of postcyborg humans in joyous community so novel—and so absolutely right as a synecdoche of the Occupy movement—that it had to be silenced.

This was not a tidy braiding of methodologies, each preserving its own identity. Rather, the methodologies almost morph into each other as, together, they move my thought along. Perhaps, in that morphing into each other, they could seem to behave like waves of acoustical energy that set all the materials in their path in sympathetically vibrating motion. Perhaps, in their mutual resonance and reverberation, they tune my thought to the particular, necessarily ephemeral details of time and place that produced the constructed interaction I have called "Occupella" on that warm November night in Washington Square Park. Perhaps my transduction of my thus-tuned thought into written words has tuned your own thought to a way of reflecting usefully on experience that more resembles the phenomenology of aurality than that of visuality. Perhaps, that is, in my analysis of the "Occupella" incident I have moved toward a kind of writing that models the processual structure of how we become knowers through sound. Perhaps.

Yet I believe this essay, like all writing, fails to do justice to sound in two ways. First, it fails to do justice to the sheer physicality of sound, which surely was a factor in creating the anxious urgency with which the police threatened Trevor's group that night. Because it does not vibrate our very skin and bones, writing can never move us in the way that Carolyn Abbate has called "drastic." Second, this essay stumbles before the paradoxical temporality of sound: sound both endures in the infinitesimal traces of its waves' impact on the vibrating bodies that produce and reproduce it and refuses to endure as what it was in any given moment. Trevor's singers, the police who rousted them, the stones of Washington Square's arch will never be who and what they were before that night; but the particular resonances of the event itself resist the desire, shared by writing, musicology, and theorizing, simultaneously to fix events in time and to render them timeless. Sound holds ephemerality and its ability to produce long-lasting but essentially impermanent change in a different kind of balance, an exquisite balance that is never still, never fully silent, never so much inscribed for all time as readying the material world to resound again, and again, always a little differently.

Perhaps writing, performativity theory, and even sound studies' reach to know sound as "a modality of knowing and being in the world" necessarily stumble in the face of sound's proliferating differences. Perhaps that is, exactly, what it is to know through sound.

ACKNOWLEDGMENTS

An early version of this essay was delivered as the keynote address to the New Zealand Musicological Association in November 2011. I am grateful to Elizabeth Hudson, Deborah Kapchen, Michelle Kisliuk, Margaret McFadden, Stephan Prock, Inge van Rijk, and Deborah Vargas for comments on that initial text.

NOTES

1. Performativity theory entered musicological discourse from gender-and-sexuality studies primarily through the citations of Judith Butler, *Gender Trouble: Feminism and the Subversion of Identity* (New York: Routledge, 1990). It simultaneously entered musicological and ethnomusicological discourse from such classic texts of performance studies as Richard Schechner, *Between Theater and Anthropology* (Philadelphia: University of Pennsylvania Press, 1986) and Victor Turner, *The Anthropology of Performance* (New York: PAJ Publications, 1988).

2. Christopher Small, *Music for the Common Tongue* (London: Calder Publications, 1987) and *Musicking: The Meanings of Performing and Listening* (Hanover, NH: Wesleyan University Press, 1998).

3. One touchstone text of such writing is Michelle Kisliuk, *Seize the Dance! BaAka Musical Life and the Ethnography of Performance* (New York: Oxford University Press, 1998).

4. Carolyn Abbate, "Music—Drastic or Gnostic?" *Critical Inquiry* 30, no. 3 (2004): 505–36.

5. Lane DeGregory, "Iraq 'n' Roll," *Tampa Bay Times Online*, November 21, 2004, http://sptimes/com/2004/11/21/Floridian/Iraq_n_roll.shtml.

6. Jonathan Sterne, *The Audible Past: Cultural Origins of Sound Reproduction* (Durham, NC: Duke University Press, 2003); Michael Bull and Les Back, eds., *The Auditory Culture Reader* (London: Bloomsbury Academic, 2004); Sumanth Gopinath and Jason Stanyek, eds., *The Oxford Handbook of Mobile Music Studies* (Oxford: Oxford University Press, 2015). For an up-to-date survey of the literature, see Jonathan Sterne, *The Sound Studies Reader* (New York: Routledge, 2012).

7. Joseph Lanza, *Elevator Music: A Surreal History of Muzak, Easy-Listening, and Other Moodsong* (Ann Arbor: University of Michigan Press, 2004).

8. Relevant touchstone texts include Friedrich Kittler, *Gramophone, Film, Typewriter*, trans. Geoffrey Winthrop-Young and Michael Wutz (Palo Alto: Stanford University Press, 1999); Douglas Kahn, *Noise, Water, Meat: A History of Sound in the Arts* (Cambridge, MA: MIT Press, 2001); and Frances Dyson, *Sounding New Media: Immersion and Embodiment in the Arts and Culture* (Berkeley: University of California Press, 2009).

9. R. Murray Schaefer, *The Soundscape: Our Sonic Environment and the Tuning of the World* (Rochester, VT: Destiny Books, 1993).

10. Feld articulated this idea in many texts. Quotations in the present text are from Steven Feld, "A Rainforest Acoustemology," in *The Auditory Culture Reader*, ed. Michael Bull and Les Back, 223–38 (London: Bloomsbury Academic, 2004).

11. See, for example, Josh Kun, *Audiotopia: Music, Race and America* (Berkeley: University of California Press, 2005); Jayna Brown, *Babylon Girls: Black Women Performers and the Shaping of Modernity* (Durham, NC: Duke University Press, 2008); and Daphne Brooks, *Jeff Buckley's Grace* (New York: Bloomsbury Academic, 2005).

12. Jennifer Stoever-Ackerman, "Reproducing U.S. Citizenship in *Blackboard Jungle:* Race, Cold War Liberalism, and the Tape Recorder," *American Quarterly* 63, no. 3 (2011): 781–804.

13. *American Quarterly* 63, no. 3 (2011); *differences* 22, nos. 2–3 (2011); and *Social Text* 28, no. 1 (Spring 2010).

14. I am grateful to Trevor Bachman, NYU class of 2012, Yoo-Jin Aun, Paul De Vincenzo, Casey Lewis, Nevin Nguyen-Tan, and Tom Scary, all members of my fall 2011 seminar "Sounds Like War!" for an extremely lively discussion of this incident.

15. A 2010 performance of Trevor's arrangement by his group, the N'Harmonics, is available on YouTube at http://www.youtube.com/watch?v=1BdGRokxSbo.

16. Rachel Beckles-Willson, "The Parallax Worlds of the West-Eastern Divan Orchestra," *Journal of the Royal Musical Association* 134, no. 2 (2009): 319–47.

17. Gina Arnold, "The Sound of Hippiesomething, or Drum Circles at #OccupyWallStreet," *Sounding Out* (blog), November 7, 2011, accessed on March 3, 2013, http://soundstudiesblog.com/2011/11/07/the-sound-of-hippiesomething-or-drum-circles-at-occupy. I am grateful to Gordon Beeferman, Josh Huddleston, and Matt McCarthy for descriptions of Occupy drum circles they heard in fall 2011.

18. A complete collection of the *New York Times*' coverage of Occupy Wall Street, accessed on September 1, 2014, is available online at http://topics.nytimes.com/top/reference/timestopics/organizations/o/occupy_wall_street.

19. See Stoever-Ackerman, "Reproducing U.S. Citizenship in *Blackboard Jungle*," for an excellent analysis along these lines.

20. For the noise code of the City of New York, see http://www.nyc.gov.html/dep/pdf/noise_code_guide.pdf.

21. Richard Kim, "We Are All Human Microphones Now," *The Nation* (blog), October 3, 2011, http://www.thenation.com/blog/163767/we-are-all-human-microphones-now#.

22. The decision, Citizens United v. Federal Election Commission, can be found online at http://www.supremecourt.gov/opinions/09pdf/08–205.pdf, accessed on March 3, 2013.

23. On Led Zeppelin, see Susan Fast, *In the Houses of the Holy: Led Zeppelin and the Power of Rock Music* (New York: Oxford University Press, 2001); Dave Lewis, *From a Whisper to a Scream: The Complete Guide to the Music of Led Zeppelin* (London: Omnibus Press, 2012); and Frank Reddon, *Sonic Book: The Impact of Led Zeppelin (Break and Enter)* (Fort Erie, Ontario: Enzepplopedia Publishing, 2008). On their characteristic recording and mixing techniques, see Barry Cleveland, "Mixing Led Zeppelin II," *Guitar Player*, May 2008, http://web.archive.org/web/20080915051359/http://www.guitarplayer.com/article/mixing-led-zeppelin/may-08/36033.

WORKS CITED

Abbate, Carolyn. "Music—Drastic or Gnostic?" *Critical Inquiry* 30, no. 3 (2004): 505–36.

Arnold, Gina. "The Sound of Hippiesomething, or Drum Circles at #OccupyWallStreet." Accessed on March 3, 2013. http://soundstudiesblog.com/2011/11/07/the-sound-of-hippiesomething-or-drum-circles-at-occupy.

Beckles-Willson, Rachel. "The Parallax Worlds of the West-Eastern Divan Orchestra." *Journal of the Royal Musical Association* 134, no. 2 (2009): 319–47.

Brooks, Daphne. *Jeff Buckley's Grace.* New York: Bloomsbury, 2005.

Brown, Jayna. *Babylon Girls: Black Women Performers and the Shaping of Modernity.* Durham, NC: Duke University Press, 2008.

Bull, Michael, and Les Back, eds. *The Auditory Culture Reader.* London: Bloomsbury, 2004.

Butler, Judith. *Gender Trouble: Feminism and the Subversion of Identity.* New York: Routledge, 1990.

Cleveland, Barry. "Mixing Led Zeppelin II." *Guitar Player.* May 2008. Accessed on March 3, 2013. http://web.archive.org/web/20080915051359/http://www.guitarplayer.com/article/mixing-led-zeppelin/may-08/36033.

DeGregory, Lane. "Iraq 'n' Roll." *Tampa Bay Times Online.* November 21, 2004. http://www.sptimes.com/2004/11/21/Floridian/Iraq__n__roll.shtml.

Dyson, Frances. *Sounding New Media: Immersion and Embodiment in the Arts and Culture.* Berkeley: University of California Press, 2009.

Fast, Susan. *In the Houses of the Holy: Led Zeppelin and the Power of Rock Music.* New York: Oxford University Press, 2001.

Feld, Steven. "A Rainforest Acoustemology." In *The Auditory Culture Reader,* edited by Michael Bull and Les Back, 223–38. London: Bloomsbury, 2004.

Gopinath, Sumanth, and Jason Stanyek, eds. *The Oxford Handbook of Mobile Music Studies.* Oxford: Oxford University Press, 2015.

Kahn, Douglas. *Noise, Water, Meat: A History of Sound in the Arts.* Cambridge, MA: MIT Press, 2001.

Kim, Richard. "We Are All Human Microphones Now." *The Nation* (blog). October 3, 2011. Accessed on March 3, 2013. http://www.thenation.com/blog/163767/we-are-all-human-microphones-now#.

Kisliuk, Michelle. *Seize the Dance! BaAka Musical Life and the Ethnography of Performance.* New York: Oxford University Press, 1998.

Kittler, Friedrich. *Gramophone, Film, Typewriter.* Translated by Geoffrey Winthrop-Young and Michael Wutz. Palo Alto, CA: Stanford University Press, 1999.

Kun, Josh. *Audiotopia: Music, Race and America.* Berkeley: University of California Press, 2005.

Lanza, Joseph. *Elevator Music: A Surreal History of Muzak, Easy-Listening, and Other Moodsong.* Ann Arbor: University of Michigan Press, 2004.

Lewis, Dave. *From a Whisper to a Scream: The Complete Guide to the Music of Led Zeppelin.* London: Omnibus Press, 2012.

Reddon, Frank. *Sonic Book: The Impact of Led Zeppelin (Break and Enter.* Fort Erie, Ontario: Enzepplopedia, 2008.

Schafer, R. Murray. *The Soundscape: Our Sonic Environment and the Tuning of the World.* Rochester, VT: Destiny Books, 1993.

Schechner, Richard. *Between Theater and Anthropology.* Philadelphia: University of Pennsylvania Press, 1986.

Small, Christopher. *Music for the Common Tongue.* London: Calder Publications, 1987.

———. *Musicking: The Meanings of Performing and Listening.* Hanover, NH: Wesleyan University Press, 1998.

Sterne, Jonathan. *The Audible Past: Cultural Origins of Sound Reproduction.* Durham, NC: Duke University Press, 2003.

———. *The Sound Studies Reader.* New York: Routledge, 2012.

Stoever-Ackerman, Jennifer. "Reproducing U.S. Citizenship in *Blackboard Jungle:* Race, Cold War Liberalism, and the Tape Recorder." *American Quarterly* 63, no. 3 (2011): 781–804.

Turner, Victor. *The Anthropology of Performance.* New York: PAJ Publications, 1988.

J. MARTIN DAUGHTRY

2. Acoustic Palimpsests

LAYER 1: OLDEST SUBSTRATE

(The Poem That Inspired This Essay)

А так как мне бумаги не хватило
Я на твоем пишу черновике.
И вот чужое слово проступает
И, как снежинка на моей руке,
Доверчиво и без упрека тает.
И темные ресницы Антиноя
Вдруг поднялись, и там—зеленый
дым,
И ветерком повеяло родным . . .
Не море ли?—
Нет, это только хвоя
Могильная и в накипаньи пен
Все ближе, ближе . . .
"Marche funèbre" . . .
Шопен . . .

And since I don't have enough paper,
I am writing on your rough draft.
And here an alien word shows through
And as did a snowflake back then on
a hand,
It melts trustingly, without reproach.
And the dark lashes of Antinoüs
Suddenly rose—and there was green
smoke
And a native breeze blew . . .
Isn't it the sea?
No, it is only pine needles
On a grave, and in the seething foam
Ever closer, closer . . .
Marche funèbre . . .
Chopin . . .

Anna Akhmatova
Translated by
Alexandra Harrington
(emphasis added)[1]

LAYER 2: SUBSTRATE

(Draft Introduction, Scratched Out in Favor of More Formal Introduction Below)

[. . . *but then lightly revised, along with the rest of this essay, in 2015 . . .*]

~~After receiving an invitation from my dear friend Deborah Kapchan to contribute to a conference panel on, as she explained it to me, "writing about writing about sound," I've been doing a lot of thinking, and writing, and thinking about writing (about sound, among other things). My thinking about writing about writing about sound—my thinking about "tearing a new sound" from our writing about sound "to sound out new perceptual possibilities," to re-use Deborah's language—my thinking, I want to say, has been deliberately playful in nature, on the theory that one of the joys of launching oneself into the realm of the "meta" is a certain freedom from the earnest solemnity that is a hallowed hallmark of ethnographic writing. I hope that this presentation, which is the result of my first attempt to write down my thoughts about writing about writing about sound, retains some of the playfulness with which my topic visited my thoughts—but, I note with interest, as I apply my playful thoughts to real situations, some of the solemnity returns. It must return, because the situations I describe are consequential for the people involved. These people, like all of us, are involved in the "serious game" (Ortner 1997) of social life, in which the "play" involves our fundamentally experimental, improvisational approach to life within cultural confines, and the stakes for each individual are high. In the same spirit, I hope to play seriously with my topic here.~~

~~This topic of mine is not really mine, of course, or at least not exclusively. My topic has been borrowed, recovered, recalibrated from the work of others. I've scraped my topic partially clean of its old connotations, and reappropriated it to serve my own purposes. You might say that my hoary topic has been recycled like an old piece of vellum, like an old draft that has become scrap paper, like a billboard that has been tagged by a graffiti artist . . . in other words, like a palimpsest. The fact that my topic has, like my words, been recycled, the fact that my topic is, in this way, like a palimpsest is actually quite felicitous, as the palimpsest happens to be my topic. (Like dialogic works about dialogue and polyphonic works about polyphony, a palimpsestic work about palimpsests performs an iconicity of style that is very stylish within our discipline, as you may have noticed . . .)~~

LAYER 3: SUBSTRATE

(Introduction, Written October 2009 for Oral Presentation at the Annual Meeting of the Society for Ethnomusicology, Before Work on the Article Commenced, and Then Revised Later)

The word "theory," it is often noted, derives from the Greek *theorein*, meaning to look at or see. The convention is to say that theories give us new ways of seeing the world. Given the academy's current infatuation with *intersensoriality* and *synesthesia*, I'm sure no one will object to us extending theory's purview further into the sensorium: th eories, we can comfortably say, give us new ways of seeing, hearing, *sensing* the world. If this is so, then metaphors, I would like to argue, are theories in miniature, *in utero*, even—and as such operate on a less expansive, tactical plane, opening small, ephemeral, but at times valuable discursive spaces in which we can think and sense the world anew. Of course, we could also define the downside of theory and metaphor by rendering explicit an obvious corollary: in providing a new way of sensing the world, a theory simultaneously occludes, if only temporarily, alternative ways of sensing the world. Metaphors, it would stand to reason, do the same thing, but less expansively, less violently. In this presentation, I'm interested in focusing on a metaphor that lays bare the layered nature of sonorous objects and auditory experience. *No, that's not quite right, scratch that*: I'm interested in using a metaphor to help us *imagine* sonorous objects and auditory experience *as layered*. This thought experiment asks if the palimpsest—a venerable (although some might say threadbare) source for metaphorical play—can be recalibrated (or "wired for sound") in order to point us toward a politics of listening that is both hermeneutically rich and deeply complementary to the ethnographic project. It proposes the palimpsest as a platform for undertaking a kind of reverse engineering of musical texts and listening activities. It positions the palimpsest as a structured micromethodology for thick description—a way to achieve interpretive thickness by uncovering the moments of inscription and erasure that lie beneath acoustic phenomena and auditory practices. Unlike the music philologist peering through editorial layers in search of the musical *urtext*, the "palimpsestuous" scholar is equally enthralled by each layer, each accretion, as well as by the gestalt effect of layeredness.[2]

I begin by dwelling briefly on palimpsests proper, and then experiment with several ways of transducing the concept of the palimpsest into the realm of the auditory. Before I commence, though, let me say this: I am aware that this project may strike some of you as paradoxical, anachronistic, or even slightly perverse. In the early twenty-first century, many of us are more inclined to think of sound as always-in-motion than we are to think of it as a stationary object (which is, one might argue, what a textual palimpsest is at its base). Decades after the decline of structuralism, the notion that sound is layered, and therefore in some general sense, fixed, feels less intuitive than the notion that sound is a dynamic force, a vibration that can "penetrate and permeate, so effortlessly becom[ing] the soft catastrophe of space" (Connor [2005] 2011, 133). Indeed, my own intellectual proclivities have tended to bend in this direction. So why then am I tethering sound to a metaphor that appears to privilege textuality, and with it, stasis? In defense of this humble thought experiment, I'll say two things. First, as I hope to demonstrate, palimpsests are less like stable objects and more like fluid processes than other texts. Second, and more fundamentally, while I am conscious of its drawbacks (several of which I discuss following), I find that the metaphor of the acoustic palimpsest simply works for me. By this I mean that it is performing some work for me; it works within the context of my work—which is, in the end, all one can ask of a metaphor.

You may know that the original palimpsests were previously inscribed sheets of vellum or other types of parchment that were reinscribed after the original writing had been erased. In the early medieval period, the original text was washed away with a mixture of milk and oat bran or scraped clean by medieval scribes using pumice dust. This practice was largely the result of the economics of the period: the value of vellum as a commodity often exceeded the economic or symbolic value of that which was written upon it. With a large manuscript such as the Bible requiring the skins of 250 sheep, it is not at all surprising that trade in used pages was brisk throughout the literate world in the centuries preceding the industrial production of paper (Mathisen 2008, 148). At the same time, some have suggested that "another motive may have been directed by the desire of Church officials to 'convert' pagan Greek script by overlaying it with the word of God."[3] I would like to keep both of these potential justifications—the pragmatic and the ideological—hovering in the background as we move forward.

Over the centuries, as the result of oxidation and other natural processes, the original texts often began to reappear beneath the newer writing. This fact made it possible for scholars of the palimpsest to engage in a kind of textual archaeology: ignoring the most recent layer, they peered back into the past, straining to read the words that had been effectively buried. In Latin, these faint textual ghosts were called the *scriptio inferior* ("underwriting") or *scriptio anterior* ("former writing"). The palimpsest is thus the result of successive acts of partial erasure

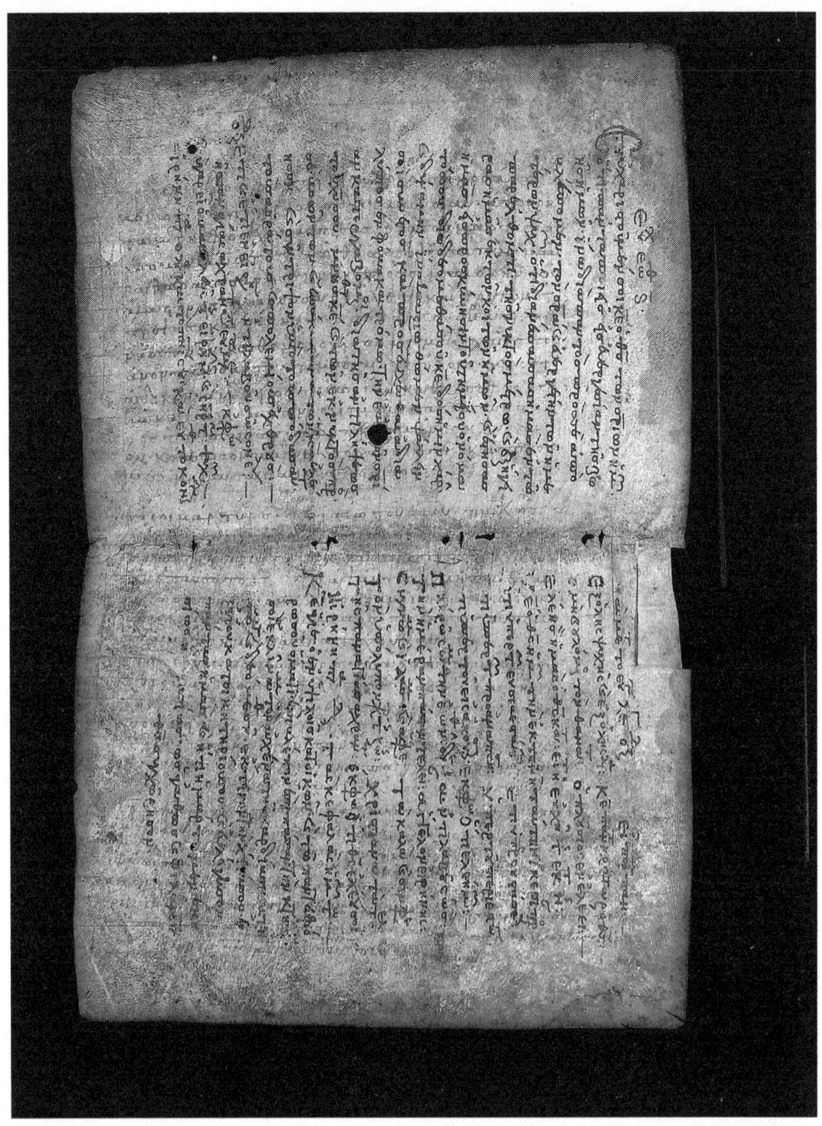

Figure 2.1 The Archimedes Palimpsest. Courtesy of the Rochester Institute of Technology. Licensed under Creative Commons Attribution 2.0 Unported Access Rights.

and inscription, acts that turn it into a "multilayered record" (*Oxford English Dictionary*), a trace of multiple histories and multiple authors.

In the late nineteenth and twentieth centuries, along with the development of new chemical techniques for uncovering the *scriptio inferior* and the widely publicized recovery of a number of historically important "lost" texts (McDonagh 1987, 210), the palimpsest emerged as a rich, interdisciplinary metaphor for the fundamentally interconnected, multiply situated, discursive nature of human experience. The acts of partial erasure and writing-upon-writing that the palimpsest presumes have inspired a vast tropology revolving around themes of temporality, memory, intertextuality, and power. For English author Thomas De Quincey (1845), the palimpsest was a textual model of human consciousness, which he imagined as a multilayered neural archive of experiences.[4] ("Such a palimpsest is my brain; such a palimpsest, O reader! is yours.") For Freud (1925), the palimpsest, or at least its structural equivalent, provides a model for the mechanism of memory, and the relationship between conscious perception and the unconscious.[5] For Russian poet Anna Akhmatova, the author of this essay's epigraph (1941–1966), the palimpsest represents the anxiety and intimacy of poetic influence.[6] For Andreas Huyssen (2003), architectural palimpsests—the visible residue of buildings that have since been razed—provide a theoretical model for reading urban spaces intertextually and recovering "present pasts" from the abyss of cultural amnesia. And for scores of street artists in my New York neighborhood, the palimpsest is the model for a radically democratic method of collaborative artistic creation, in which one artist's work becomes a colorful canvas for someone else the next day.

Closer to home for scholars of aurality, Tom Porcello's influential (1998) discussion of social phenomenology in and around the recording studio draws on the palimpsest's twentieth-century equivalent, the reel-to-reel tape, to provide new and complementary language for questioning the nature of the musical text and discussing the varied ways in which we experience temporality in music. His discussion focuses on the phenomenon of "print-through," the ghostly pre- or post-echo of musical material that has been inadvertently "transferred through adjacent layers when [analog audio] tape is wound on a reel" (485). As a recording engineer, Porcello recognized print-through as a technical problem to be avoided by winding the reel "tails-out," so that "the worst print-through comes as a post-echo and stands the greatest possibility of being masked by the program itself" (Woram 1982, quoted in Porcello 1998, 485). At the same time, as a music listener, Porcello often appreciated print-through for its ability to generate a Barthian

Figures 2.2-3 Palimpsestic street art, Orchard Street, New York City. Photo courtesy of the author.

Figure 2.4 Unintentional palimsestic street art, United Arab Eirates. Photo courtesy of the author.

"plaisir du texte," a "Dionysian strip-tease" (487) or partial presentation of the musical gesture that is to come. Drawing on these and other experiences, Porcello deploys print-through as a metaphor (1) to question the status of the musical text; (2) to "elasticiz[e] the boundaries drawn around standard conceptions of encounters with music"; and (3) to illuminate "cumulative listening experiences engendered in the mediated social spaces of musical encounter" (485–86). He also regards the act of multitrack recording more generally as structurally similar to the layering of discourses, subject positions, and identities that occurs in social interactions (488).

In a different but complementary vein, Nina Eidsheim deploys the palimpsest trope in describing the ways in which the embodied practice of singing inscribes "narratives of the body, race, class, vocal genres and practices" into "the musculature of the body" (209–10), as well as the ways that listeners hear voices—and vocal timbre specifically—in relation to all of the voices they have previously heard (212). Following the logic of Derrida's (1976, 158) maxim that "there is nothing outside the text," she asks her readers to consider the activity of singing as itself a type of inscription, a type of writing, and therefore, "a palimpsest, a constant re-writing over a prior document that may never be entirely erased . . . a struggle for power":

> If the activity of singing is conceived as inscription on an imperfectly erased canvas, writing in the midst of narratives of the body, race, class, vocal genres and practices, then the sound of singing becomes the sound, and the echo, of that fragmented palimpsest. In the case of the voice, those narratives are also inscribed into the musculature of the body, and thus the fragments are sounded as a coherent whole. (209)

Eidsheim's corporeal palimpsest provides a model for listening to voices as the result of complex histories, for hearing history—and therefore politics—within the voice's grain. It asks us to imagine the totality of the voice as comprised of multiple fragments, multiple layers that are acquired over time.

In this essay I "draw upon"—in the palimpsestic sense of that phrase—the aforementioned work in an attempt to flesh out a general concept of "acoustic palimpsest." I use this neologism to foreground the multiple acts of erasure, effacement, occupation, displacement, collaboration, and reinscription that are embedded in music composition, performance, and recording; acts that can be recovered—partially, imperfectly, but valuably—by critical listening, research, and occasional leaps of the imagination. The importance of the imaginative leap (as a research method and rhetorical strategy) has gone largely unacknowledged within the social sciences until recently. But as Avery Gordon reminds us:

> It is essential to see the things and the people who are primarily unseen and banished to the periphery of our social graciousness. At a minimum it is essential because they see you and address you. They have, as Gayatri Spivak remarked, a strategy towards you. Absent, neglected, ghostly: it is essential to imagine their life worlds because you have no other choice but to make things up in the interstices of the factual and the fabulous, the place where the shadow and the act converge. (2008, 196–97)

I want to perform a similar operation—not "to see things . . . unseen" but to hear things unheard, and barely heard. To imagine the unheard as the barely heard and strain to listen past the sonic foreground down to the ghostly echo, the faint trace of obscured selves that lie on or just beyond the periphery of audibility.

LAYER 4: SUBSTRATE

(Body, Expanded Version of Oral Presentation,
Written June 2010, Revised 2013)

What exactly is an acoustic palimpsest, other than an oxymoron? How can a mutely layered text be twisted into a sound-centered metaphor? My hope is that, like a palimpsest itself, my metaphor will emerge through a slow process of layering, an accrual of stories that I initiate and that, if it is to be remotely successful, others will continue. I present the following three stories, each of which describes a situation in which the acoustic palimpsest metaphor strikes me as apt. The first two are quite brief; the third, which builds on details discussed in the first two, is somewhat longer. These examples come directly from research projects that I'm actively working on. My suspicion is that, if I worked on other projects, other equally powerful examples would be brought to my attention. And so, to commence:

Layered Listening

In all but the most clinical of circumstances, we are confronted by sounds that emanate from multiple sources. Most music scholarship resolutely ignores the scrim of ambient sounds that accompanies the vast majority of music listening experiences. A rare exception is the work of David Beer, who, in a recent article on iPods and the "urban mise-en-scene," argues that the increasingly common practice of listening to MP3 players in noisy urban spaces does not result in the creation of a "privatized auditory bubble" as scholars such as Michael Bull (2007) have claimed. Rather, many, if not all, of our mobile music listening practices are fundamentally layered. Beer states the obvious fact that:

> [S]ound generated in [the ears of users] by the mobile music device is not the only sound they hear: they are still exposed to soundscapes of the urban territories through which they pass, and in fact, if the earphones are loud enough, may also be contributing to other people's experiences through sound leakage. (2007, 858)

Indeed, anyone who listens to an iPod in an urban area knows that music coming through headphones cannot fully drown out the sounds of a bus engine or passing police siren. And anyone who has encountered an iPod user in an elevator knows that mobile music listening can frequently become an (inadvertently) shared experience. These moments of layered listening are easy to disregard because they are ubiquitous, ephemeral, largely unconscious, and relatively benign. In other situations, however, the layering of sonic material is a phenomenon of far greater consequence. In my ongoing research on the sonic dimension of the Iraq war,[7] for example, I frequently encounter talk about the layers of sound through which military service members deployed in urban areas learned to listen for the all-important sounds of shots being fired. As an Air Force major who was stationed in Iraq once described it to me, beneath the "engine sounds, transmission sounds, road noise, static over the radio . . . and ambient noises [over headphones] . . . everybody is very much in tune, listening for gunfire or rocket fire." The focal point of their aural acuity floated from one sound source to another as they scanned the acoustic environment for signs of danger and dis-ease.

While a number of military regulations prohibited listening to music on missions, these regulations were only sporadically enforced. During the early stage of the war, before the danger from improvised explosive devices (IEDs) became acute, service members frequently listened to music to alleviate boredom while driving from one place to another or to "amp [themselves] up" to a state of heightened readiness, hyperawareness, and aggression. When music was deployed in these situations, it was often deeply buried beneath many layers of ambient sound. While rumbling along the road in an uparmored Humvee that gave off ninety-five decibels of engine noise, bantering back and forth with one's comrades, keeping one ear on the radio and another tuned for the possibility of gunfire or other signs of "action," music listening could take on a kind of ethereal quality, with the tinny strains of a jury-rigged sound system providing just enough sonic cues of a familiar song for listeners to fill in the blanks in their imaginations. Frequently, it would be necessary to tune out or turn off the music altogether, as a communication from the radio, or the soft sound of a ricochet against the hull of their vehicle, or another sound related to their mission commanded their attention. These were listening skills that they didn't have when they first deployed to Iraq. It was only over time that they learned to distinguish the often-soft significant sounds from the often-loud noises that obscured them. They became, in this sense, good analogues to the historian trying to discern a discrete text from within the palimpsest: they became experts at layered listening.

In less-violent situations, music listeners strive to keep the figure-ground relations intact, focusing on music and disregarding noise. As scholars of auditory experience, however, we can invoke the palimpsest metaphor to flip figure and ground, if only temporarily, in order to situate music listening within the sonorous matrix that accompanies and complicates it, and to take this matrix seriously as a rich cultural artifact in its own right. The effect of this move is to blur the line between the musical object and the sonorous world, to allow the cacophony of the world to rush into the study of music, and to place the politics of navigating through this complex and noisy world at the center of discussions of listening.

Music on Bones

In addition to the ambient world, recording and playback technologies create their own layers of sound that inscribe themselves on top of the music they deliver. Print-through, distortion, the pops and hiss of vinyl, and the skips and clips of digital recording constitute an acoustic layer *through which* we have trained ourselves to listen to music. However, not all of the palimpsestic dimensions of recording technologies can be apprehended with the ears alone. I have in mind a recording practice that resulted in a musical artifact whose layers were notable for being not aurally but *visually* arresting: the practice in question marked the beginning of the underground recording scene in the postwar Soviet Union.

This story—as told by one of its protagonists, Boris Taigin (1999), and others (Belyi 2008, Ivanov 2008)—begins in 1946.[8] That year, a young Soviet engineer named Stanislav Filon brought a German record-cutting machine (made by the Telefunken Company) back from the front as a war trophy. Filon used the machine to start a business in Leningrad. His shop, called "Sonic Correspondence" (*zvukovye pis'ma,* literally "sound letters") recorded the voices of customers onto discs made out of an industrial plastic called Detselit. However, according to Taigin, these pieces of "sonic correspondence" were not the primary product of Filon's shop:

> This was all a shell, an official cover. The main purpose for which the studio was built was to illegally produce what we called "fast-selling goods" [i.e., contraband] . . . After the end of the workday, when the studio was closed, that's when the real work would start! Past midnight, and often all the way through till dawn, they dubbed . . . jazz music played by popular foreign orchestras, and, most importantly, tangos, foxtrots, and romances sung in Russian by emigrants of the first and second-wave emigration from Russia. (Taigin 1999, my translation)

As Detselit phonographic blanks were relatively expensive and hard to come by, Filon and his comrades turned to other media: first, to large-format photographic film, and somewhat later to used medical X-rays. Both were soft enough to allow for inscription and durable enough to withstand the stylus on Soviet record players, but the X-rays had the extra advantage of being virtually free. The archives of the city's hospitals were always drowning in old X-rays, which they were required to periodically burn to make room for new ones. Some hospital staff members gave away the film; others sold it to Filon and Co. in bulk. And so, working with an abundant supply of recycled media that would have caused a medieval scribe, perpetually short of vellum, to salivate, the entrepreneurial Filon began to distribute recordings that looked like this:

It should come as no surprise that these musical artifacts came to be known as "muzyka na rëbrakh"—music on ribs—"muzyka na cherepakh"—music on skulls, or most popularly, "muzyka na kost'iakh"—music on bones.

After a young engineer named Ruslan Bogoslovskii successfully reverse-engineered Filon's Telefunken and started producing record cutters of his own, the practice of "music on bones" began to spread rapidly. Not surprisingly, the proliferation of homemade records on the black market attracted the attention of the government. On a single day in 1950, approximately sixty underground dubbers and distributors were rounded up for questioning, and their equipment was confiscated. Bogoslovskii received a jail sentence of three years, while Taigin

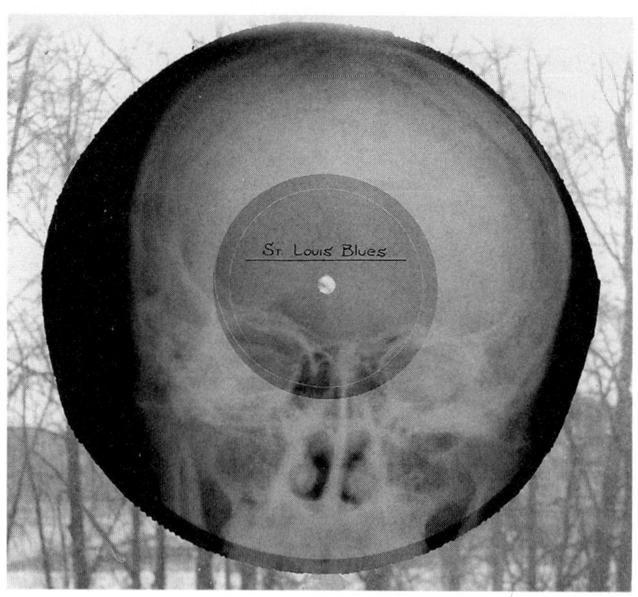

Figure 2.5 "St. Louis Blues," music on bones.
Photo courtesy of Piotr Trubetskoi and Igor' Belyi.

and one of his associates were given five years each.[9] But periodic arrests such as these, while disruptive, did not completely halt the spread of "music on bones" in the Soviet Union. What eventually did was the advent of new technology: the widespread availability of reel-to-reel tape recorders in the 1960s rendered the record-cutting business redundant, and X-ray records disappeared from view.

One of the striking things about these acoustic palimpsests—and one of the things that distinguishes them from the original, textual palimpsests—is that the X-ray's visual inscription in no way impeded the reception of the phonographic track carved into it. Unlike the vellum sheet, which was initially washed clean in order to make room for new writing, these hauntingly beautiful artifacts profit from the lack of interference between the two modes of inscription layered upon them. After even a cursory glance at these records, it appears clear that the underground record cutters were at least occasionally focused on the visually ironic, palimpsestic dimension of "music on bones." Take this as exhibit A: a record of Elvis Presley's "Heartbreak Hotel (figure 2.6)," with the hole in the middle directly over the place where the heart would be in a chest X-ray:

Or look at this somewhat more obscure and mischievous pairing of sound

Figure 2.6 "Heartbreak Hotel."
Photo courtesy of Piotr Trubetskoi and Igor' Belyi.

and image: a recording labeled "Cheek to Cheek" (figure 2.7), inscribed onto a pelvic X-ray.[10]

Or this track, of Valdir Azevedo's "Delicado" (figure 2.8), carved into a particularly fragile-looking set of ribs.

In short, it appears that the palimpsestic dimension of "music on bones" was not lost on its practitioners. In the end, how could those who made or purchased these records not take delight in the fact that the music of the nascent Soviet "underground"[11] was written on images of the human skeleton, denizen of the *literal* Soviet underground? How could they not smile at the notion that the songs of artists who were actively censored in the Soviet Union were circulating on official images of Soviet bodies?

I should mention at this point that these remarkable photographs were recently made by a gifted Russian musician named Igor' Belyi, from a rare private collection passed on to the amateur archivist Piotr Trubetskoi, who is, in my opinion, Russia's most valuable unsung hero of music preservation. Together, Belyi and Trubetskoi not only documented the "look" of "music on bones," but also its sound, making MP3 recordings of each record on a 1950s-vintage Soviet turntable. As I write

Figure 2.7 "Cheek to Cheek." Photo courtesy of Piotr Trubetskoi and Igor' Belyi.

Figure 2.8 Valdir Azevedo's "Delicado." Photo courtesy of Piotr Trubetskoi and Igor' Belyi.

this, I am listening to their MP3 of a scratchy recording of Bill Haley's 1953 classic, "Farewell, So Long, Goodbye," inscribed onto a particularly gruesome X-ray of a broken femur.[12] The scraping sound of the record player's stylus, like the scraping sound of the palimpsestic scribe's knife, compels me to remember the means of production, the hidden actors (in recording studios, equipment shops, record stores, distribution plants—and in this instance, X-ray labs, underground dubbing facilities, and black markets), the vast networks of labor and capital exchange, and the material histories that lay beneath any modern, multiply mediated musical moment. As we listen to the record, the palimpsest metaphor calls on us to listen to its history as well. That flimsy bootleg of Bill Haley emerged because of the prior participation of, minimally: a composer, a lyricist, performers, recording staff and technologies, studio and commercial spaces, a record consumer—and then, later, a record smuggler, Soviet X-ray film manufacturers, an X-ray technician, a patient with a broken leg, a hospital archivist, record dubbers, a black marketeer, and an underground consumer. Similarly, the CD gathering dust in your collection involves the participation of untold numbers of people, technologies, and resources (cf. Latour 2007). In this sense, we can understand all musical materials—scores, recordings, even live performances—to be the residue of complex networks of human and nonhuman actors, of untold dialectics between far-flung people and technologies, structures and agencies. The musical artifact is thus merely the uppermost layer of an acoustic palimpsest; scratch its surface and you will glimpse the crazy labors that hide beneath it.

Listening for Barely Audible and Inaudible Voices

Some acoustic palimpsests, such as those of the urban or wartime music listeners mentioned in my first story, are the unintentional by-products of music listening technologies (iPods, earphones, ears) being deployed in noisy environments. Others, such as "music on bones," are the more-or-less random consequence of ad hoc solutions to logistical problems of supply and demand. Others still are the intentional products of creative effort: some acoustic palimpsests are, in other words, composed. I offer as an example of this last type a recording made by a man named Iurii Kirsanov, who in 1981 was a twenty-nine-year-old officer in a KGB regiment in Afghanistan, as the Soviet Union ramped up its military presence in what would emerge as their most devastating military engagement since World War II.[13] Early in their first deployment, Kirsanov and his friend Sergei Smirnov began carrying a portable cassette recorder with them when they left their base on missions. Their objective was to create a record of the ambient sounds that were most salient in their daily life, the sounds that would later remind them of their tour of duty in Afghanistan. They recorded hours of tape, capturing the call to prayer at the local mosque, the wind whipping through the Afghan mountains, and the cacophonous sounds of military action: AK-47s, helicopters, jet aircraft, rockets.

Late one night in May 1981, Kirsanov and several friends carried his guitar and three cassette recorders into the dressing room of the battalion's steam bath. There, in the quiet, from midnight to 5:00 a.m. on two consecutive nights, they recorded an hour-length cassette of Kirsanov's compositions. Two of the tape players were used to record identical copies of the performance; the operator of the third player held Kirsanov's written scenario, which told him when to press "play" and "stop" on a tape of his ambient field recordings. The resultant trio—for guitar, voice, and tape recorder—amounted to an idiosyncratic evocation of Kirsanov's personal soundscape—not to mention a composition that unwittingly replicated the techniques of *musique concrete*—performed and recorded in the middle of a war zone.

The recording begins abruptly with several loud bursts of AK-47 fire, which slowly fade out as Kirsanov's guitar enters, playing a martial tango of the sort that gained popularity in the Soviet Union through the illicit postwar "music on bones" recordings discussed previously. These imbricated introductory gestures, "played" on two very different "instruments," precede the entrance of Kirsanov's voice, singing a song that references the grim violence of the Afghan war:

Здесь под небом чужим, под кабульской лазурю,
Слышны крики друзей, улетающих вдаль
Ах, как хочется мне, заглянув в амбразуру,
Пулемётом глушить по России печаль.

Zdes' pod nebom chuzhim, pod kabul'skoi lazuriu,
Slyshny kriki druzei, uletaiushchikh vdal'
Akh, kak khochetsia mne, zaglianuv v ambrazuru,
Pulemëtom glushit' po Rossii pechal.

Here, beneath the foreign sky, beneath Kabul's azure blue,
I can hear the cries of my friends as they fly off into the distance.
Oh, how I want, having peered through the embrasure
To drown out, with a machine gun, my longing for Russia.

This verse powerfully evokes the wartime sense of alienation, frustration, and aggression that has been common among soldiers throughout history. Interestingly for the discussion at hand, it does so in language that foregrounds sound: the audible cries of the narrator's departing comrades fuel his desire to "drown out" (*glushit,* also "silence," "kill") his longing with a loud and deadly burst of gunfire. Even in the absence of the ambient machine-gun track, we could begin to read the lyrics of this song as a palimpsest of sorts, one that involves an act of acoustic inscription and erasure: sound silencing sadness. But the presence of an actual recording of machine-gun fire renders this palimpsest thicker, more complicated, and significantly more chilling than it would be otherwise. To my ear, the combined effect of the song text and the ambient track, of the poetics and the ballistics that underwrite this recording, is to lend an aura of immediacy, authority, aggression, and realism to it that words and music alone could scarcely accomplish.

Kirsanov recorded the gunfire in 1980 outside Shindand, Afghanistan, and between each burst you can hear the echo of the report as it bounces off a mountain in the distance. A sense of space is embedded in that echo, and that sense follows me throughout the recording. On successive listenings, I find myself focusing less on the words, the melody, or even the gunfire—less on the phenomenal surface, if you will—and more on the stark contrast between the wide-open acoustic space of the ambient recordings and the claustrophobic, tin-can-like space of the steam bath in which Kirsanov's voice and guitar were recorded. The different sets of echo and decay that characterize the two recording venues bespeak two different arrangements of wartime bodies: one, nestled within the relative protection of a military base; another, exposed to the vertiginous chaos of the battlefield. This audible difference, this sonic residue of resonant spaces, constitutes another layer that one can tease out of this palimpsestic recording.

I first encountered Kirsanov's recording several years ago, around the same time that I began thinking about palimpsests. The lyrics I quoted above, combined with the rudimentary multitracking undertaken in the recording, were more than enough to prompt me to think of it in the palimpsestic terms of overwriting. More recently, however, I played Kirsanov's tape to my friend Madina Goldberg, a professor of Russian history who grew up in the USSR. Her immediate reaction, on hearing one verse of Kirsanov's tango, was to ask if the song was written in the 1930s or 1940s. Rather triumphantly—because I so seldom know something that she doesn't know—I revealed that it was written in 1980. Undaunted, Goldberg insisted that she had heard the same song in a much older recording. After doing a series of online searches together, we realized that she was right: Kirsanov's tango is indeed a version of an earlier piece. Unwittingly, I had selected as my subject a song that was significantly more multilayered than I had thought!

According to a Russian-language article written by V. M. Soldatov (2004), the most widespread version of this tango was attributed to the famous émigré singer Piotr Leshchenko (1898–1954). One of the most popular underground pieces in the 1950s, this song, titled "The Cranes" ("Zhuravli"), narrates the profound yearning of an emigrant for his native Russia. I have emphasized the lines that are duplicated in Kirsanov's version:

> **Здесь под небом чужим** я как гость нежеланный,
> **Слышу крик** журавлей, **улетающих вдаль.**
> Сердце бьётся сильней, летят птиц караваны.
> В дорогие края провожаю их я.
>
> **Zdes' pod nebom chuzhim** ia kak gost' nezhelannyi,
> **Slyshu krik** zhuravlei, **uletaiushchikh vdal'**
> Serdtse b'ëtsia sil'nei, letiat ptits karavany.
> V dorogie kraia provozhaiu ikh ia.
>
> **Here, beneath the foreign sky,** I am like an unwanted guest,
> **I hear the cry of** the cranes **flying off into the distance.**
> My heart beats stronger, the caravan of birds flies off,
> I accompany them [with my gaze] as they head for [my] dear homeland.

The first verse of Kirsanov's Afghan tango attains an additional measure of clarity when we listen to it within the context of this earlier piece. Kirsanov clearly used the earlier verse as a template for his version, retaining its melody (roughly), 50 percent of the words from the first line, and 80 percent of the words from the second. But the changes he makes to these lines are just as striking. He discards the second half of line one ("I am like an unwanted guest") reinscribing it with a phrase that situates the tango in Afghanistan ("beneath Kabul's azure blue"). More ominously, Kirsanov transforms "I hear the cry *of the cranes* flying off into the distance" to "One can hear the cries *of my friends* flying off into the distance."

VERSION 1: *From "The Cranes," as sung by Nikolai Markov:*

Slyshu	krik	zhuravlei,	uletaiushchikh	vdal'
I hear	[the] cry	of the cranes	flying off	into the distance

VERSION 2: *From "Here Beneath the Foreign Skies," as sung by Iurii Kirsanov:*

Slyshny	kriki	druzei,	uletaiushchikh	vdal'
Are audible	[the] cries	of [my] friends	flying off	into the distance

If the image in the first version is relatively clear—the cranes are flying off to the emigrant's homeland, returning to the place from which he is banned—the image in the second is strange. The phrase "friends flying off into the distance" would generally conjure up the image of people on an airplane, but if his friends were on a plane, he wouldn't be able to hear their cries. Were they "door gunners" shouting to him from a helicopter? Perhaps. Or could the cries be the kind of theatrical screams that we have grown accustomed to in B-grade war and action films, as bodies struck by explosions fly through the air? Or are the "friends, flying into the distance" actually those who have already shuffled off this mortal coil, and the "cries" the imagined voices of the dead ascending into heaven, as cranes lift off into the sky? For me, all of these scenarios remain latently present in the recording. But knowing that this line is inherited from an earlier version of the song provides an explanation for the ambiguity embedded within it. At the same time, like the palimpsestic poem that serves as my epigraph, Kirsanov's adaptation opens up an intertextual relationship with the earlier lyric: by imagining the older song text as hazily visible (or better, audible) beneath the newer one, we can muse upon the structural similarities that soldiers in the Afghan war share with émigrés longing for their homeland. More specifically, we can acknowledge the faint presence of the effaced image of the cranes, an image that would likely be on the minds of Kirsanov's listeners, who would be acquainted with the older tango. If I were to describe my own reaction to the palimpsestic penetration of the cranes into the description of Kirsanov's comrades-in-arms, I would probably point out the inadequacy of language in these circumstances, but then venture that it left me with a vaguely poignant feeling and an inchoate image of human bodies, elongated, gracefully floating away, like the cranes themselves.

There are still more layers to peel back: in particular, two details about the earlier tango are worth mentioning. First, émigré songs such as this were not distributed by the state-owned Soviet music industry in the 1950s. While the tango had been popular in Russia throughout the first half of the twentieth century, more than one generation of Soviet censors saw it as the crystallization of Western decadence, a tortured "music for impotents" (Edmunds 2004, 24).[14] Thus, it is not at all surprising that "The Cranes" was not mass-produced on Detselit at the government-owned Melodiya studios, but rather on X-rays, utilizing the underground "music on bones" format that I discussed previously. Once again, we must add another layer of inscription and erasure to our archaeology of Kirsanov's song.

Second, you will recall that I originally described "The Cranes" as being *attributed* to the famous émigré singer Piotr Leshchenko. It turns out that the version of the song that was so widely distributed on used X-rays was actually sung not by Leshchenko himself but by another vocalist who worked as a Leshchenko impersonator. In a recent (2004) reminiscence, V. M. Soldatov explains that he "first heard ['The Cranes'] in 1955, on a 'music on ribs' disk. . . . The name 'Leshchenko' was handwritten on the record." Only later did he discover that Leshchenko *had never recorded* "The Cranes." The version he owned, it turns out, was likely produced by an ensemble called "Jazz Tabachnikov," which released forty pieces sung by a man named Nikolai Markov, "whose voice was almost identical to the voice of the famous singer" (Savchenko 1996, 220, quoted in Soldatov 2004). Markov's name, symbolically overwritten by Leshchenko's, had been effectively erased from this recording. Erased, but only temporarily: with time, scholars and aficionados succeeded in discerning the identity of the singer despite the layer of false advertising that covered it.

At this point, I almost wish I could say that was it, that we have reached the bottom, the urtext upon which all the (equally interesting) others were written. But we are not there yet: for I must tell you that there were actually over ten different versions of "The Cranes," including a well-known one that dates from the 1930s, and a satiric remake set in Stalin's GULAG ("Pesennik Anarkhista-podpol'shchika"—"Songbook of an underground anarchist," n.d.). Moreover, all of these different versions were preceded by a poem written by Aleksei Zhemchuzhnikov in 1871, the first quatrain of which reads:

Сквозь вечерний туман мне, под небом стемневшим,
Слышен крик журавлей всё ясней и ясней . . .
Сердце к ним понеслось, издалёка летевшим,
Из холодной страны, с обнажённых степей.

Skvoz' vechernii tuman mne, pod nebom stemnevshim,
Slyshen krik zhuravlei vsë iasnei i iasnei . . .
Serdtse k nim poneslos,' izdalëka letevshim,
Iz kholodnoi strany, s obnazhënnykh stepei.

Through the evening fog, beneath the darkening sky,
I can hear the cry of the cranes ever clearer and clearer . . .
My heart is carried away to them as they fly in
From a cold country, from the naked steppes.

Kirsanov's "cry of my friends" ("kriki druzei") thus rests atop well over a century of "cries of the cranes" ("krik zhuravlei"). To make matters even more complicated, Zhemchuzhnikov did not originate the "cry of the cranes" trope around which the poem was built. The symbolically loaded cry of the cranes is likely to have been in oral circulation for hundreds of years before it became memorialized in written verse. As a result, rather than ending our archaeological investigation of Kirsanov's palimpsestic text with a definitive original, we must simply watch, and listen, as the "cry of the cranes" recedes into the mists of the Russian oral poetic tradition. As Clifford Geertz would surely have said, there is no end to the palimpsest of intertextuality: when it comes to language, "It's turtles all the way down."[15]

Returning to Kirsanov's recording, I want to relate a few final palimpsestic moments before moving on. At one point in the tape, Kirsanov performs a song that narrates the experience of a "door gunner" on a helicopter. This track begins, predictably, with a recording of a helicopter in flight. Toward the end of this ambient recording, beneath the percussive wash of the rotors, a muffled shout is clearly audible. The exact words are impossible to decipher, but it seems clear that they are in Russian and so should belong to one of the Soviet troops fighting in Afghanistan in 1980. (My Russian friends agree, but cannot identify the words either.) Listening again, I begin to have my doubts: the echo of the voice sounds too clear and drawn out to have been recorded at the same time as the helicopter. Is this a recording that Kirsanov lifted from a Soviet war film? Possibly. Regardless of its provenance, this voice screaming beneath the white noise of a helicopter in the war zone is arresting.

In the end, though, it is another much more subtle voice that haunts me. Relatively recently, after having reviewed the tape over two dozen times, I was surprised to discover a second voice hidden within the ambient recordings that are woven into Kirsanov's songs. A song titled "A Battle Thundered Away on the Outskirts of Kabul" ("Boi gremel v okrestnostiakh Kabula") begins with another recording of gunfire, this time with two automatic weapons firing. Buried deep in the mix, in the middle of this gun battle—or is it merely target practice?—one can barely detect the sound of a human voice. The voice appears for a single instant, as a single undecipherable syllable wedged in the silence between two bursts of gunfire.

Who was the owner of this voice? A fellow Soviet soldier? A member of the Mujahideen? An innocent bystander? We will never know. But this short vocal pip adds yet another layer of complexity to what is already a maddeningly complex musical artifact. Kirsanov presents us with a song about wartime, composed and performed in wartime, which includes the actual mechanized sounds of wartime, along with the faint trace of a human voice amidst the violent noise of war. Like the phenomenological palimpsest in my first example, this recording, composed from multiple sounds emanating from multiple sources, offers us the possibility to listen *through* the most obvious signals, recovering from the background partially effaced inscriptions that normally go unnoticed. By performing the palimpsestic operation—by bringing the anonymous voice into the foreground—we can open up a consideration of the many humans who were enmeshed in the Afghan war.

To my ears, Kirsanov's multitracking powerfully evokes the layers of "precarious lives" (Butler 2004) that are both the *subject* and the *context* of his compositions, as well as the *objects* of the kind of fundamental erasure that only organized violence can accomplish. At the same time, his lyrics describe and endorse multiple acts of violent overwriting that have both sonic and corporeal consequences: "Akh, how I want . . . to drown out, with a machine gun, my longing for Russia," for example. Similarly, in another song:

> The dust billows up, and with the rustling sound of our wheels
> We slice through the silence of the dawn. . . .
> There's our target: we head straight into battle.
> The KPVT [machine gun] performs its solo recital.
> ("The March of the Cascade Detachment")

Kirsanov's protagonists, slicing through the silence of the dawn, certainly don't want us to hear the voices of the enemy. They prefer to erase them, along with their own sadness, with the deafening cascade of the guns. And yet in the tape, the literal voice of someone on the battlefield escapes the gun's roar and presents itself, Horton-Hears-a-Who fashion: softly, unnoticed by all but the most attentive, but nonetheless powerfully asserting the humanity of its owner. Of course, as I alluded to earlier, it is precisely this paradox—the existence of multiple layers inscribed by multiple authors, and the repeated (albeit unsuccessful) attempts to erase that which came before you—that is the defining characteristic of the palimpsest. From this standpoint, we might say that the task of the palimpsestual listener is to discern both the things that a recording encourages us to remember and the things it urges us to forget, the things that are insistently audible and the things that have long been silenced.

———

And it is here, on the shifting hermeneutic ground of this weird accretion of inscriptions and erasures, that my imagination takes its leap. Inspired by Kirsanov's multilayered recording, I imagine a palimpsestic tape that fully captures the Afghan war in all of its troubling acoustic richness, the parts of the war that Kirsanov heard and the parts he was unable to hear.

In a story cowritten with a friend in the same year Stanislav Filon brought his Telefunken home from the German front, Jorge Louis Borges described an ancient empire whose obsessive cartographers produced a 1:1 map of the empire itself. Here is the story in its entirety (the opening ellipsis is his conceit):

> . . . In that Empire, the craft of Cartography attained such Perfection that the Map of a Single province covered the space of an entire City, and the Map of the Empire itself an entire Province. In the course of Time, these Extensive maps were found somehow wanting, and so *the College of Cartographers evolved a Map of the Empire that was of the same Scale as the Empire and that coincided with it point for point.* Less attentive to the Study of Cartography, succeeding Generations came to judge a map of such Magnitude cumbersome, and, not without Irreverence, they abandoned it to the Rigours of sun and Rain. In the western Deserts, tattered Fragments of the Map are still to be found, Sheltering an occasional Beast or beggar; in the whole Nation, no other relic is left of the Discipline of Geography[16] [my emphasis].

What would a Borgesian acoustic palimpsest of Kirsanov's Afghanistan sound like? In order to attain the absolute, exhaustive, one-to-one fidelity of the map in the story, we could imagine such a recording beginning with the multitrack layering of Kirsanov's tape, but pushing past the current threshold of audibility, allowing us to hear the sounds of everyone who was ever involved in the Afghan war. Just as the map would show us every pebble, every grave, every blade of grass in the empire, this impossible recording would capture every breath of wind and every whistled melody within the Afghan theater of operations. We would hear all of the sounds of vehicles and weapons, mountains and cities, the sounds of soldiers and civilians, perpetrators and victims and bystanders. We would hear the sounds of the displaced, of the dying, and of the dead. We would hear the voices of those represented in Kirsanov's song, and the voices of those whom Kirsanov's song passively ignores or actively effaces. This ultimate acoustic palimpsest would capture the *scriptio superior* of representation—that is, the fusion of instrumental music and sung text that we call "song"—but it would also reveal a *scriptio inferior* consisting of the multiple contexts and complicated networks that precede, surround, and are brought into being by a song's performance. It would be an infinitely layered recording that would allow us to listen to history itself. It would enable a panacoustical politics of listening, with all the granularity and dynamism that term implies. Borges's impossible mapping project is precisely the quixotic goal to which I am striving when I incorporate the imagination into my acoustic palimpsest metaphor. This activity creates its own pitfalls, including the structurally important fact that it is destined to failure;[17] but as a thought experiment, I find it sharpens my appetite for unearthing unheard and barely heard presences—Gordon's "ghostly matters"—that would otherwise go unnoticed.

Returning from my imagined recording to the actual cassette tape that Kirsanov made in 1981, I conclude with a final moment of palimpsestic irony. At the conclusion of the late-night recording session, Kirsanov's tape was circulated among his friends in his detachment. In time, dubbed copies were passed along to neighboring military garrisons. According to one account, officers who were nearing the ends of their tours of duty would play Kirsanov's tape to newly arrived troops in order to prepare them for "the reality of Afghanistan."[18] Copies of Kirsanov's tape found their way to the nearby military hospital, and its patients, once released, were likely to be carrying a copy in their duffle bags as they returned to their posts in Afghanistan or their homes in Soviet cities. Customs officers at the Soviet-Afghan border confiscated many of these copies, however. As Kirsanov tells the story:

> There was some unpleasantness with a certain person in the political section of the detachment's Command [Headquarters] in Kabul. I heard through the grapevine that some of my songs had received unfavorable (*nelitsepriiatnyi*) reviews, and [had prompted] threats to "settle the score with that crooner" (*razobrat'sia s etim pevunom*).

Kirsanov suspected that a line in the dirgelike song "Remote Kabul" had generated the unfavorable attention:

> Cry, motherland, sob with sorrow.
> [Your sons] have left, they have abandoned you.
> The Party pointed out the road they should take.
> "Go [it said], and fulfill this sacred command:
> Make sure that the Motherland can peacefully go to sleep."

These lines transparently refer to the young Soviet conscripts who were sent to Afghanistan and, it is clear from the previous verse, died there. Were Kirsanov's superiors offended by the frank statement that the Communist party had sent its sons to their inevitable death? Or were they disturbed that the lugubrious tone of the song stood in stark contrast to the marshal grandeur of official songs about the Afghan war? In a reminiscence recently published on an Internet forum devoted to his Afghan song cycle, Kirsanov attempted to convey the tenor of the complaints leveled against him:

> "How could he?! An officer in the KGB looks ironically upon our most sacred [party]! What kind of ideas is he planting in the minds of our politically vulnerable soldiers?!" (This was the general tone of the panegyrics I was receiving.)

In reaction to the unvarnished critical edge of a few songs within a repertoire that was generally sympathetic to the Soviet cause, the KGB leadership in Moscow stripped Kirsanov of one of his medals, placed him on a list of "untrustworthy" individuals, and, Kirsanov and his friends surmise, ordered the customs officers to confiscate any Kirsanov tapes that they found in the possession of soldiers crossing the borders. A member of the KGB forces who fought in Afghanistan in the mid-1980s recalls:

> I remember returning from my first tours of Afghanistan, when the Customs officers opened and listened to even the cassettes of mine that were in their

original wrappers, to see if there were any "Afghan" (i.e., Kirsanov) songs on them. I remember how a nurse in Shindand showed some soldiers who were traveling with her a clever trick for outwitting Customs: she unwound the cassettes and rewound them backwards, so that when they listened to it they would hear something muffled and indistinct.

The attempt to erase Kirsanov's tape from the aural history of the period was initially successful. With no official distributor and only limited bootleg copies reaching the USSR, most Soviet citizens never learned of the tape's existence. Other more politically acceptable recordings ended up articulating the tenor of the time, at least until the advent of Perestroika and the gradual reduction of the state's desire and ability to censor. But like a persistent *scriptio inferior,* Kirsanov's cassette eventually emerged as a subtly subversive text, ready to be read by those who were astute enough to discern its presence in the background. His recording presented a counterhistory of the war, one that emphasized the toll of the war on all of its participants, its perpetrators and victims, including those the author himself sought to erase.

With its conspicuous layering of music and ambience, the ethos of Kirsanov's project was overtly palimpsestic from the start. In the end, though, I want to argue that *all* sonorous events and listening acts take place within environments that, once you scratch the surface, reveal themselves as densely layered, and that some layers inscribe themselves over others in an attempt to erase the past. This is the difference between the dynamic and essentially *political* trope of the palimpsest and the more passive layering of Geertz's "thick description." The metaphor of palimpsestic listening urges us to seek out and recover the hidden layers of agency and history and creativity and politics that underwrite and overwrite all sound experiences. It asks us not only to appreciate the composite effects of this layering, yes, but also to acknowledge that the acts of making and listening to music always involve inscription *and* erasure, inscription and erasure, inscription and erasure, inscription and erasure, inscription and erasure . . .

LAYER 5: SURFACE

(In Place of a Conclusion, Some Final Thoughts That Occurred to the Author after Writing the Body)

By this point, I have stretched the palimpsest metaphor to encompass a truly broad and somewhat bewildering range of phenomena. As I look back on my text, I see that a taxonomy of palimpsest categories would have been helpful to bring order to the conceptual disarray. Without attempting an exhaustive list, and somewhat late in the game, let me suggest that acoustic palimpsests may be:

Textual: when words (or notes) are erased and reinscribed with other words (or notes). Kirsanov's rewriting of "The Cranes" would be an example of this, as would multiple musical settings of a single poem, or the composerly revisions that are the subject of musicological sketch studies.

Auditory: when sounds from multiple sources occur simultaneously. Masking effects, or the complete drowning out of one sound by another, are possible here. My example of the layers of noise through which people listen for significant sounds during wartime employs the palimpsest metaphor in purely auditory terms.

Intermedial: when a work is translated into a different medium (e.g., poems reinscribed as song texts, novels reinscribed as operas or films), and the new version obscures the existence of the original. Zhemchuzhnikov's poem disappearing amidst the rhythm of Markov's tango is an example of this type of intermedial reinscription and erasure. Ravel's orchestral "Pictures at an Exhibition" obscuring Mussorgsky's pianistic original is another.

Technological: when a work is inscribed onto a recording medium, and the trace of a former work is still discernible. The ghostly sound of the original track on a rerecorded tape, the X-ray visible beneath the grooves of a "music on bones" record, and the extremely common technique of multitrack recording all qualify.

Authorial/performative: when the original author or performer is obscured by another. Markov's voice being marketed as Leshchenko's is an example of this, as would be the Milli Vanilli scandal of the early 1990s or, I suppose, the transformation of Israel Isadore Baline into Irving Berlin.

Symbolic: when an act of erasure and reinscription is described within a work. Kirsanov's lyric "Akh, how I want to drown out, with a machine gun, my longing for Russia" is a symbolic representation of palimpsestic erasure and reinscription.

Ideological: when an act of erasure is the result of a political decision. Censorship of music and, more broadly, silencing of voices (by killing, imprisonment, or marginalization) can be understood palimpsestically. Musical nationalism can be framed as an attempt to inscribe an ideological orientation on a populace through sound.

Corporeal: when history (in the form of genetics or lived experience) is inscribed into the body. Nina Eidsheim imagines the voice as a corporeal palimpsest.

Memorial: when a sonic event is absorbed into one's memory, a memory that is itself an accrual of remembered experiences, some of which are ineluctably erased by others. When this happens, the event becomes embedded in the existential palimpsest that is the listener's consciousness.

If we were to compile all of the layers that we have discerned in Kirsanov's recording, beginning with the oldest and proceeding more or less forward in time, and label them according to these categories, this is the kind of multilayered record we would find:

Layer 1: [textual]
A poem is written [drawing on folk motifs] by Aleksej Zhemchuzhnikov.

Layer 2: [textual/intermedial/authorial]
The poem is changed [partially erased, partially overwritten] and put to music [inscribed into a new medium]. It begins circulating in live performance. The authorship of the poem and the music is effectively erased.

Layer 3: [textual]
Multiple variations [partial erasures and reinscriptions] of text and melody begin appearing.

Layer 4: [technological/authorial]
A recorded version appears in "music on bones" format, inscribed on used X-rays. This version is sung by Nikolai Markov, whose identity is effectively erased and reinscribed as Piotr Leshchenko. The "music on bones" version circulates widely.

Layer 5: [textual/authorial]
During the first years of the Afghan war, the text is changed [partially erased, partially reinscribed] several times, by

several people, including Kirsanov. Kirsanov emerges as "author" of his variation.

Layer 6: [symbolic]
His lyrics describe an act of erasure and overwriting: drowning out his longing for Russia with the sound of his machine gun.

Layer 7: [auditory/technological]
Kirsanov's tape involves layering ambient sounds from the Afghan theater of operations underneath his recorded performance.

Layer 8: [auditory]
The ambient recordings all but completely erase the voices of those with whom and against whom he is fighting. Occasionally, the voices of local Afghans and anonymous others can be discerned beneath Kirsanov's voice and guitar.

Layer 9: [corporeal]
All of the voices that are layered in this recording are themselves layered artifacts, bespeaking the unique genetics and histories of their owners.

Layer 10: [ideological]
Kirsanov's recording is partially "erased" by censors, who confiscate copies of his tape at the Soviet border.

Layer 11: [ideological]
His song and the entire genre of Afghan war songs are "overwritten" by other musical works describing the Cold War

in politically acceptable terms. These works occupy the airwaves and reduce the possibility that Kirsanov's songs will influence the public perception of the war.

Layer 12: [memorial]
Everyone who comes in contact with this song (including, most recently, you who are reading this essay) writes it onto his or her memory, if only temporarily. This kind of inscription involves the potential for overwriting other memories; it is also itself constantly vulnerable to erasure.

LAYER 6: SUPERSTRATE

(Marginalia, Scattered throughout Manuscript)

Allow me to pull the curtain aside for a moment: As I look back on this palimpsestic operation, with the various layers of Kirsanov's song splayed out and pinned back like a frog's innards on a dissection table, I must admit that I feel a strange sense of incompletion, even dejection. As exhaustive as I've tried to be, my acoustic palimpsest of "Here beneath a foreign sky" lacks many of the elements and practices that I, as an ethnographer, have tended to find most important: testimonies from those who found this song valuable; fine-grained analysis of musical moments, notice paid to participatory discrepancies, groove, and so on; broader reflections on cultural resonance—I could go on and on. And here's something that I find really shocking: I actually corresponded with Kirsanov a few years ago, and I couldn't really find space within the palimpsest model to write about our conversation. This leaves me with the suspicion that the palimpsest might be best employed as a research methodology, rather than a mode of representation. Might it make sense to imagine the object of investigation as a palimpsest, see how many layers can be discerned within it, and then imagine it as something else, and something else again, *before* the writing process begins?

In any event, as I prepare to step away from this essay, I want to sketch out a few final thoughts about the acoustic palimpsest metaphor. Consider these to be the most important of the marginalia that proliferated on the pages of my latest draft. They consist of several overlapping and at times contradictory generalizations about palimpsests, and a rudimentary list of the costs of deploying the metaphor:

> *There is something violent about palimpsests.* The twin acts of erasure and reinscription that are the palimpsest's minimal condition can easily be construed as an aggressive move with respect to the past. The desire to erase the past and start afresh is one of the hallmarks of modernism, and the palimpsest metaphor retains some of the violent energy of this movement. While the persistence of the *scriptio inferior* points toward the impossibility of fully erasing history, the palimpsest is nonetheless infused with the desire to do so. Thus, one of the images that the metaphor is capable of conjuring is that of a text that has been ruined, violated, or even "murdered."[19]
>
> *There is something intimate about palimpsests.* One can choose to ignore the atmosphere of violence I just described, and instead imagine the palimpsest as a congenial relation between two or more texts. Just as the narrator of Anna Akhmatova's poem experiences a feeling of intimate communication by writing upon her friend's rough draft, so can we experience a closeness, a sensual proximity even, when we encounter the multiple layers of a palimpsest. The "music on bones" records represent one kind of felicitous marriage of visual inscription and sonic inscription. Kirsanov's multitracked recording—with the layers consciously interacting with one another rather than attempting to drown each other out—would be another.
>
> *There is something uncanny about palimpsests.* As Sarah Dillon says of Thomas De Quincey's palimpsests: "The resurrective activity of palimpsest editors always involves uncannily bringing the dead back to life: the footprints of the hunted wolf or stag are traced *backwards,* back to the start of the hunt, *before* the game was killed . . ." (26). The acoustic palimpsest metaphor thus encourages us to think of audible phenomena as complexly layered *and* to imagine the traces of human activities that have been silenced. Imagining these silences as faint but legible presences rather than absences or nonentities is akin to resurrecting the dead.

There is something transgressive about palimpsests. The original textual palimpsests involved texts that we weren't supposed to see, but that pushed through, that crossed back over the threshold of visibility. Acoustic palimpsests often involve sounds that we weren't supposed to hear: sounds related to the body, to technological mediation, to the neutral background, to the inaudible politics that undergird all sonic situations. The palimpsest metaphor encourages us to listen for the quietest of sounds, and to imagine erased sounds stubbornly pushing back through the threshold of audibility as well.

The palimpsest metaphor is far from perfect. For all that it brings into focus, the acoustic palimpsest produces a number of distortions and omissions, each of which deserves consideration. Here, briefly, are a few of the more serious limitations that I have noticed:

1. *It deals with temporality in a problematic way.* Textual palimpsests involve layers of writing that were put on one after another, with the most recent one always dominating. The palimpsests that inspired this metaphor thus encourage a unidirectional historical perspective: palimpsestic texts acquire their layers one after another, as time marches forward. You will have noticed by now that the audible and inaudible layers of which I speak have no such temporal unity joining them together. This lack of correspondence weakens the vitality of the metaphor.
2. *It fails to deal with motion convincingly.* Sound is experienced as vibration, as action, as something subject to attack and decay. The palimpsest metaphor attempts to freeze what is in essence an evanescent experience and present it as a more or less stable, layered object. At times, such as in the "music on bones" example, this aura of stability is justified. At others, such as the layered listening example, it is obfuscatory.
3. *It presumes a privileged vantage point from which all sounds can be heard.* To imagine an acoustic palimpsest is to adopt something akin to an omniscient stance. While this stance is relatively common in music scholarship, it obscures the radical situatedness of sound. "Listening to the palimpsest" is an imagined activity, and thus is not representative of any individual's actual listening experience.
4. *It treats the world as a text.* The palimpsest, a metaphor derived from the hyperliterate West, shamelessly treats aurality as a subgenre of textuality,

> denying it an epistemology of its own. While this position may be in alignment with the critics of phonocentrism, the scriptist bias of the palimpsest metaphor is certainly a problem, and this problem is rendered all the more acute when the object of investigation is not a literary text but a fluid series of sounds.

So there you have it, a number of the pros and several of the cons surrounding this thought experiment, this theory-in-utero. I hope there are more of the former and am certain there are more of the latter that haven't yet occurred to me. I would like to think that, used a bit more judiciously and less expansively than I have here, the acoustic palimpsest's greatest utility lies in its ability to encourage a kind of listening that embraces complexity, values history, and draws attention to the hidden dialectics of inscription and erasure that lie beneath all musical moments.

"I would like to think that." Indeed, I *would* like to think that. But I find in the end that my metaphor's inherent limitations prevent me from arguing this concluding point more emphatically. As I read back over this text, doubts proliferate: is the acoustic palimpsest really a sound way to write about sound? Is it sound or unsound sound writing? Having reached the end of this essay, I find myself wishing I could start over again, in the hope that the next time I might get it right. (Tell the truth, colleagues: how many of you have never felt this perverse desire?) But wait: perhaps my palimpsest metaphor can rescue me from the predicament in which it has placed me: *The original text was washed away with a mixture of milk and oat bran or scraped clean by medieval scribes using pumice dust . . .*

Having inscribed this layered text, this meditation on erasure, can I erase what I've written so far? Can I wipe out my treatment of Kirsanov, and Filon, and soldiers in Iraq, and iPod users, only to try again to capture their essence tomorrow? Like a medieval scribe with a scraping knife, can I *unwrite* this text? In doing so, can I compel you, dear reader, to *unread* it?

Of course I can~~not~~.

[Delete all.]

[Restart.]

LAYER 7: SUPERSTRATE

(Epigraph, Written in Pencil on the Back of the Last Page, with Several Words Erased and Rewritten in a Different Hand)

In that Empire, the craft of **Sound Engineering** attained such Perfection that the **recording** of a **single song** comprised the **sounds of all the versions that had come before it**. In the course of Time, those Extensive **tapes** were found somehow wanting, and so the College of **Sound Engineers** evolved a **recording** of the Empire whose **multiple tracks** were those of the history of the Empire and coincided with it point for point. Less attentive to the Study of **Sound**, succeeding Generations came to judge a **recording** of such Magnitude cumbersome, and, not without Irreverence, they abandoned it to the Rigours of sun and Rain. In the western Deserts, tattered Fragments of the **master tape** are still to be found, Sheltering an occasional Beast or beggar; in the whole Nation, no other relic is left of the Discipline of **music studies**.

NOTES

1. Alexandra Harrington, *The Poetry of Anna Akhmatova* (London: Anthem Press, 2006), 226–27.

2. According to Gérard Genette (1997), the term *palimpsestuous* was coined by Philippe Lejeune.

3. See, for example, the palimpsest article in the 2010 *Encyclopaedia Britannica Online*, http://www.britannica.com/EBchecked/topic/439840/palimpsest. Strangely, I have found this exact quote in several publications, including peer-reviewed journals, without quotation marks or proper attribution (e.g., Rapantzikos 2005; Nethersole 2005; Balas et al. 2003). Without endorsing this behavior, I will only note that the irony created by scholars of palimpsests plagiarizing a text about palimpsests is of a decidedly postmodern (not to mention palimpsestic) flavor.

4. In a section of De Quincey's autobiography (*Suspiria de Profundis*, 1845) titled "The Palimpsest," the author metaphorically links the reinscribed parchment with human cognition, memory, and history—and this was written eighty years before Freud's "mystic writing pad" (see note 5)! As Josephine McDonagh (1987) writes of De Quincey's text, "[His] initial account of the palimpsest as a literal agent of history tells how it contains texts from different historical periods in a single parchment: in De Quincey's example these are a Greek tragedy, an early Christian 'monkish legend,' and a twelfth century romance. The palimpsest is the 'library' or 'archive' through which 'the secrets of ages remote from

each other have been exorcised'" (143). It then becomes a model for the human mind in general. De Quincey asks, "What else than a natural and mighty palimpsest is the human brain?" (144), linking historical and psychological models (208).

5. Freud's brief and idiosyncratic "Notes on the Mystic Writing Pad" does not deal with palimpsests per se; nonetheless, it is regularly, almost ritualistically, cited in literature that explores the palimpsest's metaphorical significance (see, for example, McDonagh 1987; Dillon 2005 and 2007; Elsaesser 2009; Derrida and Mehlman 1972). In this essay, Freud proposed that the human perceptual apparatus functions roughly like the "mystic writing pad," a child's toy tablet with a celluloid cover, upon which one can create text or images with a stylus. Lifting the cover wipes the slate clean, but leaves a visible trace of the inscription on the wax or resin layer underneath it. Similarly, Freud argued, the conscious mind "has an unlimited receptive capacity for new perceptions and nevertheless lays down permanent—even though not unalterable—memory-traces of them" in the unconscious. Sigmund Freud, "A Note upon the Mystic Writing-Pad," trans. James Strachey, in *General Psychological Theory: Papers on Metapsychology,* ed. Philip Rieff, 212 (New York: Touchstone, 2008).

6. In the dedication of her major work, "Poem without a Hero" (*Poema bez geroia*), which serves as the epigraph to the present essay, Akhmatova explains to Osip Mandelstam, the dedicatee, that her poem is written as a palimpsest on top of one of his drafts. That she does this in a passage rife with allusions to Mandelstam's poetry only increases the "palimpsestuous" (Dillon 2005, 254) nature of their relationship.

7. See Daughtry 2014 and 2015.

8. Taigin's (1999) article, "The Rise and Fall of the Golden Dog," is the source of the historical account that follows.

9. All three were released in connection with a sweeping amnesty in 1953 following Stalin's death.

10. It turns out that this record is mislabeled. The actual recording on the record is an instrumental version of "Smoke Gets in Your Eyes," orchestra unknown.

11. In Russian the original term was "*podpol'naia muzyka,*" literally "underground music," with the word for "underground" providing a nice echo of Dostoevsky's "Notes from the Underground" (*Zapiski iz podpol'ia*). Much later, the English calque андеграунд ("andegraund") began to displace the older term.

12. Bill Haley and the Comets, "Farewell, So Long, Goodbye," 1953. Undated "music on bones" recording from the private collection of Piotr Trubetskoi. Reproduced online by Igor Beliy, http://beliy.ru/private/na_rebrah/19_farewell_so_long.mp3.

13. In this section I draw on two biographical sketches of Kirsanov by retired KGB Colonel Viktor Verstakov. The first, originally published in Verstakov's autobiography, *Afganskii dnevnik* [Afghan diary] (Moscow: Voennoe Izdatel'stvo, 1991), is available at

http://kaskad-4.narod.ru/Dnevnik_Verst.html. The second is an article originally published in the *Gazeta Moskovskogo okruga PVO "Na boevom postu,"* no. 77 (May 7, 1992) and titled "*S chego nachinalas' afganskaia pesnia?*" ["From what did Afghan songs emerge?"]. This article was republished in 2003 on the website *Avtomat i Gitara* [Automatic weapon and guitar], a website wholly dedicated to the songs of Soviet soldiers, and is available at http://avtomat2000.narod.ru/Verstakov.html. This biographical data was confirmed and expanded in personal correspondence with Iurii Kirsanov himself in 2008.

14. "The American-European origins of the tango and fox-trot made them all the more susceptible to (the Russian Association of Proletarian Musicians') charge that this music was a 'narcotic,' the masked weapon of the capitalist wrecker" (Nelson 2004, 223).

15. Surely the most-quoted excerpt of Geertz's *Interpretation of Cultures* (1973, 28–29) is this: "There is an Indian story—at least I heard it as an Indian story—about an Englishman who, having been told that the world rested on a platform which rested on the back of an elephant which rested in turn on the back of a turtle, asked (perhaps he was an ethnographer; it is the way they behave), what did the turtle rest on? Another turtle. And that turtle? 'Ah, Sahib, after that it is turtles all the way down.'" In addition to being essentially about layers and therefore at least latently palimpsestic, Geertz's story is apropos here because of his interpretation of it: the infinite succession of turtles is, for him, a reminder that "cultural analysis is intrinsically incomplete. And, worse than that, the more deeply it goes the less complete it is. It is a strange science whose most telling assertions are its most tremulously based, in which to get somewhere with the matter at hand is to intensify the suspicion, both your own and that of others, that you are not quite getting it right." This sense of always "not quite getting it right" is one that I would like to embed within my palimpsest metaphor, with all of its erasing and scribbling over.

16. Jorge Luis Borges and Adolfo Bioy Casares, in J. L. Borges, *A Universal History of Infamy,* trans. Norman Thomas de Giovanni (London: Penguin Books, 1975), 131.

17. Borges didn't believe in the possibility of perfect mimesis or absolute representation; rather, his map served as an allegory for "the paradoxes and slippages involved in any project of perfect duplication" (Peters 2008, 1). Borges scholar John Durham Peters sees the story as "designed, ultimately, to provide oxygen and exit from totalitarian systems," rather than as an idealistic project for total representation (ibid.). My imaginary acoustic palimpsest is offered in a similar spirit: it is only because the project is patently impossible that it is safe to strive for it.

18. Ogryzko 2000, 26.

19. Sarah Dillon notes that "palimpsests are not dusty palaeographic objects but uncanny harbingers to the present of the murdered texts of former ages" (2007, 13).

WORKS CITED

Balas, Costas, et al. "A Novel Hyper-Spectral Imaging Apparatus for the Non-Destructive Analysis of Objects of Artistic and Historic Value." *Journal of Cultural Heritage* 4, no. 1 (2003): 330–37.

Beer, David. "Tune Out: Music, Soundscapes and the Urban Mise-en-scène." *Information, Communication and Society* 10, no. 6 (2007): 846–66.

Belyi, Igor. "*Plastinki na rëbrakh*" ("Records on Ribs"). *LiveJournal.* 2008. Accessed on July 12, 2009. http://bujhm.livejournal.com/381660.html.

Borges, Jorge Luis. *A Universal History of Infamy.* London: Penguin Books, 1975.

Bull, Michael. *Sound Moves: iPod Culture and Urban Experience.* London: Routledge, 2007.

Butler, Judith. *Precarious Life: The Powers of Mourning and Violence.* London: Verso Books, 2004.

Connor, Steven. "Ears Have Walls: On Hearing Art." In *Sound: Documents of Contemporary Art.* Edited by Caleb Kelly. London: Whitechapel Gallery, and Cambridge, MA: MIT Press, 2011, 29–39. Originally published in *FO(A)RM,* no. 4 (2005): 48–57.

Daughtry, J. Martin. "Thanatosonics: Ontologies of Acoustic Violence." *Social Text* 119 (2014): 25–51.

———. *Listening to War: Sound, Music, Trauma, and Survival in Wartime Iraq.* New York: Oxford University Press, 2015.

De Quincey, Thomas. "Suspiria de Profundis." In *Thomas De Quincey: Confessions of an English Opium Eater and Other Writings.* Edited by Grevel Lindop. Oxford: Oxford University Press, 1998.

Derrida, Jacques. *Of Grammatology.* Translated by Gayatri Chakravorty Spivak. Baltimore: Johns Hopkins University Press, 1976.

———, and Jeffrey Mehlman. "Freud and the Scene of Writing." *Yale French Studies* 48 (1972): 74–117.

Dillon, Sarah. 2005. "Reinscribing De Quincey's Palimpsest: The Significance of the Palimpsest in Contemporary Literary and Cultural Studies." *Textual Practice* 19, no. 3 (2005): 243–63.

———. *The Palimpsest: Literature, Criticism, Theory.* London: Continuum, 2007.

Edmunds, Neil. *Soviet Music and Society under Lenin and Stalin: The Baton and the Sickle.* New York: Routledge, 2004.

Eidsheim, Nina. "Voice as a Technology of Selfhood: Towards an Analysis of Racialized Timbre and Vocal Performance." PhD diss., University of California, San Diego, 2008.

Elsaesser, Thomas. "Freud as Media Theorist: Mystic Writing-Pads and the Matter of Memory." *Screen* 50 (2009): 100–13.

Freud, Sigmund. "A Note upon the Mystic Writing-Pad." In *On Metapsychology: The*

Theories of Psychoanalysis. The Penguin Freud Library, vol. 11. Translated by James Strachey. 1925. Reprint, London: Penguin, 1991, 427–34.

Geertz, Clifford. *The Interpretation of Cultures.* New York: Basic Books, 1973.

Genette, Gérard. *Palimpsests: Literature in the Second Degree.* Translated by Channa Newman and Claude Doubinsky. Lincoln: University of Nebraska Press, 1997.

Gordon, Avery. *Ghostly Matters: Haunting and the Sociological Imagination.* Minneapolis: University of Minnesota Press, 2008.

Harrington, Alexandra. *The Poetry of Anna Akhmatova.* London: Anthem Press, 2006.

Huyssen, Andreas. *Present Pasts: Urban Palimpsests and the Politics of Memory.* Stanford: Stanford University Press, 2003.

Ivanov, Boris. "*Mesto v istorii*" ("A Place in History"). *Novoe Literaturnoe Obozrenie* 6 (2008): 295–305.

Latour, Bruno. *Reassembling the Social: An Introduction to Actor-Network-Theory.* New York: Oxford University Press, 2007.

Mathisen, Ralph W. "Palaeography and Codicology." In *The Oxford Handbook of Early Christian Studies.* Edited by Susan Ashbrook Harvey and David G. Hunter, 140–68. Oxford: Oxford University Press, 2008.

McDonagh, Josephine. "Writings on the Mind: Thomas De Quincey and the Importance of the Palimpsest in Nineteenth-Century Thought." *Prose Studies* 10 (1987): 207–24.

Nelson, Amy. *Music for the Revolution: Musicians and Power in Early Soviet Russia.* University Park: Pennsylvania State Press, 2004.

Nethersole, Reingard. "Reading in the In-Between: Pre-Scripting the 'Postscript' to *Elizabeth Costello.*" *Journal of Literary Studies* 21, nos. 3–4 (2005): 254–76.

Ogryzko, Viacheslav. *Pesni Afganskogo pokhoda* [Songs of the Afghan campaign]. Moscow, 2000.

Ortner, Sherry. *Making Gender: The Politics and Erotics of Culture.* Boston: Beacon Press, 1997.

"*Pesennik anarkhista-podpol'shchika*" [Songbook of an underground anarchist]. N.d. http://a-pesni.org/dvor/zuravlinadkolymoj.php.

Peters, John Durham. "Resemblance Made Absolutely Exact: Borges and Royce on Maps and Media." *Variaciones Borges* 25 (2008): 1–24.

Porcello, Thomas. "'Tails Out': Social Phenomenology and the Ethnographic Representation of Technology in Music-Making." *Ethnomusicology* 42, no. 3 (1998): 485–510.

Rapantzikos, K. "Hyperspectral Imaging: Potential in Non-Destructive Analysis of Palimpsests." *Proceedings of the IEEE International Conference on Image Processing (ICIP),* Genoa, Italy, 2005.Savchenko, B. A. *Estrada retro* (*The Retro Stage*). Moscow: Iskusstvo, 1996.

Soldatov, V. M. "*Zhuravli v ispolnenii Nikolaia Markova i 'Dzhaza Tabachnikov*" ("The Cranes in the Performance of Nikolai Markov and 'Dzhaz Tabachnikov'"). *Blatata.com.*

2004. Accessed on February 29, 2016. http://www.blatata.com/2007/09/01/zhuravli-v-ispolnenii-nikolaja-markova.html.

Taigin, Boris. "*Rastsvet i krakh 'Zolotoi sobaki'*" ("The Rise and Fall of the 'Golden Dog'"). *Pchela,* no. 20 (May–June 1999). Accessed on February 29, 2016. http://www.pchela.ru/podshiv/20/goldendog.htm.

Verstakov, Viktor. *Afganskii dnevnik* (Afghan Diary). Moscow: Voennoe Izdatel'stvo, 1991.

———. "*S chego nachinalas' afganskaia pesnia?*" ("From What Did Afghan Songs Emerge?"). *Gazeta Moskovskogo okruga PVO "Na boevom postu,"* no. 77 (May 7, 1992).

Zhemchuzhnikov, Aleksei. "Osennie zhuravli" ("Autumn Cranes"). In *Russkaia poeziia XIX—nachala XX v* [Russian poetry of the nineteenth and early twentieth centuries]. Edited by N. Nikushkina. Moscow: Khudozhestvennaia Literatura, 1987.

MICHELLE KISLIUK

3. Writing the Magnified Musicking Moment

In this essay I give some sustained attention to the significance of magnified musicking moments. These are the moments that crystallize, in heightened miniature, aesthetic and interpersonal sentiment fused with cultural and existential affect. In a flash they tend to multiply and refract centripetally and centrifugally. Then they pass. The sensation that they are fleeting is a part of their power and poignancy.

> Suddenly, there was room for a million different pronunciations of this moment and I could not tell where the kaleidoscope ended and the sound began. It seemed that each of us carried this instant in our mouths; singing our particular syllable, tinting the expression. We each gave the notes a different weight, so that some sailed through the space between us and others sank into our flesh or bounced off the yellowing plaster on the ceiling. The song became a communal narrative, originating in me. In Kelly. In Margot. In the teacher. There was no part of it that did not belong to each of us; to all of us. But it wasn't easy. Every hum was a negotiation. (Woodly 2001, 2)

At the end of this chapter I return to the longer piece in which Deva, my former student, describes further this magnified instance of singing. Moments such as this are familiar and often cherished by many people, but they are rarely addressed directly in musical scholarship. I suggest here that understanding better how to approach these moments in writing could be important for the continuing development of the ethnography of musical performance. We have not so far been well trained in the academy to address these moments as foci for the transmission of "sound knowledge" (Kapchan, this volume), while in fact they may provide a conceptual locus for informed understanding. I am advocating here for the microevocation of minimalist sound events—for an ethnographic focus on microcosms of observed experience that when, perhaps *only* when rendered in poetic specificity, allow us to think and feel in depth about sound textures, musical interactions, and heightened experiences.[1] Digging down into the ethnographic at this microlevel can allow for greater socioaesthetic insights, that unfurl into multiplex meanings and implications when pulled from what was otherwise packed and hidden within a moment. I explore in this essay how such moments might be addressed, even written into identifiable form, by poetically hypersituating reactive and interactive routes arriving at a sonic, social, and sensual presence. This focus might, I hope, compel writer-researchers to critically ground themselves in the writing while taking the vulnerable turn toward poetics required to evoke emotional resonances. The concept I explore is not developed here into a full ethnographic rendering. Rather, I consider the kinds of moments and the kinds of writing that could become the focus of more extended treatment.

WHY MUSICKING?

Unlike the noun *music,* the verb *musicking* (after Small 1998) emphasizes that music is at once enacted and experienced. Musicking directly opposes the language and attendant ideology that encodes "music" as an object, and is especially appropriate given that this essay (and this volume) contributes to the broader project of destabilizing the objectification and reification of expressive life by carving out pathways of knowledge that have thus far been marginalized in academic discourse. What's more, musicking, as defined by Small, reminds us that music is always more than what is sounded. Musicking is an activity of consequence, where issues of broad socioaesthetic significance may be at stake.

I wish to focus specifically on moments of participatory engagement with "humanly organized sound," John Blacking's (1973) working definition for "music." As Blacking reminded us, "It is the human content of humanly organized sound that 'sends' people" (Blacking 1973, 34). Any sound that we as humans perceive is, in a sense, "humanly organized" by the very fact of and in the very moment of its perception. Therefore, my paradigm in this essay is in dialogue with the field of sound studies, which has opened a significant new frame of critical perception regarding what we might call "musicking." But I emphasize in this essay the concurrent experience of *making* sound (especially with others) as well as perceiving it. As one recent purveyor of community musicking explains:

> Music changes when other people enter the scene, often miraculously and for the better. The same note I was playing on the guitar by myself an hour ago sounds drastically different when it combines with a drummer's beats. The note I'm singing might sound like a different note altogether when somebody sings an unexpected harmony. Or, that note I played might gain a brand new energy when I know somebody else is listening or whispering "bravo"! Theoreticians describe the interactions of musical overtones, but mostly what I feel is the interactions of energies. Often these energies add up to much more than the sum of their parts. What's more, they create a combined, unpredictable magic that can only be experienced once, for next time it will change. Shared music, in short, is ephemeral, a product of the here and now. (Weisenberg 2011)

During these moments, sound enables mutual, if fleeting, connections and interactions between people that resonate on many levels. And although one can surely have a silent magnified moment of experience with memorable impact, sound tends toward synesthesia—the crossing of multiple senses and modes of experience—and as I will address, it can also stretch and alter the perception of time and of the copresence of living things in ways that are arguably particular to sound.[2]

AN APPROACH TO WRITING

Writing a magnified musicking moment is to explore overdetermined conditions and sudden correspondences, where multivocal meanings bubble to the surface, overflowing into a kind of transcendence. There is a special correlation worth keeping in mind between layered, textured, interactive musical practices and the rendered writing of layered microcosms that *emerge* intra-actively from such practices (Barad 2003). The writer delves into thick description (Geertz 1973), bringing readers along into her embodied consciousness (Merleau-Ponty 1962) by evoking the immediacy of intra-active sounding and listening. She takes care to describe the aural and kinesthetic, personal and interpersonal details that fleetingly crystallize emergent meanings. At first grounded in the writer's position, the metadescription can move concentrically outward into overlapping, widening ethnographic repartee, resulting in interpretive tension that multiplies into refracting, open-ended meanings that spin out from the momentary microcosm. The challenge is to both identify such occasions of heightened significance *and* to write them into a parallel palpability.

The approach I am outlining here assumes that the writer is in some manner a participant in the musicking that she also wishes to engage ethnographically. In several of the examples that follow I cite my own writing, clustering my examples around bluegrass and on musicking in the rainforest of central Africa, as these are the areas I am most experienced in and have written about. I also include writing by other authors on these and related genres, as it is crucial to offer a variety of voices. But each is from an experience-centered position, which invites personalized, vulnerable, and even playful poetic narrative that can bring readers into the frame while allowing for multiple interpretations.[3] I will often quote at length, because it is in the details and sometimes in the development of the cited writing that the examples of these musical moments become meaningful. As Susan Stewart notes, "Because of the correspondences it must establish, writing about the miniature achieves a delirium of description" (Stewart 2007, 46).[4]

MAGNIFIED MOMENTS BEYOND LINEAR TIME

The ethnographic effort I propose also falls within the movement toward embodied, multisensory research and writing that a number of ethnographers have been engaged in (e.g., Stoller 1989; Csordas 1994; Sklar 2001). They include contributors to this volume on sound writing and others, a few of whom I will cite in this discussion. But even within the subcategory of senses-focused ethnographic writers, attention to the significant but ephemeral microcosmic moments of performance has been slim. V. S. Ramachandran observes that "the most interesting aspects of human conscious experience have received the least attention" (1998, 1854—here he refers to research on the neurobiology of synesthesia, which I address later). One reason for this scholarly inattention is, I think, because topics such as synesthesia or musicking moments demand a kind of emotional and psychological labor requiring coaxing and courage—like facing the discomfort of recalling an elusive or disquieting dream. They demand conscripting into creative service the very consciousness that prefers to evade self-scrutiny, but which usually offers substantial rewards when we manage to lure it out of its cozy hiding places. Another reason people resist putting exceptional moments into writing is that these may be felt as exceedingly private, protected aspects of our lives. The idea of setting them out for strangers to scrutinize, the fear of reducing or trivializing a cherished and fluid memory that has become a part of oneself, can dampen an impulse to expose these moments in writing. And although there are "intense pleasures [in] moment chasing" (McKinney 2004, 1)—

these pleasures are felt during the musicking (and in freely remembering it), but maybe not again until the conceptual and perhaps painstaking part of a research and writing process is over and one has reentered the poetic domain. So part of the writing process I am advocating for here might become more uncomfortable than other kinds of writing.

One of my goals with this essay, then, is to encourage ethnographers (myself included) to push past resistance and devote to these moments the intellectual heart and creative mind required to render them with the life force that they merit. And right there is another key—ethnographic language moves, following convention, into hegemonic visual metaphors that so often imply, as I just have, that one is "rendering a scene" or giving the "big picture." But when the focus is devoted to one or a series of micromoments, suddenly the visual is no longer so predominant. This shift is important: breathing into and expanding those musicking instances brings kinesthetic perception, aural and tactile sensation, and memory into a present that bursts suddenly beyond linear time.[5]

An embodied radical empiricism (Jackson 1989) is the research medium and poetics is the rendering tool that grounds the ineffable as it flutters momentarily in our grasp. The poetic response might be in writing, or it could be through other expressive modes including more musicking—metamusicking. So right away we are at the edge of the conventional academic realm (Taussig 1992), even threatening to slide off that edge. But we urgently need to hang on, as scholars and not only as scholars, but as creative, ephemeral beings unfettered by an idea of "proper" discourse. In this realm, we might be not only moved to tears, but also compelled to understand and describe how and why we have been so moved, and why it matters.

WHEN SOUND AND SYNERGY MOVED THEM TO TEARS

Two well-known and innovative musical ethnographies of the late 1970s and early 1980s have elements that especially prefigure, I think, attention to the kind of moments and the kind of writing I am talking about. One is Paul Berliner's *The Soul of Mbira* (1978), and the other is Steven Feld's *Sound and Sentiment* (1982). By beginning to address, via their own writing, the transportive emotional power that the musics they are describing have on the people whom they write about—and on themselves—they moved musical ethnography a step closer to what we don't quite have yet, issuing a summons to write our way into the most resonant occasions of performance. Berliner's book expressively and rigorously addresses Zimbabwean Shona *mbira* practices, bursting with musicking that lingers just beneath the text while thoroughly informing it. And he does not choose to delve as deeply as he might have into the particularity of the events that inform his rich ethnography. In a later chapter, when the focus is on spirit possession during religious ceremonies, most of the description, while elegantly written and nuanced, is also normative and generalized. But instances of spirit possession are notoriously difficult to describe ethnographically. They reside within the mysteries of human consciousness, and at a far point on the spectrum of transcendent musicking (to which I will return later). Berliner deserves to be lauded because this ethnography goes further than most had, or have since, toward grounding ethnographically the emotional complexities of trance-based musical experience.[6] But in fact, as Devin McKinney has observed, it is not possible within *conventional academic discourse* to address "some fleeting convergence of sound that excites terror, captures delight, opens the soul, tilts the universe." So the task we give to ethnographers cannot be to "define something whose nature it is to elude us" (McKinney 2004)—as that of a dream. The task is rather to inscribe it on another plane, to meet the magnified moment in the poetic realm in which it already exists.

In his now-canonical book *Sound and Sentiment* (1982) about Kaluli in New Guinea, Steven Feld approaches his topic near the end of the book in a way he had not done earlier, allowing himself to tumble, almost as an afterthought, toward poetics and metaphor in his own writing. Though he addresses metaphor as a topic of analysis throughout, until these final pages he does so mostly in dry, academic terms, by way of structural linguistics and formal analyses. But that approach renders the material relatively lifeless, because "metaphor not only pervades the language people use about emotion-laden experience, but also . . . is essential to the understanding of most aspects of the conceptualization of emotion and emotional experience" (Kovecses 2000, 20).[7] So when we ourselves engage in metaphoric communication as we write about metaphoric communication, we are both conceptualizing emotion and constituting aspects of our experience in the process—piecing together little metaphor dwellings in which to tuck and shape affective experiences that would otherwise remain abstract (see also Fernandez 1991). Feld's influential work is well known, especially for the Kaluli aesthetic of "lift up over sounding" (e.g., Feld 1982, Feld and Keil 1994). But *Sound and Sentiment* has not been cited or emulated as much as it might have been for the actual turn at the end of the book toward authorial poetics.

Referring to his artistic photograph near the end of the book, Feld writes, "The image is a man, a bird, a bird as a man, a man as a bird." He continues, admitting that he feels he has "picked these things to pieces" and now must "conclude by seeing them as one. . . . I wish this one to carry the 'underneath' that analysis must coexist with synthesis if ethnographers are to witness and feel the emotional dimensions of cultural form and expression" (238). With this statement he anticipates, and briefly realizes, the poetic turn I am calling for here. Feld's challenge—apparent in his willfully schizophrenic voices in the book—is recognizable in my paraphrase here of Devin McKinney, who is addressing pop music reception, but whose observations are broadly applicable:

> The most powerful [musical] moment flies past, feeds on memory, occupies the unconscious; but still, its parts are nameable. . . . The critic-mechanic dismantles the moment and names parts; the mysterian is appreciative that the moment is never reducible to those parts alone. In the fusion of the mechanical and the mysterious is the singular wildness of . . . music, its resistance to rational sense, coherent politics, systems of order—and there's the fix: as critics we rely on such things to order our own discourses. To the extent we define the . . . moment in these ways, we kill it; to the extent we honor it, we'll be unable to say, finally, what it is, to stamp it with any definitive meaning. Seeking to define the indefinable moment in terms that do it justice, then, means cruising a road to nowhere: loving the ride, savoring the moment, searching for landmarks, scoping the landscape—and avoiding the terminus of a definitive interpretation. . . . But therein lies the challenge of living up to this music. It's the road (real or metaphorical), not the house at the end of it. (McKinney 2004, 1)

Popular music scholarship, with some of its roots in journalism, has left room for writers such as McKinney to invoke poetics. This is also true of travel writing, another popular correlate to ethnography (see Pratt 1992). Both music journalism and travel writing are often denigrated by the academy, whether by musicology or anthropology, because such scholars may wish to distance themselves from relatively undisciplined, superficial, commercial, or indulgent journalistic productions. But if we are to continue to develop what Raymond Williams urged, that in the "practice of analysis we have to break from the common procedure of isolating the object and then discovering its components. On the contrary, we have to discover the nature of a practice, and then its conditions" (1980, 47), then a different kind of ethnographic music writing should be added to our repertoire. A different approach to scholarship altogether is called for: a creative nonfiction that overlaps with ethnography of performance, such as the sound writing suggested by this volume. Can a creative/poetic discourse be welcome as a legitimate (if antistructural) scholarly discourse? Can training in such skills find a place? I am not insisting that all musical scholarship heed this call—if it did our efforts would no longer be antistructural as they need to be. I am calling, though, for a healthy, supported niche for this kind of discourse so that when the material indicates, students and scholars, poets and performers are not hindered by a prejudice that favors by default the distanced approach of academic convention.[8]

BLUEGRASS: METAPHOR AND METAPERFORMANCE

Writing effectively about actively sounded, kinesthetic experience requires metaperformance, otherwise it necessarily falls flat—like a paper lantern that expands into shape only when infused with air and space, breath and dimension. Poetic metaperformance inhales the life into the ethnography of performance. Writing as metaperformance first must be rich, multilayered, personally invested description, insofar as vividly rendered, resonant micromoments can lead organically to analysis and synthesis, opening up layers of meaning beyond what a bare-bones description might offer. But effective writing in this magnified musicking mode is necessarily a multisensory evocation that is at once an aesthetic and intellectual poesis, theory and practice—research, writing, and performance together. And though I emphasize the transcendent category in the current discussion, mundane moments or failed musicking can be as equally if differently revealing.[9]

The examples I draw upon in the rest of this essay delve into poetic metaperformance located within a musicking moment. The following two examples focus on bluegrass. Writing from one's own experience, as I have noted, must of course be part of a grounded approach (Kisliuk 2008a)—writing that both stirs reader-listeners and generates unpredictably refracting new metaperformances in its wake.

I live in the foothills of the Blue Ridge—where many narratives place the birth of bluegrass—but my own bluegrass and old-time music education started in Boston, where I grew up. I learned from a range of people such as Joe Val (who spoke with a heavy Boston accent) and native northerners (Bela Fleck, Orin Starr, Stefan Senders, and members of the Boston Bluegrass Union). As a young teenager I was drawn to the uniquely intense, if temporary, feeling of community at bluegrass festivals, especially late at night in the campgrounds. So as a graduate student I pursued as a thesis topic the question of what makes some jam sessions click, how jammers use a "special kind of courtesy" particular to successful jams. I recently began thinking about bluegrass again (Kisliuk 2010) in terms of the topic of this essay, returning to this particular moment almost thirty years later.

"LOVE ME, DARLIN', JUST TONIGHT"

Please come with me into the multisensory field of a late-night jam session. I leave out material leading up to and drawing from this moment (what Schechner 1985, after V. Turner, would call the warm-up and the aftermath, with their important fragilities and ambiguities)—readers can access these in the longer article (Kisliuk [1988] 2011). For now, let's jump to the core of it. The scene is Bill Monroe's Bean Blossom Bluegrass Festival, summer 1984, sometime after midnight:

> "You're turning in?" Greg asks, keeping the beat. "That's un-American!" he jokes, in the spirit of all-night jam sessions. . . . Two of the older, neighborly spectators are getting ready to leave, and through the din of plucked strings one of them says to Greg, "I really liked your pickin', it was real good."
>
> Everyone plucks strings absent-mindedly, perhaps wondering if we can regain the precious tuned-in feeling. I start to fool with the beginning of a Ralph Stanley banjo tune in an attempt to keep up the Stanley idea. Everybody suddenly goes silent and Greg starts to back me up, stopping momentarily to be sure of the chords, but picking it up right away, putting in parallel runs and fill-in echoes. I stop short; Greg's backup is so nice that it takes me by surprise. I wasn't expecting such sudden attention. "It's just a Ralph Stanley banjo thing that I just . . ."
>
> "Oh," says Ron sympathetically in his quiet voice, "it's hard to do Stanley. I don't know why but nobody can do it just like him." Ron starts to noodle around. Greg follows him and soon they're playing a lively Stanley tune. They glance at me but I indicate with a head shake that I don't know the tune. Ron starts to sing it. I play some soft backup while Greg joins Ron for a high harmony on the chorus:
>
> Love me darlin' just tonight,
> Take these arms and hold me tight.
> Tomorrow you may hold another;
> Love me, darlin', just tonight.

Greg lets his voice trail off on the high part in classic "high lonesome" style. Ron plays a simple, clear banjo break, and then sings the next verse in a soft, raspy voice:

Tomorrow you say that you'll be leavin',
I hope you know the way that's right.
I pray to God that you won't leave me;
So love me darlin' just tonight.

This is one of the finest moments we've had all evening, and since it's so late the silence around us presses in, magnifying each sweet sound and heightening every feeling. This is the kind of moment jammers strive for. The song is about ephemeral love, but it has some unspoken correspondence to our more immediate situation: The delicate feeling with us now could pass or be disrupted at any moment, and even if we could sustain it, our jam session alliance is necessarily temporary. Like all powerful music, bluegrass can be a manifestation of pure love of life, and of course life itself is ephemeral too—ephemeral love, ephemeral jam session, ephemeral moment, ephemeral life. Although these metaphors may not be consciously apparent to us as we play, the feeling of them is apparent, as is the fact that Ron and Greg, both of them master jamming artists, are finally in control of the musical and social atmosphere. . . . For a moment Ron can't remember the last verse. Greg chuckles; it doesn't matter anyway. But then Ron remembers it:

Try to find true love in your heart,
Tomorrow we may not have to part.
But if you feel you must leave me,
Love me, darlin', just tonight.
(Kisliuk, [1988] 2011, 205–20)

This example brings us back to the topic of metaphor, and specifically to metaphoric processes in language. Lakoff and Johnson point toward this idea of refracting multiplicity, that is, when metaphors overlap and intercorrespond (Lakoff and Johnson, 1980, 97), such as when the lyrics of the song parallel the immediate aesthetic and social experience of the musicking moment. This overlapping recalls the Feld/Kaluli "lift up over sounding." We actually need this kind of layered metaexperience in order to grasp meaning in our lives.[10]

Moreover, there is an interdependent dialectic at play between quotidian/mundane experience and expression, and heightened/transcendent experience and expression—musical instances such as the jam session moment I describe can be seen as elevated pauses within everyday processes.[11] Jason Toynbee comments on this "oscillation between mundane and sublime":

> The concept of sublime helps us to understand precisely the duality of [musical experience], the fact that it may be both mundane and extraordinary at the same time. In popular music, voice and texture can suddenly tip over into the sublime, that is to say something awe-inspiring.
>
> . . . Far from being opposed to it, the concept of the sublime radically opens up our understanding of the everyday experience of music. (Toynbee 2004, 1)

What we are talking about, then, goes into and beyond the domain of metaphor, toward the more visceral aesthetic realm of synergy, correspondences, and synesthesia—this last being an actual perceptual effect, not simply a memory association, symbolic link, or analogy (Ramachandran 2001).[12]

Staying with the bluegrass theme—but with a difference—I quote Lee Bidgood from his 2011 dissertation on bluegrass practices in the Czech Republic. These are two contiguous excerpts of ethnographic sound writing that illustrate instances of unanticipated synergy. Bidgood describes his sensation of blurred physical, social, temporal, and spiritual boundaries with members of the Czech bluegrass band Reliéf. The second of the two excerpts is in the context of making live music in an unexpected place, while the first begins with Bidgood listening to his field recording:

> I played for the first time a live recording of Reliéf singing "There is a God" through the stereo system I had just set up at my desk. . . . It was only when I corrected for the low output of my computer and turned the volume dial nearly to its limit that I really heard it—the grinding of voice on voice, not just knowing that they are singing in close harmony, but feeling that process of "singing close" in my ears, in an electric sizzle down my neck and into that familiar warm resonance in my chest—that was it! . . . The powerful, intimate experience of Reliéf's singing is indeed transporting—both aesthetically, spiritually, and in the sense of place. Resonating with their quartet sound, we are squeezed into the matrix of their close-harmony sound, swept up from our intimate listening space to church, to the Southern United States. The shadows of our actual location fade, and we rest in a perfectly harmonized space of concord.[13]

But in the gospel material they play with life-and-death words, with intimations of eternity. As they sing in "There is a God," they "see and know" the reason for their confident faith. The words still trouble me. It took an experience of my own to drive home the ways that singing can blend powerfully with the lyrical content of a song and, through performance, lead to something greater than their sum. (Bidgood 2011, 202–3)

Here Bidgood is offering a vivid example of those concretely physical sensations—the cross-activation (Ramachandran 2003) of the senses, a synesthetic correspondence—which magnifies the relationship between social and physical sensibilities, historical resonances, and spiritual and environmental surroundings. Residents of the former Soviet bloc, these Czech musicians are atheists who struggle to come to terms, in performance, with the religious roots of the music to which they are devoted. This tension serves as an unexpected route to a moment of transcendence. Bidgood continues:

My singing moment happened on a trip outside of Prague in May, 2008. . . . On a Saturday morning, we went for a walk, and ended up at the Church of Saint Nicholas on the outskirts of town, a graveyard chapel built in the early 14th century. This church . . . had lived through the (proto-Protestant) wars of the 14th century, seen the counterrevolution and the 30-Year's War roll through. And now it welcomed us.

The elderly caretaker gave Svatka the keys,[14] and we let ourselves into a dusty, deserted sanctuary that glowed as the morning sunlight filtered in. Our hushed voices and the clanking of the huge medieval keys echoed invitingly. Zbyněk snapped his fingers, appraising the acoustics. I was itching to make music with these people whom I had only heard . . . on stage. . . . That was [why] I had ridden with Zbyněk and Svatka all the way down from Prague. We stepped into a space that practically asked us to fill it with song. As we stood on the verge of song, the appropriate material immediately presented itself, both because of the place [church] but also because of the tradition of gospel a cappella singing. . . .

As we sang, the spaces of the church building lifted and blended our voices, carrying them farther than we could have taken them ourselves.

[This] moment flip[ped] my experience around . . . bridged language and other cultural divides, brushed aside . . . the complex history that distinguishes Czech from U.S. bluegrass, and crossed any number of other boundary lines. . . . The persisting resonances of this singing moment challenge my instinct to separate along [my] normal boundaries, and offers wider understandings that might not separate "sacred" from "secular," but [rather] acknowledge that the two are seldom all that separate. (Bidgood 2011, 204–5)

The stakes become clearer if at this point we take into account the significance and power of transcendent musicking as potentially liminal, antistructural moments that can, sometimes in a flash, reshape social hierarchies and shake up the status quo whether in interpersonal, localized social dramas or potentially in larger, farther-reaching ways that challenge and rebalance social life. We can ask, are these moments latently or explicitly actually present in a particular scene, whom do they serve, and under what performative circumstances?

FEELING AND WRITING "CORRESPONDANCES"

CORRESPONDENCES[15]

Nature is a temple in which the living pillars
Sometimes emit confused words;
Man passes there through forests of symbols
That observe him with familiar glances.

Like long echoes that blur in the distance
In a shadowy and deep unity,
Vast as the night and vast as light,
Perfumes, sounds, and colors intermingle.

Some scents are as fresh as the flesh of children,
Sweet as the sound of oboes, green as pastures
—And others rotted, rich, and triumphant,

Spanning like infinite things,
Such as amber, musk, resin, and incense,
Singing the flight of spirit and senses.

CORRESPONDANCES

La Nature est un temple où de vivants piliers
Laissent parfois sortir de confuses paroles
L'homme y passe à travers des forêts de symboles
Qui l'observent avec des regards familiers.

Comme de longs échos qui de loin se confondent
Dans une ténébreuse et profonde unité,
Vaste comme une nuit et comme la clarté,
Les parfums, les couleurs et les sons se répondent.

Il est des parfums frais comme de chairs d'enfants,
Doux comme les hautbois, verts comme les prairies,
—Et d'autres, corrompus, riches et triomphants,

Ayant l'expansion des choses infinies,
Comme l'ambre, le musc, le benjoin et l'encens,
Qui chantent les transports de l'esprit et des sens.

Charles Baudelaire (1852–1856)

I first read this poem in a French class in college and was steamrolled flat by it.[16] This was at a time when I was also learning West African drumming and dancing,[17] and learning about interpretive anthropology (e.g., Geertz 1973).[18] This combination, with the idea of correspondences at the core, launched my interest in the transdisciplinary synthesis of the creative and intellectual, the spiritual and practical.[19] And as one poetic correspondence or synergy tends to spark multiple others, during this fertile time of cross-resonance in my early twenties, I wrote this poem about a magnified moment of Ewe drumming:

AGBADZA (A POLYMETRIC POEM)

Barrel, tilted, held between your knees.
Deer skin facing you. Two sticks,
To meet the skin with force
Answer a call
When the player beats the double bell

Ko dzi koko dzi ko dzi ko dzi

Vujo! Strength of ancient blood flows in
Blood! Yes, Agbadza is ours alone!
Kidiki! Kidiki! Your drum cries
Cutting through the mesh of beaded gourds.

Ko dzi koko dzi ko dzi ko dzi

Rumble, as the sogo plays a roll
Floating on the pattern of the bell
With kagan inside, a call begins
Now and lifts you out, around the drums.

Michelle Kisliuk (1980)

It is tempting to launch into a literary analysis of Baudelaire's "Correspondances" in relation to synesthetic experience, but a textual approach would distract from the topic and approach at hand.[20] Rather I will carry the themes of "Correspondances" into the remaining examples of magnified musicking—continuing to meet poetry with poetics—like answering transcendent moments with more metaperformance (see also Taussig 1993, xvi).[21]

SYNESTHESIA, KINESTHETIC EMPATHY, AND MUSICKING MOMENTS

Neuroscientist V. S. Ramachandran focuses on the phenomenon of synesthesia, which is currently drawing more attention in neuroscience and elsewhere than it has in the past, but that was first identified as a distinct process decades after the time of Baudelaire. Ramachandran explains that Frances Galton (1880) first reported a condition called synesthesia when he noticed a number of people in the general population, otherwise completely normal, who had experienced sensations in "multiple modalities in response to stimulation of one modality. For example, musical notes might evoke distinct colours" (Ramachandran 2003a, 49). Developing our understanding of the phenomenon of synesthesia is important, I think, for coming to understand the power of magnified musicking moments.

Trenley Anderson is a classical clarinetist, an aspiring musicology student, and also a sound-color synesthete, who responded to an earlier draft of this essay by describing a musicking moment of her own:

> The first two chords of the Eroica symphony can be shocking for anyone. Loud, sharp, and sudden, for decades they have caused thousands of concertgoers to jump in their seats. On stage playing my two opening notes, I did not jump in my chair, but I was "jumped" in a way similar to the way in which a car is jumped: as I emphatically belted these two notes on my clarinet, I felt the familiar white shock of the explosions of sound around me. My heart racing from the jolt, I could recover while the all-too-familiar opening theme spun its

> orange thread through my mind—until it reached the unexpected C-sharp, a piercing green made even more agitated by a cellist's wrong note. . . .
>
> Following our jolt we all moved subtly from side to side. The melody we played seemed to superimpose itself on our dance. Its arabesque curved to a point of emphasis, and at this point we all leaned forward together and then relaxed back to normal positions with the resolution of the phrase. We had not arranged this choreography in advance; it seemed to be a part of the music. It was our communal embodiment of the music and it functioned as expressive communication. We did not have to discuss which note of that phrase should be emphasized. Through body language we felt the music together and circulated its energy within and from our woodwind section.
>
> As the first movement of the symphony passed by me I saw that my experience of time was suspended in a new and special way. . . . As if in a car watching blurs of color go by my window, I travelled across the landscape of the stage and through time. With my neighbor I moved in a gesture to express an accented note—a landmark. Perceiving the style of his gesture, I adjusted my next accent with more energy to match his. In a magical and timeless moment our synchronized accents perfectly matched.
>
> His solo, which spun out of this accent, was a white ray of color sparkling with bright red, light blue, and gold—colors characteristic of his unique clarinet sound and of his personality. He danced and sang his monologue. Then he invited the rest of the section to join him, and suddenly in my mind timbre, pitch, color, and personality became one, first for each of us as individuals, then, as we blended, for the entire group. In that radiant moment we all blended perfectly and time, without any coloristic differentiation and measurement, seemed to cease.
>
> That moment, while ephemeral, seemed to energize our performance for the rest of the evening. (Anderson 2012)

While a synesthete such as Trenley can offer particular insight, Ramachandran and Hubbard's research (2001, 52) suggests that under certain circumstances people who are not clinically synesthetes nevertheless experience synesthesia because of basic structural neural links in our brains. They explain that,

> In addition to clarifying why artists might be prone to experiencing synesthesia, our research suggests that we all have some capacity for it and that this trait may have set the stage for the evolution of abstraction—an ability at which humans excel. The TPO [junction of the temporal, parietal, and

> occipital lobes] is normally involved in cross-modal synthesis. It is the brain region where information from touch, hearing and vision is thought to flow together to enable the construction of high-level perceptions. (Ramachandran and Hubbard 2003b, 58)

This is where heightened magnified musicking moments come together with the structures of metaphor and the experience of synesthesia.

In the late 1970s neurobiologist Barbara Lex published related research that caught the attention of performance studies scholars at New York University at that time (including Richard Schechner, one of my mentors). Lex (1979) found that when people enter possession or trance, there is a sudden neural spilling over of interconnections back and forth between the right and left hemispheres of the brain that otherwise operate somewhat separately. During these trance states, the experience of time and memory is disrupted, and among other phenomena, boundaries between self and others are altered (similar to *communitas*—V. Turner 1969; E. Turner 2012; also Blacking 1973 as discussed earlier—and to the magnified moments that are the subject of this essay). Ramachandran and Hubbard's explanation of synesthesia refers to a cross-activation process (2003a, 51), wherein boundaries among senses are dissolved, where "a kind of spillover of signals occurs" (2003b, 59). Deep similarities among these processes emerge: correspondences, metaphor, synesthesia, gestalt, the spilling of memory into an expanded present, trance (left to right brain interplay). And the neurobiological research of Ramachandran and Hubbard among others "suggest[s] that the nonarbitrariness both of synesthesia and of metaphor . . . arise because of constraints imposed by evolution and by neural hardware" (Ramachandran and Hubbard, 2001, 51–52).[22]

CASCADING CORRESPONDENCES: ECHOES FROM AFRICAN FORESTS

Colin Turnbull, writing about musicking and communal experience in the Congo basin rain forest in the 1950s and 1960s, brought nuanced and evocative life to the singing and ceremonies of the BaMbuti pygmies. This writing engendered what could be considered an entire genre of writing and other productions about adventurous encounters with "pygmies."[23] Turnbull's most famously moving and detailed descriptions are of the Molimo ceremonies that he witnessed and took part in, and especially his captivating descriptions of musical sound, interactions, and transporting moments in *The Forest People* (1962). My own inspiration from Turnbull came first from reading his books as an undergraduate (at that same fertile time in which I was reading Baudelaire, Feld, and Berliner), and later when he taught briefly in my graduate program in Performance Studies at New York University in the late 1980s. During that time Turnbull prepared an essay in which he responded to the innovative thinking of Victor Turner and Richard Schechner, who were linking ritual studies in anthropology with theories and practices in contemporary theater (especially experimental or avant-garde). Embedded in his discussion, Turnbull offers a focus on sound that had not yet been articulated by Turner or Schechner, emphasizing that sound can provide "a royal road to the liminal condition, and the feelings it evokes can become highly significant for the fieldworker if he allows them, if not the sound itself, to move him both physically and spiritually" (Turnbull 1990, 77).

Perhaps if Turnbull had had access to the neurobiological underpinnings offered since by scientists such as Ramachandran, and if a poetic, experiential response to field experience had found its place in ethnographic training and reception at that time, his approach could have been more nuanced and more ethnographically persuasive during his own time.

I conclude this essay by sliding down a cascade of correspondences that flow first from Turnbull and the Mbuti, then to me with BaAka, and further from me to my students (and then onward and elsewhere along with them). I have sought in my ethnographic work to delve into the practical aspects of the musicking of Central African forest people, paired with a critical approach to embodied, evocative writing. *Seize the Dance!* (Kisliuk 2000) is focused on the lives of forest people from the Central African Republic—a region over five hundred miles away from where Turnbull was located (Ituri, former Zaire). In that book I include descriptions of flashes of musical insight, some very brief, leading to more extensive musicking episodes. This first example took place when I was practicing BaAka singing while taking a walk by myself in the forest. As I learned something important about BaAka singing, an echo of Turnbull too was mixed into the sound that the trees sent back to me with my own voice:

> After a while I thought I was getting the open-throated sound a little better: one should not taper off the phrases but project them out brightly, letting the notes ring through the trees while listening for the echo. I found that the close interaction of BaAka song with the surrounding forest weaves singing and listening into a simultaneous process . . . I never did hear BaAka discuss this experience overtly, probably because the melding of song and soundscape is so complete as to seem self evident. (Kisliuk 1998, 10)

Several months after this encounter with my own echo, I was living in a BaAka camp. At first I was just trying to get a handle on what to listen for during large dance events when many voices were elaborating on a song, the core of which was difficult to discern. The dance was a hunting dance called Mabo, and one of the most popular Mabo songs at the time was "Makala." One day I had an epiphany of sorts:

> I was walking to our camp on my way back from [Bagandou] village. Along the path I came upon Djongi's daughter, Mokoti, and some younger children. As they scurried along in front of me, Mokoti sang out the phrase of a song. I recognized then that it was the main theme of one Mabo song very popular at the time, "Makala." (Kisliuk 1998, 98)

These two incidents—hearing my own echo and then hearing Mokoti's young voice in the forest—helped build to this next one. It is no coincidence that the occasions that stand out for me are the ones in which I am fully participating, especially—as Turnbull notes—when dancing as well as singing, and often after long periods of waiting for the right time to join in:

> After a while the distracting novelty of my dancing seemed to wear off. The focus shifted from me to the whole group, or maybe I just relaxed to the point where I could notice the whole group. "Oka, oka!" people called out, meaning "let's go!" (literally, "listen!").
>
> My senses tingled: I was finally inside the singing and dancing circle. The song was "Makala," and singing it came more easily to me while I danced. As I moved around the circle, the voices of different people stood out at moments, affecting my own singing and my choices of variations. Ndami sang a yodeled elaboration I had not heard before. I could feel fully the intermeshing of sound and motions and move with it as it transformed, folding in upon itself. This was different from listening or singing on the sidelines because, while moving with the circle, I became an active part of the aural kaleidoscope. I was part of the changing design inside the scope, instead of looking at it and projecting in.
>
> The physical task of executing the dance steps melded with the looking, listening, smiling, and reacting that kept us all dancing. Since our camp was built on a hill, it took extra effort to dance the full-soled steps while going up or down hill. Running the bottom of my foot inchworm-like across the ground required the sturdy support of many muscles in my leg. All this while trying to stay loose enough to follow through with my whole body [as I had been

> instructed to do earlier by Ndoko] and keep up with the beat. As I continued to dance, trying to refine my step, I noticed more fully the inward and delicately grounded concentration of the movements, like the *mboloko* antelope. Someone cried out, "sukele!" ("sweet!" an interpretation of the French, *sucre* [sugar]). (Kisliuk 1998, 101)

A magnified musicking moment might be fleeting but memorable, or could last for minutes, or could surface intermittently over hours and days. The experience can be deeply personal or broadly collective. I witnessed the latter one day in Bangui, the capital of the Central African Republic. The popular singer and composer Thierry Yezo (of Le Formidable Musiki) had just died of AIDS. The entire city echoed in memoriam with his song "Mami Wata." All day and into the night the song emanated in unison from thousands of transistor radios, wafting up with the smoke and ash of cooking fires from family compounds and the dust stirred by taxi tires (Kisliuk 2008b).[24]

STREAMS AND EDDIES

My students have taught me about the "twice behaved behavior" of performance (Schechner 1985), when a moment of musicking is infused with a presence from the past. Making music and dancing with students has also taught me fresh things about differing perspectives within a collective experience. This magnified moment in performance was poetically rendered by pianist and scholar (and my former student) Kelly Gross:

> Emphasizing the varying contours of vocal lines by singing different melodies from my neighbor feels so new to my body, as does singing in general. As a young pianist, I was urged to express myself musically with that instrument alone, and to leave the singing to others. Since learning to sing these beautiful and intricate BaAka songs of the Central African Republic, I have felt increasingly more comfortable in this newly acquired expressive mode.
>
> Now as my voice simultaneously blends and contrasts with my classmates, I smile as I sing. The polyphonic texture is so wonderfully lush and thick, that sometimes I can hardly differentiate the various parts we have learned. Many of us are creating new melodies and complementing the overall texture with improvised variations and yodels. The themes cycle again and again with some overlapping parts. After dropping down to a lower register (registers which tend to be neglected this semester due to our 21:3 ratio of women to men) I

hear the lower melody immediately resonate in my ears. I figure that someone nearby has to be singing the same line. My eyes search the lips of others until I find Laura's (one of the ensemble's most long-standing members) and find that she's singing the same melody. Her smiling eyes lock with mine. (Gross 1999, 2)

Kelly reappears in Deva Woodly's "sensational" (Hahn 2007) prose poem excerpted at the beginning of this essay and continued here. Deva illustrates just how much the interpersonal is synesthetically interconnected, while her piece brings together the themes I have explored in this essay:

MORE THAN MEASURE FOR MEASURE

The smell of things was human and I leaned against my friend Kelly, picking lint off my loose pants. The black cotton was soft and damply sweaty from the . . . dancing that had come before.

We were tired and the song started slowly.

. . . We swayed into one another and Bakele was gentle as it continued.

"Yo yaya eeha, eeyeh."

I smiled at Margot as she began to yodel, she was sitting across from me, her mouth open wide. She was small, her dark hair falling out of the careless knot at her neck. She pushed the tonal improvisations up from her center, the cries grew to twice her size after they passed her lips. Margot answered my smile, but the subtle expression around her eyes and mouth was not one of amusement. Something about her seriousness made me close my eyes. Concentrate. For a moment I was quiet, my hands pressed together at the end of a cycle of clapping.

At first, the song was little more than a collection of oddly pleasant measures that floated and spun on the air. I imagined lively cartoon notes drawn on a rebellious score. The lines of the bass clef wriggling and jumping to meet the treble clef, the tone and cadence flirting, playing, and then returning to its original place. I started singing again, extemporizing on the theme Kelly sang as she lightly tapped her bare foot on mine. The light syncopated touch fit in and under the rhythm of Bakele and I discovered that my body was part of the music. The song was not my voice or Kelly's. It was not even the sound of Margot grown double.

As I sat with my eyes closed, fingers pushed out straight and pressed together, I discovered that the music had color and shape. Not the animated approximation I had invented before, but a dynamic hue that began the same color as the dark behind my eyelids. And then, a wide white circle formed on the canvas on the back of my closed eyes. The faint, dull white that tumbles across vision truncated by a bright flash of light. The color of echoes. The circle grew thicker and brighter and the song went on. Loud and slow. We were taking our time. Kelly breathed deep beside me. A purple point formed in the center of the bright white circle beneath my closed eyes and almost immediately the spot of color bloomed into a kaleidoscope. The song separated into an infinite swell of rhythm and melody. Every tone was there, sung and unsung. (Woodly 2001, 1–2)

At this stirring juncture Deva informs us that I, the teacher, stopped to critique the singing and broke the spell. Deva writes, "Behind my eyes, fading, was the colorsound; the echoblush. I missed it already" (2001, 2). I was pitifully unaware of the feeling that was transpiring for others, if not for me. Despite what Blacking says about the sociality of musical affect, sometimes not everyone feels the same thing. The correspondence may not always transfer from one person to another. I have found that the role of instructor can be paradoxical, since "letting go" and being open is key, but is not usually the role of an instructor among students. I try continuously to level that field on the fly, to allow for moments of unanticipated combination and innovation, though only sometimes I succeed.

During the humid Virginia summer of 2010, a group of my former students gathered. We cooked meals together at my house—telling about individual pains and successes that had aged us. And we danced Elamba in our old classroom at the University of Virginia (the one I still teach in almost every day). Instruction was unnecessary; they were already experts. We sat on the ever-inadequate greenish linoleum floor. I sang close among them with my eyes closed, at once with them in the moment and also transported to other moments with BaAka: outside, on the ground, singing among the trees and loud insects, lifted out of time and place then as now, when suddenly Lamika tapped my arm. I opened my eyes to find her tying the Elamba skirts for dancing around my waist. I was not any kind of stranger here, this was a seamless letting go. Ordinary and extraordinary.

By delving into musicking moments as performing ethnographers, as scholars with freely poetic imaginations, we can train ourselves to better understand and be carried by the power of these moments: then dance them, play with them, sound them, and write them.

NOTES

1. Susan Stewart, theorizing on the phenomenon of the miniature, suggests that "the depiction of the miniature moves away from hierarchy and narrative in that it is caught in an infinity of descriptive gestures" (Stewart 2007, 47).

2. On the topic of copresence and sound, see the recent work of Jeff Todd Titon (2013).

3. While the limiting parameters of this topic are blurred, I keep my discussion focused mostly on the experience of participatory creation more than on reception.

4. The kinds of moments I address fall within what Victor and Edith Turner have pointed to in broader theories of liminality and communitas (e.g., V. Turner 1969; E. Turner 2012).

5. This is not the same kind of erasure of boundaries between past and present as in the infamous "ethnographic present" (Fabian 1983). The kind of past/present blur that I am speaking about, to the contrary, makes manifest the expansive unity of selves and others, pasts and presents, a theme I will take up again subsequently.

6. See Judith Becker's important comprehensive work (2004). For examples of recent and successful efforts in the ethnography of possession trance that venture into poetic realms, see the work by Katherine Hagedorn (2001) and Deborah Kapchan (2007), who also appear in this collection, and by Steven Friedson (especially 2009). We should also remember the pioneering work of Maya Deren in the 1950s, and of course the astounding life and work of Zora Neale Hurston in the 1930s.

7. This is reminiscent of Carlos Castaneda's parody of structuralism in Appendix B of *The Teachings of Don Juan* (1968). Castaneda got the irony of trying to pin down the ineffable with inadequate and often pretentious academic tools (see also Turner 2012, 21).

8. Speaking to anthropologists, Colin Turnbull (1990) pointed in this direction decades ago, emphasizing the correlation between the depth of participation and the depth of understanding.

9. In a longer essay about bluegrass jam sessions, I have detailed several contrasting incidents that missed the mark and jams that failed altogether (Kisliuk [1988] 2011). Addressing a number of such differently affecting moments can work collectively within a musical ethnography to offer readers their own path of insight through layers of socio-musical description.

10. In terms of writing style, Lakoff and Johnson themselves might well have illustrated their findings more effectively had they tossed the academic rhetoric in favor of some more choice metaphors of their own.

11. This parallels Zen Buddhist philosophy and practice.

12. Unless we insist that (polysemous) metaphors (and metonyms), memories, and analogies are also, or at least can be, actually physically felt, physiologically manifested phenomena—as dreams are and as theatrical, musical, and spiritual experiences can be.

13. Readers can access a video of Reliéf singing "There Is a God" at http://www.youtube.com/watch?v=uv8m-OMckgI.

14. Svatka is not a member of Reliéf, but Zbyněk is. Svatka is a bassist and singer; she has played in bands with Zbyněk in the past (Bidgood, personal communication, January 2012).

15. This is my own translation.

16. This was in a course with professor and poet Georgette Pradal, who was also my mother's mentor in French literature. I recently learned that both Victor and Edith Turner read Charles Baudelaire's poetry since before they were married in 1941 (Edith Turner, personal communication via e-mail, January 2012). The title of Victor Turner's book, *The Forest of Symbols,* is a reference to a line in "Correspondances."

17. This was with David Locke, in his ensembles both at Tufts University and in Boston. In a course on dance ethnology, Professor Locke also introduced me to the terms *synesthesia* and *kinesthesia,* which individually and in relation to each other intrigued me immediately. I touched on these ideas in an undergraduate thesis (and performance piece), but have not had a chance to truly explore them since until preparing this essay so many years later.

18. Also, I was reading and meeting Paul Berliner (and Ephat Mujuru) and Steven Feld, and studying Buddhism and aesthetic philosophy.

19. I am grateful to the late, wonderful theater artist Julie Portman for suggesting to me then that what I was struggling to articulate as my interest is called "aesthetics."

20. See Dorra (1994, 8–11) for a brief but effective analysis of this poem and the intellectual context in which it was written.

21. Alan S. Weiss has written about Baudelaire's idea of correspondences in relation to sound art and architecture (see Weiss 2002).

22. Kinesthetic empathy is yet another neurobiological element at play here. Ramachandran, in addition to his work on synesthesia, studies mirror neurons in the human brain that enable us to use our kinesthetic sense to empathize with the physicality of another being, to the point where our brains respond in the same way whether we ourselves are moving or when we are watching another living being move, touch, or be touched (Ramachandran 1998). I suggest that sound can also can have these kinesthetic qualities.

23. See, for example, Louis Sarno (1993). Turnbull's influence has been significant and widespread; Steven Feld mentions that as his teacher Turnbull influenced him profoundly (e.g., Feld 1990, ix). See also a recent feature film based on the life of Louis Sarno, *Oka!* (2011), which channels Turnbull's writing as much as it does Sarno's life.

24. You can hear the song at http://www.youtube.com/watch?v=sUyoNx3vvK8 (see also Kisliuk 2008).

REFERENCES

Abrahams, Roger D. "Review of Victor Turner and the Construction of Cultural Criticism: Between Literature and Anthropology by Kathleen M. Ashley, 1990." *American Ethnologist* 21, no. 4 (Nov. 1994): 994–95.

Anderson, Trenley. Unpublished prose, University of Virginia, 2012.

Armstrong, Robert Plant. *The Affecting Presence.* Urbana: University of Illinois Press, 1986.

Barad, Karen. "Posthumanist Performativity: Toward an Understanding of How Matter Comes to Matter." *Signs: Journal of Women, Culture, and Society* 28, no. 3 (2003): 801–31.

Baudelaire, Charles. "Correspondances." In *Les Fleurs du Mal.* 1857. Reprint, Paris: Levy, 1868.

Becker, Judith. *Deep Listeners: Music, Emotion, and Trancing.* Bloomington: Indiana University Press, 2004.

Berger, Peter L., and Thomas Luckmann. *The Social Construction of Reality: A Treatise on the Sociology of Knowledge.* Garden City, NY: Anchor Books, 1966.

Berliner, Paul. *The Soul of Mbira.* Chicago: University of Chicago Press, 1978.

Bidgood, Lee. "'America Is All Around Here': An Ethnography of Bluegrass Music in Contemporary Czech Republic." PhD diss., University of Virginia, 2011.

Blacking, John. *How Musical Is Man?* Seattle: University of Washington Press, 1973.

Burke, Edmund. *A Philosophical Enquiry into the Origin of Our Ideas of the Sublime and Beautiful.* Edited by J. T. Bolton. 1757. Reprint, Notre Dame: University of Notre Dame Press, 1968.

Cantwell, Robert. *Bluegrass Breakdown: The Making of the Old Southern Sound.* 1984. Reprint, Urbana: University of Illinois Press, 2003.

Castaneda, Carlos. *The Teachings of Don Juan: A Yaqui Way of Knowledge.* Berkeley: University of California Press, 1968.

Csordas, Thomas. *Embodiment and Experience: The Existential Ground of Culture.* Cambridge: Cambridge University Press, 1994.

Dorra, Henri. *Symbolist Art Theories.* Los Angeles: University of California Press, 1994.

Downey, Greg. "Synesthesia and Metaphor—I'm Not Feeling It." *Neuroanthropology* (web blog), June 5, 2008. Accessed on February 29, 2016. http://neuroanthropology.net/2008/06/05/synesthesia-metaphor-im-not-feeling-it/.

Fabian, Johannes. *Time and the Other: How Anthropology Makes Its Object.* New York: Columbia University Press, 1983.

Feld, Steven. *Sound and Sentiment: Birds, Weeping, Poetics, and Song in Kaluli Expression.* 1982. Reprint, Philadelphia: University of Pennsylvania Press, 1990.

Feld, Steven, and Charles Keil. *Music Grooves.* Chicago: University of Chicago Press, 1994.

Fernandez, James, ed. *Beyond Metaphor: The Theory of Tropes in Anthropology.* Stanford: Stanford University Press, 1991.

Fleck, Bela. "Throw Down Your Heart: V01.3." Audio CD recording (Rounder) and DVD documentary film. Directed by Sascha Paladino. 2008.

Friedson, Steven. *Remains of Ritual: Northern Gods in a Southern Land.* Chicago: University of Chicago Press, 2009.

Geertz, Clifford. *The Interpretation of Cultures.* New York: Basic Books, 1973.

Gross, Kelly. "Energy, Interaction, and the Sound Vortex: Performance of BaAka Song and Dance." 1999. Unpublished student paper quoted in Michelle Kisliuk and Kelly Gross. "What's the 'It' That We Learn to Perform? Teaching BaAka Music and Dance." In *Performing Ethnomusicology: Teaching and Representation in World Music Ensembles,* edited by Ted Solis. Los Angeles: University of California Press, 2004.

Hagedorn, Katherine. *Divine Utterances: The Performance of Afro-Cuban Santeria.* Washington DC: Smithsonian Institution Press, 2001.

Hahn, Tomie. *Sensational Knowledge: Embodying Culture Through Japanese Dance.* Middletown, CT: Wesleyan University Press, 2007.

Hall, Stuart. "Notes on Deconstructing the Popular." In *People's History and Socialist Theory.* Edited by Raphael Samuel. London: Routledge, 1981.

Jackson, Michael. *Paths Toward a Clearing: Radical Empiricism and Ethnographic Enquiry.* Bloomington: Indiana University Press, 1989.

Kant, Immanuel. *The Critique of Judgment.* Translated by Jack Creed Meredith. 1790. Reprint, Oxford: Clarendon Press, 1969.

Kapchan, Deborah. *Traveling Spirit Masters: Moroccan Gnawa Trance and Music in the Global Marketplace.* Middletown, CT: Wesleyan University Press, 2007.

Kisliuk, Michelle. "Agbadza: A Polymetric Poem." Unpublished poem, 1981.

———. *Seize the Dance! BaAka Musical Life and the Ethnography of Performance.* 1998. Reprint, New York: Oxford University Press, 2000.

———. "(Un)Doing Fieldwork: Sharing Song, Sharing Lives." In *Shadows in the Field: New Perspectives for Fieldwork in Ethnomusicology.* Edited by Gregory Barz and Timothy Cooley. 2nd ed. 1997. Reprint, New York: Oxford University Press, 2008a.

———. "The Intersection of Evangelism, AIDS, and Mami Wata in Popular Music in Centrafrique." In *Sacred Waters: Arts of Mami Wata and Other Divinities in Africa and the Diaspora,* edited by Henry John Drewal, 413–22. Bloomington: Indiana University Press, 2008b.

———. "Anything Special about a Bluegrass Jam Session?" Unpublished paper delivered at "Fire on the Mountain: A Bluegrass Symposium," Harvard University, January 2010.

———. "A Special Kind of Courtesy: Action at a Bluegrass Festival Jam Session." In *Roots Music,* edited by Mark F. DeWitt, 205–20. 1988. Reprint, London: Ashgate, 2011. Reprinted from *TDR: A Journal of Performance Studies* 32, no. 3 (fall 1988): 141–55.

Kohler, Evelyne, Christian Keysers, M. Allessandra Umilta, Leonardo Fogassi, Vittorio Gallese, and Goacomo Rizzolatti. "Hearing Sounds, Understanding Actions: Action Representation in Mirror Neurons." *Science* 297 (August 2, 2002): 846–48.

Kovecses, Zoltan. *Metaphor and Emotion: Language, Culture, and the Body in Human Feeling.* Cambridge: Cambridge University Press, 2000.

Lakoff, George, and Mark F. Johnson. *Metaphors We Live By.* Chicago: University of Chicago Press, 1980.

Lawler, James. *Poetry and Moral Dialectic: Baudelaire's "Secret Architecture."* Madison, NJ: Fairleigh Dickinson University Press, 1994.

Lex, Barbara. "The Neurobiology of Ritual Trance." In *The Spectrum of Ritual.* Edited by E. G. d'Aquili, C. D. Laughlin, and J. McManus. New York: Columbia University Press, 1979.

Marks, Lawrence. *The Unity of the Senses: Interrelations among the Modalities.* Cambridge, MA: Academic Press, 1978.

McKinney, Devin. "The Mechanics and Mysteries of the Pop Music Moment." Abstract of paper delivered at the "Writing What You Hear" panel, Experience Music Project Pop Conference, Seattle, Washington, 2004.

Merleau-Ponty, Maurice. *The Phenomenology of Perception.* 1962. Reprint, London: Routledge, 1995.

Pratt, Mary Louise. *Imperial Eyes: Travel Writing and Transculturation.* London: Routledge, 1992.

Ramachandran, V. S. "Consciousness and Body Image: Lessons from Phantom Limbs, Capgras Syndrome and Pain Asymbolia" in "The Conscious Brain: Abnormal and Normal." Special issue, *Philosophical Transactions: Biological Sciences* 353, no. 1377 (Nov. 29, 1998): 1851–59.

Ramachandran, V. S., and E. M. Hubbard. "Synesthesia: A Window into Perception, Thought and Language." *Journal of Consciousness Studies* 8, no. 12 (2001): 3–34.

———. "The Phenomenology of Synesthesia." *Journal of Consciousness Studies* 10, no. 8 (2003a): 49–57.

———. "Hearing Colors, Tasting Shapes: People with Synesthesia—Whose Senses Blend Together—Are Providing Valuable Clues to Understanding the Organization and Functions of the Human Brain." *Scientific American,* May 2003b, 53–59.

Sarno, Louis. *Song from the Forest.* New York: Houghton Mifflin, 1993.

Schechner, Richard. *"Restoration of Behavior" in Between Theatre and Anthropology.* Philadelphia: University of Pennsylvania Press, 1985.

———. *The Future of Ritual.* London: Routledge, 1995.

Schieffelin, Edward. *The Sorrow of the Lonely and the Burning of the Dancers.* New York: St. Martins Press, 1976.

———. "Performance and the Cultural Construction of Reality." *American Ethnologist* 12, no. 4 (1985): 707–22.

Sklar, Deidre. *Dancing with the Virgin: Body and Faith in the Fiesta of Tortugas, New Mexico.* Berkeley: University of California Press, 2001.

Small, Christopher. *Musicking: The Meanings of Performing and Listening.* Middletown, CT: Wesleyan University Press, 1998.

Stewart, Susan. *On Longing.* 1993. Reprint, Durham, NC: Duke University Press, 2007.

Stoller, Paul. *The Taste of Ethnographic Things.* Philadelphia: University of Pennsylvania Press, 1989.

Taussig, Michael. *Mimesis and Alterity.* London: Routledge, 1993.

ter Hark, Michel. "Coloured Vowels: Wittgenstein on Synesthesia and Secondary Meaning." *Philosophia* 37 (2009): 589–604.

Titon, Jeff Todd. "Thoreau's Ear." Paper delivered to theannual conference of the Society for Ethnomusicology, Indianapolis, Indiana, Nov. 13–17, 2013.

Toynbee, Jason. "Do You Believe? Notes on the Sublime in Popular Music." Abstract of paper delivered at the "To Sublime Effect" panel, Experience Music Project Pop Conference, Seattle, Washington, 2004.

Turino, Thomas. *Music as Social Life: The Politics of Participation.* Chicago: University of Chicago Press, 2007.

Turnbull, Colin. *The Forest People.* 1962. Reprint, New York: Touchstone Books, 1987.

———. "Liminality: A Synthesis of Subjective and Objective Experience." In *By Means of Performance: Intercultural Studies of Theater and Ritual,* edited by R. Schechner and W. Appel. Cambridge: Cambridge University Press, 1990.

Turner, Edith. *Communitas: The Anthropology of Collective Joy.* New York: Palgrave Macmillan, 2012.

Turner, Victor. *The Ritual Process: Structure and Antistructure.* 1969. Reprint, Hawthorne, NY: Aldine de Gruyter, 1997.

Turner, Victor, and Edith Turner. "Performing Ethnography," in *TDR: The Drama Review* 26, no. 2 (summer 1982): 33–50.

Weisenberg, Joey. "Jewish Singing: A Practical Guide to Fostering Communal Music." HuffPost Religion blog. *Huffington Post,* May 31, 2011. Accessed on February 29, 2016. http://www.huffingtonpost.com/joey-weisenberg/jewish-singing-fostering-_b_868788.html.

Weiss, Alan S. *Varieties of Audio Mimesis.* Berlin: Errant Bodies Press, 2008.

Williams, Raymond. *Problems in Materialism and Culture.* London: Verso Books, 1980.

Woodly, Deva. "More Than Measure for Measure." Unpublished prose poem, University of Virginia, Charlottesville, 2001.

PART TWO

Memoir and Metaphor as Method

ALEX WATERMAN

4. Listening to Resonant Words

Writing sound is an act of transcription—a writing across. Phonography (*phōnē* "sound, voice" and *graphē* "writing") is the effort to get sound on *and* off a surface (cylinder, plate, wire, page, screen, and so on) in order to notate it by describing its movements, transmissions, and transactions. Phonography first brings to mind the *phonograph*—the mechanical instrument that could both record (inscribe) and play back (re-sound). Another example of phonography was the phonetic notation and shorthand system developed by Isaac Pitman, which inscribed speech onto the page in as direct a fashion possible by representing the sounds, *not* the letters.[1] Phonography can be reimagined in the context of this chapter as an instrumental model and metaphor for how sound writing can be both an inscriptive/prescriptive and a descriptive/resonant practice. This chapter seeks out ways in which our sound writing might incorporate techniques and methodologies from visual, musical, and poetic practices.

Scripts, scores, and poems are forms that use words in the generation of visual or sonic compositions, or both. Some forms of "sound writing," such as concrete poetry (see Ian Hamilton Finlay that follows), have few or no playback possibilities. Letters are seen and syllables are heard in the silent and privatized imagination of the reader or spectator. The arrangement of words as sculptural objects or type on the page evokes sensorial correlations for the viewer, but the words are not meant to *come off* the page or resonate. Their senses are made through the silent production of the reader no matter how "loud" the typography might be.[2] In sound poetry on the other hand (e.g., Henry Chopin, Isidore Isou, Bob Cobbing), words are read phonetically, registered by the scanning of the eye, not as syncretic objects (on their way to forming a new language) but symbols for the vocal production of consonants, vowels, gutturals, fricatives, openings and closings of the mouth, wet explosions of saliva, the smacking of lips, or the cold roughness of fast inhalations against bared teeth.[3]

Marjorie Perloff writes in the introduction to *The Sound of Poetry/The Poetry of Sound*, "The term *poetry* has come to be understood less as the lyric genre than as a distinctive way of organizing language—which is to say, the *language art. Poetic* language is language made strange, made somehow extraordinary by the use of verbal and sound repetition, visual configuration, and syntactic deformation."[4]

Most of the surfaces we write upon are not unique but multiple, virtual, or transitional. Our words are stored as data in hard disks and across servers or "clouds"; they rarely if ever exist on a single computer. Pages and screens each map out radically different geographies for our language to inhabit. Writing is composed of marks, moving type, monotype, or computer fonts, which move and perform in very different ways depending on whether they are on the page or on the screen. Because *sound* moves and *makes us move* in very different ways depending on the space that it occupies, the material and process that we use *to write* is of considerable importance. As Charles Olson wrote while reflecting on the machine he most often engaged with in his practice:

> It is an advantage of the typewriter that due to its rigidity and its space precisions, it can for a poet indicate exactly the breath, the pauses, the suspensions even of syllables, the juxtapositions even of parts of phrases, which he intends. For the first time the poet has the stave and bar a musician has had. For the first time he can, without the convention of rhyme and meter, record the listening he has done to his own speech and by that one act indicates how he would want any reader, silently or otherwise, to voice his work.[5]

BRIDGE

If music is one way that a social body sounds together and scores are a way to make a social body *move* together (or apart) over time by way of transmitting sound in written form, then how might we produce sonorously resonant words, for (silent *or* sonorous) reproduction by the reader? Can our ideas be *scored* for the reader?

LISTENING TO LISTENING

Listening to listening (is) sensing sense: making sense of what we hear. Listening to how we hear, and perhaps most important, realizing how unique an experience of listening can be in relation to who we are and where we are at the moment of listening.

Jean Luc Nancy's book *Listening* (2007) posits that listening is an *act of resonance*. When we listen, we are hearing the resounding of sound. We are part of this resonance, and in our making of sound we are re-sounding and receiving our own transmissions. Instead of describing or analyzing creative processes, could we imagine our listening as composing? Listening as a way of thinking and being in the world that trains us to listen and reproduce sound *together*, thus repositioning the critical act as a *social act of reading* sounded out in the moment of performance? Would this writing about sound *resound* differently?

LISTENING TO *NATURA MORTA*, LONDON 2010

In April of 2010, I was in London when Iceland's Eyjafjallajokull volcano erupted. All flights were cancelled, and I was stranded in London as the city was having its first splendid days of spring. They were strange days. I was drifting in a zone between the unexpected pleasure of having ample time off and the guilt-ridden and anxiety-plagued state of mind caused by hovering deadlines and my worries about my wife Elisa, who was in her ninth month of pregnancy. Would I get back in time for the birth?

I was also without a place to stay; but as luck would have it, my friend Celine was out of town, and she let me crash at her flat, a beautiful place, high up in the Lubetkin Spa Green Estate, on Rosebery Avenue across from Sadler's Wells Theatre.

After arriving and fixing a cup of tea, I sat down to listen to some music. The light was pouring into the living room, and the camera obscura in Celine's window captured the steeple across the street and the trees that lined the avenue, projecting them upside down on the small crystal screen. I opened the windows, and the joyful, raucous sound of children playing at the school next door poured into the room.

It started to sink in that I had something truly rare on my hands: time to reflect. I plugged my iPod into Celine's stereo and began to listen to *Natura Morta* by Walter Marchetti.[6] As I sat on the couch gazing out the window, it occurred to me that this act of listening felt more vivid and immersive than usual. I wanted to inscribe these feelings and document my listening, so I took out my field recorder and pressed record.

In recording my listening, I was recording the ambient sounds of the day onto/into the "original" performance of Walter Marchetti. The soundscape of the interior of the apartment and its acoustics were captured while being mixed with the sounds of children, traffic, and birds outdoors. In *listening* to this recording, a whole new chain of events transpires: the process of transcribing the listening becomes transposed to other acoustics and is apprehended by other bodies that receive the sound but also absorb, reflect, and interfere with it. The recording of listening contains an imprint of time that one can (possibly) recognize, though it may be hard to know the season, temperature, and time of day.

What can we "see"—by echolocation or fantasy—from this act of listening? Do we "hear" the dimensions of the room and the height of the building? Are we able to assess the amount of spillage from exterior to interior and judge distances and proximities? How many people are listening? How do we know? (We hear coughing, sniffing, and various other bodily sounds, but what do these sound sources tell us?)

Jean-Luc Nancy writes:

> What does to be listening, to be all ears, as one would say, "to be in the world," mean? What does it mean to exist according to listening, for it and through it, what part of experience and truth is put into play? What is at play in listening, what resonates in it, what is the tone of listening or its timbre? Is even listening itself sonorous?[7]

In other circumstances, when we are "listeners-listening-live," we can feel how music and sound have an impact on our bodies by way of vibration and the signals that the inner ear sends back to the sounds that enter our ear canals. Some frequencies flutter in our ears as they clash with the tones of our inner ear. Other sounds tickle our hairs, and yet others make our skin crawl. We can physicalize and recognize these phenomena, but as Nancy writes, "What part of experience and truth is put into play?" What resonates inside of listening? What is *its sound?*

If listening is an act of resonance, then we are listening to the resounding of sound. We are not only a part of this resonance, but even in our making of sound we are re-sounding and receiving our own transmissions.

In composer Alvin Lucier's piece, "I Am Sitting in a Room," "the natural resonant frequencies of the room (are) articulated by speech," so that the room's resonance is made resonant in itself, through a simple process of recording and re-recording that eventually removes the original articulations of the voice and captures more and more of its sounding in the acoustics of the room. The subject sits in a room reading and recording his reading, played back into the room; then he records and plays back the recording and record again and again and again, the voice eventually disappears, and we are left with the resonance (of the room). This is the re-sounding of (captured) listening that results in the loss of the subject's original performance. A feedback loop allows us to amplify the space around the subject and learn what the room does with the resonance of our listening, as we attend to the room's own resonance. It could be argued that subjectivity is *not lost* but transferred.[8] The room becomes the subject (where *I* = *a room*).

When one is listening, one is on the lookout for a subject, something (itself) that identifies itself by resonating from self to self, in itself and for itself, hence outside of itself, at once the same as and other than itself, one in the echo of the other; and this echo is like the very sound of its sense.[9]

As Lucier has noted, he might have achieved similar results had he proceeded in another manner, but his more laborious approach allows for a gradual process to unfold versus achieving the expected results in a more expedited fashion. Listening to the voice evanesce and gradually be superseded by the room sound is to attend to very gradual changes in the sonic environment, as one might watch a sunset on a beach when one has no other place to be—feeling the minute changes in light by stages (civil twilight, nautical twilight, "Clair de Lune," astronomical twilight . . .).

> I was interested in the process, the step-by-step, slow process of the disintegration of speech and the reinforcement of the resonant frequencies. Actually, when Mary (Lucier) and I visited the Polaroid Company in Cambridge—Mary, as you know, did a visual analog to the tape by subjecting a Polaroid snapshot to a similar reductive process—the art director, when he saw the end result, said, "I could do that in one step." He just didn't understand that what we found interesting was the gradual process itself.[10]

In a roundtable with Gordon Mumma and Carmen Pardo at La Casa Encendida, in March of 2008, Alvin Lucier spoke more broadly of his compositional goals and the listener:

> People say to me, "When I listen to your music I'm thinking of how I'm listening not to the music itself but I'm thinking of how I'm experiencing it." The focus is in a different place. It's not in the object of the music itself; it's in the individual person thinking about how they're listening. If I've accomplished that then I think I've done something worthwhile.[11]

This graphing and grafting over and graphing again of sound sources are a "writing across" (transcription) that is not *linear.* It is everywhere around and not just across and over other sounds, it is inside of and interpenetrating all sound and yet also determining the quality of "silence" that the room will have when the piece is over. When we hear a room's re-sounding, do we thereafter imagine it as always already outside and inside of every sound that we make in that room?

> In terms of the gaze, the subject is referred back to itself as object. In terms of listening, it is, in a way, to itself that the subject refers or refers back. Thus in a certain way there is no relationship between the two. A writer notes: "I can hear what I see: a piano, or some leaves stirred by the wind. But I can never see what I hear. Between sight and hearing there is no reciprocity.[12]

In contrast to this statement by Nancy, Susan Howe writes: "Font-voices summon a reader into visible earshot."[13] Howe's "conflation of voice and print" opens up a potential reciprocity that Nancy has foreclosed in his essay. It is through understanding what Howe means by "font-voices" that this opening is possible. Her meaning emerges out of the "wilderness" of the archive and the library. It is there that one finds voices from the past printed on the page in fonts and typefaces (*characters* on a page) that allow us to imagine their sounding in other ways. The "font-voices" mark from where these voices first sounded and give us an impression from which to imagine their re-sounding.

Alvin Lucier, in conversation with Robert Ashley in 1977, remarked:

> The way I work, without sounding too pretentious, is what happens after print . . . Webern, Schoenberg, and post-serialism are so connected with print, so connected with writing notes. And if you don't write in notes you get off the page. You're not thinking on a page, and if you're not thinking on a page, you might not think in two dimensions . . . See, I don't think of technology as technology. I think of it as landscape.[14]

Our modern-day computer takes words and parses and fragments—organizes and makes them searchable—then translates and recompiles them into language or speech once more. Our computers are a hybrid, evolved form of typewriter and television. The fusion of these two technologies makes pages and screens interchangeable, creating new landscapes for sound writing.

As Robert Ashley has said, television brings to the viewer an impossible landscape all at once. We can see the minutest detail and the whole picture in lightning-fast sequences. Baseball games on television can be another way for us to imagine the power of word processing, in that word processors allow us to shift scenes, perspectives, search for action and characters, zoom in and out, and edit together a total sensorial experience for the reader/viewer.

If we return to Celine's apartment and the listening to the listening of *Natura Morta* by Walter Marchetti, *knowing* that we are listening to a recording allows me to imagine another chamber inside this chamber—that of the recording device. Like Celine's camera obscura on the windowsill, which seems to draw the outside world into its confines and reproduce it in etched detail, an inverted exterior on a tiny field of crystal, my recording device draws in and amplifies her room; but it is *not* the room, but rather a kind of outline of my listening. If we were to take the acoustic information we hear from the recording and attempt to reconstruct the space, it would be a little like asking an architect to reconstruct the interiors depicted in a painting by a Flemish master. We would end up with a fantastically distorted room.

Scoring Sound Writing?

As John Cage has said, "Composing's one thing, performing's another, listening's a third. What can they have to do with each other?"[16] We speak of scores in broad terms as being *prescriptive and descriptive,* referring to whether they are documenting sounds, performances of sounds, actions, language, and so on (descriptive), or on the contrary, whether they give a set of instructions or orders and timings within which a sequence of actions or sounds is to be produced (prescriptive). Because of the different types of training involved, alphabetic literacy and musical literacy have often remained quite far apart from one another. We generally learn to speak before we learn to write, but in many Western musical traditions the opposite is true: it is a perverse situation in which we learn to read music and then learn how to play our instruments, or at best we struggle to read and learn technique simultaneously.

One attempt, among many in the twentieth century, to undo this paradigm was the composition of verbal and graphic scores. Beyond their expansion of musical language and the creative possibilities that it opened up for composers and musicians, it also opened up musical production to other types of performers and readers. One of the most famous proponents of graphic and verbal notation was the British composer Cornelius Cardew (1936–1981).

Michael Nyman, writing about Cornelius Cardew's music from 1961 to 1971, says, "Cardew has always conceived of notation (in his own works) not as an end in itself or a means of unlocking *sounds,* but as a way of engaging the most valuable resource of any music—people. Notation can *make you move*[17] . . . The notation *should* do it. The trouble is, he [Cardew] feels, that just as you find your sounds are too alien, intended 'for a different culture,' you make the same discovery about your beautiful notation: no-one is willing to understand it, no-one moves."[18]

Experimental scores can be viewed as both models for producing music and social models for assembling networks and communities. As Nyman points out, the most important resource in any music is people. How a notation makes a people move or not may or may not be the fault of the notation, there must also be a willingness on the part of the reader. If the notation or what it produces seems intended "for a different culture," Nyman implies that there will be resistance. In looking at the study of notation as a possible site from which to propose new methodologies for sound writing, we should remember the labors of Wittgenstein as he explored the logical limits of language. As he wrote, "To imagine a language is to imagine a form of life." When the sounds or the writing feel too removed from our "culture" as Nyman writes, we are likely to feel it has nothing to do with our lives.

Because of the priority it gave to works that were open or indeterminate, British and American experimentalism (Cardew, Parsons, Cage, Wolff) left openings for the musicians to assemble the works themselves. It is only through playing out the material, reshaping and resetting it for the particularities of the group that is performing, and the place where one is performing, that the works become realized. The social forms that are produced by experimental music process are in some cases a more important product than the music produced. Experimental scores often encourage elaborate conversations in order to generate a reading for a performance. The notion that conversation *is* production is something that can be extrapolated from this practice and put to use in many other types of artistic and academic production.[19]

REFRAIN

> Sound essentially emanates and expands, or is deferred and transferred . . . sonorous time takes place immediately according to a completely different dimension, which is not that of simple succession (corollary of the negative instant). It is a present in waves on a swell, not in a point on a line; it is a time

> that opens up, that is hollowed out, that is enlarged or ramified, that envelops or separates, that becomes or is turned into a loop, that stretches out or contracts, and so on.[20]

Does Nancy's notion of "sonorous time" arriving on the swell of a wave collapse upon itself or rather *engulf* itself? Or does it break into particles that can never reassemble themselves into a wave ever again?

IAN HAMILTON FINLAY

In the work of Ian Hamilton Finlay, the spatial, chromatic, and rhythmic typesetting of words create a visual harmony that interacts with the reader's visual and syntactic understanding of the composition. Implicit in this arrangement is the silent production of the reader. Words remain *on* the page. Type and fonts do *not* articulate speech, mark out breaths, or provide dynamic contours or pitch information. Finlay's work *concretizes* words, making them into a kind of visual music that is not to be heard. Words are fixed in their place in order that they move within the autonomous and fixed space of the reader's mind.

Ian Hamilton Finlay is most famous for his garden in Scotland, known as Little Sparta. The garden is conceived largely as a set of poems, containing many sculptures that range from one-word poems to poems composed of multiple words or short phrases. The garden-as-poem (or poem-as-garden) requires the reader's engagement on foot (like a score, it makes people move). The landscape around the words, or the landscape itself *as word* (tree, pond, clearing, leaves) changes seasonally; the materiality of the words in the landscape also changes over time as the sculptures are covered with moss or lichen, or slowly erode away as they are exposed to the elements.

The poem in figure 4.1 is from a series of works that Finlay made in the 1960s, on the word "wave." In this particular work, the English word is translated to Latin (*unda*). The work goes beyond the simple pun, as its form references not only water, but also sound and light. On the concrete curves, we see sinusoidal waves in blue moving across the five sections. The concrete itself is in the shape of a crest, and it alternates between concavity and convexity in relation to the viewer. The blue sinusoidal wave intersects the word (UNDA) as it moves across the concrete curves from left to right. The anagrammatic transformation of the word renders new words: UNAD, UDNA, NUDA, UNDA, two of which—NUDA and UNDA—mean "naked" and "wave," respectively. The other

Figure 4.1 Ian Hamilton Finlay's *Unda*. This picture was taken at the Max Planck Institute in Stuttgart in 2010, while I was in residence at the Künstlerhaus Stuttgart with a group of artists, as we began working on a collectively produced book based on Cornelius Cardew's verbal score from 1967, *The Tiger's Mind*. The project was conceived by Beatrice Gibson and Will Holder, and was a continuation of work that Beatrice, Will, and I had produced collaboratively on musical scores as models for conversation and artistic production.

two resist translation and are possibly nonreferential. If this is the case, then the words themselves have a dual nature: sense and nonsense, like the wave that itself has two natures: wave and particle. As the sculpture faces south, the light shines through the space between each wave/particle. The play between light and water and wave and particle is given further meaning because of its location (Max Planck[21] Institute).

I took my colleagues out to see the garden at the institute on a crisp late winter morning. It was a long beautiful walk through the university campus and out through the fields. I had decided to record the walk there, and later I transcribed the conversations and the commentary about what we were seeing along the way. As we stood in front of the sculpture, we talked about Ian Hamilton Finlay's work. Will Holder, our resident expert on his work, spoke about concrete poetry and how words are carried by the landscape and do not serve as mere objects in the landscape.

WILL HOLDER: Like Mallarmé, the diagrammatic or what was on the page became a model of social relations. Syntax became a model for social structures. I think it [concrete poetry] was a failure because it became an academic preoccupation, the diagrams didn't directly translate or relate to society or to the "real world."

BEATRICE GIBSON: They became too abstract, or too formal?

WH: Too formal, or . . . governed by a set of conditions which can only exist on the page, literally and figuratively. [Ian Hamilton] Finlay has a huge garden now. When he first started it, it was quite small, but he bought up pieces of property from surrounding farmers in Scotland. It's really beautiful because it's chronological, going from this kind of work, outwards to (something) much more semantic I think, literally the placing of texts in the landscape and not texts as an object in the landscape. There's still this tension because he still uses very physical reproduction techniques such as stone carving and wood carving.

BG: So in other words, there would be an object inscribed with typography in the landscape, and the landscape is organized formally?

CELINE CONDORELLI: There are no words as such, to be seen?

WH: Oh, there absolutely are, but the words aren't as much the objects themselves as the words are "carried" by objects in the landscape, if that makes sense.

CC: [*Speaking about the garden where we were standing*] The pathways here have a similar wavelike structure (to the sculpture) and there's a creek that runs behind it that is also sinusoidal.

WH: I think this is (all) about feedback, about the wave coming in and going out again, and meaning coming in and going out again, and constantly being distorted by the things it's constantly referring to, and back and forth. A lot of his work is involved in describing elemental or natural phenomena like the sea or the wind, and man's position in relation to them. This is why boats figure so prominently in his work. There was also a period where he was working a lot with words and images about war and man's position as maker and breaker of the earth. Maker and breaker of rules that govern the earth, or physicality . . . But again, this is a semantic destruction I'd say. He looks at warfare and the cycle of war and the inevitability of violence in relation to revolution . . . how they go hand in hand. He pursued this for a long time, the relationship between violence and revolution and how it's

> prescribed and described and documented. In other words, how violence is legitimated through text, in the name of progress.

As one walks through the garden at the institute, following a winding stream leading to a pond, one encounters the next sculpture. In order to get to it, the spectator walks over the stream, stepping on three concrete stepping stones, and then skirting the perimeter of the pond in order to reach the sculpture.

It is a concrete lectern (sounding board) that is planted in the pond itself with a pedestal that the spectator can step out onto in order to stand at the lectern and read the inscription in Latin: HIC IACET PARVULUM QUODAM EX AQUA LONGIORE EXCERPTUM (Here lies a small excerpt from a larger body of water).

Walking back past the UNDA sculpture toward the exit, one passes the third sculpture/poem: a low curvilinear wall with a bench facing a standing concrete half-pipe, like the ones that compose the UNDA piece, with a circle of water at its base. The bench faces south toward the light and a clearing in the forest, but the viewer who takes a seat has her or his view obstructed by the half-pipe. As the landscape is omitted, the ears open to what is all around. The wave blocks one's vision, yet forces the viewer into a position of reflectivity where one might imagine the landscape behind the wave/screen. The channel of the half-pipe partially encloses a dark circular pool, suggesting an auricular form (the pool as ear canal), or perhaps the half-pipe is a curling page upended and standing over an inkwell.

The concrete screen, a wave with full opacity, reflects sound waves off its surface and thus enlightens the spectators to the forms all around them. If the viewer moves around the bench, turning away from the view, the binaural image of their listening changes, as well as moving in and out of the wind, filtering its noise in and out of the sonic image. It's a brilliant synthesis of all of the ways that UNDA can be understood. As poem, all the senses engage in order to reveal the multiple layers of meaning. It is a poem that must be walked through, stepped out onto, and sat on or in. It scores one's movements and soundlessly[22] reveals its composition to the reader. To engage the poem with a group of us was to unfurl a winding single file form composed of bodies, stopping along the way to read together and re-sonate what Finlay had created.

As Ian Hamilton Finlay wrote to Michael Schmidt in 1979:

> It is not only by drawing pictures that one can use language in a non-discursive way, and the difficulty lies precisely in this, that our time has seen only the

> *pictures* and has not understood that the *non-discursive* is the essential bit . . . and that "Commentary" is not something supplied in a gratuitous manner . . . Indeed, our age does not understand what language *is* (always supposing that there is only *one* language).[23]

Perhaps the fact that we are so limited in *how* we use language, and also *which* language we are using, perpetually disorients us from getting closer to an understanding of either music or sound. How can we move to the next level as we try to *tear a new sound from our listening*?[24] Instead of continually shuffling through different types of speech forms and adapting to each new situation, is there another strategy for taming the sounds we capture as we bring them back from the wilderness?

SUSAN HOWE'S "WRITING ARTICULATIONS OF SOUND FORMS IN TIME"

Susan Howe's poems and essays are full of voices and inscriptions intoned and imprinted by other writers. In Susan Howe's chapter for the volume, *The Sound of Poetry/The Poetry of Sound*,[25] she gives an account of reading early American testimonies and histories. Her chapter title reads like a definition of the very activity of writing she engages in, "Writing *Articulations of Sound Forms in Time*."

These articulations are typographical renderings of a language that in its fits and starts; its inexactitudes; its shorthand, abbreviations, and colloquialisms; its obsolescent syntax and worn-out accents contains life-giving force for a poet such as Susan Howe. It is through the voices and breath of these writers from the past that she takes up the pen anew.

> During the 1980s I wanted to transplant words onto paper with soil sticking to their roots—to go to meet a narrative's fate by immediate access to its concrete totality of singular interjections, crucified spellings, abbreviations, irrational apprehensions, collective identities, palavers, kicks, cordials, comforts. I wanted jerky and tedious details to oratorically bloom and bear fruit as if they had been set at liberty or ransomed by angels.[26]

As Thoreau speaks of Nature as a place for "absolute freedom and wildness," Howe writes that she wants to "speak a word for libraries as places of freedom and wildness." In the quietude and reflective pause that the silence of librar-ies offer, Howe finds pages filled with rows of wild wheat that are there to be reaped. She walks through stacks and hears the vocalizations of past speech forms that stutter, twang, and grind against our aural imaginations as we try to submit them to domestication and certainness of orientation on our pixelated screens.

To map the world is to write across our own histories, tell stories, and navigate desires. For Susan Howe, however, it is the indeterminism that the words from ancestors render when they clash against our more measured and clinical modernity: their typographical gregariousness is so un-tame-able and crude that it cannot be made to resonate as a "muffled discord from distance," as the sacred sounds of the swamps in Thoreau's writing[27] might once have done.

> Each page is both picture and nonsense soliloquy replete with transgressive nudges. It's a vocalized wilderness format of slippage and misshapen dream projection. Lots of blank space is essential to acoustically locate each dead center phoneme and allophone tangle somewhere between low comedy and lyric sanctity.[28]

Howe describes beautifully in her analysis how we inscribe certain sounds through one grammar and/or syntax and others through entirely different ones. As she has written elsewhere, "Emily Dickinson suggests that the language of the heart has quite another grammar."[29]

Will *sound writing* take upon itself the task of creating a new typology, or will it discover a genealogy that grows around a practice that is more transparent—like a listening that is an opening and making vulnerable of one's self?

Order suggests hierarchy and category. Categories and hierarchies suggest property.

> My voice formed from my life belongs to no one else. What I put into words is no longer my possession. Possibility has opened. The future will forget, erase, or recollect and deconstruct every poem. There is a mystic separation between poetic vision and ordinary living. The conditions for poetry rest outside each life at a miraculous reach indifferent to worldly chronology.[30]

Before the page disappears, as one day it must, we should consider how our present scholarship around voice and vocality, the study of sound, and our writing of sound, are all crucially linked. We must also come to terms with what it will mean, some years from now, when we say that we are "writing."

The materiality of sound: air pressure and waves emerge from string lengths, tubing, pipes, voltage, or digital binary code, and so on, but *onto what* and *from where* sound graphs itself or transcribes its movements across space determines how we understand its meaning. It locates us in the world and forms our language around our experience of listening to sound. How we write sound and how we write our listening to sound will bear witness to who we are and the world that we are presently rendering through our perceptual cartographies. As Susan Howe writes at the beginning of *Souls of the Labadie Tract*:[31] "True wildness is like true gold; it will bear the trial of Dewey Decimal."

We must not only listen to who is speaking and from where, we must listen to our listening, transcribe and prescribe perceptual geographies, and grapple with the ever-updating technology of language. Our writing moves and makes move, it sounds out and resounds our thoughts and makes us more aware of how we receive and perceive and process our thoughts, when the ear is the primary organ that is orienting us.

Let's sound out our new words together, making a *sound writing* that might yet become a general theory of harmony in a world that could renew itself by listening to its listening.

CODA

My family and I lived in Tehran, Iran, in the years 1976 through 1979—the period at the end of the shah's power and the beginning of the Iranian Revolution. My father was a naval officer ordered to work with the Iranian navy, teaching them how to navigate the new ships that the United States had sold them.

The house we lived in was a modern concrete construction with bars on the windows and a high concrete wall around the perimeter. Like slicing open a geode, the interior was surprising. Its colors and forms were in no way belied by its outer casing. The circular entrance hall had a tiled floor and a round glass atrium in its center open to the sky above. Light poured onto the tall lush plants inside the glass column, and the walls around the hall were mirrored, creating a dazzling play of light and colors. In this hall I would ride my tricycle, circling around the vitriform column, hundreds of reflected counterparts riding with me, across curved surfaces.

The nursery where I slept had a window that looked out onto the entrance hall, and it was there that I would stand in my crib watching the light on the plants and contemplate the rhythm of the tiles as the luminous colors would dart from floor to wall and back, an eternal dance of my waking hours. The rest of my family lived in the back of the house, facing out onto a concrete yard. Cocooned and insulated from the noise of the street, I slept oblivious to nightly power outages and loud protests on the streets.

My eldest brother had an old school desk in his room, where he would work on his homework. I have the most distinct picture of his room in my mind, though I've not had my memory verified—so I imagine his room as distinctly monastic and emptied of objects: white walls, a single bed, plain sheets, and an old desk against the wall next to the window. Just outside his window is the swimming pool where I fell in, almost drowning one afternoon when my other brother left the child gate open and I ventured out to walk the perimeter of the pool, balancing along the edge like a tightrope walker.

In dreams I had throughout my youth, my eldest brother's window composed for me the first wide shot of a filmic replay of this traumatic experience. In the dream I always move through this window and out past the concrete terrace to the pool. The shot shifts to a close-up of my feet, slowly moving back and forth between my steps and the mesmerizing blue of the water. And finally, my small form topples into the water and the cold and airless embrace of water filled with sunlight. Space in all directions offers no resistance to my body. I sink deeper.

The story continues with my middle brother (who had left the gate open) jumping in the pool to pull me out. After saving my life, he is scolded by my mother. This part is not part of my cinematic recall. I remember it as imagery that is generated by words. I've been told the end to the story, whereas the sun-filled water and the shots leading up to that moment are composed by my own memory. Or so I like to think.

One night my eldest brother was reading on his bed when he heard the protesters in the street shouting. They were far away, but he could hear the sound of their pounding feet and the din of their cries in unison. To him they sounded distant yet imminent. He began to cry uncontrollably, terrified that they were marching on our house. He went into my parents' room to be consoled, but my mother could not hear what he was hearing and couldn't console him.

It turned out that there was no protest and no marching that night. No shouts from the rooftops. It was a quiet autumnal evening, and only the sporadic sounds of passing cars or the lonely whine of a scooter could be heard on the street.

My brother insisted that our mother come to his room to hear the protest. They went hand in hand to the room. It was quiet. Mother couldn't hear anything at first.

Exasperated and sobbing, he asked once again, "Can't you hear them marching? They're coming!"

Silence. Then, Mother heard a periodic and measured clicking sound. From where was it coming?

Searching the room for sound sources, she opened the lid of the school desk. Inside were hundreds of tiny ants marching in single file. Their tiny steps in unison tapping out a foreboding homophony—distant yet imminent—bringing news of the approaching revolution that would tear us from our home. I would be told that we were going on vacation and would not return to the nursery where I'd gazed on the hyaline surfaces of the circular hall of plants, where boys rode tricycles on the walls.

Hearing takes us out of our bodies and out into the night of things unknown, as it also provides us intimacy and comfort when we can return once more to our breath under the blanket, finding a reciprocal pleasure in the warmth that it spreads under the sheets and the rhythmic certainty of selfhood that it sounds out.

ACKNOWLEDGMENT

"Acoustic Palimpsests" appeared in *Music and Politics* and is reprinted with permission.

NOTES

1. James Corner (1999) underlines the difference between *imaging* and *picturing.* Imaging "exercises agency . . . actualizing emergent realities" and picturing is an "act of representation: 'to picture' or 'depict.'"

2. The early work of Mallarmé, Apollinaire, the Futurists, and the Lettrists are examples of how dynamic the page can be.

3. For an excellent book on sound poetry and text-sound composition, see *Literally Speaking* (Göteborg, Sweden: Bo Ejeby Edition, 1993).

4. Marjorie Perloff and Craig Dworkin, eds., *The Sound of Poetry/ The Poetry of Sound* (Chicago: University of Chicago Press, 2009), 7.

5. Charles Olson, cited in Erberto F. Lo Buc, "John Cage's Writings," *Poetics Today* 3, no. 3 (1982): 65–77.

6. Walter Marchetti, *Natura Morta* (Vicenza, IT: Cramps Records, 1980). CD, album.

7. Jean-Luc Nancy, *Listening* (New York: Fordham University Press, 2007), 5.

8. Lucier's piece leaves us with the room resonance, but the system is subject-dependent. The room is articulated by voice, not the other way around:

> Now, things made are *not* objects, but subjects, so imbued by human thought. As such, I see them as "living." A work cannot make itself. Makers do that. An observer is *necessary* in order to further its livingness. This chain is implicitly interactive, and interactions are *dependencies*. Living systems are subject-dependent, and not object-dependent. Thus to deny, to disengage, to dismiss is not only to do so to some existential work, but also does so to its maker, and to its dismisser. Quite literally, one can dismiss one's one existence! (Kenneth Gaburo and David Dunn, *Publishing as Eco-system: David Dunn and Kenneth Gaburo Collaborate on Discussing the Eco-system* [Lebanon, NH: Lingua Press, 1983].)

9. Nancy, *Listening,* 9.

10. Alvin Lucier, *Chambers: Scores by Alvin Lucier* (Middletown, CT: Wesleyan University Press, 1980), 34.

11. Xavier Guell Lopez and Carmen Pardo Salgado, eds., *The Limits of Composition?* (Madrid: La Casa Encendida, 2009), 61.

12. Nancy, *Listening,* 10.

13. Perloff and Dworkin, *Sound of Poetry,* 12.

14. From "Landscape with Alvin Lucier" in Robert Ashley's fourteen-hour television opera about seven American composers. Each "Landscape" consisted of a conversation between Ashley and one of the composers. These conversations were later transcribed and published in Robert Ashley, *Music with Roots in the Aether* (Cologne, DE: MusikTexte, 2000). This passage appears on pages 82–83 of the book.

15. This quote first appeared in a June 1955 article titled "Experimental Music," in the British publications *The Score* and the *I.M.A. Magazine*, London.

16. Emphasis of the author.

17. Michael Nyman, *Experimental Music: Cage and Beyond* (New York: Cambridge University Press, 1974), 115.

18. See Beatrice Gibson and Will Holder, *The Tiger's Mind* (London: Sternberg Press, 2013). In *The Tiger's Mind*, Beatrice Gibson invited five other artists (including myself) to participate in producing a book and film from our structured conversations. Cornelius Cardew's verbal score from 1967 (of the same title) scored our daily meetings and dialogues. Instead of representing individual voices in the final text, all of our voices are combined into a singular, imaginary author's voice. This author's voice is also employed for the narrative voice-over in the film. All participants produced elements of the film as well: special effects, sound and Foley, music, script, and sets.

19. Nancy, *Listening,* 13.

20. From the website for the Max Planck Institutes Stuttgart: "The research interests cover a broad spectrum from fundamental to performance-oriented physics, chemistry

and materials science. The depth and breadth of expertise and infrastructure in Advanced Materials concentrated in Stuttgart (which ranges from chemical synthesis and nanofabrication techniques to advanced experimental and analytical methods) is matched by few institutions or locations around the world."

21. By "soundlessly" I mean that it *allows* for all other sounds around it to be *read in its place*.

22. Ian Hamilton Finlay to Michael Schmidt, December 7, 1979, in *A Model of Order: Selected Letters On Poetry and Making*, ed. Thomas A. Clark (Glasgow: WAX366, 2009).

23. Merleau Ponty; quote appears in the abstract for Deborah Kapchan, *Theorizing Sound Writing* (this volume). Kapchan (2009).

24. Perloff and Dworkin, *Sound of Poetry*.

25. Ibid., 201–2.

26. Ibid., 202. "Hope and the future . . . [are] not in lawns and cultivated fields, not in towns and cities, but in the impervious and shaking swamps." As Howe writes, Thoreau enters "each swamp as a sacred place, a *sanctum sanctorum*."

27. Ibid., 203.

28. Susan Howe, *My Emily Dickinson* (New York: New Directions, 1985), 13.

29. Ibid., 13.

30. Susan Howe, *Souls of the Labadie Tract* (New York: New Directions, 2007).

REFERENCES

Ash, Jesse. "The Figure of Speech: The Politics of Contemporary Chatter." PhD diss., Goldsmiths, University of London, 2010.

Ashley, Robert. *Music with Roots in the Aether: Interviews with and Essays about Seven American Composers*. Vol. 7. Cologne, DE: MusikTexte, 2000.

———, Will Holder, and Alex Waterman. *Yes, But Is It Edible?* Vancouver: New Documents, 2014.

———, and Ralf Dietrich. *Outside of Time: Ideas about Music*. Cologne, DE: Musiktexte, 2009.

Cardew, Cornelius. "Notation: Interpretation, Etc." *Tempo* 1, no. 58 (summer 1961): 21–33.

———. "A Scratch Orchestra: Draft Constitution." *Musical Times* 110, no. 1516 (June 1969): 617–19.

———. *Treatise Handbook*. London: Edition Peters, 1971.

———. *Scratch Music*. London: Latimer New Dimensions, 1972.

———, Eddie Prévost, and Richard Barrett. *Cornelius Cardew: A Reader*. Harlow, Essex: Copula, 2006.

Cavarero, A. *For More Than One Voice: Toward a Philosophy of Vocal Expression*. Stanford: Stanford University Press, 2005.

Cole, Hugo. *Sounds and Signs: Aspects of Musical Notation.* London: Oxford University Press, 1974.

De Certeau, Michel. *Culture in the Plural.* Minneapolis: University of Minnesota Press, 1997.

———. "Vocal Utopias: Glossolalias." *Representations* 56 (fall 1996): 29–47.

———, L. Giard, and P. Mayol. *The Practice of Everyday Life.* Minneapolis: University of Minnesota Press, 1998.

Gibson, Beatrice, and Will Holder, eds. *The Tiger's Mind.* London: Sternberg Press, 2011.

Howe, Susan. *The Birth-Mark: Unsettling the Wilderness in American Literary History.* Middletown, CT: Wesleyan University Press, 1993.

———. *My Emily Dickinson.* Vol. 1088. New York: New Directions, 2007.

Hultberg, Teddy. *Literally Speaking: Sound Poetry and Text-Sound Composition.* Göteborg, Sweden: Bo Ejeby Edition, 1993.

Kostelanetz, Richard. *Text-Sound Texts.* New York: William Morrow, 1980.

Kotz, Liz. *Words to Be Looked At: Language in 1960s Art.* Cambridge, MA: MIT Press, 2007.

LaBelle, Brandon, with Christof Migone. *Writing Aloud: The Sonics of Language.* Vol. 1. Los Angeles: Errant Bodies Press, 2001.

Laske, O., and K. Gaburo. "On Composition Theory as a Theory of Self-Reference." In *Allos.* Edited by K. Gaburo. La Jolla, CA: Lingua Press, 1980, 426–31.

Lucier, Alvin. *Chambers: Scores by Alvin Lucier.* Middletown, CT: Wesleyan University Press, 1980.

———. *Reflections: Interviews, Scores, Writings.* Cologne, DE: MusikTexte, 1995.

———. *Music 109: Notes on Experimental Music.* Middletown, CT: Wesleyan University Press, 2012.

Lyons, Matthew, Debra Singer, and Alex Waterman, ed. *Between Thought and Sound.* New York: Kitchen, 2007.

Mumma, Gordon. "The Once Festival and How It Happened." *Arts in Society* 4, no. 2 (1967): 381–99.

Notley, Alice. *Coming After: Essays on Poetry.* Ann Arbor: University of Michigan Press, 2005.

Nyman, Michael. *Experimental Music: Cage and Beyond.* New York: Cambridge University Press, 1999.

Olson, Charles. *The Maximus Poems.* London: Cape Goliard Press, 1970.

Perloff, Marjorie, and Craig Dworkin. *The Sound of Poetry/The Poetry of Sound.* Chicago: University of Chicago Press, 2009.

Rothenberg, Jerome, and Pierre Joris. *Poems for the Millenium.* 2 vols. Berkeley: University of California Press, 1995.

Spoerri, Daniel, Robert Filliou, Emmett Williams, Dieter Roth, and Roland Topor. *An Anecdoted Topography of Chance.* London: Atlas Press, 1995.

Stein, G., and C. Van Vechten. *Selected Writings.* New York: Modern Library, 1962.

Stewart, George R. *Names on the Land: A Historical Account of Place-Naming in the United States.* Boston: Houghton Mifflin, 1958.

Sumner, Melody, Kathleen Burch, and Michael Sumner. *The Guests Go into Supper.* Oakland, CA: Burning Books, 1986.

Waterman, Alex, ed. *Agape.* New York: Miguel Abreu Gallery, 2007.

Weiss, Allen S. *Phantasmic Radio.* Durham, NC: Duke University Press, 1995.

———. *Unnatural Horizons: Paradox and Contradiction in Landscape Architecture.* Princeton: Princeton Architectural Press, 1998.

———. *Breathless: Sound Recording, Disembodiment, and the Transformation of Lyrical Nostalgia.* Middletown, CT: Wesleyan University Press, 2002.

———. *Varieties of Audio Mimesis: Musical Evocations of Landscape.* Vol. 3. Berlin: Errnat Bodies Press, 2008.

Williams, Emmett. *An Anthology of Concrete Poetry.* New York: Ultramarine, 1967.

Wolff, Christian. *Writings and Conversations.* Vol. 5. Cologne, DE: MusikTexte, 1998.

Films

Gibson, Beatrice. *The Tiger's Mind.* London: LUX, 2012. 23 min., HD video. For more information: http://www.lux.org.uk/collection/works/the-tigers-mind.

———, and Alex Waterman. *A Necessary Music: A Science Fiction Film about Modernist Social Housing.* London: LUX, 2008. For more information: http://anecessarymusic.org/info.html. To watch online: http://www.ubu.com/film/gibson_music.html.

TOMIE HAHN

5. Sound Commitments

Extraordinary Stories

WARNING: "Sound Commitments" was written to be performed and is meant to be read out loud. It addresses the profound art of writing about sound, of sound writing. Hahn addresses the paradox of representing—*re*-presenting the ephemeral experience of sound—as a compelling challenge, particularly in the digital age of media. Join in the performance. Explore the presence of text, the vulnerability and ephemerality of embodying text, by listening to each sound formed by your voice. In this way you will be sharing the text while also experiencing and altering Hahn's fieldwork experiences.

So profound is sound,
So powerful is music and experience
We desire to commit it to paper.

Like a great blue heron facing you in stillness, the lush expanse of experience appears narrowed, flattened in text, virtually disappearing into typographic symbols. But when she flies, how extraordinary!

When we create "cultural translations" of our experiences, it has been argued that we must be aware of the lenses we peer through, so that we do not order/organize the culture according to our own logic, and even the limitations of our language.
So profound is sound,
So powerful is music and experience
We desire to commit it to paper.

To text . . .
A veritable natural history museum of experience, frozen in time
As a form of transmission
Messages to the future.

And somehow, despite our passion for experience, we continue to transmit textual supremacy as a means of measuring academic merit . . .

Tan profundo es el sonido
Tan potente es la música y la experiencia
Queremos cometer al papel.

When we write—sound—the object that emerges potentially enhances, pales, perverts, sways, betrays.
Words of caution.

Objectified in text, a sound or movement departs from the body and enables a transmission that demands interpretation, interrogation, and reconstitution. And for some, text as portable object is perceived as a threat to the life of the ephemeral practice.

What of the mystery of presence?
. . . the ordinary?
. . . and the extra-ordinary in flight?

It's been fascinating to me that a number of ethnographers have had extraordinary encounters while in the field, yet frequently these stories are not incorporated into their ethnographic texts. Often, they are discouraged from disclosing these experiences because of the stigma the extraordinary bears and the repercussions that may follow, particularly in academic circles. So, I have been collecting stories, keeping their identities anonymous.

Sit back and let me tell you a story . . .

> I had been working on the topic of my master's thesis (on language and music) for several years when my primary teacher developed emphysema. Through the long and drawn-out process of dying and death, he kept me on

edge by deliberately withholding information and offering small tidbits here and there, each one so tantalizing that I began to realize that we were on the tip of an iceberg whose depths I would never plumb. I knew that with his passing, an entire lifetime of knowledge would evaporate and that I was the last chance he had to make his knowledge public. I wrote down every word and focused on what was between the lines. We quarreled about little things, and he would go for days without wanting to see me or speak to me because of some real or imagined mistake on my part. It was hell. And he died. The last time I saw him, he told me to take up his teachings so that his work wouldn't go to the grave with him. I promised him that I would follow his wishes, feeling simultaneously blessed and cursed.

After a few months, I began the process of working on the writing aspect of my thesis. Things started to pick up for me, and the analysis of the songs came together smoothly. One night, he appeared in my dream. In shock, I said, "But you're supposed to be dead!" He said, "Now, don't start that!" He then said that I'd completely botched my analysis earlier that day. He gave me some tips on what I should have said, then ordered me to wake up and write it all down. I changed my analysis according to what he dictated to me. About a week later, he showed up again in another dream (completely out of the blue) and asked for changes in a couple more points. He also gave me some new examples from songs I hadn't studied yet. This process continued for a total of six visits, at which time the thesis was relatively complete. Through the process of editing, revision, and final acceptance, my dreams were empty of his visits. Of course, I was hoping for an eventual "Congratulations! Now it's correct!" from him, but he would never have said that in real life either!

Note the multiple layers of textual vigilance residing here . . .

Despite such a powerful experience, the story was unpublished, and until recently, untold. In the story the teacher had been "deliberately withholding information."

Yet later, in life and in dreams, he was concerned about the correct documentation of the musical notation. The legacy. The tradition.

I imagine most of you have had teachers who wonder *what* we are writing . . . our transformation of experience to object.

Yes?

Recently, while studying *mikyo,* esoteric Buddhist mudra and mantra, I learned there are "mistakes" deliberately inserted in the ancient text as a safeguard. How delightful! This firewall reveals how potent these sound and movement experiences can be. Some view the mistakes as an authoritative control over transmission. Yes, and for good reason.

What a predicament!

While this practice illuminates the nature of embodying these sounds and gestures through ritual . . . the transmission through my own words and practice is out of bounds. The abbot smiles broadly at me . . . knowing we'll be working through this dilemma.

I comprehend my mission when reading Walter Ong's inspiring words: "Writing is a technology that restructures thought." I take to heart the passages from ethnographers' writings concerning their own struggle . . . Talal Asad reminds us:

> (But this) pushing beyond the limits of one's habitual usages, this breaking down and reshaping of one's own language through the process of translation, is never an easy business, in part because (if I may be allowed a hypostatization) it depends on the willingness of the translator's *language* to subject itself to this transforming power. (Asad 1986, 157)

So profound is sound,
So powerful is music and experience
We desire to commit it to paper.

REFERENCES

Asad, Talal. "The Concept of Cultural Translation in British Social Anthropology." In *Writing Culture: The Poetics and Politics of Ethnography,* edited by James Clifford and George Marcus. Berkeley: University of California Press, 1986.

Ong, Walter J. "Writing Is a Technology That Restructures Thought." In *The Written Word: Literacy in Transition,* edited by Gerd Baumann, 23–50. Oxford: Clarendon Press, 1986.

6. Traffic Patterns

I keep coming back to Edmund Carpenter's work. The vast quietude of the Arctic cuts through his book *Eskimo Realities.* At the outset, he contrasts the visitors' perspective with the residents' perspective, at the bottom of two otherwise blank pages. A formidable stretch of white hangs over the text.

> From the writer's point of view, the Arctic has no favorable qualities, unless its severity be counted as such. It is a barren, empty land, largely comfortless and desolate. The endless tundra stretching from sea to horizon has an austere, monotonous charm, a certain cold, clean-edged beauty. Yet throughout it is hard on man. (6)
>
> To the Eskimo, however, it is home, the earth's most favored place. They have no desire to go elsewhere; they are content with this, country which contains enough walrus and seal to satisfy most of their needs. (7)

Two pages, facing one another, a paper landscape wider than a 16:9 film image, with just a few lines whispering across the low horizon. As the sound of these words fades, I can hear the blankness of the page, spreading out around me.

I ask myself, how might I use the page to convey the soundscapes of the Kathmandu Valley, and make room for both visitors' and residents' perspectives? Where Carpenter uses text, image, and layout to express a steady serenity, I am going to need to communicate a jangly hubbub.

There are two ways to get there.

ROUTE NO. 1

New roads are always possible, but most roads are packed down by a history of travel and are paved over with layers and layers of materials. The history of sound includes the history of studying sound; the history of studying sound includes the history of writing about sound; the history of writing about sound includes a history of questioning how to write about sound; and the history of sound technologies compels us to wonder if writing about sound is really necessary when other modes of representation may convey the sounds studied more immediately or accurately. Walking this road now, one can't help but notice that scholars of all sorts are increasingly writing using digital and multimedia formats, and that we are increasingly reading from various kinds of screens rather than from the page. And observing this, we have to ask, why would we wish to theorize and experiment with the print medium?

Why write, rather than do something else? To answer this question, it is helpful to think about the range of something elses available. Along with digital and multimedia formats, we might also consider "intermedia," the term introduced by Dick Higgins in the 1960s to encompass the ways people were working between the arts, or "mixed media," a designation more closely associated with visual art. Along with these are single-medium formats such as CDs and DVDs, although these have multimedia components. Some imprecision exists over what "media" people mean sometimes. Are we talking about the specific format of presentation—265-page book, 45-rpm record, 35-mm film? Or are we talking about the stuff of which a presentation is composed—"encaustic, oil, and collage on fabric mounted on plywood, three panels, 42 ¼ 5 60 ⅝" (107.3 5 153.8 cm)," the basic recipe for Jasper Johns's *Flag*?[1] Sometimes a medium is a format; sometimes it is a component. An overview of the work of the Canadian artists General Idea observes that their "works in all media interrelate—video, performance, installation, and publishing."[2] These are formats. But Nicholas Cook, in his book *Analysing Musical Multimedia* (1998), considers the art song, words plus music, an instance of musical multimedia. These are components. Meanwhile, architects, whose work is profoundly multimedia in a sense, hardly use the term.

I don't want to advance my own new and improved definition of *media* or any combination thereof, nor do I care to debate the relative merits of different media. But I do want to think about some different ways of putting some media together. Some practices have been more prevalent than others. As Dick Higgins notes, "I cannot, for example, name work that has consciously been placed in the intermedium between painting and shoes."[3] Text, sound, and image are the three media that form the core of ethnographic work on sound appearing in print, as audio recording, and as video recording.[4]

Print ethnomusicology relies predominantly on text, but makes room for sound and image. By text I mean quite simply *text as text,* not Lady Gaga's "Telephone," Wong Kar-Wai's *In the Mood for Love,* or my Asics running shoes as text.[5] In early print work, sound, of course, is the focus of the text; but sound also appears in image form, as transcription. More compact audio recording media allowed for sound itself to be included as an adjunct to the text. With CD-ROMs and companion websites came the potential to incorporate sound and image more dynamically, although a full integration with the text still had to be more or less performed by the reader. It was necessary for text to jump over into the digital realm to join together more completely with image and sound, although the digital print work that more seamlessly melds together text, sound, and image has not yet been widely used in ethnomusicology,[6] and publishers haven't yet figured out how to market such works.[7]

Text and image have been part of audio recordings for some time, and ethnomusicologists have made excellent use of liner notes with records and booklets with CDs. Here the media roles were reversed—text was included as an adjunct to sound. (And images were typically an adjunct to the text, except on the cover of the album, where text was more often an adjunct to the image.) Digital audio has certainly made it very easy to package sound together with text and image, but the download culture that has emerged in the interstices between music production, device production, music consumption, and device consumption has bypassed the possibilities of integration of text, sound, and image for the conveniences of mobility of sound. While the nature of what Jacob Smith has called "unscreened media"[8] means that there is a lot of screen space left over for other things, we instead typically use the screen for other purposes while listening, or simply transfer to a screenless device.

There is great apparent potential for combining text, sound, and image in documentary films and videos on music, or at least there has been since the introduction of more portable recording equipment. Our commonsense assumption with film is that the image is central, with sound and text playing ancillary roles. Michel Chion has made a good case for the centrality of sound,[9] but many a film music composer will be happy to acknowledge the subservience of music to action and dialogue, while many a screenwriter will be happy to tell you about the primacy of the text. (Some of the texts of documentary films and videos constitute stages in the production process: a script is converted into sound and image, and a written part for a narrator is converted to a voiceover along the way. But there are often visible texts as well: subtitles, for instance, or text that identifies, explains, or elaborates on something presented in sound or image.) Carol Vernallis, in her book *Experiencing Music Video* (2004), offers a useful way of thinking about media relations in film and video work, observing that any parameter of a work can emerge out of the mix at any time and suggesting that we attend to the shifting relations between parameters. Oddly, the documentary film on music all too often comes off like a screened text—that is, with the text too far up in the mix.

While different formats make different kinds of room for text, sound, and image, all three tend to work together, regardless of the format chosen. It is worth considering the question of how working predominantly in one medium might get you somewhere. When you experiment in one medium, one thing you tend to do is employ that medium in multiple ways. The musical term *heterophony*—multiple ways of stating the same thing—might be a more pertinent analogy here than the polyphonic or the polysemic. Thinking about the use of text, sound, and image in ethnographic work on music, where might heterotextual, heterophonic, and heterovisual approaches get you? What have been some of the effective experiments in staying within text, or sound, or image, yet employing that medium in multiple ways?

There are a number of important heterotextual experiments worth noting: Lila Abu-Lughod's use of storytelling, Steve Feld's dialogic editing, and Louise Meintjes's use of narrative takes and mixes that echo the takes and mixes of the recording studio.[10] In their work, doing ethnography becomes more closely linked to writing ethnography, helping bring us as readers within earshot of Bedouin storytellers, Kaluli singers, and Zulu musicians. There is a pleasurable sense of multiplication in works such as theirs, as the voices within their texts perform a kind of "lift-up-over sounding" in conversation with both subjects and readers.

There are not nearly as many heterophonic experiments in ethnomusicology as we might imagine. Steve Feld's *Voices of the Rainforest* recording (1991), in which Kaluli voices and instruments constitute only a few of the tracks of the "Bosavi rainforest groove," is one, where the experiment in compressing "a day in the life of the Kaluli and the rainforest" into one CD is less significant than the effort to enact and perform "how Kaluli hear this world." Some composers and performers also incorporate field recordings and ethnographic study into their work. Annea Lockwood's *A Sound Map of the Hudson River* ([1989] 2003), for example—commissioned as an installation for the Hudson River Museum in Yonkers—also exists in CD format, in which the Hudson is broken up into movements identified by the location of the mostly natural but sometimes human sounds recorded. And on *Dialects* (no date), by Electric Kulintang (percussionist Susie Ibarra and her husband, Roberto Rodriguez), sounds recorded in the Philippines merge with Susie's performances on the *kulintang* and merge with Roberto's programmed beats and other sonic materials.

Heterovisual experiments in film and video certainly abound, but it is quite unusual for an ethnographic filmmaker to work only with images: a heterovisual approach is more frequently paralleled by heterophonic and sometimes heterotextual approaches. We might, though, look at films that were silent by necessity, such as Ernst Lubitsch's *So This Is Paris* from 1926, or films that were silent by choice, such as Maya Deren and Talley Beatty's *A Study in Choreography for Camera* from 1945.[11] In these films, the filmmakers employ multiple visual styles (and careful editing between them) to create a kind of dance ethnography—the former of a large group, the latter of an individual. Or at least the presence of the camera as observer puts these somewhere between ethnography and choreography.

What these experimental approaches share is the tendency for one medium to cross over into another. Isabelle Raynauld and Michel Chion have pointed out to us how in silent film images we could see words even without the help of intertitles and hear diegetic sound in our heads precisely because there was no diegetic sound.[12] Image evokes word and sound. And sound evokes image and word—the *Dialects* album, for example, is described on Electric Kulintang's now-defunct website as "cinematic in many ways, telling short stories and poems to its listeners."[13] And text evokes sound and image—which goes without saying, almost. Such experimental approaches move us toward a more nuanced sense of the room for play between text, sound, and image.

Why would we wish to theorize and experiment with the print medium in the digital age? Why write, rather than do something else? I have circled back to my earlier questions in a way that edges on being tautological. We write to evoke sound and image, so rather than use sounds and images themselves, we write. We might say that in print we can evoke sound and image in ways that sound and image themselves are incapable of doing. We might say that in writing we create a presence by first establishing an absence. To be more precise, we write tautologies. We take the sounds we hear and double them, triple them, multiply them into heterotextual, heterophonic, and heterovisual copies that honor the complexity and vivacity of the original.

Audio recording, film, and video have the remarkable capacity to grab our attention, to arrest our senses. Text, in the absence of sound and image, has the capacity to open up the senses. It may be that text is one of the best places we have in which to bring more free play into the interplay of media.

ROUTE NO. 2

My first route circled around the larger questions addressed in different ways by the contributors to this book. This route traverses a particular spot on the page—the place where we stop writing to insert some other kind of written message, such as a table, a diagram, a map, an illustration, a transcription.

Representations of sound in print may be textual or pictorial. In text we represent sound in a variety of ways, through words that sound—onomatopoeia—as well as through the words we use to walk around sounds and observe their properties—for instance, we might talk about singers having scratchy, gravelly, sweet, or rich voices. Text both connects us directly to sound and carries us in a roundabout way to sound. In picturing sound on the page, we plot aural dimensions of sound onto the visual dimensions of the page. Pictorial representations may be prescriptive, descriptive, or inscriptive. The first two are familiar enough ways of thinking about the uses of different kinds of musical notation: either a notational method prescribes what to do (specifies what sounds to make) or it describes what was done (specifies what sounds were made).[14] In using musical notation, a writer assumes a competent reader with access to a real or imaginary sounding device, with a capacity to recreate the sound either in performance or in thought. A third kind of representation of sound I am calling inscriptive: it is the attempt to engrave the sound itself into the page, the effort to make the page vibrate with the acoustic presence of the sounding body.

Most of the materials we insert into our texts are both textual and pictorial. In order to think about how to expand the potential of the space where we stop writing with words alone, it is useful to consider other kinds of works that move between the textual and the pictorial. Poetry often sits at the intersection between the two. Poets routinely take stock of the room available on the page: the placement of words matters, and their proximity to other words matters. Text can additionally be turned into picture, as Dick Higgins's wonderful collection of *Pattern Poetry* (1987) shows.

And altering the size and shape of words in poetry can convey temporal and acoustic dimensions: for instance, in the early twentieth century, the Italian Futurists, in their *parole in libertà* (words in freedom), experimented with the pictorial disposition of words on the page, hoping to capture new sounds and liberate the conventional poetic text. While they did perform their work, this was also text for performance by the reader: even silent reading could not avoid being a performance.[15]

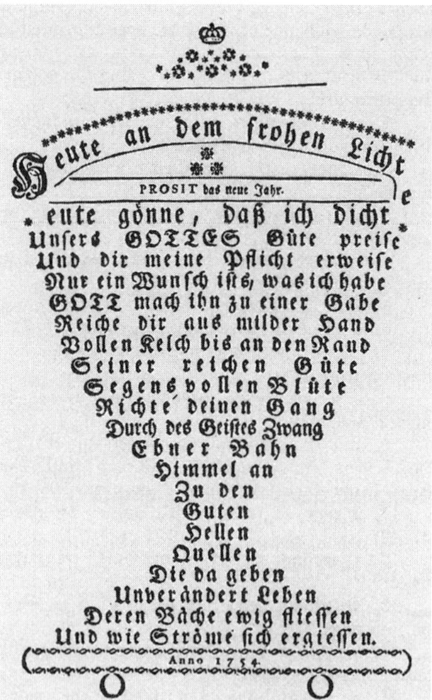

left Figure 6.1 Anonymous, New Year's chalice (1754). Dick Higgins, *Pattern Poetry* (1987). Courtesy of State University of New York Press. *right* Figure 6.2 F. T. Marinetti, free-word poem from *Canta Giovinezza* (1934). Willard Bohn, *The Other Futurism* (2004).

Outside of poetry a wide variety of artists have shuttled between the textual and the pictorial. In the second half of the twentieth century, much work in the fine, popular, and commercial arts experimented with such hybrid means of expression. Composers have made pictorial musical scores, such as James Tenney's *A Rose Is a Rose Is a Round* (1970), in which words and notes circle around a hand-drawn rose, and William Hellermann's *to the last drop* (1976), in which musical notes come pouring out of a bottle tilted into the top-left corner of the page.[16] Vocal music especially invites imaginative arrangements of text, notation, and image on the page, and here should be mentioned works written by and for singers such as Cathy Berberian, Joan La Barbara, and Meredith Monk; "vocal music" might also include texts arranged on the page for performance, such as John Cage's "Julliard Lecture" (1952).[17]

Children's books have long been a place where writer and illustrator inhabit the page together. In handwritten works, such as Shel Silverstein's *Uncle Shelby's*

Feldman writes his music sometimes on music paper
and other times on graph. In a series of pieces called
Projections, written on graph paper, he indicates only
high, middle, and low in reference to pitch.
A player is free at the instant of playing to
play any note in the register indicated

It acts in such a way
that one can 'hear through' a piece of music just as one
can see through some modern buildings or see through a wire
sculpture by Richard Lippold or the glass of Marcel
Duchamp

— in his ear where he
will find a metal ball , to toss it on the road in front
of them , so that, as the horse goes on to say, we may
be led by it. This, too, giving himself and his quest
up to the aimless rolling of a metal ball, the hero, un–

Figure 6.3 John Cage, "Juilliard Lecture" (1952). John Cage, *A Year from Monday: New Lectures and Writings* (1963). Courtesy of Wesleyan University Press.

Figure 6.4 Roy Lichtenstein, *Emeralds* (1961). Copyright by the Estate of Roy Lichtenstein. Used by permission.

ABZ Book (1961), text and image sometimes cross into each other's worlds, much as music weaves its way in and out of the diegetic sound world of a film. Comic strips and comic books open up space in the image for words, using speech and thought bubbles somewhat like the subtitles of a silent film to anchor and propel action. Magazine advertisements succeed on their capacity to pull text and image together suggestively, and billboards do likewise with much larger spaces. All of these spaces also spilled out of the commercial world into the work of pop artists.[18]

An experimental bent entered into ethnography, as well, most notably in Dennis Tedlock's representations of sound and silence in oral poetry in *Finding the Center* ([1972] 1999) and *The Spoken Word and the Work of Interpretion* (1983), and of course, in Edmund Carpenter's exploration of the expressive potential of empty space.

NEPALI FICTIONS

Experimental work tests possibilities, opens up possibilities: its place in the natural sciences is well known and widely accepted; in the arts, humanities, and social sciences, though, its place is perhaps just as well known but less widely accepted. Beyond the academic disciplines, experiment is the method

"What are you DOING?" that's what he asked her. "Well,
I'm winnowing," she said.
"What are you winnowing?" he said. "Well

•

pigweed and tumbleweed"
that's what she told him.
"Indeed.
What's that you're saying?" "Well, this is
my winnowing song," she said.
"NOW SING IT FOR ME
so that I
may sing it for my children," he said.
Old Lady Junco
sang for Coyote:

YUUWA HINA YUUWA HINA
YUUWA HINA YUUWA HINA
YU HINA YU HINA
(blowing) PFFF PFFF
YU HINA YU HINA
(blowing) PFFF PFFF

That's what she said.
"YES, NOW I
can go, I'll sing it to my children."
Coyote went on to Oak Arroyo, and when he got there
MOURNING DOVES FLEW UP
and he lost his song.

Figure 6.5 Andrew Peynetsa, "Coyote and Junco" (1965). Reproduced from Dennis Tedlock, *Finding the Center: The Art of the Zuni Storyteller,* 2nd ed. (1999). By permission of the University of Nebraska Press. Copyright 1999 by Dennis Tedlock.

of the marginal, the subaltern, the dispossessed. The possibilities it tests or opens up act as a form of social and cultural critique. Experiment is, of course, part of hegemony as well: winning consent and maintaining power require a good deal of creative exertion. But it is by definition one of the primary tactics of resistance, which must constantly seek to provide alternatives to current hegemonic configurations.

In these experimental inscriptions of the soundscapes of the Kathmandu Valley in Nepal, I merge the ethnographic and the phonographic, the humanistic representation (straddling the artistic and the scientific), and the sonic representation (linking the textual and the pictorial).[19] Each has, as its starting point, a recording I made. The inscriptions move between ideals of presence and critiques of change, between Nepali ideals and critiques as I have been able to apprehend them and the ideals and critiques of visiting observers such as myself. The inspiration for these inscriptions comes from the many ways I have seen people in Nepal work to establish spaces of sonic sensibility in the midst of the sonic overload of the city. In opening up pockets of acoustic pleasure, they resist the hegemony of urban noise and suggest alternatives.

Near the end of my first visit to Nepal in 1987, I made a few recordings at various spots around Kathmandu. For one of these I walked along the narrow road lined with shops that runs from the northeast corner of Durbar Square to the southwest corner of the spread of ritzy hotels and upscale shops surrounding the royal palace. (On the map I had at the time, the middle, oldest part of Kathmandu looks like a slightly tilted square of streets and buildings with a diagonal line clearly drawn from lower left to upper right. Ring Road, which surrounds the cities of Kathmandu and Patan—at what seemed a great distance then—is mostly off the map.)

I only began studying the Nepali language in earnest five years later, so the sound that initially stood out to me the most was the interruption of an older British fellow who, observing my activity, wryly commented as he walked past me, “Really listening in, huh?” His laughter bounced along behind me. While this is still the most prominent vocal sound because of his proximity to my microphone, when I listen to the recording now I hear more the bits of conversation, mostly in Nepali and Newari, coming from all corners. And threaded through this conversational fabric is the language of bells and horns, as people on bikes and cycles and in cars and three-wheeler tempos make their way down the street, and as pedestrians ring temple bells in passing. The more widely ranging melodies of speech and bells contrast sharply with the narrow pitch range of the horns.

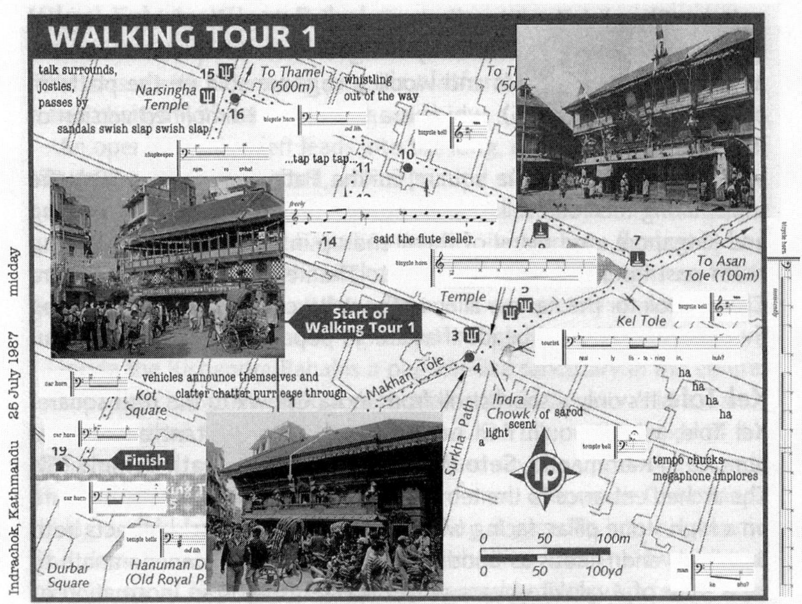

Figure 6.6 Inscription No. 1: Indrachok, 1987.

Two days later. The solid darkness of another cloudy monsoon night shook with the sound of drums moving past my bedroom window—just like yesterday, just like the day before. But this morning, rather than waiting for the tumult to recede and sleeping a bit longer, I peeled back the mosquito netting and took my ears along behind the drummers up to Swayambhu, the large stupa that looks east over the Kathmandu Valley. When I arrived, drums, harmonium, cymbals, and numerous meshed but distinct voices already were gathered in a small pavilion, open on the side facing the stupa. I sat in back, but in a spot where I still could see the musicians who initiated most of the *bhajans*—devotional songs, in this case, Buddhist—and opened my tape recorder.

Not long after I sat down, a brass band came past. The thickening overlap between the sound of men singing *bhajans* and the sound of the brass band made me think of the Charles Ives records that my father sometimes played around dinnertime. The crescendo of the band as it got closer brought a momentary halt to the singing; as it faded into the distance, the lead singer and the lead drummer initiated the *bhajan* singing again. What I heard as a great chasm between these two tracks of sound is not so apparent to the Nepali ear. The intent of each track

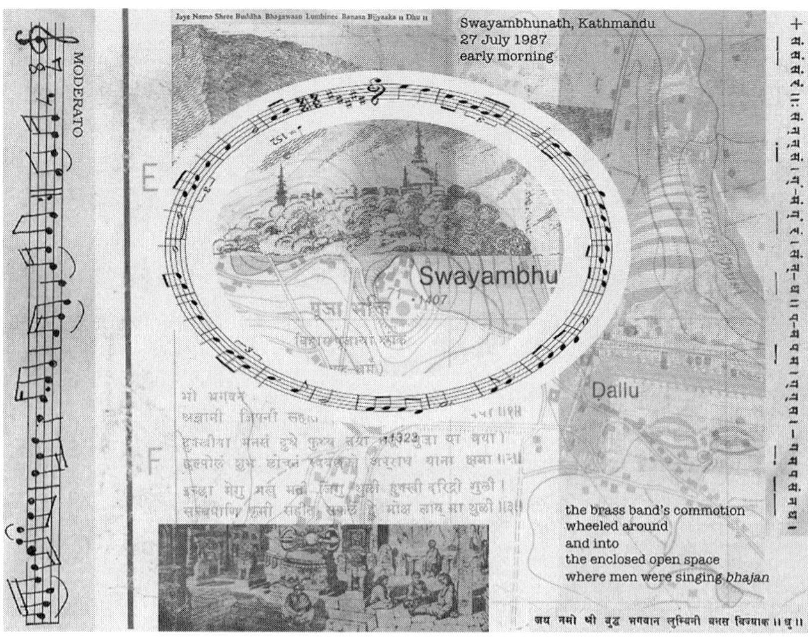

Figure 6.7 Inscription No. 2: Swayambunath, 1987.

is similar. Brass bands may be more common at weddings in South Asia, but in this case they were playing a spirited version of a devotional tune associated with Swayambhu itself and played during *Gunla,* the Buddhist auspicious period that begins in the bright fortnight of the month of *Sravan* (July-August).

In 1995 I lived in Sanepa, a neighborhood of Patan (also called Lalitpur), just south of Kathmandu. One day I was out in Bhaktapur, then a half-hour minibus ride to the east, for a drumming lesson. We saw a clip of the chariot of Machhendranath being pulled through the streets of Patan on the TV news, and my teacher said I should be sure to hear the *dhimay* groups that play for the procession, noting that their repertoire is different from what he knew.

In *Monk, Householder, and Tantric Priest: Newar Buddhism and Its Hierarchy of Ritual* (1992), David N. Gellner explains:

> The three biggest festivals of the year in Lalitpur are Mohani (Np. Dasai), Swanti (Np. Tihar), and "The Festival" (*jatra*), i.e., the chariot festival of Karunamaya-Matsyendranath. . . . Karunamaya's chariot festival is particularly associated with the city of Lalitpur and its district, but is big enough and important enough

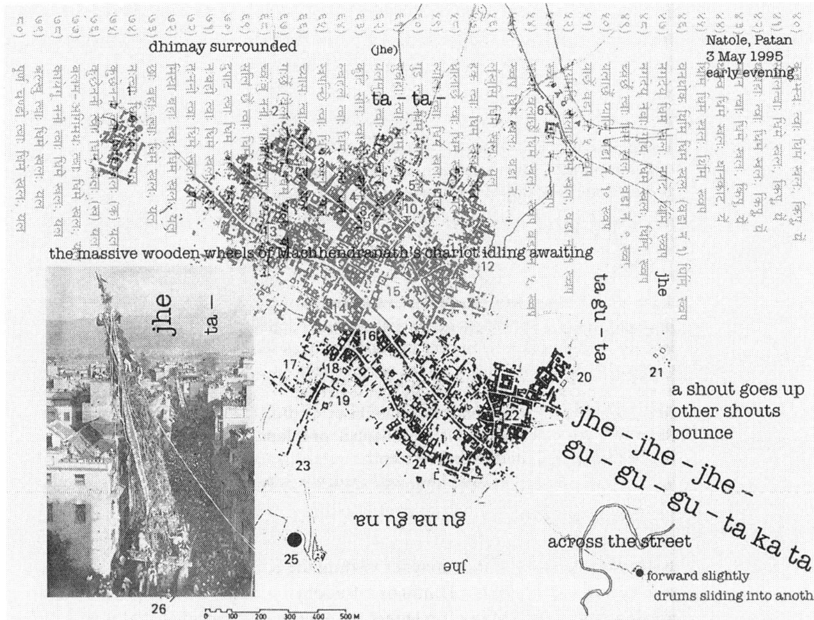

Figure 6.8 Inscription No. 3: Natole, 1995.

to have spawned smaller imitation shrines in Kathmandu, Thimi, Nala, and Dolakha. It is a local festival which has spread. (214)

I don't know how many conversations I've had in Nepal about how things have changed. The air used to be cleaner. It used to be easier to get around to visit friends and relatives. There used to be fewer buildings, more gardens, less traffic, more peace and quiet, less noise, more room.

Maybe the fact that I can only get there every few years precipitates these kinds of conversations. Certainly my time away makes me aware of how things have changed. On my first visit to Kathmandu, I landed at night in a cow pasture of an airport and took a solitary taxi through darkened streets to a quiet guesthouse. When I left in 2007, I almost missed my flight, as my taxi inched, stopped, inched, stopped, inched along the smog-shrouded, *ekdam* jam-packed *bhaeko* road.

New Road is closer to the heart of Kathmandu, running from Basantapur (which tourists and locals alike know as Durbar Square) to the west to the Tundikhel (or "parade grounds," though mostly I've seen impromptu soccer games there, not parades) to the east. New Road is in part new because it is one of the roads that is wide and straight enough that you can see from one end to the other. This makes for little shade. And the rebar-and-concrete buildings on either side catch the sounds of traffic and hurl them back into the street. Another thing that makes it new is that it has separate sidewalks with metal railings to keep pedestrians from weaving through traffic. It is always a relief to step into a shop or to swing off down a side street.

Lately, I've spent more time on the outskirts of town. My friend Kishor Gurung, a classical guitarist and son of the well-known musician Amber Gurung, had a house built in Bansbari, just beyond Ring Road to the north. My singing teacher Dilip Nath had a house built in Kalanki, just beyond Ring Road to the west. When I visited the construction sites in the 1990s, both seemed like idyllic retreats, but both have since been surrounded by new construction and partially engulfed by the sounds of the city.

Kishor invited me to come for a conference in 2003, and generously secured a place for me to stay at Malpi International College in Maharajgunj, just down the road from his house, just inside Ring Road.

THE FACTS OF KATHMANDHU

In my first route to these five inscriptions, I circled around the ways text, sound, and image collaborate; and in my second route, I followed a line across the printed page, taking it as a space in which potential resonances could be explored. I did not do everything that I said such work might do; the circumambulation of route no. 1 and the traverse of route no. 2 were not meant to lead simply to my own inscriptions, but beyond. My aim here has not been to liberate a particular space in the ethnography of sound merely so that others can come along and either fill that space in like manner or tear that space open further. An experimental bent exists, rather, as tautological proof of the inexplicable value of openness. With *Eskimo Realities,* Edmund Carpenter inspired me to try to use the page in new ways to record multiple voices, bring distant moments in time together, and map the Kathmandu Valley idiosyncratically as a sounding place and not as a mute topography.

Carpenter brings his study of Eskimo art to a close with the myth of Sedna, a former Eskimo girl who now rules all creatures from the bottom of the sea. A drawing of Sedna appears in white lines in the upper-right quadrant of a black page. Turn the page and we are on the penultimate page of the book, now back to a small patch of black text on a white page.

Figure 6.9 Inscription No. 4: New Road, 2007.

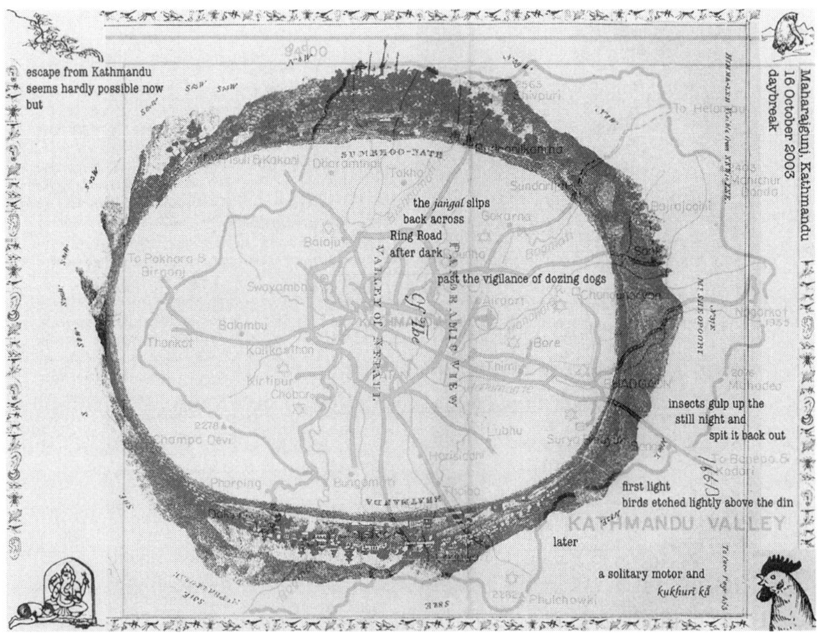

Figure 6.10 Inscription No. 5: Maharajgunj, 2003.

The last part of the Sedna myth reveals the role of art. There is a maze of the past to be entered and come out of alive, bringing the innocent to safety. And in this maze there lives the monster dog whose name is Death. Find the door that opens the past. Unravel the ever-tangling threads of time. Rescue the innocent. And beware the dog. (216)

On the last page, Carpenter describes how an *angakok,* or shaman, does this. But here is where my path stops. We are not shamans, but as ethnographers we know well the maze of the past, and as writers we are compelled to find ways through.

ACKNOWLEDGMENTS

Thank you especially to Bob Moore, whose four-semester course at the University of Southern California, "Analysis of Post-Tonal Music" (1989–1991), pushed my thinking about the relation between the musical score and musical sound, and to Steven Feld, whose one-semester course at the University of Texas at Austin, "Anthropology, Performance, Aesthetics, Style," in spring 1994, pushed my thinking about the relation between the ethnographic text and visual and aural art.

INSCRIPTION CREDITS

Figure 6.6: Inscription No. 1: Indrachok, 1987: Map: From Hugh Finlay, *Nepal,* 5th ed. (Melbourne: Lonely Planet Publications, 2001). *Top photo*: Akash Bhairab temple at Indrachok, labeled "House Front, Katmandu," in Perceval Landon, *Nepal,* vol. 2 (New Delhi: Asian Educational Services, 1993). Originally published 1928. *Middle photo*: Akash Bhairab temple at Indrachok. Courtesy of Andrées de Ruiter. Original digital image published at http://www.nepal-dia.de/K-Kathmandu-Tal/k-Gassen_von_Kathmandu/k-gassen_von_kathmandu.html. *Bottom photo*: Akash Bhairab temple at Indrachok. Courtesy of Axelle Bergeret-Cassagne. Original digital image published at http://www.flickr.com/photos/58791115@N05/5566518835/. Transcription of street sounds: From the author's field recording, July 25, 1987.

Figure 6.7: Inscription No. 2: Swayambhunath, 1987: Map of Swayambhu: From the map *Kathmandu City* (Munich: Arbeitsgemeinschaft für vergleichende Hochgebirgsforschung, 1979). *Top print*: "Part 5 of a View of the Himaliya Mountains," from Francis Buchanan Hamilton, *An Account of the Kingdom of Nepal* (New Delhi: Asian Educational Services, 1990). Originally published 1819. Bottom print: "Temple of Adi Buddha at Sambhunath," from H. Ambrose Oldfield, *Sketches from Nepal,* vol. 2 (Delhi: Cosmo Publications, 1981). Originally published as *Sketches from Nipal* in

1880. Photo: By Frederick Ayer in Michel Peissel, *Tiger for Breakfast: The Story of Boris of Kathmandu* (New Delhi: Time Books International, 1990). Originally published 1966. *Transcriptions*: "Jaya namo sri buddha" by Vijay Kumar Sunam, in *Classical, Traditional and Folk Tunes of Nepal* [Nepalka sastriya, pauranik git ra lok dhunharu] (Kathmandu: Savardhikar Sagrahakartama Suriksit, 1993). Transcription: Brass band rendition of the same from the author's field recording, July 27, 1987.

Figure 6.8: Inscription No. 3, Natole, 1995: Map: By Niels Gutschow, and photo by Stephen D. Ryan, in David N. Gellner, "Monk, Householder, and Tantric Priest: Newar Buddhism and Its Hierarchy of Ritual," *Cambridge Studies in Social and Cultural Anthropology* 84 (1992). *Excerpt*: From a list of *dhimay* groups in the Kathmandu Valley published in *Dhime hanejya: smarika* (Kathmandu: Jyapu Mahaguthi, 1994). *Transcription*: *Dhimay* performance from the author's field recording, May 3, 1995.

Figure 6.9: Inscription No. 4, New Road, 2007: *Map*: From Prakash A. Raj, *Nepal on $4 a Day*, 1975–76 ed. (rev. from 1973 ed. of *Nepal on $2 a Day*) (Kathmandu: R. C. Joshi, 1975). *Upper photos*: New Road taken as stills from the author's video recording, June 27, 2007. *Photo*: Durbar Square, "Street Scene. Kathmandu. c. 1895," from Adrian Sever, *Nepal under the Ranas* (New Delhi: Oxford and IBH, 1993). *Background print*: Kasthamandap from H. Ambrose Oldfield, *Sketches from Nepal*, vol. 1 (Delhi: Cosmo Publications, 1981). Originally published as *Sketches from Nipal* in 1880. *Print*: "Gateway to Katmandu" from Pradyumna P. Karan and William M. Jenkins, Jr, *The Himalayan Kingdoms: Bhutan, Sikkim, and Nepal* (Princeton, NJ: D. Van Nostrand, 1963). *Peak Pro 7 rendering*: Sound of traffic on New Road, from the author's video recording, June 27, 2007.

Figure 6.10: Inscription No. 5: Maharajgunj, 2003: Map: Kathmandu Valley from *Nepal* (Kathmandu: Mandala Maps, n.d.). *Print*: "Panoramic View of the Valley of Nepaul" from Colonel Kirkpatrick, *Account of the Kingdom of Nepaul* (New Delhi: Asian Educational Services, 1986). Originally published 1811. *Prints on the border*: From the Nepali second-grade schoolbook *Mahendra mala* (Bhaktapur: Janaka Shiksha Samagri Kendra, 1983). Based on the author's field recording, October 16, 2003.

NOTES

1. Jasper Johns. *Flag* (1954–55). MoMA Collection (online). http://www.moma.org/collection/works/78805.

2. General Idea. Video Art in Canada (online). http://www.videoartincanada.ca/artist.php%253Fid=11.htm.

3. Dick Higgins, "Intermedia" (1966), reprinted in *Esthetics Contemporary* (1989).

4. There are, of course, other formats for presenting ethnographic work on sound, such as performances and conference papers. My focus here, however, is on material formats (or stable digital formats) that exist separately from their author(s).

5. Angus Fletcher disparages the critical turn toward textual analysis in *Colors of the Mind: Conjectures on Thinking in Literature* (1991): "Often in recent criticism we have seen a pretense that no author is doing the thinking; there is only a text. Critics personify the textual as if each text could write itself or as if each text were the automatic product of some magical, corporate, cultural machine known as ideology. Furthermore, these personifications mutate and reproduce, anything at all can be text, or be so called" (11). Quoted in Vernallis 2004, 201.

6. *EOL* (*Ethnomusicology OnLine*) is, of course, one place where some of this work is published, though even here some of the articles could just as easily have been printed.

7. Alexandra Juhasz comically described the general bafflement of MIT Press over how to market her open-access video book, *Learning from YouTube* (2011), at the workshop "New Media Futures" at the annual meeting of the Society for Cinema and Media Studies in New Orleans, March 11, 2011. The video book is available at http://vectors.usc.edu/projects/learningfromyoutube/.

8. Jacob Smith, "Problems of Unscreened Media" (paper presented in the session "Placing Sound," annual meeting of the Society for Cinema and Media Studies, New Orleans, March 13, 2011).

9. See Chion 1994 and 2009.

10. See Abu-Lughod 1993; Feld 1996; Meintjes 2003.

11. A stunning dance sequence from *So This Is Paris* (1926) is excerpted on *Light Rhythms: Music and Abstraction,* part of the seven-disc set, *Unseen Cinema* (2005). *A Study in Choreography for Camera* (1945) and other short works of Maya Deren are collected on *Maya Deren: Experimental Films* (1986).

12. Raynaud 1997, cited and discussed in Chion 2009.

13. Electric Kulintang (website, now defunct), accessed on June 28, 2011, http://electrickulintang.com/. For more on Electric Kulintang and Susie Ibarra's other projects, see http://www.susieibarra.com/susieibarra/projects/.

14. In noting this basic difference, I am glossing over the complexities of graphic representation and its uses. The terms *prescriptive* and *descriptive* were used by Charles Seeger in 1958 in an article in *Musical Quarterly* called "Prescriptive and Descriptive Music Writing," reprinted in Seeger 1977, 168–81. Ter Ellingson discusses and elaborates these terms in *Ethnomusicology: An Introduction,* edited by Helen Myers (Ellingson 1992a and 1992b).

15. See, for example, Filippo Tommaso Emilio Marinetti's contribution to the single issue of the journal *Canta giovinezza* that appeared in Padua in 1934, reprinted and translated in Bohn 2004, 91–93. For more on futurist performance, see Kirby 1971.

16. See Johnson 1981.

17. Reprinted in Cage 1963, 95–111.

18. For a selection of writings on pop art, see Madoff 1997. Certainly, text was already

creeping onto the canvases of artists earlier in the century; see, for one precedent, Robert Rauschenberg's *Mother of God,* from around 1950, in the SFMoMA Collection (online), accessed on April 2, 2016, https://www.sfmoma.org/artwork/98.299.

19. While I am using the term *soundscape* in reference to R. Murray Schafer's *The Soundscape: Our Sonic Environment and the Tuning of the World* ([1977] 1994), it is probably impossible to refer to any "-scape" without also echoing Arjun Appadurai's consideration of "five dimensions of global cultural flow which can be termed: (a) ethnoscapes; (b) mediascapes; (c) technoscapes; (d) finanscapes; and (e) ideoscapes" (Appadurai 1990, 6–7).

PRINT WORKS CITED

Abu-Lughod, Lila. *Writing Women's Worlds: Bedouin Stories.* Berkeley: University of California Press, 1993.

Appadurai, Arjun. "Disjuncture and Difference in the Global Cultural Economy." *Public Culture* 2, no. 2 (1990): 1–24.

Bohn, Willard. *The Other Futurism: Futurist Activity in Venice, Padua, and Verona.* Toronto: University of Toronto Press, 2004.

Cage, John. *A Year from Monday.* Middletown, CT: Wesleyan University Press, 1963.

Carpenter, Edmund. *Eskimo Realities.* New York: Holt, Rinehart and Winston, 1973.

Chion, Michel. *Audio-Vision: Sound on Screen.* Edited and translated by Claudia Gorbman, with a foreword by Walter Murch. New York: Columbia University Press, 1994.

———. *Film, a Sound Art.* Translated by Claudia Gorbman. New York: Columbia University Press, 2009.

Cook, Nicholas. *Analysing Musical Multimedia.* Oxford: Clarendon Press and New York: Oxford University Press, 1998.

Ellingson, Ter. "Transcription." In *Ethnomusicology: An Introduction,* edited by Helen Myers, 110–52. New York: W. W. Norton, 1992a.

———. "Notation." In *Ethnomusicology: An Introduction,* edited by Helen Myers, 153–64. New York: W. W. Norton, 1992b.

Feld, Steven. "Waterfalls of Song: An Acoustemology of Place Resounding in Bosavi, Papua New Guinea." In *Senses of Place,* edited by Steven Feld and Keith H. Basso, 91–136. Santa Fe, NM: School of American Research Press, 1996.

Fletcher, Angus. *Colors of the Mind: Conjectures on Thinking in Literature.* Cambridge: Harvard University Press, 1991.

Higgins, Dick. *Pattern Poetry: Guide to an Unknown Literature.* Albany: State University of New York Press, 1987.

———. "Intermedia." In *Esthetics Contemporary,* edited by Richard Kostelanetz, 173–76. Buffalo, NY: Prometheus Books, 1989.

Johnson, Roger. *Scores: An Anthology of New Music.* Selection and commentary by Roger Johnson. New York: Schirmer Books, 1981.

Juhasz, Alexandra. *Learning from YouTube.* Design by Craig Dietrich. Cambridge, MA: MIT Press, 2011.

Kirby, Michael. *Futurist Performance.* With manifestos and play scripts translated from the Italian by Victoria Nes Kirby. New York: E. P. Dutton, 1971.

Madoff, Steven Henry, ed. *Pop Art: A Critical History.* Berkeley: University of California Press, 1997.

Meintjes, Louise. *Sound of Africa! Making Music Zulu in a South African Studio.* Durham, NC: Duke University Press, 2003.

Raynaud, Isabelle. "Présence, fonction et représentation du son dans les scénarios et les films de Georges Méliès (1896–1912)." In *Georges Méliès, l'illusionniste fin de siècle?* edited by Jacques Malthète and Michel Marie, 201–17. Paris: Presse de la Sorbonne Nouvelle, Colloque de Cerisy, 1997.

Schafer, R. Murray. *The Soundscape: Our Sonic Environment and the Tuning of the World.* Rochester, VT: Destiny Books, 1994.

Seeger, Charles. *Studies in Musicology 1935–1975.* Berkeley: University of California Press, 1977.

Silverstein, Shel. *Uncle Shelby's ABZ Book: A Primer for Tender Young Minds.* New York: Simon and Schuster, 1961.

Tedlock, Dennis. *The Spoken Word and the Work of Interpretation.* Philadelphia: University of Pennsylvania Press, 1983.

———. *Finding the Center: The Art of the Zuni Storyteller.* Translated by Dennis Tedlock from live performances in Zuni by Andrew Peynetsa and Walter Sanchez. 2nd ed. Lincoln: University of Nebraska Press, 1999.

Vernallis, Carol. *Experiencing Music Video: Aesthetics and Cultural Context.* New York: Columbia University Press, 2004.

Audio Works Cited

Annea Lockwood. *A Sound Map of the Hudson River.* Lovely Music, [1989] 2003. CD.

Electric Kulintang. *Dialects.* Plastic Records, n.d. CD.

Voices of the Rainforest. Rykodisc/360° Productions, 1991. CD.

Video Works Cited

Maya Deren: Experimental Films. Mystic Fire Videos, 1986. VHS.

Unseen Cinema: Early American Avant-Garde Film 1894–1941. Image Entertainment, 2005. 7 DVDs.

CAROL MULLER

7. In My Solitude

Jazz Song as "Sound Writing"

In my solitude, you hold me with reveries of days gone by.
In my solitude, you taunt me with memories that never die.

Lyrics from "Solitude" by Duke Ellington

All men, at some point in their lives, feel themselves to be alone . . .
To live is to be separated from what we were in order to approach what
we are going to be in the mysterious future. Solitude is the
profoundest fact of the human condition.

Octavio Paz

The recording session in the Barclay Studios in Paris for the Dollar Brand Trio was the result of a surprise decision made by Duke Ellington, then A and R man for Reprise Records, Frank Sinatra's label in 1963. Ellington responded to the persistence of a beautiful young South African woman who had lingered backstage at one of his performances in Zurich, Switzerland, the week before. She begged him to come and listen to her musical partner, Dollar Brand, and his South African drummer and bass player. They were performing a few blocks away at the Africana Club. Ellington was so moved by what he heard coming from South Africa that he met the group in his hotel room the following morning and invited them to Paris. While the young woman, Bea Benjamin, was modest about her singing, when asked what her place was in the group, she told Ellington that she sang sometimes. At Ellington's request in the studio that morning, the young South African began the recording session. She had not known what to expect or what she would be required to perform that day, though she had been working on a wide range of popular tunes, including a selection of Ellington and Strayhorn songs, before leaving South Africa.

Quickly reminding herself of the lyrics written by Rogers and Hart, the South African born jazz singer, Beatrice (Sathima Bea) Benjamin, began to sing, "If they ask me, I could write a book" in the Reprise Recording Studio in Paris in February 1963. Her musical partner, Dollar Brand (known as Abdullah Ibrahim after his conversation to Islam in 1968), accompanied her on piano, with South Africans Johnny Gertze on bass, Makaya Ntshoko on drums, and Danish Svend Asmussen playing pizzicato violin around her melody. American musicians Billy Strayhorn and Duke Ellington would support her on piano on other tracks recorded that morning. This was the second recording session for Benjamin in about five years—the first had taken place in Cape Town, South Africa, in 1959 and resulted in an acetate recording called *My Songs for You* by Beatty Benjamin (and compiled by Swiss graphic designer Paul Meyer). In 1976 she recorded another long-playing disc titled *African Songbird,* where she experimented with extended musical form (two songs, each taking up a full LP side). It wasn't until she established her own label, Ekapa Records, that Sathima Bea Benjamin began to create a distinctive and enduring place for herself as a singer, bandleader, and record producer.

One of nine children, Sathima had rarely been on her own, early on using music as a space of solace, a personal place where she imagined herself singing to an audience, which she began to do at about the age of ten. She would walk on stage, during the intermission at the movie theater, and sing the songs of Hollywood musicals in her own style. As a jazz musician she had regularly created moments of solitude, moments to remember, imagine, and "sing inside" amid the demands of everyday life. When her life became too busy, the singer, composer, producer, wife, manager, activist, and mother would use water running into the kitchen sink as a space to imagine into being her style and repertoire of jazz songs. It was being alone at the sink that constituted a space of solitude for the singer; there she remade domestic space into a place for reflection, remembering, and imagining new possibilities for old repertoires of songs.

A South African school teacher by training who mostly sang jazz in clubs on weekends, Sathima's life to that point had been profoundly enriched by the literature she had read in neighborhood libraries in Cape Town, much of it focused on African American experience in the United States. It had similarly been shaped by the music broadcast on radio; heard in movie theaters; performed live at home, on the city streets, and in the wider community; and listened to on records in South Africa. If she had written a book herself, it would have been both about her love for her musical partner, Dollar Brand, and her love for jazz, as two interrelated pieces of her story. While Sathima and I ultimately did coauthor *Musical Echoes: South African Women Thinking in Jazz* (2011), it has been through the medium of jazz song that she has most profoundly inscribed her story, even if the contours of the journey were rarely conducive to recording and releasing her work until she settled in New York City and created Ekapa Records in the late 1970s.

After leaving South Africa in February 1962, Sathima and Abdullah spent close to two decades in a period perhaps best called a state of musical migrancy in Africa, the Americas, and Europe. Benjamin and Brand/Ibrahim announced the launch of their own record label in New York City. The label, Ekapa, was the Xhosa name for being from the Cape (province), South Africa. While Abdullah would make most of his recordings on other labels with just a few on Ekapa, the label became the vehicle for a dozen sound recording projects led by Sathima Bea Benjamin and funded by Abdullah's successes elsewhere. In the spring of 1997, Sathima launched *A Morning in Paris,* the highlights of her time with Ellington, Strayhorn, Asmussen, and the Dollar Brand Trio in Paris in 1963, at a live performance in the Weill Recital Room at Carnegie Hall in New York City, and in a recording discussed later on.

Sathima's story is told through her recorded output from 1963 through 2007, roughly divided into four categories: those recordings that introduce her to a global audience by paying tribute to her mentors and significant others (*A Morning in Paris, Sathima Sings Ellington, Memories and Dreams,* and *Dedications)*; those that speak to the antiapartheid movement abroad (*WindSong* and *LoveLight)*; recordings that articulate her place in a contemporary African diasporic community (*African Songbird* and *A Southern Touch)*; and those that interrogate the archive of global jazz and her position in that archive (*Cape Town Love, Musical Echoes, Sathima Bea Benjamin: Embracing Jazz, The Best of Sathima Bea Benjamin,* and *Song Spirit)*. In other words, we will come to know something of Sathima's story through close listening to her voice in jazz. And then Sathima explains why and how she uses the language of jazz to tell her story. I conclude with a brief reflection on Sathima's form of autobiographical sound writing in jazz. Here "sound writing" is constituted less as the representation of musical utterance in notation, as it is an inscription of the self and memories of home in the sounds and voice of South African jazz. Here the archive of a globally circulating archive of twentieth-century popular song is reconstituted as the repertory of the South African singer in diaspora.

"Sathima" translates as "the one who listens," and it is the name that was given to then "Bea Benjamin" by her compatriot bass player Johnny Dyani, while both were in exile, traveling between Europe and the United States in the 1970s. The name pays tribute to the woman's compassion, care, and willingness to listen to the struggles of the young Dyani, but it also speaks of the manner in which Sathima engaged with popular song, and ultimately moved into the improvisational language of jazz. Listening to the sounds around her and recalling and transforming them have long been the means by which Benjamin incorporated remembered sounds from home as personal inscription once she left South Africa.

Sathima's earliest memory of her own music making was that it was inserted into the crevices or secret spaces of everyday life. The first source of such activity was her grandmother's radio and the popular songs that streamed out of the box daily while she did chores in the kitchen, cooking, cleaning, and ironing clothes. These songs were intended to work as background music, but Sathima recalls being deeply moved by the words and melodies and wanting to sing them herself. As a young girl Sathima secretly created a repertoire that she sang in competitions held during intermission at the movies, even though listening and gathering songs was a forbidden pleasure—Sathima's grandmother did not know the girl was singing these songs in public from about age eleven, and it had to be kept secret. Even so, this music transformed the daily schedule of cooking, ironing, and cleaning from the mundane into the memorable and musical.

At the time Sathima's repertoire included such songs as "Somewhere Over the Rainbow" performed by women from England and America. "You began by copying, by sounding just the same as Joni James or Ella Fitzgerald," Sathima recalled, "but eventually you had to move away from that. Eventually you had to sound like yourself. No two singers are the same." Sathima ultimately stopped singing those songs when she became more aware of the politics of race and colored/mixed racial identity; but they were the first signs of the possibilities of travel through music, and they were first heard in the kitchen, a place in which Sathima would spend much of her time when she settled in New York City in the mid-1970s to raise her children.

This body of vocal material was supplemented with the dance-hall melodies originally played by several saxophones in Cape Town's dance bands; in remaking the music years later, Sathima assumed the line of the saxophone and then found the words in New York City's sheet music stores. Finally, she would add to her repertoire the music she gleaned from recordings of Billie Holiday and Duke Ellington that traveled to South Africa in the postwar period. Once Sathima left South Africa, she would add to the remembered repertoires songs she recalled from the extended family that had traveled to Cape Town from the British island of St. Helena in the Atlantic Ocean, starting in the late nineteenth century. They would gather around the piano to sing together and around the gramophone to listen to the tunes of British music hall from the 1920s and 1930s, remembered as the music of her grandmother's youth; and while the adults never attended church, several of the children participated in Wayfarer missionary services held in Sathima's grandmother's garage. As such, Sathima's songbook has been formed from a complex layering of musical and human travel, whose destination in the mid-twentieth century was Cape Town, South Africa, but later circled back to some of the original sites of the music's production.

"I sing those old songs from the 1920s. When I teach these songs to American musicians, they say 'Where did you find this, what is it?' They don't even know the music and it is actually from here. It went to Cape Town, and I am bringing it back to musicians in New York City. We give the song jazz changes, really hip changes underneath the melody, and I swing it. And then it sounds like I wrote it, but I didn't. It's just my memories of Cape Town that come back to me in New York City. All these musicians have this 'fake' book. And they go through it and choose a song. I don't have a fake book. I don't even own one. Whatever I'm singing is in my repertory because I have heard it before and then it comes to mind again. There's a reason it comes to mind, and then you have to sing it."[1]

PAYING TRIBUTE: TWO ELLINGTON RECORDINGS AND OTHER DEDICATIONS

A Morning in Paris *([1963] 1997)*

Sathima's first recording made after leaving South Africa was *A Morning in Paris,* recorded in 1963 with Ellington, Strayhorn, Svend Assmussen, and the Dollar Brand Trio. The songs Sathima sang in this recording session are largely the popular songs of the era, or those written by Ellington or Strayhorn. They were standards from what had come to be called the American Songbook, popularized by singers such as Ella Fitzgerald and Sarah Vaughan. Each song is focused on the idea of love in some fashion—longed for, lost, found, or hoped for—and it is the subject of love and the loss of love, which are key to Sathima's repertoire to this day. To showcase Sathima's voice, Ellington urges the musicians to create a lean instrumental texture, first bowed then plucked violin playing from Danish violinist Svend Asmussen, with a spare bass line in much of the recording from

South African drummer Johnny Gertze. The musicians leave considerable space within the instrumental frame for the singer to project her own style and to tuck the words into musical phrases that demonstrate a particular approach to pitch, modulation, and timing. From the start, we are struck by the sheer presence of Benjamin's voice—never forced, often quite delicate and wistful—and words, which are impeccably enunciated. In this recording Sathima is the melody that everyone else has to work around.

The musicians, all men, are clearly listening to what she does, and responding to her musical calls with often extraordinarily delicate and beautiful melodic and harmonic materials. The music supports or overlaps with the richness of tone quality and timbral possibility in her own voice. While she intuitively grasps the complex harmonic language that underpins her jazz melodies, she conveys vulnerability. It is hard not to read the words as autobiographical.

What lacks musically in this session are three elements that become hallmark qualities of Benjamin's voice as a jazz singer and leader of her own ensembles. First, there is little independence of line or function for the bassist.[2] Once Sathima starts to compose her own materials, we discover that it is often a bass line that comes first, before other musical materials. And bass players are given enormous latitude to be playful and wickedly creative, "singing" their own countermelodies to Sathima's voice—as she would hear in the freer playing of South African bassist Johnny Dyani. While the bass player becomes much more than the mere shape of harmonic progression, we have no inkling of that dimension of her performance in this earlier moment. Second, Sathima demands of her drummers a particular sound that is more percussive, some call it a qualitatively "African" feel—they bring brushes, use their sticks to create a dry woody timbre in the rhythmic outline of a piece, and often make the drums seem to "speak." On occasion, she requires the drummer to sound out what is known in South African jazz as the Cape Town rhythm, or *klopse* beat, to mark place through rhythmic articulation. Third, Sathima gives her trio considerable freedom to solo: to express themselves musically inside the improvisational format. That is simply not her prerogative in the Paris context.

African Songbird *with Dollar Brand (1976)*

Located in the improvisatory spirit of free jazz, this recording included South African and American musicians playing three of Sathima's originals: "Africa," "Music," and "African Songbird," and was reissued in 2013 by Matsuli Music.

Sathima Sings Ellington *(1979)*[3]

While every recording Sathima produces on Ekapa includes at least one Ellington composition, the next recording she makes is an album dedicated to all Ellington tunes. Once Sathima settled in New York City with two young children in 1977, recording became her primary mechanism for "reinventing herself" as a jazz musician and constituting a feeling of home in the music itself. She could not travel as easily with two young children and no wider family network to support her. Sathima tells the story of her decision to produce her own recordings: "It occurred to me that I could make a record. I really didn't know anything about it. I decided to do an album of Ellington songs because I figured, well, they don't know me here. Let me do something that is familiar. I was very unsteady with my own compositions, and I was very shy about them." With Ekapa established, Sathima could, in her words, let her records "do a little traveling" for her, in much the same way that American musicians had sent their music to South Africa since the 1920s. This was how she first heard the music of Billie Holiday and Duke Ellington.

Financially supported by Abdullah in exchange for managing his travels, Sathima made her first self-produced long-playing record at Downtown Studios in New York City. It came, however, after a difficult personal moment. Sathima had presumed Abdullah would perform with her on Ellington's piano, in both the original live performance of Ellington's works and on the recording, but Abdullah had refused. He told her that she was in New York City and should find her own musicians with whom to perform. (*Note:* She has died since this piece was first written.) Sathima recalled how devastated she felt, walking the streets of New York City, feeling as if she had just been thrown away. Abdullah, however, believed it was a turning point for Sathima, the moment he insisted that she stand on her own as a musician and bandleader. She gathered together one group of musicians for the live performance—including Onaje Allen Gumbs on piano and Buster Williams on bass—and another group for the recording. Onaje Allen Gumbs played piano, Vishnu Wood, bass, John Betsch on drums, and Claude Latief on congas. There was no bass in this rendition—a remarkable absence in contrast to the presence of the bass in Sathima's original music. Abdullah produced but did not perform on the album.

The album, *Sathima Sings Ellington,* contains seven Ellington standards: "In a Mellow Tone," "Prelude to a Kiss," "Sophisticated Lady," "Mood Indigo," "Lush Life," "I Let a Song Go Out of My Heart," and "Solitude." Accompanied by a group of African American male musicians, she described making the record in this way: "The recording session, which started around midnight and ended up in the early hours of the morning, was extremely relaxed and enjoyable. Please do not think me presumptuous when I say that there were moments during the session when I felt 'HIS' [i.e., Ellington's] spirit very strongly—and that was beautiful."[4]

"I did it, I went into the studio and I did it," Sathima commented to me in the early 1990s. She continued, "You know, Abdullah would say to me, I remember him saying this to me long ago, that I didn't realize the gold within myself. He said that a long time ago. The problem was that in my mind he was the overwhelming force; it took me a long time to come out from under—actually he will take credit that he established me as a jazz singer when we arrived here in New York City. And he is proud of that fact. But, you know Carol, while I learned much from Abdullah, each of the recordings I have made has been my own concept and project."[5]

Once the studio session was complete and the tapes edited into an album, Sathima recalls, "I sat there with a couple thousand LPs and I said, 'What am I going to do with all this?' So I had to get the courage and say, now where are all the critics in this jazz music business? I am going to write a little note, package it, and send it to them. They can either look at it, or throw it in the bin. Then I waited six months. I got feedback. I almost fell off my feet. It was so positive! I couldn't believe it. Then a distributor approached me. Everybody said this is an artist-owned independent company: this is what this woman has done. If you want to know anything more about this woman, here is the contact information. So this small company called me. That was how I found out I needed a distributor! It was just trial and error. I was actually very naïve. They came to me: that is how the stuff got out there."[6]

What we hear in this music is something new. In all of Sathima's recording projects, there are very few songs that she sings more than once. "In My Solitude" is one exception. She sang it straight with Ellington accompanying her in the 1963 Paris recording, but here, in the April 1979 tribute to Ellington, she takes the song in a completely different direction. And her trio does the same, a point I return to in my reflection on the dialectics of solitude that follows.

Dedications *(1982)*

"And that success inspired me to do my second album on Ekapa, *Dedications*,[7] which I recorded in New York in January 1982." *Dedications*, reissued by a Japanese label as a CD in 2005, is "in many ways Sathima's musical autobiography," writes jazz critic Fred Bouchard, "joining the past with the future . . . Part of the beauty of this album lies here: when you listen to people tell you their life stories, it lets you reflect on your own life in new ways" (2005, liner notes to *Dedications*).

While the CD reissue of *Sathima Sings Ellington* has Sathima's own composition, "African Songbird," and as suggested previously she recorded the LP *African Songbird* in South Africa in the mid-1970s, *Dedications* is the first Ekapa recording to include Sathima's own compositions. These are the songs "Music" and "Africa." The remaining contents include songs that she remembers as favorites of important people in her life. She dedicates the first three songs: "Love's Old Sweet Song," "Ah! Sweet Mystery of Life," and "One Day When We Were Young" to her St. Helenian grandmother, "Ma Benjamin," who raised Sathima, her sister, and her brother for many years. All three songs were written in the days of British colonialism, were popular around the time of World War I, and were favorites of Sathima's grandmother. She reinvents three standards from her youth over a "Cape Town/klopse" rhythm; dedicates the Cole Porter tune "Every Time We Say Goodbye" to her then husband Abdullah; inserts her two originals "Africa" and "Music" discussed subsequently; and closes out with Eubie Blake's "Memories of You," a song she recalled hearing played on alto saxophone by legendary South African musician Kippie Moeketsi, and on recordings of Eubie Blake himself.

Sathima explained her use of an earlier repertoire of popular songs as almost like a living archive, or human reissue: "I bring the old songs back, I love doing that. I enjoy researching very, very old songs that nobody is singing any more. I think about how I can present this, how I can do it differently without offending the composer. There is a very old song that has recently come to me. It is called 'Prisoner of Love,' I don't even know who sang it, but it must have been some vocal group from long, long ago. These are songs from like 1945. I do these things because I actually heard them broadcast on the BBC. There were singers like Vera Lynn. They had very good diction. That said, you can't live in the past, to be extraordinary you have to live for the moment and think about tomorrow. There isn't any yesterday. You can reflect and have memories, but they must be used to project something new. That is what I like to do with the music, I take something old and make it new."[8]

Sathima also talked with me about "Music" and "Africa" in 1989. "I don't know when 'Music' started, but it was probably a long time ago. It surfaced in 1974 when I was on a visit home to South Africa. Maybe it was being back on the African soil, being with family, and looking at my life from another perspective. Having been there, gone away, and gone back. I was also going through a lot of personal difficulty, keeping a marriage together, having a four-year-old son, and not being able to sing. I think that was the third song that came after I realized I could write songs, though I kept it inside me for a long time. When I decided to record it in 1985, I gave it to the musicians and they just dived into it. We hardly rehearsed. We just went into the studio. They are real pros. They know more about this stuff than I do. As for 'Africa': that song expresses how I imagined we would feel when we did finally go back home—as it became possible to do in the 1990s. I once tried to sing that in Cape Town, in the 1970s. Somebody wrote a review and said, 'Well we don't know exactly what Africa she's singing about.' And I said to Abdullah, 'Now I know one thing, it is time to leave. It is definitely time to leave.' But I would sing it here in the United States and people would understand. It's funny how things work out." In contrast to the lack of recognition in the 1970s, each time Sathima sings "Africa" with Africans and African Americans in the audience now, it becomes the anthem of the event, eliciting deeply felt emotions to the message, the musical texture, and perhaps also the sense of longing for Africa as a place and sensibility.

"Soon after recording *Dedications,* I was in Europe and I came home to find a letter that said, 'You are being considered for a Grammy nomination.' I told Abdullah that I thought they had the wrong person. They said that you have to send eight copies of your record to the Academy of Recorded Sound immediately. Of course, it was a foregone conclusion that someone with a small label and only their second recording wasn't going to get the award. But I was happy that I was being considered seriously by the critics. That nomination inspired me to do another album I called *Memories and Dreams,* which has my 'Liberation Suite.' I was stunned because it just took off."

DELVING INTO THE POLITICAL

Memories and Dreams *(1986)*

An unlikely title for an album in which Sathima moves directly into the political on side A of the LP—"Nations in Me, New Nation a Comin'," "Children of Soweto," and "Africa" are combined to create Sathima's "Liberation Suite," which could be read as a parallel to the "Freedom Now Suite" composed by Max Roach with Abbey Lincoln performing in the 1960s. The particular subject matter, while tied to issues of race, frames the project as a specifically South African political struggle. Sathima is a women of mixed racial heritage; in South Africa under apartheid she was classified by the regime as "Cape Coloured"—her original identification on her passport said "mixed St. Helenian." The Cape Coloured category erased all forms of prior history. "Nations in Me" addresses what it means to have "many nations" in one's body, and to sing about it as a positive and rich heritage rather than a shameful form of miscegenation. "Children of Soweto" honors those who participated in the Soweto Uprising of 1976, a political movement that changed the direction of the antiapartheid struggle internally and internationally. Sathima responds as a woman and mother to the strength of Soweto's children. And "Africa" we have heard before—the anthem to new forms of African diasporic experiences and longing.

Side B presents four songs of love and sentimentality: "Till There Was You," "I'm Getting Sentimental over You," "In a Sentimental Mood," and "Day Dream" (the last two, once again, songs by Ellington), honoring her musical mentor, but also keeping in focus the personal in times of political challenge and the central focus on love in all aspects of daily life.

WindSong *(1987)*

"The success of *Memories and Dreams* inspired me to do 'WindSong,'" Sathima commented to me in the early 1990s. This is the album in which Sathima claims she found herself musically, and self-consciously asserts herself as a woman as well. In my view, "WindSong" reaches the highest levels of artistry, of musical freedom in the free jazz sense, and of emotional depth. Sathima recalled:

> I start off the album with the old African American spiritual, "Sometimes I Feel Like a Motherless Child." For twenty-five years I used to start all my shows with that old song. This was while my mother was alive even though she was away from me. It was as if I was singing the song to her, telling her how much I missed her as a child. But now she is no longer alive I can't sing that song anymore. I also used to sing it at funerals a lot. But it's not coming from that faraway place that it used to. It's over now.
>
> "WindSong" is the song and the name of the group I used to take with me when I occasionally traveled in the 1980s. That song is my space capsule: it is what I am really all about. It is about keeping your heart in tune and attuned to what is really happening. And I believe there is a song that blows on the

wind. You will only hear it if your heart is open. It is subtle and nuanced, and it carries tenderness and compassion in its sound. I am really old-fashioned, you know, because I believe that women and mothers have to catch tenderness and compassion and give it to their children, both boys and girls. These qualities are lacking in the world, but I have to believe that the Creator lets compassion blow on the wind. You can see that it is gone here in the United States, but in Africa you still can find it. Africa is always a little bit behind, but I have one foot here, and one foot there.

I dedicated that album to the struggles of women and children in South Africa. And I used the photographs of my daughter Tsidi and myself for the cover to represent all women and children in the struggle.

"WindSong," and "Music" came at about the same time. First came a bass line, then the rhythm, and then the words. Much later the melody came too. I didn't have a melody: I just walked around with this bass line and words for a long time. But the musicians all love going into that music: there's so much space in "WindSong." It leaves so much space for everybody. There is a structure, but it's also very open. You have to listen to each other: we cannot just ignore each other. They have to listen to me. I have to listen to them. Because the musicians I perform with have worked with themselves, they know how to listen to each other. And we have fun, we swing a little, I let everyone play a part, and then I take it out again. Everything is very spiritual because I can't write anything down. When the musicians are like this I know they are ready for "WindSong," musically and spiritually, and they embrace it.

The third song on side A is "Lady Day," a stunning and early tribute to Billie Holiday, whom Sathima never met in person but came to know intimately through the autobiography of Holiday, *Lady Sings the Blues: The Searing Autobiography of an American Musical Legend.*[9] In the late 1950s, she had felt a certain kinship and place in jazz because of the kind of voice, personal story, and invocation of the blues that Sathima believed she shared with Billie Holiday.

Side B contains two swinging standards, Victor Herbert's "Indian Summer" and Harold Vicars's "Song of Songs," which create a protective shell around "Dreams," another Benjamin original. Kenny Barron is on piano, Buster Williams on bass, and Billy Higgins on drums. Musically speaking, this is Sathima's dream trio—there is an audible affinity and sensitivity, and exquisite levels of whimsical creativity, in their responses to the standards on side B, but even more so, to the Benjamin originals. Sathima's voice opens up a rich palette of tone and timbre, and a musical fabric in which all are equal players. "WindSong" is an extraordinary work of political consciousness expressed in a nest of emotionally evocative, at times heart-wrenching vocal power.

LoveLight *(1988)*

Sathima recorded *LoveLight* in 1987, and it was distributed by Enja Records (Germany) in 1988. South Africans in exile in Europe in the 1960s and 1970s were known for the tributes they paid to other American and South African musicians through the music they wrote. Sathima has three tribute songs that came to her, one for Duke, the one for Billie Holiday on *WindSong,* and a suite-like song for the now fallen political hero Winnie Madikizela Mandela, the ex-wife of then political prisoner Nelson Rolihlahla Mandela. In the late 1980s Winnie Mandela was both celebrated for her brave fight against the apartheid regime, particularly as the wife of then still-imprisoned Nelson Mandela, but rumors about her darker side were beginning to circulate. Putting out "LoveLight" with the opening track as a tribute to Winnie Mandela was a risk, but Sathima was not afraid of stirring debate and controversy.

When the song "Numzamo: Winnie Mandela" came to Sathima, Winnie Mandela was under house arrest, and there were no signs that Nelson Mandela would be released from prison anytime soon. Winnie Mandela, who relentlessly opposed the apartheid regime, had just published the autobiographical text, *Part of My Soul Went with Him.*[10] Another side to the woman would emerge in the early 1990s, but Sathima's tribute to Winnie Mandela should be read in light of the political context of the mid- to late 1980s in South Africa. As Sathima recounted:

> There was all this controversy around Winnie Mandela just as I was about to release *LoveLight,* which has her song on it. I was told not to release the CD. But it's a good sign for me if something is going to be problematic, because I am used to having to survive against the odds. I did a lot of interviews about that song and have always asked, why can't we look at her track record of good things and not just her errors? What about the impact of solitary confinement on her personality? She could have chosen to do different things with her life, but for twenty-seven years she put her life on the line for Mandela. She survived a long separation with Nelson in prison, and raised her children alone. She is human, and anyway, most of the time, we are just pawns in this big game.

Compositionally the "Song for Winnie" just arrested me. It woke me up from my sleep, and I had to call Don Sickler, the jazz arranger and trumpeter, and say, "Please write this down." Then I had to get Buster [Williams]. I just had this song for Winnie. I didn't have the first part, the Nomzano thing, so I went and did that other part. I had Buster Williams write it down. It was an extremely difficult song. We wrote it and then I came home, and when I was making the children's supper, the Nomzamo part came. So I had to call him again. And I said, "This is the bass line."

Anyway, it took a long while to write the song for Winnie Mandela because it came in three sections. I put an appeal out to God, or the Higher Spirit, or Creator. I wanted to write this song for Winnie, because I absolutely identified with her. I could feel her pain. I wanted to write this song, but it was the most difficult song I have written. It came in bits and pieces, so it is a complicated piece, like a mini suite. It has different sections because women have different sides to their personalities. You could have three husbands and still they wouldn't know all about you. We are very mysterious—how could we expect our husbands to understand us? (Someone is going to kill me for this, I am sure!) I could see many sides to Winnie Mandela, her connection with Nelson—what a wonderful love to survive all that. I could see her political views: I could see her as an African woman representing womanhood across Africa.

I just remembered the pieces as they came. As I washed the dishes, it would go through my mind. I have a very tiny kitchen, but at least when I am in there, running the water, I can't hear anyone else. I use that time to sing without actually singing, to sing inside. I wash dishes a lot. I use that place, it's a private place in a large apartment where there are no other private places for me. It makes me feel comfortable, and relaxed. I am never just washing dishes: I think a lot as I work. And running water is very soothing.[11]

As with all Sathima's earlier projects, *LoveLight* includes a balance of her originals; in addition to Winnie Mandela's song, there are "Music" and "African Songbird"—the latter two are discussed in the *Sathima Sings Ellington* reissue—and "Gift of Love," her tribute to Duke Ellington. Four standards round out her selections, learned from her mother: "You Are My Heart's Delight," "I'll See You Again," "Long Ago and Far Away," and "You Don't Know What Love Is," each masterfully rendered by the quartet, with Larry Willis on piano, Buster Williams on bass, Billy Higgins on drums and talking drum, and Ricky Ford playing tenor sax. *LoveLight*—the essence of one's being centered in the heart and reflected in the way you live—and the album is dedicated to Sathima's mother, who died just after the album was recorded on September 5, 1987.

AFRICAN DIASPORIC TIES

Southern Touch *(1989)*

Southern Touch, Sathima's sixth album, was written in response to the trip she made to Europe, where she was rather aggressively asked why she always sang love songs and not explicitly political material if she was from South Africa. One of the musicians turned to the person interrogating Sathima and replied, "Can't you hear she's from Georgia, in the United States?" Sathima recalled how grateful she was for his support, and decided to document the ties between the two Souths—that of the United States and South Africa. This is the moment in which she creates explicit connections between the struggles of the old African diaspora—those who endured slavery—and the new African diaspora, specifically the diaspora caused by the apartheid regime in South Africa.

In conversation with students at Marymount College in Tarrytown, New York, in November 1990, Sathima talked about *Southern Touch:* "I am calling it *Southern Touch* because jazz originated here in this country in the Deep South with African Americans. It didn't come from anywhere else, and African Americans came from Africa. It wasn't jazz as we know it, it was a cry, it was pain; the pain is the same in South Africa and the traumas have been similar, if slightly different. And the connection is there music-wise. That's how it unfolded for me. And the music actually should be spontaneous. You have to have your stuff together, and you have to come through what I have to get there. I couldn't have started with jazz: I had to grow into it. It's a process. You have to be patient with yourself, and it's the friends and people who are on the path with you, with the music, who will nurture you, guide and help you. It's in the sentence they say, or a look they give you that lets you know everything is okay."[12]

The *Southern Touch* repertoire begins with very old songs from the southern parts of the United States: W. C. Handy's "Loveless Love/Careless Love"; "Street of Dreams" by Victor Young, written in 1932 but popularized by Bing Crosby and Ella Fitzgerald; Sammy Cohn's "I've Heard That Song Before," a song recorded in 1939 by Harry James and popularized later by Bing Crosby; three others popularized by Hollywood films; and tributes to Ellington, "I Let a Song Go Out of My Heart," and Strayhorn, "Lush Life," both of which she recorded before. This time, however, while she doesn't fundamentally change her arrangement of the tune, her voice is in a more equitable dialog with her dream team of musicians: Billy Higgins on drums, Buster Williams on bass, and Kenny Barron on drums.

RETROSPECTIVE: CLAIMING A PLACE IN GLOBAL JAZZ

Cape Town Love (1999)

Cape Town Love was the first recording made in the context of postapartheid South Africa. Its purpose for Sathima was to provide the opportunity for the musicians who had nurtured her as a young singer in Cape Town to record with her. The project was triggered by a fax sent by Abdullah Ibrahim, after he heard pianist Henry February (already seventy in the recording) performing in the Cape. Despite a lifetime as a gifted professional pianist and teacher in Cape Town, February had never been recorded. Abdullah suggested that Sathima think about including him in her trio. Her goal quickly transmuted into more than mere documentation. *Cape Town Love* became the moment for Sathima to return home: to pull from deep within her the songs she remembered so vividly in exile, from her childhood and young-adult life, but had never performed with American musicians. This was the time to make visible, for the record as it were, the "home" she had carried within for so long. This was her chance to go back to the music that had been the vessel pushing her out of the movie theater at intermission and into the world of professional singing. Henry February had been a key force behind that move.

Cape Town Love was recorded on March 18 and 19, 1999. The compact disc has eight songs, though two more were made when the musicians returned to the studio with a Cape filmmaker producing a documentary on Sathima Bea Benjamin. The musician who most vividly recalled the songs of the post–World War II period was, of course, Henry February, but it didn't take bassist Basil Moses long to recall the melodies. Drummer Vincent Pavitt was younger, so did not necessarily remember the tunes, but he certainly could play with a "Cape Town" rhythmic feel. Once again, Sathima puts such a fresh spin on these decades-old melodies that it is easy to imagine the quaint romantic sentiment in the singer triggered her compositional spirit—you may even think she wrote these songs herself. She did not; rather, these are her echoes of a repertoire of American and British origins sounding out from the southern part of Africa.

The *Cape Town Love* cover contains a black-and-white photographic image of the musicians whimsically inserted into a larger frame of Khoisan rock paintings from the Kagga Kamma reserve in the Cape. Sathima and her Cape Town trio are sitting on a couch taking a break for tea. Bass player Basil Moses listens to what drummer Vincent Pavitt has to say. Sathima has the familiar white china cup and saucer in her hand. Sathima smiles as she raises the steaming liquid to her lips. Pianist Henry February, the oldest and most intense member of the group, is surprised by the flash of the camera. He stares ahead, perhaps thinking about the food in the wax wrapping nested in the palm of his hand. Longtime friend and renowned photographer George Hallett, remembered from the old Kew Town library days, dropped by to capture these contingent moments in the photographic image, and to work with Sathima in conceptualizing the visual project.

Like the cover of the recording, the songs themselves work as a kind of palimpsest of twentieth-century popular song. Each of the songs performed on this recording comes out of Sathima's memories of her life before she left South Africa. Songs that circulated globally through Hollywood movie soundtracks—the musicals in particular—and through radio broadcasts and recordings were heard performed live by local dance bands, in community halls and elite jazz clubs, in talent shows held at intermission in the movie theaters, in school performances, and in church halls all located in the city of Cape Town, South Africa. When dance band musicians such as February and Moses performed many of these songs in the dance band context, they played them straight and in strict time, keeping the beat for the dancers. Now it was time to do more than just keep time—here was a moment for the musicians to set their scores free, to liberate their minds from the strictures of ballroom dance, and to play! And play they did in the Milestones Studio at the foot of Table Mountain. Out of the archive of human memory and into the present through freshly made performances, *Cape Town Love* sets down, for future generations to hear and recreate in new contexts and historical moments, popular songs of the early twentieth-century transatlantic world.

Musical Echoes *(2002)*

In 2002, several years after receiving the words and melody of "Musical Echoes" in a dream, Sathima traveled from New York City to Cape Town to record the song and produce a CD of the same name. Her trio included American Steven

Scott on piano and South Africans Lulu Gontsana on drums and Basil Moses on bass. This was her second recording celebrating the transatlantic relationship between South African and African American jazz musicians. The repertoire once again dug into the archive of transatlantic popular music and jazz compositions: three Ellington tunes, Gershwin, Noel Coward, and Irving Berlin, among the composers whose work was rendered locally for global consumption. The original song, "Musical Echoes," was Sathima's own. Though on this recording she is older, more reflective, her voice sounds as youthful as ever. It has no politics, just simple statements about the transatlantic connections between jazz and its echoes elsewhere in the world: jazz and its capacity to transform moments of sorrow and loss into exquisitely crafted, spontaneous musical statements about love in the face of suffering. It is full of South African blues: the music that made so many continue to love, to sing of love, and to keep on striving for its place in their lives.

And finally, there are three retrospective compilations: *Sathima Bea Benjamin: Embracing Jazz* (2000), compiled by Lars Rasmussen; *Song Spirit* (2006), compiled by Sathima with each of the pianists she has worked with represented by one track of her singing; and the *Best of Sathima Bea Benjamin*, created over the last decade to celebrate a lifetime as a singer of jazz.

IN HER OWN WORDS: SOUND WRITING IN JAZZ AS A SOUTH AFRICAN STORY?

In 1999, on a return trip to South Africa, Sathima expressed her beliefs about the early history of jazz in this way: "Jazz," she commented, "is a cry. It is a survival skill for the spirit. I think it must have started with a woman who just let out a wail. Then came the accompaniment."[13] Why jazz? For Sathima, jazz is personal music, a vehicle in which to express your very existence, to state what you feel about life. As she told the students in a class I taught at Marymount College in Tarrytown, New York, in 1990:

> My message here is be true to yourself. . . . Listen to my song "Music," because the most important thing is to find your own sound. And when you do, everything gets easy. I wrote "Music" because we must all find our own individual sound. We all went through listening to other singers; you want to sound a little bit like them, or you just start in a vacuum.
>
> The reason I am doing jazz is it affords you a certain amount of freedom of thought, freedom to be different and unique. And it dares you: it lets you pull

out whatever courage you have. You have to take risks. That's the whole thing. I could have inherited this courage; I think even things like that come through in the genes. My mother had to take risks. Just growing up in South Africa not being white, you learned how to survive and take risks. My grandmother taught me to be careful and stay out of trouble, but eventually I rebelled against that; that whole rebellion thing led me to jazz. I saw that as music of rebellion: maybe it wasn't, but I think it really was.

The music doesn't speak to my head, it speaks to my heart, and I listen only to that. I have never been able to listen to what my head tells me. If I had, my whole life would have been different. This is where the music resides: within my heart. In my head I remember it all, but the music is all in my heart. They all say it must come from the heart. I think all jazz musicians, if they are jazz musicians, this is how we operate, and that is why it is such a dear music.

For Sathima, three key elements define her compositional and musical processes: intuition, spontaneity, and inspiration (i.e., coming from the heart, in the moment, and without the mediation of music writing):

I am just an inspirational composer; I don't sit down at a piano and say, 'I am going to write a piece.' It just comes, and sometimes it doesn't come for a long time. I don't write down my own music. When I have a song, I have to ask somebody to write that down, and you go through that whole process. But I think if I learned to write, I would be interfering with my antennae, and I don't want to do that. I gravitate to musicians like drummer Billy Higgins because he can hear subtleties and nuances, and he can help you punctuate them. It's wonderful to have someone like that in your orbit. And he's paid his dues.

When do I compose? I find that when I am walking through the streets and it's crowded, I get a lot of things because people impact on you. I don't have to walk down a lonely country road. It works for me to take long walks, even a subway ride. When I am standing on the platform waiting for a train, nobody can hear me singing. If I want to try something out, I try it out there and nobody hears it. Remember, Carol, when my children were young I used to take them to school—for almost ten years I did this every day during the school year. I had to go by subway or by bus, but always chose the subways to take them there, and then I would walk back at least a mile and a half each day, early in the morning. There were never many people about, so you are fresh, and then lots of things come to you.

All my compositions start musically with the bass line. Then I go to bass players Buster Williams or Onaje Allan Gumbs, and he says, "Do you know how difficult it is to write these bass lines?" Because there are spaces in between; and if they play it wrong, if someone doesn't write it down the way actually, they can look at that as a guide, but sometimes it confuses them. What they have to do is actually feel and learn the bass line. Like in "Africa," you know. [Sathima hums the line.] There is a space there. Some musicians just cannot accommodate that space in their minds. They have to stamp their feet in between there so they don't play in the wrong place. If you don't play it as written, it is pretty horrible. It's the space in between that gives it that whole feeling. This is in both "Africa" and "WindSong."

I haven't done "WindSong" for a long time because it's the same thing—the musicians don't get it. They just don't hear the space. I tell them it's like an extension, it's like the male and then the female takes over. I don't know how to explain it to these guys. But if they play it like that, exactly like I am singing it to you, it sounds very corny. I don't like to come down hard on the musicians. But they feel bad and they say, "What is she talking about?" It's not about the notes, it's just a feeling. That's why I love Steven Scott. He will say, "You need to listen." Buster will tell Onaje, "Just listen to what she is doing: just be quiet. Sathima says how it should be done." We have to do it that way, because if they don't, oh, it's so horrible; I will start and can't wait to finish it.

My music is about essence and feeling. I can't write the feeling in the music down. The musicians, when they look at it and they start dissecting it and say, "Oh, my goodness!" Even my husband will say to me, "This is a really expensive song, Sathima." It's very difficult because I get impatient if I have to take someone on a gig when I can't get the real guys, and they can't play my music. And I say, "But it's so simple," and my husband says, "It's not so simple. Besides the feeling, what is required technically is not that simple."

Once Abdullah said I should go to school and learn how to write music because I always have to share the credits with others. I say that if I go to school and learn how to write down the music, I am entering into another way of doing the music. I might not get the inspiration anymore. Inspiration is dear to me. This is what I rely upon, that God will send or he won't send a song to me. So I was scared to do it; I am still scared, and I won't do it. I don't mind giving the credits to the pianists who helped me write my music down, I really don't mind. Well, music doesn't belong to me anyway, or to them. I would say to the pianists, "How much do you want from me for writing my song down?"

They say they don't want money, they just want the credit, so there is obviously something in that.

It's hard to explain how I write my music. The only way I can is to say that you have your antennae ready and they have to be clean. They have to be like laser beams so they attract—it's like what I call a "lovelight." In "WindSong," there's a lovelight. I don't have any control over this: I am just a channel of the music from the Creator. The antennae are actually inside. They have to be inside and then it comes. I think we are dealing with something that is very divine; that's not something that you can study. I don't know when a song will come. I just keep living my life until the Creator sends me something. So my heart must be clean.

When I sing the words of a song, for me it's a story being told with the lyrics and the sound. It's a story you are telling. Everything has to make sense. I don't suddenly just sing a song. I will figure out what the story is here. That impacts on where I am going to put the accents and which word is more important in the line. Every song is a story. How on earth did you get this gift of storytelling in song? It comes to me when I am meditating in motion. I think about songs when I am walking in streets here amid all kinds of people. I do not retire to some place and say, "Okay, I'm gonna write or sing a particular song." It's not about that. It's very divine and inspirational.[14]

"How do you prepare for a performance, do you just go out there and sing?" a student at Marymount College asked Sathima in 1990. Sathima responded:

I usually go out and sing by myself. The guys say, "Are you going to do that thing again where you just go out solo? Because we know the music, we can start with you." And I say, "Yes, I am going out alone because I have to draw the audience in to myself, and then you can come out and join me." The first three notes are crucial. I have a certain strength, and we are going to have a beautiful time together. You learn to stand on your own two feet, to harness your energy, and go out there and do it. That is my approach. Everything I do is about love.

I want my music to always feel spontaneous. Duke Ellington believed in one take. That means the dials are set, you call the tune, and you do it.[15] He said you only repeat yourself, you only do a second take if there is a technical hitch. I still do my recordings in that way. I learned that from Duke Ellington. I prepare myself beforehand, and I go into the studio knowing exactly what I want to do and I do it. He said if you do it twice, it's already a bad thing, and if you do it three times, you will sound like a bad imitation of yourself. I think he is right, absolutely right. Jazz music should be extremely spontaneous—you have a plan ahead, but when it happens it is spontaneous.

That is the bond I naturally work toward. That is what I want to achieve. It's not that I am this fantastic musician; while I think its true I have a great sound, that's not the most important thing. The most important thing is when I have my guys around me. They are males: I want to touch them in such a way, because I am sensual, but without a hint of sexuality. It's not about sex. I want to keep the purity. The point is I am working with three men, and I am letting them touch their fragile and feminine side, and they do it in spite of themselves. Men are just naturally macho, and I say I am the one who has to stand out in front; you are behind me, you are going to embrace this song just like I do. I think I achieve that.

I need to feel the embrace and to embrace back. The music for me is about love and how it travels. There are so many different ways to love. Love is supposed to be merciful. The basis of everything I do, in life and in my music, is love, a little capsule of tenderness and compassion I am trying to put that into my sound. That is the most natural thing to me.[16]

FINAL REFLECTIONS

Earlier I mentioned the one anomaly in Sathima's recorded output: the radical transformation of the melody of Ellington's song "In My Solitude" from the 1963 studio rendition, where Sathima sings the melody, to the practically new song (with the same words) she renders with herself as bandleader in 1979. Outside of the words, the song bears little resemblance to what she sang on the earlier recording; there is no parallel transformation to a song in any of Sathima's other material. In addition, "In My Solitude" in both arrangements is the only tune in which Sathima doesn't step aside and allow the male instrumentalists to feature without her. She sings from beginning to end, without any solo breaks for the instrumentalists. One has the sense as a listener that this is Sathima's song: this is her moment.

Over the two decades I have worked on Sathima's material, I have often wondered about the extent to which "In My Solitude" is an autobiographical statement for Sathima. But because the song is written as a conventional love song—a song about a subject longing for love—I have hesitated to read anything further into its words. Listening recently to the complete recorded output[17] revealed the distinct arrangements created by Sathima and suggested that "Solitude" was an early vehicle of personal experimentation and expression. Out of this musical gesture, or kind of sound writing, I am suggesting that we might set the song apart, reading its words and music as something more than mere romantic longing.

First, let us discuss briefly the two musical arrangements. In the Paris 1963 rendition, Sathima places herself in the lineage of American jazz singers. She is accompanied by Ellington on piano, with Danish pizzicato violinist Svend Asmussen weaving his sounds around her melody. While the bass player and drummer come from South Africa, there is nothing overtly South African in their sound. Rather, this rendering of Ellington's song by Sathima is clearly in the mode of torch and jazz singers like Helen Merrill and Ella Fitzgerald. In the 1979 version something very different is happening both in the melody and the musical arrangement. The song is performed with voice and percussion, using the drum kit and congas; the only parallel to this kind of arrangement is Sathima's haunting rendition of the African American spiritual "Sometimes I Feel Like a Motherless Child." Clearly "In My Solitude" is reaching out in its musical rendering to two very distinct communities, locating its subject very differently. The first harnesses the transnational language of a kind of jazz cosmopolitanism; there is a "this could be performed anywhere" feel to the 1963 version. In contrast, the much clearer location of the second song is in an imagined African space that incorporates its West African percussive and rhythmic routes/roots. It is this juxtaposition—of the words of solitude nested in the sounds of particular communities—that speaks to Octavio Paz's "dialectic of solitude."

In Paz's thinking, solitude enables one to come to terms with difference—how different one is in relation to others. It is not a state of inferiority, but rather a retreat in order to come to terms with difference. In popular language, solitude is identified with suffering, and suffering with the lack of capacity to love freely. There is no way in which solitude and communion can exist together.

It is easy to see how solitude is central to Sathima's selection of song repertoire, the transformation of style and intention over her lifetime: from a youthful longing for love in a condition of solitude, through a greater self and political awareness and the accompanying maturation of voice and musicality—in terms of South African liberation and the transnational African diasporic community—into a more reflective, echoing mode as she reaches the latter years of her life. It is here that I suggest she moves from an individual living with the tensions of the dialectic of solitude—pulled simultaneously in opposite directions by the luxury of solitude and the necessity and longing for communion and community—to a broader understanding of the shared nature of the human journey.

While Sathima and I have metaphorized her musical journey through the acoustical image of the echo and the visual image of the palimpsest, what Sathima's autobiographical sound writing suggests is that song creation and performance constitute an etching of a journey in sound that celebrates the recuperation of a fleeting community. Like the groove of the long-playing record, the original media of musical inscription for Sathima, the words and melody of a song remembered from multiple pasts create pathways of possibilities for the singer and her male musicians in the immediacy of spontaneous performance. Perhaps ironically, even in the company of musicians, Sathima's voice still seems to float above the musical texture. One hears a vocal solitude in the moment of musical utterance, despite the sensitive and careful listening by musicians such as Buster Williams and Basil Moses on bass, Kenny Barron and Steven Scott on piano, or Billy Higgins on drums. These moments of solitude, of invoking the spirit of prior performances, are nowhere more evident than at the start of all her live performances, which she always opens alone, out front, in a kind of acoustical solitude. She tunes her spirit to the music, and invites the audience to listen closely to her. Hers is the orphaned voice that has passed through many places. She summons its energy, and invites musicians and audience alike to listen carefully and embrace and be transported by her voice.

NOTES

1. All citations here are drawn from Muller and Benjamin 2011, chap. 5.

2. Perhaps with the exception of the bridge in track 7, "The Man I Love," where the bass occupies a more prominent place, creating a bridge from the slow ballad of the first section into a double-time upbeat swinging second section.

3. There are two versions, the initial release and a reissue on CD, with three additional songs from later recordings.

4. Bea Benjamin, "Liner Notes," *Sathima Sings Ellington*, 1979.

5. Sathima Bea Benjamin, interviews with the author, March–April 1990.

6. Sathima Bea Benjamin, conversation with the author, Marymount College, Tarrytown, New York, November 1990.

7. *Dedications* was reissued in 2005 on compact disc by Celeste Company (Japan).

8. Quote derived from Maxwell Campbell, "Interview," *All About Jazz* (April 2008): 13, accessed on April 20, 2016, http://www.allaboutjazz.com/interviewer-newsletter-april-2008-by-john-kelman.php.

9. Billie Holiday and William Dufty, *Lady Sings the Blues: The Searing Autobiography of an American Musical Legend* (New York: Penguin Books, 1956).

10. I recall reading the book myself and being completely taken by Winnie Mandela's story of courage and brutal struggle against the apartheid regime.

11. Sathima Bea Benjamin, interviews with the author, March–April 1990.

12. Sathima Bea Benjamin, conversation with the author, Marymount College, Tarrytown, New York, November 1990.

13. Sathima Bea Benjamin, as reported by Jill de Villiers, *Citizen* [South Africa], June 24, 1999, p. 33.

14. Sathima Bea Benjamin, conversation with the author, New York City, 1999.

15. Graham Lock, *Blutopia: Visions of the Future and Revisions of the Past in the Work of Sun Ra, Duke Ellington, and Anthony Braxton* (Durham, NC: Duke University Press, 2000), 10.

16. Sathima Bea Benjamin, conversation with the author, Marymount College, Tarrytown, New York, November 1990.

17. While I have had the complete collection of her recordings, they have been in several different formats; so while I listened closely to the long-playing records when I first met her and transferred them onto cassette tape, these media have become obsolete. Now with the capacity to download LPs into iTunes, the process has become a lot easier. I have been able to view the complete body of work in a single format, with all the titles clearly visible, making direct comparison a very simple process.

REFERENCES

Feld, Steven. *Jazz Cosmopolitanism: Five Musical Years in Accra.* Durham, NC: Duke University Press, 2012.

Holiday, Billie, and William Dufty. *Lady Sings the Blues: The Searing Autobiography of an American Musical Legend.* New York: Penguin Books, 1956.

Lock, Graham. *Blutopia.* Durham, NC: Duke University Press, 1999.

Mandela, Winnie. *Part of My Soul Went with Him.* Edited by Anne Benjamin and adapted by Mary Benson. New York: Norton, 1985.

Muller, Carol Ann, and Sathima Bea Benjamin. *Musical Echoes: South African Women Thinking in Jazz.* Durham, NC: Duke University Press, 2011.

Paz, Octavio. *The Labyrinth of Solitude and Other Writings.* New York: Grove Press, 1985.

Rasmussen, Lars. *Sathima Bea Benjamin: Embracing Jazz.* Copenhagen: Booktrader, 2000.

Recordings Cited

Beatty Benjamin. *My Songs for You.* (1959)

Sathima Bea Benjamin. *A Morning in Paris* ([1963] 1997)

Sathima Bea Benjamin with Dollar Brand. *African Songbird* (1976)

Bea Benjamin. *Sathima Sings Ellington* (1979)

Sathima Bea Benjamin. *Dedications* ([1982] 2005)

Sathima Bea Benjamin. *Memories and Dreams* (1986)

Sathima Bea Benjamin. *WindSong* (1987)

Sathima Bea Benjamin. *LoveLight* (1988)

Sathima Bea Benjamin. *Southern Touch* (1989)

Sathima Bea Benjamin. *Cape Town Love* (1999)

Sathima Bea Benjamin. *Embracing Jazz* (2000)

Sathima Bea Benjamin. *The Best of Sathima Bea Benjamin* (2001)

Sathima Bea Benjamin. *Musical Echoes* (2002)

Sathima Bea Benjamin. *Song Spirit* (2006)

PART THREE

Theorizing Sound Writing

ANNE K. RASMUSSEN

8. Women Out Loud

Religious Performance in Islamic Indonesia

SOUNDING THE SCENE: SOUTH JAKARTA, INDONESIA, AUGUST 2014

I am with my longtime consultant, colleague, and friend, Hajjah Ibu Maria Ulfah,[1] in the living room of her home on the sixty-ninth anniversary of Indonesian independence from the colonial rule of the Netherlands (*hari kemerdekaan*), August 17, 2014. Ibu Maria's neighborhood, Ciputat Baru, is decorated with red-and-white flags, and in addition to the national pageantry that is playing live on television, low-key, grassroots celebrations are going on in neighborhoods all over the country, a vast archipelago of seventeen thousand or so islands in an arch spanning about thirty-two hundred miles. Independence is one aspect of "imagined community" in this country comprised of hundreds of different ethnic groups and languages; religion is another (Anderson 1983). Ibu Maria and I are seated on the couch with a huge, encyclopedia-sized volume spread across our laps. We are exploring a multimedia educational Qur'an that, with the touch of a digital pen on a color-coded text, takes the student to audio recordings of nearly every aspect of each and every verse of the Qur'an, including: recitation (both melodic, *mujawwad,* and nonmelodic, *murattal)*; *tajwid* (rules for pronunciation, phrasing, and sectioning of the text); *maqamat* (Arab melodic modes); Indonesian and English translations of the Arabic text; associated *hadith* (recorded traditions of the Prophet Muhammad and his companions); and *tafsir* (commentary, explanation, and interpretation). The most incredible feature of this, the latest development in a parade of didactic devices for learning to recite and understand the Qur'an in Indonesia, is that the digital pen is also an MP3 player and speaker. Touch the color-coded or numbered place in the book, and the device recites, translates, explains, and coaches in a way that ensures that eye and ear work together in the experience of hearing and understanding the recited Qur'an.

Scholarly works that treat the Qur'an in context, as it is experienced among Muslims and people in the Islamicate world, emphasize its orality (see, for example, cited works by Crow, Ergin, Frishkopf, Gade, Graham, Hirschkind, Lee, Nelson, Rasmussen, and Sells). The word *Qur'an* means "recitation," and while it may be read (in the original Arabic or in translation), it is more commonly and by necessity recited (by the reader) and heard by everyone. Ergin, in her explication of the soundscape of sixteenth-century Istanbul mosques, summarizes the ideology to which scholars refer:

> One needs to perceive the text acoustically in order to understand its message. Ideally, one should read and hear the text at the same time, bringing together two different modes of perception for a multi-sensorial communication of the message. However, even a cursory acoustic perception of the Qur'an in the background will bestow blessings upon the hearer. (Ergin 2008, 212)

Ibu Maria positions the magic pen over a page of the giant book and taps on the fourteenth verse of the chapter Āl 'Imrān, an apparently random choice:

> The love of desired objects, like women and children and stored up reserves of gold and silver, and pastured horses and cattle and crops, appears attractive to people. All this is the provision of the hither life; and it is Allah with Whom is an excellent abode. (Qur'an 3:14; translation Khan 1991, 49)

We listen to the passage. She then taps on the Indonesian translation, the English translation, the associated *hadith,* the explanation of *tajwid,* then back to the recitation. It catches me by surprise. Without warning I hear the voice of Pak Moersjied Qori Indra, whose rich baritone with its full, nasal resonance brings with it a wave of sensation and memory. His melodic *mujawwad* recitation in the Arab scale, *maqam hijaz* is a model exposition of Arab melody, something that requires no replay, no analysis—although one can be made,[2] no words—although volumes will be written. In that moment, the sounded is heard, understood, and signifies on multiple levels. Although I have lost touch with Pak Moersjied, the resonance of his voice sends me to my first class with this fine reciter some fifteen years earlier.

The first time I heard a *tawashish* in the context of a class at the *Institut Ilmu al-Qur'an,* it was literally "music to my ears." The melodic line in the Arabic musical mode, *maqam sabà,* caused my hair to stand on end. As I listened to the voice of our guru, I appreciated the resonant nasality that was enhanced by his exacting pronunciation of the Arabic text. I was able to imagine the movement through time of the musical mode that Pak Moersjied sang in terms both of the melody's intervallic content and its progression through the various stations of the *maqam* as it is realized in Arab music performance practice. For me, this performance was powerfully moving. If I listen to a recording of this song, or perform it myself, it has the same effect. An audition summons a sensorium of emotion and memory that is challenging to capture in words on a page, though we try with Sisyphean stubbornness.

Pak Moersjied, a *qar'i,* or master reciter of the Qur'an, and our teacher, performed the Arabic poem *Ara it-Tayiran* ("I See a Bird"), then wrote the text on the board in Arabic, and subsequently invited his class of about fifteen college-age women (and me) to sing the song, phrase by phrase, until we mastered the Arabic poetry and the specific melodies that were assigned to each line of the text.[3] The myriad affective musical and social elements that spoke or, more appropriately, sang to me were many. First was the power of our teacher's voice: present, nasal, focused, and loud. Second was his relaxed demeanor. Learning to recite the Qur'an was, I thought correctly, serious business; but Pak Moresjied's class seemed fun, and the college-age women I was among seemed to think so too![4] Third, I could perceive and appreciate the intervallic content of *maqam sabà,* with its neutral or half-flat second degree, a note called *sika* in Arabic; its distinctive flattened fourth degree of the scale, which then leads to an augmented second degree between the fourth and fifth scale degrees; and somewhat later on, a modulation that tonicized the sixth degree, Bb, which became the ground note (*qarar*) of *maqam Ajam,* a musical mode whose intervallic content is like a Bb major scale. Are you with me? It doesn't matter. This kind of music-theory metalanguage means nothing to the students of recitation with whom I shared this singing. In Indonesia, such rules of melody, their adherence to the system of Arab musical techniques and aesthetics, and the way that melody "is applied to" (*mengaplikasikan*) the sacred text of the Qur'an are activated only when sounded. In this context, theory is sounded, not written. This is sound theory.

Beautiful but formulaic melodies were assigned to each line of text of this classic Arabic poem, a *tawashih.* These melodies were characteristic of a performance practice I knew from my own experience of Arab music, experience that I accumulated a half a world away from Jakarta, Indonesia, in places such as California, Michigan, New York, and Virginia. Dramatic and improvisatory embellishment of the melody with trills and slides was expected of everyone as we learned the *tawashih* with the performance practice of Arab singing. The result in class was a heterophonically textured, almost cacophonous wall of noisy singing, redolent with participatory discrepancies and the thick texture that invites anonymous yet collective participation by all.[5]

STUDYING THE SOUNDS OF ISLAMIC INDONESIA

My contribution to this volume attempts to translate into words the experience of learning through hearing, something that affected me profoundly when I lived in Indonesia. I was in the country—based in its teeming capital city, Jakarta, with a population of nine million people and at least, or so it seems, that many cars and motorcycles—in order to learn through *doing fieldwork*, beginning tenuously in 1995 and 1996, continuing throughout the year in 1999, and on various occasions during the 2000s up to this writing. My project aims to document and interpret various kinds of Islamic performance: Qur'anic recitation, liturgical and paraliturgical song, and popular instrumental and vocal music that is activated with the syntax of Arab musical styles and informed by several Arab world, Indonesian, and global trends and traditions.[6] My work is notable for the recognition of the vibrant and creative performance of religion in Muslim Indonesia and its introduction of professional and amateur women and their students, who are reciters, teachers, and specialists in the communication of religious knowledge (Rasmussen and Harnish 2011; Rasmussen 2010, 2009, 2005, 2001). The power, presence, and permissibility of women's voices in the Islamic soundscape is something that was made known to me through hearing knowledge and is something that I have tried to convey in my writing and presentations, with or without the soundprints of those voices that might be made accessible though experience, live demonstration, or recordings. In the second chapter of my monograph, titled "Hearing Islam in the Atmosphere," I discuss the public practices of listening that I observed, overheard, absorbed, and eventually shared along with the creation of the Islamic soundscape, something I found to be an essential aspect of Islamic culture in Indonesia, or at least my experience of it as a musician and ethnomusicologist. At that time, I did not conceive of my work as an acoustemology, to recall Steven Feld's initiative, as outlined in his 1996 publication, to "argue the potential of acoustic knowing, of sounding as a condition of and for knowing, of sonic presence and awareness as potent shaping forces in how people make sense of experiences" (97). I associated Feld's ideas with his field site of indigenous people, waterfalls, and exotic birds in Papua New Guinea; Feld's ideas did not seem applicable to urban Jakarta, a place to which most ethnomusicologists are not attracted.[7] Nor were "sound studies" or "sound writing" officially on my radar or within earshot; although in retrospect, I believe that in the translation of my experience and understanding into words, I have been tempting these three methodologies for some time.

To make a move toward sound studies has strategic legitimacy in the contexts I describe. Claims about "music and Islam" (a phrase that personifies and gives agency to both entities in a way that misrepresents each of them) are always controversial. Approaching the topic of "music and Islam" requires what has become a ritual for writers: a review of the permissibility of music during the time of the Prophet Muhammad based on the interpretation of the Qur'an and the *Sunnah* (the social and legal practice of Muslims), and the interpretation of this corpus by subsequent communities of believers, from the Abbasid Caliphate to the present-day Taliban.[8] This prerequisite literature review should then be followed by the explanation that in Arabic thought, music (*musiqá*) is a category separate from singing (*ghina*) and chanting, or recitation (*tilawa*). Thus, things that sound "musical" to the outsider, whether they be a scholar, journalist, or musical tourist, and that may be described as "music" according to certain epistemologies, may not even actually be "music" at all in local or Arabic-informed dialects, including those in Muslim Indonesia. In the context of Indonesian Islam, a great deal of which transpires in the Arabic language, it is then important to signal which aspects of Arabic thought about anything, music or women for example, have been imported along with the language and which have not. Among Indonesians in the business of religion, music is a marked category that generally means song with instruments; however, adherence to categories of music, song, and recitation are not rigid, as numerous instances in my ethnography reveal.

Given the distinction between the categories "music," "song," and "recitation," exchanging the term "music" for "sound" therefore, for the analysis of any Muslim context, may be seen as a welcome development. We can make similar acclamations about UNESCO's category of "intangible cultural heritage," which takes the emphasis off "music" in sensitive Islamicate-world contexts and replaces it with the vague and more encompassing term "cultural heritage." Sound studies and perhaps by extension sound writing cover all of the bases, from sound to music and beyond. The "sonic universe," to quote soundscape studies pioneer

R. Murray Schafer (1993, 5), and as a field of inquiry "sound studies," can potentially encompass the interdisciplinary collection of scholars and approaches, both native and non-, that are necessarily involved in the creative expression of religious culture in any context. Furthermore, sound studies and sound writing invite those who are intimidated by or bored with the category "music" and all of its trappings. On top of the music literacy that is required for the music scholar, there is a lexicon of musicological metalanguage, an example of which was deployed in the fourth paragraph of this essay, that seems to be created by and for those who reside in the "special domain" of music (Stokes 1997, 1). Playing music and singing as a methodology for fieldwork and teaching is also not required for sound studies and its products.

While referring to Qur'anic arts and the music that is associated with Islamic culture as "sound" is safe, it seems to be a demotion. The analysis of sound seems to me to emphasize the scientific, the random, and the natural aspects of our lifeworld rather than the very purposeful, rehearsed, public, and in many cases artistic and virtuosic repetition that constitutes Jakarta's Muslim soundscape, however it is overheard. Furthermore, the Muslim sound world in Indonesia also extends decidedly to the musical and to music. Songs that have structured, repeated melodies and forms are well beyond the domain of "language performance," to borrow Frishkopf's apt descriptor, such as the *tawashih* described at the outset of this essay (2009). And when musical instruments, composition, arrangement, and production enter the mix, we are squarely in the domain of music. To reiterate, scholars of Islam insist on its orality: on the importance of sound and of hearing as a methodology for knowledge; on the existence of the text as one that is sounded in recitation and not merely read; and on transformative experiences through movement and sound as it is heard, spoken, recited, chanted, sung, shouted, and played (either on instruments or through speakers) that are central to the experience of the religion, from the mundane repetition of daily ritual, to the quest for and encounter with states of elation, ecstasy, rapture, trance, and union with the divine. Rather than ask how to theorize sound writing, perhaps we should be asking why we are still struggling with writing at all when the limitations of the medium, particularly as applied to sound worlds, have long been exposed (see, for example, Blacking, Stokes, Small). One depressing response to this question may be the admission of compliance with a Western, male, logocentric hegemony of economy and power that offers little variation to its system of just reward. With the variety of media that we have had at the ready for more than a century, why just write?

HEARING, LISTENING, LEARNING, KNOWING

The singing I experienced when among reciters and their students in Jakarta and elsewhere in Indonesia meant something to me, in part because I spent the formative years of my life as an adult musician acquiring a hearing literacy in and for Arab music, through first observing and then absorbing "techniques of the body" (Mauss 1934). Although I am an outsider to the tradition, understanding Arab music through both cognitive and kinesthetic channels has been my ambition and passion since the late 1980s, beginning in graduate school and as a methodology for fieldwork, research, and teaching. My learning experience resonates with that of many who work *through* music. Virginia Danielson, whose monograph on the Egyptian singer Umm Kulthum is an invaluable guide to the musical values and aesthetics of twentieth-century Cairo, writes of the process of acquiring cultural literacy in Egypt:

> I came into the society of musicians in Cairo as one who had to be taught why Umm Kulthum's singing was good singing. I did not become, in the course of my years in Egypt, an objective observer of cultural expression: My story, and the language of my interpretation of Umm Kulthum's story is that of a Western musician and academic who learned to love and value Arabic singing. (1997, 3)

Like Danielson who, in the course of her research on the Egyptian singer Umm Kulthum (d. 1975), had to be taught by Egyptians, both people on the street as well as connoisseurs who patronized and performed the music of Umm Kulthum, *why* this singer and her music were so good, I had to learn how to hear, listen to, perceive, and eventually love Arab music through being musical. Experience as a singer and instrumentalist flourished in expansive ways during graduate school through work with two fine musicians: a mentor, A. J. Racy, and a colleague, Scott Marcus. Arab musicality facilitated my first explorations as an ethnomusicologist *doing fieldwork* by interviewing, listening, and playing music among Arab musicians and audiences in Massachusetts, New York, Rhode Island, Michigan, Chicago, and California. As a college professor, I have taught through practice and performance since 1991. While my fingers and voice learned to do what they needed to play the Arab lute, the *'ud,* and to sing, and I trained my mind to understand the music though mastering various literatures, this new context in Indonesia introduced me to the challenges and opportunities of an embodied musicality.

My relationships in Indonesia were more often than not facilitated by a mutual involvement in Arab music. In fact, this common interest became a *fieldwork hook.* In my research process, our musical performance and talk about that performance constituted one of the strongest sites of meaningful exchange and still does. Arabic singing and discourse about music is a common middle ground. Oddly, it isn't a native discourse either for me or for the Indonesians who make the performance of Arabic melody and text a priority, but Arab music is something we are keen to talk and know more about.

Our pursuit of Arab music, although different in orientation, represents a kind of egalitarian meeting place. Arabic language performance, studying the musical *mujawwad* style of Qur'anic recitation, singing songs in Arabic for any number of public events, writing popular songs *bernuansa Islam* (with Islamic flavor), as some of the college-age women I came to know did, and just listening to Arab music with Indonesians has been the medium through which I learn about Islamic performance and the people for whom it matters in Jakarta and in a number of places throughout the archipelago to which my initial contacts in Jakarta led me.[9] By participating in its performance, I have learned about Indonesian Islam. Learning through listening, and then hearing, and then, ideally, knowing, makes up for the inadequacies of the linguistic sophistication I possess either in Indonesian or, particularly in Arabic, this language of aesthetic and intellectual prestige that all of this performance is *about.*

In studying *qira'a,* the performative, melodic, *mujawwad* style of Qur'anic recitation, during the early stages of this project, the intensity of the experience was almost overwhelming. To practice channeling the word of God through the body, with language that is thought to be so beautiful that it could only come from a divine source, was profoundly stunning. I often felt that I played the part of an *enfant sauvage,* the wild child, who has special needs and disabilities but whose senses are also heightened, intensified, and ultraperceptive.[10] Listening to the performative music of the Jakarta soundscape was one way I could train myself to be literate in Indonesian culture. Hearing knowledge complimented the race to understand this place through the medium of *bahasa Indonesia,* the national language, and through the mountain of texts in history, anthropology, and music that I was trying to digest in this exciting and overwhelmingly challenging stage of the project.

LISTENING TO THE JAKARTA SOUNDSCAPE

In his "critical genealogy" of the now quotidian term *soundscape,* originally coined by R. Murray Schaeffer (1993), Ari Kelman notes that rather than to curate a particular soundscape, which was Schaeffer's original intent, "Scholars of sound ask how does sound circulate and how does it contribute to the ways in which we understand the world around us" (Kelman 2010, 215). While I didn't understand everything in the Jakarta soundscape, my auditory perception of the environment became sharper as time went on, and I became willingly dependent on my hearing perception. Sounds that were at first perplexing, comical, or annoying later became commonplace and acquired meaning for my family and me. I eventually began to trust my ears and to welcome the call of the knife sharpener or the broom salesman, who passed by our house walking their cart full of wares through the neighborhood alerting potential customers of their passing. I began to hear the difference between the engines of the three-wheeled *bajai* and various sizes of motorcycles, cars, and trucks, especially those that frequented the spaces I habitually occupied. I came to expect the jingle of the ice cream vendor, the rumble of the Toyota *Kijang* pulling into the driveway at about six in the evening, the morning din of the nursery school on the corner. Ever present were the nocturnal *musang* (civit cats) on the roof, and the growling and yowling of feral cats in the act of procreation (*sedang kawin*—getting married), and the chorus of dogs, often inspired by the morning call to prayer. The sounds of Islamic ritual and recreation, apprehended aurally, were what opened my mind to the possibility of a project on the performance of Indonesian Islam: of groups of women practicing recitation down the street; Umm Kulthum on the radio; religious music videos on television; our houseman (*penjaga)* practicing the recitation of the Qur'an in the garage in the evening; and the rhythms of five mosques that were in earshot of our house in the Jalan Banka complex of the Kemang Raya neighborhood of South Jakarta. Intimidating yet alluring, these sounds eventually measured out the day in more and more predictable ways. In fact, once I knew which sounds interested me, I was able to filter my soundscape, to "orchestrate my environmental acoustics" Schaeffer (1993, 4), excluding sounds that were interruptive or meaningless or inviting them back in only when I had the time or inclination to savor them.[11]

The term *soundscape,* which has come to capture our imagination as a comprehensive auditory landscape in which background noise is foregrounded as aesthetic texture with sonic valence, is actually a radical revision of the term.

In his attempt toward "Rethinking the Soundscape," Kelman (2010) reminds us that the original definition of soundscape as conceived by R. Murray Schafer, the Canadian composer who originated soundscape studies, is more specific:

> His notion of "the soundscape" is far from the broad, descriptive term that it has since become. . . . it is suffused with instructions about how people ought to listen; and it traces a long dystopian history that descends from harmonious sounds of nature to the cacophonies of modern life. Schafer's soundscape is not a neutral field of aural investigation at all, rather, it is deeply informed by Schafer's own preferences for certain sounds over others. (Kelman 2010, 214)

Ethnomusicologists who encourage students to "become alive to their soundscape" (Titon 2008, 2010 Introduction) would agree that the identification of individual voices in the complex texture of a sonic environment involves "making informed distinctions about sound (as) a social process in which context plays a crucial role" (ibid., 230; see also Corbin 1999, Wainwright and Wynne 2007).

Deborah Kapchan takes the mere acknowledgment of and identification of or within sound environments several steps further with her introduction of the phrase "literacies of listening." Kapchan asks how we can acquire the ability to learn other cultures through participating in their sound economies (Kapchan 2009). In her account of experiencing Sufism in France among a group of female *Faqirât* (Sufi ascetics, literally, "poor ones"), she writes:

> My focus shifts away from the role of discourse and towards the importance of the auditory in enacting transcendent experiences of the sacred. Examining how ways of listening (like ways of speaking) structure perception and create an ethnos of religious community, I argue for the primacy of listening and memory in developing auditory "literacy." (Kapchan 2009, 67)

Kapchan's quest for a literacy of listening takes us beyond the mere recognition, identification, and categorization of sounds to sonic knowing, sensation, and memory. Her notion of listening literacies is one that connects nicely with Christopher Small's action, "musiking," a concept that glosses interaction and communication through the medium of music and musicality, the latter made manifest in reception, reaction, and communication about music and, I will extend, about sound.

THE AFFECTIVE POWER OF ARAB MUSIC IN INDONESIA

In my description and analysis of Arabic Indonesia, I try to convey the experience of *tarab,* the Arabic-language concept that indexes aesthetic excellence and communal elation borne of both repertoire and performance practice and that has at its core performative interaction (Racy 1991). *Tarab* unfolded, for example, during an evening when two champion reciters who had invited me to Medan, Sumatra, brought me to a *Haflah al-Qur'an,* or more literally, a "Qur'an party." At this event alternation between recitation and singing among women and men was replete with communal ecstatic indulgence among a vociferous group of about sixty participants gathered for the occasion. Their responses, in the Arabic language, of encouragement and acclamation became part of the performance. Audience response was even part of my performance, singing and playing on the *'ud.* That my hosts, Yusnar Yusuf and Gamal Abd al-Nasr Lubis, and I listened to cassettes of Umm Kulthum during the hour drive to and from the "Qur'an party" only enhanced this musical road trip. From the back seat I was able to observe and absorb the way they engaged with the recordings, singing along and commenting, and also to join in this ritual of pleasurable and interactive reception myself. This evening and many other occasions confirmed for me the proximity between Islamic ritual and music. When reciters—men and women, professionals and amateurs—consistently show interest in musical performance and collaborations with me, their enthusiasm for "musiking" is clear (Small 1998). Many instances in the research process helped to confirm that for many reciters, a seamless flow—from recitation, to singing, to music, and back again—is the norm and not the exception.[12]

Simultaneously, and to complement new experiences of Arab music in Indonesia, the entire soundscape gradually became a close consultant: Hearing Islam in Indonesia is not an option; it is a certainty. Architecture in Indonesia, even in Jakarta, is porous, and the sonic dimension of the built environment is interpenetrating. Neighborhoods are acoustically accessible and penetrable. And because even the smallest group will amplify their activities, pushing them into the public space, sometimes with a great deal of distortion, my access to or at least observation of innumerable contexts was enabled through orality. I could often hear where I could not go; and as I learned more about the sound sources of Islamic Indonesia, I was able to more accurately guess at the biographies of the sounds I heard. The "insight," or more accurately "in-hearing," into religious and social life that such a permeable physical environment offered, turned my ears into "cognitive organs" that invited me to "reach beyond the noise," a reach that Alice Cunningham Fletcher made when listening to Native American ritual—one she likens to the then quotidian experience of listening to scratchy, noisy wax-cylinder recordings. Through hearing practices I was able to, as ethnomusicologist Veit Erlmann writes, "conceptualize new ways of knowing in a culture and of gaining a deepened understanding of how the members of a society know each other" (Erlmann 2004, 3).

My education came through the soundscape, but my progress as a student of this sonic landscape was enabled and enriched in multifold ways by my ability to participate in it, not only as a musician and an ethnomusicologist, but also as a female voice.

WOMEN'S VOICES

Among the most salient features of both the continuous localization of Islam in Southeast Asia, as well as of the Islamization of the Indonesian Muslim ecumene is the public participation of females. I was able not only to study this phenomenon, but perhaps partially in the spirit of *dakwa* (from the Arabic, *da'wa,* to strengthen or promote religious faith and practice) to become a participant. Not long after I started visiting the Institut Ilmu al-Qur'an, I was encouraged to seek out Maria Ulfah, in part because she was a woman and a respected teacher, but also because as a woman, reasoned an acquaintance—then assistant, and now colleague, Dadi Darmadi—"my voice would be better matched to hers." It was this nudge that led me to practice regularly with the young women that Maria Ulfah was coaching and to begin to take into my body the rigorous work of Arabic language performance in Indonesia. The challenges of recitation are the criteria for which it is judged and comprise the separate elements of its aggregate aesthetic affect. The long, melismatic, single-breath phrase is prized, so a line of recitation will be preceded by a long pause and a deep belly breath, the phrase, and then a dramatic release and gulp of air after a line's delivery. Maria Ulfah's recitations tended to begin on the lowest grumble, for example, the note A or G an octave and a half below middle C. As the phrases developed, the range expanded until we all were trying to hit an E-flat or F an octave and a half above middle C in our chest voices. There is the description and it is accurate. But no sound writing can tease out the sensation of making or hearing this progression of sound with your body. The challenges of *tajwid,* the system that governs the pronunciation and sectioning of the text, was my great weakness; however, by mimicking my teachers (students included), I became more and more aware of the nuances of pronunciation, articulation, duration, and effects of timbre, such as nasality, that are employed in the course of language performance. I was able to "go with the flow," as in Turino's explication of "flow," where skill level is balanced with the inherent challenges of recitation (2008, 4). I sat close to the women around me, close enough to feel the vibration of their breath and the warmth of their bodies, and absorbed their demeanor, breathing with them and vocalizing with them, trying to share the sensation as they physically enacted, through practice and repetition, the sacred and challenging text. Finally, the construction of melody-in-time and its adherence to the performance practice conventions of the Arab *maqamat* (musical modes) was a most important location for auditory knowledge and expression.

In channeling the word of God through the human body, Qur'anic reciters—women or men—activate an inner spirituality: the melding of the mundane and the sublime toward a personal experience of the Divine. While the objective is to recreate the archetypal, the result is unapologetically personal, as the voice, more than any other human performing apparatus, is always identified as belonging to a particular body (see Rasmussen 2011). Nevertheless, in spite of the fact that these are particular women's bodies with their distinct voices activating powerful, individualized, and highly specialized performances, there are a number of ways in which a woman's personal and physical individualism is obscured.

First, although it may be represented as a solo and individual act, the performance of language in an Islamic context is actually a "communal endeavor."[13] The performer of Qur'anic recitation or devotional song is doing something that everyone has practiced and experienced (see Sells 1999, Marcus 2007). Second, the performed text is immutable. The delivery can vary widely depending on the person and the context, but there are no surprises in the words. Hirschkind helps us to understand the importance of orality by juxtaposing the logocentric process of persuasion by argument with hearing with the heart:

> That Muslim scholars have been relatively uninterested in elaborating an art of persuasive speaking owes in part to the way revelation affected their conceptions of the efficacy of speech. . . . The message itself has been articulated in the most perfect of possible forms, the Qur'an. This is made evident in many parts of the Qur'an where the failure to heed the words of God is attributed to a person or community's inability or refusal to hear *(sam')*. (2004, 134)

Even melody as a concept is thought to be "already out there" only to be taught, practiced, mastered, and applied in performance. The eminent musician and scholar of Arab music A. J. Racy, in his work on "musical ecstasy," the Arabic term is *tarab,* tells us that because modal improvisation is "tuneless" or "compositionally neutral," this "safeguards religious texts from the imposition of external, or humanly contrived compositional creations. Tuneless music allows the sacred words themselves to structure the performance as well as to accommodate the desirable melodic embellishments of the talented reciter" (Racy 2003, 97).

No matter how perfect the message, however, it is always preferable to have it transmitted by the beautiful voice of the talented reciter (Rasmussen 2010, chap. 3). Nina Ergin, in her study of the soundscape of Ottoman Istanbul (2014), delves into the records of Istanbul's numerous mosques to discover explicit directions for reciters who have "the capacity in reading the Qur'an with a beautiful voice." The directives of mosque patrons elaborate that "every one of them will read from the holy Qur'an with a soul-caressing voice in a way that will awake pleasure in the listener" (ibid.).[14] To revisit Hirschkind, quoted previously, reception through hearing by listeners (Arabic: *sami'a*) is as much a part of the aesthetic complex as is performance. Often demonstrated through physical and sounded behavior, reception, as it is embodied and performed, of this ideally perfect message (with its compositionally neutral but optimally sublime melody and rendered by a soul-stirring voice), then becomes the site where meanings, individual and collective, take shape.

In Arab music the notion that the performer and audience constitute a "feedback loop" (Racy 1991) is an ideology and practice with deep historical roots. Danielson writes of reception as an articulated and crucial component of performance. She remarks that the musical authorities of early nineteenth-century Cairo all count audience as among one of three to five components of music; the others generally include text, melody, rendition, and in the case of instrumental music, composition and accompaniment.[15] Although the lineage of these ideas is tenuous, the reciprocal and symbiotic relationship between performer and audience (including other performers) is deeply embedded in overlapping traditions of sacred and secular and has significant implications for our consideration of audition and of sound knowledge, as it is described by this volume's editor, Deborah Kapchan: "a non-discursive form of affective transmission resulting from acts of listening" (Kapchan, this volume).

In a recent visit to Jakarta, Dadi Darmadi, an anthropologist and professor at the Islamic National University (UIN, Universitas Islam Negri) and affiliate of the Center for the Study of Islam and Society (PPIM, Pusat Penilitian Islam dan Masharikat) recalled the formative power of Ibu Maria's voice when he was a young man and serious contestant in various recitation competitions. He clarified that even if people weren't studying with Maria Ulfah, her cassettes and didactic recordings permeated the market of eager reciters beginning in the 1980s. Her voice was in the air and in your ear, he remembered. Pak Dadi's remarks remind us that women who can be heard although not always seen have a long history in Islamic contexts and in other situations, where the appropriateness of women's public performing bodies may be problematic (see also Ergin 2014).

There is no question that virtuosity and excellence is cultivated, practiced, noticed, and rewarded among men and women, some of whom achieve star status; yet I suggest that mechanisms are in place that deemphasize the female reciter as superstar so that women may escape any accusations of being self-absorbed divas. In this way the women are always working for the good of the community. Just as Indonesian female reciters work in the business of religion and at the service of the state, women's voices elsewhere seem to serve similar nationalist projects. Amanda Weidman, for example, explicates the situation for female would-be divas of South Indian classical music in the early twentieth century (2008). Her study describes a process whereby women's voices were cast as "natural," thus excusing a new cohort of emergent professional singers—often invisible to the public, thanks in part to the recording industry—from any indulgent behavior in the physicality and emotionality of Indian singing. Notions of the "natural" female voice were conflated with ideas of God-given talent and the child virtuoso, further removing the female singer from the hard work and creative agency that are thought to accompany artistic work. These "politics of voice" aligned with the emergence of the Indian nation that, as in the case of Indonesia, harnessed the power and labor of women for the agendas of male statecraft (see also Suryakusuma 1996 on the Indonesian case, Mooallem 1999, and Rasmussen 2010, chap. 6). This new natural, meaningful female voice allowed respectable middle- and upper-class women to pursue music and deemphasized the role of the female singer, heretofore fulfilled by the *devadasi*, unmarried female devotees of the temple.

Alessandra Cucci's work with female *shikhat* (plural from the honorific term for female *sheikh*) of rural Morocco elucidates a scenario where women's voices are described as "embodying the countryside" (2012). To explain why a voice is said to "smell like the soil," she writes that singers are not valued for their individual talents:

> The voice of these *shikhat* is instead valued exactly because it is a marker and an expression of a collective identity, rather than for its individuality or for its power to express a singer's own identity. Its timbre, which is said to embody or perhaps *must* embody coarseness or roughness, allows the audience to be transported via the senses—hearing, smelling, tasting, and more importantly, touching—to the rocky soil on which it all began. (Cucci 2012, 18)

I suggest that these examples align with the Indonesian case, not because of similarities in voice qualities; in fact, the registers and timbres of Moroccan *shikhat,* South Indian classical singers, and Indonesian women who recite the Qur'an are all remarkably different, suggesting that there is much to pursue should we switch our focus from "ideologies of language to ideologies of voice" as Weidman proposes (2008, 136). Rather, the connection I hear is one where the power, intimacy, hard work, and individual accomplishment associated with women who sing is given license to operate within the constraints of patriarchal societies.

In channeling the Word of God through the human body, Qur'anic reciters—women or men—activate the Sufi objective of inner spirituality: the melding of the mundane and the sublime toward a personal experience of the Divine. As elsewhere in the Islamicate world, the Muslim soundscape in Indonesia is difficult to legislate because it both represents and activates the intersection of hearing, knowledge, piety, and power through individual and collective experience. Through a national competition system, however, banks of judges, ranking criteria, and a point system scientifically distill the experience of recitation into an objectively measurable act. The competition system is yet another uniquely Indonesian institution that invites and controls women's participation and for measured periods of time amplifies and channels the Islamic soundscape in all of its glorious variation.

An exercise in nationalism, the *Musabaqah Tilawatil al-Qur'an,* or MTQ, celebrates the diversity of Indonesia under the umbrella of Islamic unity and tolerance. The production of competitions at various regional and national levels is overseen by a department within the national Ministry of Religion, the Institute for the Development of Qur'anic Recitation (*Lembaga Pengembangan Tilawatil*

Qur'an, or LPTQ). As stipulated in the national planning guide, eighteen ongoing competitions take place during the weeklong festival. These include recitation by male and female adults, teenagers, children, and the blind; calligraphy; team quiz contests; team presentations combining recitation, translation, and interpretation; contests in the seven styles or dialects of reading; and memorization. The colorful and celebratory nature of the event is impressive, as is the fact that 50 percent of the contestants in all categories are female. Add to this parades, opening and closing ceremonies, speeches, and performances by any number of reciters at the ready, and music and dance groups who perform Islamic and regional arts, and the result is an impressive demonstration of the "festivalization of religion" (Rasmussen 2010, chap. 4).

With its attention to hierarchical judging and material reward, the state-sponsored competition may inadvertently control the inherently mystical aspect of internalizing and collectively experiencing God's word. In the context of competitions, the performance act is rigidly proscribed. It seems as though contestants—both male and female—are concentrating so hard on producing a flawless recitation that the technical aspects of their recitation overshadow any emotion. Furthermore, because they are being judged on *adat* (or proper behavior, including the way they are dressed, the way they enter and exit the stage, and the way they carry and place the Qur'an on its stand), a contestant will minimize any extraneous physical action or emotional display.

I submit that government patronage of religious festivals and competitions is a function of both tolerance and control of the Islamic soundscape and what it might represent. In the Indonesian Islamic context, the performance of language and music embodies not only the power of persuasion, but also the temptation of elation for all who produce and experience the sound. The festivalization of religion tempers this society teetering on the brink of religious ecstasy through national competitions with banks of judges, ranking criteria, a point system, prizes, and media hype. Here feeling, emotion, interiority, reception, and participation are erased from the board, and objective perfection is theoretically and practically privileged.

WOMEN, KNOWLEDGE, POWER

Since the early days of its introduction to the archipelago, the Arabic language, witnessed and apprehended through the aural and oral media, has represented and activated learning, knowledge, and power. When women and girls are present in the soundscape, their voices contribute to the acoustic colonization of space, whether they are seen or not. Competence in the language of their religion leads to knowledge and power in other social spheres. Doorn-Harder's work reveals the ways in which access to Qur'anic texts through both traditional education, often in the context of the *pesantren,* or Muslim boarding school, along with the modern methodology of *ijtihad,* new and reasoned interpretations of Qur'anic text, has enabled women to discourse substantively on the issues that affect the control of women's intellects and physical bodies—from access to education and the workplace to polygamy and rape (2006).[16] Doorn-Harder does not, however, address the door that is opened to ecstatic states, hearing as knowing, and extralinguistic communal and physical experience that may be facilitated by accessing religious texts.

Letting Arabic "live on the lips" of Muslims in the words of Graham (1987) allows Indonesians—whether they understand Arabic or not—to both feel the language and let others experience it. The roots of women's involvement not only in access to religious texts but also in their interpretation and their presentation as lectures, lessons, recitations, and artistic performance are long. The power and beauty of these texts when recited or alluded to in song, as well as the mystery surrounding their sound, both in their divine origin and human creation, ensures that the reception of such texts occurs on the cognitive level of the mind, the emotional level of the heart, and the spiritual level of the soul. That women in Indonesia are so prominent as reciters, particularly when compared their numbers elsewhere, may be a function of their "talent" for sounding the divine while being controlled by patriarchal institutions of society and state.

AFTERTHOUGHTS

My goal in this essay has been to give the reader a sense of what it was like for me to learn through listening and to test the parameters of learning by communicating through sound, as a woman and among both women and men. That my experience was noisy, "redolent with participatory discrepancies," loud, and musical should come across in my sound writing. I have also suggested some of the reasons why the voices of women and girls are a significant presence in the Jakarta soundscape. Hardly an exception, their voices have helped to define the culture of Islamic "noise," to use Attali's alternative to the sound-music continuum, in the country with more Muslims than any other in the world, in ways that are both aesthetically valued and politically salient. I have also questioned why, when generations of scholars of Islamic culture have insisted on the primacy of sound throughout the history and contemporary experience of the Muslim religion, we hobble ourselves with the singular medium of academic writing. Even as innovative as the sound writing in this volume is, are we not in part worshipping a false idol, the one that the academy has presented to us as the only one with value? In "The Splash of Icarus," the introduction to this volume, Kapchan tells us that while there are a few ways to write about music, ethnopoetics is the only sound writing that attempts to "evoke its SOUND on the page." Reviewing writing as a "recent technology," perhaps still in development, our colleague insists, "It is not writing that is a prison house per se, but our modes of perception, of listening and translation, that must be broken through" (Kapchan this volume). While I struggle to break through, I wonder if as scholars, we are all complicit in the hegemony of the written word, where the mistrust of aurality and orality and the prestige of literacy exclude sound knowledge for both capitalist and ideological reasons. After all, we have (once again) become more and more of an oral culture, fueled by bits and bites of hearsay and local knowledge, some of it viral, some of it crowd-sourced, all of it trending in one way or another. It is only within the last ten years or so, of my academic consciousness, that social fields have converged to bring on a serious conversation about forms of communication that might prove as effective, yet remain as prestigious, as the written word. Such considerations are often prefaced with serious doubts about the sustainability of academic publishing, combined with such revelations as "given the options afforded by digital media," or "unleashing the potential enabled by new (digital) technologies," as if it is our *technologies* that will enable us to understand things in new ways, ways that aren't written down. Yet if we look at our *listening* practices today compared with the revelations and forecasts of a variety of voices from the phonograph's naissance at the turn of the twentieth century, I see more similarities than remarkable developments.

Mark Katz's compilation of primary documents about the phonograph at the turn of the twentieth century, source readings from voices of the past, demonstrate the various receptions of and imaginative uses for the phonograph among men and women of the day (Katz, Taylor, and Grajeda 2012). Their writings demonstrate that listeners were excited about listening alone, rather than in social collectives; that the phonograph afforded the listener a variety of musical options with which to nurture and develop an eclectic ear; that listening in the home to *any* style of music could happen at *any* time of day or night; that a listener could now choose between radio and recorded music, or of course listen to the latest recordings on the radio; that speeches, poetry, literature, and famous voices could constitute “a well-stocked oratorical cellar” for the connoisseur of good words. Listening could happen communally in formal settings, as in a private salon, at parties to compliment socializing, and to facilitate dancing. Testimonies of the time divulge that people harbored a passion for recording themselves and listening to those recordings right away, a technology that was as possible with a cylinder recording as it is with a smartphone, and that making good (studio) recordings was really hard work. None of these voices from over a hundred years ago strike me as old-fashioned, naïve, or passé. In fact, these voices from a century ago seem to predict and recite many of the listening practices we sustain as central to our consumption of recorded sound today, all of them facilitated by the latest technologies. It makes one wonder, when we can see a century of consistency in our listening practices and our abilities to circulate sound in complement to writing, why sound knowledge, learning through listening and through participating in the practice of humanly organized sound, has not been able to achieve either the exchange value or the use value of the written word. It is clear that however open-minded our institutions, those of us who traffic in music and sound still occupy, as Martin Stokes writes, a “precarious periphery” where “music is still considered a domain of special, almost extra-social, autonomous experience” existing “somehow outside of the ‘real-life’ of which social reality is assumed to consist” (1994, 1). Perhaps, as Herschkind has illuminated, our hearts and minds are not open and ready to hear a more perfect message.

NOTES

1. A word about names and people is in order here. *Hajjah* is an honorific title that indicates that a woman has completed the pilgrimage to Mecca, the *Hajj*. *Ibu* means woman, mother, Mrs., and is generally used to preface women's names; for example, I am Ibu Anne. I am deeply indebted to Hajjah Ibu Maria Ulfah; her husband, Dr. Mukhtar Ikhsan; and her sons Rifki and Labib and Labib's wife, Novi, for hosting me in their home in August 2014. Ibu Maria became the most important consultant for my work on women's roles and the culture of Qur'anic recitation in Indonesia over the course of my fieldwork in the late 1990s and subsequent visits to Indonesia up to the present.

2. An analysis of the reciter's exposition of the *maqam Hijaz* would mention the intervallic relationships of the *maqam*, with its characteristic augmented second between the second and third pitches of the scale, along with at least three “accidental” notes employed by the reciter within a rather short phrase (the leading tone of the fourth degree, the sharped seventh degree of the scale, and the penultimate flatted fifth degree of the scale).

3. For a transcription into musical notation and a transliteration and translation of the text, please see Rasmussen 2001.

4. Absent from my academic description are the jokes, the cajoling, the flirtation between the teacher and his female students, and the instances of collective empathy, where the mistake of a good (or even not so good) effort was met with group laughter or a knowing sigh.

5. Here I combine references to both Charles Kiel's term *participatory discrepancies* and Tom Turino's discussion of participatory music making.

6. Arab language performance: the call to prayer, recitation, collective ritual and paraliturgical song, and religious popular musics are informed by several streams of Arab music, including trends both contemporary and ancient from the Arabian Peninsula, particularly Saudi Arabia and Yemen, and the more mainstream musical practices of Egypt and the Eastern Mediterranean, which began to be disseminated via mass media in the early twentieth century. See Rasmussen 2010 for a fuller account.

7. The lion's share of the work of ethnomusicologists and anthropologists of music is focused on courtly and regional Gamelan traditions and on popular music and theater. It is fair to say that all ethnomusicologists pass through Jakarata, but few chose the city as their research site—with the exception of Jeremy Wallach, whose book *Modern Noise, Fluid Genres: Popular Music in Indonesia 1997–2001* derives from the author's experience in Jakarta.

8. See Shiloah and Freemuse for accounts of both.

9. My book of 2010 includes a useful map of my research sites (xxii). Numerous cities and villages on the Island of Jakarta figure into my project, including the famous cities of Yogyakarta, Surakarta, Bandung, and Surabaya, but also less well-known places including Gontor, Lamongan, Jember, Madiun, and Jombong. Various invitations also took me to Sumatra (Indralaya in the south and Medan in the north), Palankaraya, Kalimantan, and Palu Sulewesi. I was fortunate to be a guest at nine different Islamic boarding schools, where the soundscape became both a consultant and informant.

10. Here I make reference to the 1970 French film by director François Truffaut.

11. On several occasions I gave lectures to Jakarta expats, in which I included an invitation to listen to the Islamic soundscape and particularly the call to prayer. On more than one occasion I was stopped in the grocery store or elsewhere by someone in the audience who confessed that they now listened to the call to prayer with completely different, and educated, ears. No longer did they just tune it out, rather, they tuned it in. I have received similar feedback from students who have traveled abroad and sent me an e-mail about hearing the call to prayer in situ after being introduced to it in one of our classes.

12. During my stay in Jakarta, in August 2014, I was asked to perform four times over the course of ten days (playing the *'ud* and singing). For one of those performances,

Maria Ulfah and I rehearsed two songs by Umm Kulthum, one that we had performed in the past and another that was new to me. I stayed up late, searched on YouTube, and rehearsed over and over with Ibu Maria, in the house and in the car, until I had learned the Umm Kulthum song composed by Ahmad Rami, *Ifrah ya Albi*, to her satisfaction.

13. I borrow this phrase from Scott Marcus, who describes his conversations with several neighborhood men who give the call to prayer in Cairo. He writes, "Giving the *azan* is, as a consequence a communal endeavor" (Marcus 2007, 9).

14. Used by permission of the author, Nina Ergin.

15. Kamal Husni, the son of Egyptian composer Dawud Husni and himself a *hafiz al-turath* (a custodian of the musical heritage frequently called upon as a teacher), articulated five major components of traditional song: text (*al-nass*), composition (*al-lahn*), rendition (*al-ada'*), instrumental accompaniment (*al-alat al-musahiba),* and audience (*al-jumhur).* Kamil al-Kula'i also indicated that "qualities of voice, proper delivery, and demeanor for the singer, and proper listening incumbent upon the audience" are essential to a good performance, and musicologist Mahmud al-Hifni cited listening (*al-istima'*) as one of the four pillars of the musical renaissance of early twentieth-century Cairo. It is thought that such concepts, particularly the notion of reception as key to performance, are consistent "through the ages" of the Arab world (Danielson 1997, 11).

16. Doorn-Harder studies the two large Muslim social organizations of Indonesia, Nahdlatul Ulama and Muhammadiyah and their women's organizations.

REFERENCES CITED

Attali, Jacques. *Noise: The Political Economy of Music.* Minneapolis: University of Minnesota Press, 1985.

Carlyle, Angus. *Autumn Leaves: Sound and the Environment in Artistic Practice.* Paris: Double Entendre, 2007.

Crow, Douglass Karim. "Sama': The Art of Listening in Islam." In *Maqam: Music of the Islamic World and Its Influences.* Edited by Robert Browning. New York: Alternative Museum, 1984, 30–33.

Cucci, Alessandra. "Embodying the Countryside in 'Aita Hasbawiya (Morocco)." *Yearbook for Traditional Music* 44 (2012): 107–28.

Danielson, Virginia. *The Voice of Egypt: Umm Kulthum, Arabic Song, and Egyptian Society in the Twentieth Century.* Chicago: University of Chicago Press and Cairo, Egypt: American University in Cairo Press, 1997.

Doorn-Harder, Pieternella van. *Women Shaping Islam: Reading the Qur'an in Indonesia.* Chicago: University of Illinois Press, 2006.

Ergin, Nina. "Ottoman Royal Women's Spaces: The Acoustic Dimension." *Journal of Women's History* 26, no. 1 (2014): 89–111.

Ergin, Nina. "The Soundscape of Sixteenth-Century Istanbul Mosques: Architecture and Qur'an Recital." *Journal of the Society of Architectural Historians* 67, no. 2 (2008): 204–21.

Ergin, Nina. "A Sound Status Among the Ottoman Elite: Architectural Patrons of 16th-Century Istanbul Mosques and Their Recitation Programs." In *Music, Sound, and Architecture in Islam,* edited by Michael Frishkopf and Federico Spinetti. Austin: University of Texas Press, forthcoming.

Erlmann, Veit. "But What of the Ethnographic Ear? Anthropology, Sound, and the Senses." In *Hearing Cultures: Essays on Sound, Listening and Modernity,* edited by Veit Erlman, 1–20. Oxford: Berg, 2004.

Feld, Steven. "Waterfalls of Song: An Acoustemology of Place Resounding in Bosavi, Papua New Guinea." In *Senses of Place,* edited by Steven Feld and Keith H. Basso, 91–136. Santa Fe, NM: School of American Research Press, 1996.

Freemuse (website). Accessed on March 1, 2016. www.freemuse.org.

Frishkopf, Michael. "Qur'anic Recitation and the Sonic Contestation of Islam in Contemporary Egypt." In *Music and the Play of Power in the Middle East, North Africa and Central Asia,* edited by Laudan Nooshin. London: Ashgate, 2009.

Gade, Anna M. *Perfection Makes Practice: Learning, Emotion, and the Recited Qur'an in Indonesia.* Honolulu: University of Hawai'i Press, 2004.

Graham, William A. *Beyond the Written Word: Oral Aspects of Scripture in the History of Religion.* Cambridge: Cambridge University Press, 1987.

Harnish, David, and Anne K. Rasmussen, eds. *Divine Inspirations: Music and Islam in Indonesia.* Oxford: Oxford University Press, 2011.

Hirschkind, Charles. "Hearing Modernity: Egypt, Islam, and the Pious Ear." In *Hearing Cultures: Essays on Sound, Listening and Modernity,* edited by Viet Erlmann, 131–52. Oxford: Berg, 2004.

Kapchan, Deborah. "Learning to Listen: The Sound of Sufism in France." *World of Music* 51, no. 2 (2009): 65–90.

Katz, Mark. "Sound Recording" and "Readings." In *Music, Sound, and Technology in America: A Documentary History of Early Phonograph, Cinema, and Radio,* edited by Mark Katz, Timothy Taylor, and Tony Grajeda, 11–28 and 29–136. Durham, NC: Duke University Press, 2012.

Keil, Charles. "The Theory of Participatory Discrepancies: A Progress Report." *Ethnomusicology (A Special Issue: Participatory Discrepancies)* 39, no. 1 (1995): 1–9.

Kelman, Ari Y. "Rethinking the Soundscape: A Critical Genealogy of a Key Term in Sound Studies." *Senses and Society* 6, no. 2 (2010): 212–34.

Lee, Tong Soon. "Technology and the Production of Ilamic Space: The Call to Prayer in Singapore." *Ethnomusicology* 43, no. 1 (1999): 86–100.

Madanipour, Ali. *Public and Private Spaces of the City.* London: Routledge, 2003.

Marcus, Scott L. *Music in Egypt: Experiencing Music, Expressing Culture.* New York: Oxford University Press, 2007.

Mauss, Marcel. "Les Techniques de Corps." *Journal de Psychologie* 32, nos. 3–4 (1934).

Mooallem, Minoo. "Transnationalism, Feminism, and Fundamentalism." In *Between Women and Nation: Nationalism, Transnational Feminisms, and the State.* Edited by Caren Kaplan, Norma Alarcón, and Minoo Moallem. Durham, NC: Duke University Press, 1999.

Nelson, Kristina. *The Art of Reciting the Qur'an.* Austin: University of Texas Press, 1985.

Olwage, Grant. "The Class and Colour of Tone: An Essay on the Social History of Vocal Timbre." *Ethnomusicology Forum* 13, no. 2 (2004): 203–26.

Ong, Walter J. *Orality and Literacy: The Technologizing of the Word.* 1982. Reprint, London: Routledge, 2000.

The Qur'an. Translated and with an introduction by Muhammad Zafrulla Khan. New York: Olive Branch Press, 1991.

Racy, Ali Jihad. *Making Music in the Arab World: The Culture and Artistry of Tarab.* Oxford: Oxford University Press, 2002.

Racy, Ali Jihad. "Creativity and Ambience: An Ecstatic Feedback Model from Arab Music." *World of Music* 33, no. 3 (1991): 7–28.

Rasmussen, Anne K. "The Qur'an in Daily Life: The Public Project of Musical Oratory." *Ethnomusicology* 45, no. 1 (2001): 30–57.

Rasmussen, Anne K. "The Arabic Aesthetic in Indonesian Islam." *World of Music* 47, no. 1 (2005): 65–90.

Rasmussen, Anne K. "The Juncture between Composition and Improvisation among Indonesian Reciters of the Qur'an." In *Musical Improvisation: Art, Education and Society,* edited by Bruno Nettl and Gabriel Solis, 72–98. Chicago: University of Illinois Press, 2009.

Rasmussen, Anne K. *Women's Voices, the Recited Qur'an, and Islamic Music in Indonesia.* Berkeley: University of California Press, 2010.

Schafer, R. Murray. *The Soundscape: Our Sonic Environment and the Tuning of the World.* Rochester, VT: Destiny Books, 1993.

Sells, Michael A. *Approaching the Qur'an: The Early Revelations.* Ashland, OR: White Cloud Press, 1999.

Shiloah, Amnon. "Music and Religion in Islam." *Acta Musicologica* 69, no. 2 (1997): 143–55.

Small, Christopher. *Musicking: The Meanings of Performing and Listening.* Middletown, CT: Wesleyan University Press, 1998.

Stokes, Martin. "Introduction: Ethnicity, Identity, and Music." In *Ethnicity Identity and Music: The Musical Construction of Place,* edited by Martin Stokes, 1–27. London: Berg, 1994.

Suryakusuma, Julia I. "The State and Sexuality in New Order Indonesia." In *Fantasizing the*

Feminine in Indonesia, edited by Laurie J. Sears, 93–119. Durham, NC: Duke University Press, 1996.

Turino, Thomas. *Music as Social Life: The Politics of Participation.* Chicago: University of Chicago Press, 2008.

Weidman, Amanda. "Stage Goddesses and Studio Divas in South India: On Agency and the Politics of Voice." In *Words, Worlds, and Materials Girls: Language, Gender, Globalization,* edited by Bonnie McElhinny, 131–55. Berlin, DE: Mouton De Gruyter, 2008.

KATHERINE JOHANNA HAGEDORN

9. "Where the Transcendent Breaks into Time"

Toward a Theology of Sound in Afro-Cuban Regla de Ochá

DANCING TOWARD DEATH: AN INTRODUCTION TO *BABALÚ AYÉ*

The helpless imposition of the body's angles: bent knees, sharp elbow, hunched shoulders, jutting chin. Eyes bulging and head rolling, the figure lurches from side to side, just about to topple: he is the picture of disease. Oddly, he is also smiling. This is how Cuban folkloric dancer Jesús Ortíz portrays Babalú Ayé, *oricha* (deity) of smallpox and healing: a diseased body dancing toward death.

Cuban anthropologist and Ochá priestess Natalia Bolívar Aróstegui describes the arrival of Babalú Ayé during a possession performance:

> When he arrives, he almost always looks sickly, twisted and bent over with gnarled hands. He limps and hobbles and feels so weak, and he almost falls over. His speech is muddy, and his nose is full of mucous. His movements recall those of a feverish sick person. Sometimes he acts as though he were trying to scare away the flies and other insects that are alighting and perching on his sores. He also thrusts the *já* [brush broom] into the air, a gesture of cleaning, sweeping away bad things. (Bolívar-Aróstegui 1994, 259–260, author's translation)

Anthropologist Anthony Buckley describes the Yoruba antecedent of this Cuban *oricha* as "the god of smallpox, a ferocious and vindictive god who not only causes smallpox, but who is also responsible for a form of madness" (Buckley 1985, 187). Epidemiologist Abbas Behbehani writes that efforts to eradicate smallpox in Nigeria and in Benin were met with suspicion because "the Yorubas worshipped the smallpox god Sopona who was believed to be very stubborn and unappeasable" (Behbehani 1983, 494). Africanist Robert Farris Thompson notes that Babalú Ayé is known as the "wrath of God" in West Africa and in its diaspora (Thompson 1993, 217).

Perhaps it is not surprising, then, that *oricha* worshippers in Africa and the diaspora do not call this deity by his "real" name (a name that evokes hot earth, according to Buckley), for fear of invoking the infectious diseases he spreads. Instead, they refer to him by a variety of flattering pseudonyms that remind me of the many names people use for the Judeo-Christian God. He is referred to as Oba (the king), Obalùayé (king of the world), Olùayé (lord of the world), Olóde (owner of the outside), and in Cuba, Babalú Ayé (Father, lord of the world) (Buckley 1985, 189), and more commonly, San Lázaro. It is significant that none of these names touches on the pain and havoc wreaked by epidemic diseases such as smallpox. This is a powerful instance of euphemism, from the Greek *euphemia* ("good speech"); naming the deity is tantamount to summoning his horrors, so the speaker uses "good speech" instead.

It is within this context of good speech that I make the claim that the performance practices dedicated to this multinamed deity in Cuba comprise a series of reinforced utterances that both invoke Babalú Ayé/San Lázaro and allow his worshippers to know him in a sounded, yet largely nonsemantic, way. Through the simultaneous performance of dedicated drummed patterns, sung invocations, danced rhythms, and other bodily gestures, and the remembrance of the deity's many *patakíes*—or sacred narratives—Babalú Ayé/San Lázaro is both known and praised. Reinforced utterances are thus a kind of sounded inscription that both call forth and appease this great deity. The combination of these utterances conveys theological meaning quickly and palpably. I argue that these instances (and they are not all that common within the liturgy of Ochá) not only crystallize the relationship between the *orichas* and the rhythmic gestures that represent them, but convey essential theological knowledge about specific *orichas* without requiring specialized semantic knowledge.

BABALÚ AYÉ AND THE DISRUPTION OF BEAUTY

My godfather created a blog on Babalú Ayé a couple of years ago called "Baba Who? Babalú!" Every few weeks he would post a thought—a "bean" as he called it, after one of Babalú Ayé's ritual foods, speckled beans—about the significance of Babalú Ayé in our lives. In October 2010 he posted a picture of a little child with a great big *moco* (glob of mucous) hanging from his nose. This is classic Babalú, I know—the *mocos* hanging from the *naríz,* the *catarro* that produces lots of *flema*—but still, I was struck by the contrast between the toddler's cuteness and that swinging stalactite. This disrupted my sense of the little one's impermeable beauty, that soft light that radiates from so many toddlers. And it made me contemplate the disruption of beauty caused by infectious diseases, particularly those that cause eruptions on the skin. The pockmarks on smooth skin tell the history of the disease.

In Cuban Regla de Ochá, Babalú Ayé/San Lázaro has a broad profile. He not only spreads disease, he offers the possibility of a cure; and he has been merged with the biblical Lazarus, who is crippled and poor, and with the Jesus who grants the prayers of the desperate for health and healing. Babalú Ayé/San Lázaro does not communicate the same unmitigated wrath among Cuban worshippers as he does among West African worshippers. Perhaps it is his association with the beleaguered and benevolent Catholic San Lázaro in Cuba, perhaps it is his solid position in Cuban popular culture (who can forget Ricky Ricardo's nightly invocation of "Babalú" as he played the bongó? or Miguelito Valdés's rendition of Margarita Lecuona's song "Babalú," which became a nightclub standard during the 1940s?), or perhaps it is the West's almost-religious belief in pharmaceuticals, but Babalú Ayé/San Lázaro is both reviled and revered in Cuba as a healer. Nonetheless, he remains deeply associated with human suffering of all kinds and is widely venerated throughout the year, but especially on his festival days, December 16 and 17.

On these festival days, worshippers of San Lázaro/Babalú Ayé dress up as the deity—wearing sackcloth or burlap, torn clothing, bandages on their limbs—thus embodying infirmity, poverty, and physical suffering. If they are able, these adherents make a pilgrimage to the temple of San Lázaro/Babalú Ayé in Santiago de las Vegas, about seventeen kilometers outside the city center of Havana, taking the Avenida Rancho Boyeros, and about one kilometer from the AIDS sanatorium. The pilgrims make a *promesa,* a promise to endure physical suffering during his feast days in exchange for their own health or that of a loved one. Publicly performing suffering, they attach bricks or other heavy objects to their feet as they walk, scrape along on their backs, walk on their knees, or drag themselves on their torsos—an embodiment of the suffering they want San Lázaro/Babalú

Ayé to take from them. Those believers who make this hardship-laden journey are comprised of all combinations of Christians, *oricha* worshippers, and practitioners of other religions. Along the pilgrimage, people sing songs in honor of San Lázaro/Babalú Ayé, ranging from the *oricha* praise song "Mole Yansa" to the spiritist song "Yo saludo to' los santos, en el nombre Babalú. Ekua, Ekua, Babalú Ayé, Ekua," to the Catholic praise song "Alabaré a mi señor, alabaré a mi señor, alabaré a mi señor," to the familiar cry "Viva San Lázaro!" (Hagedorn 2002). They keep time with bricks, hands, and stones all the while, never missing a beat, while their keepers (friends, family, companions) walk ahead, sweeping their path clean with palm fronds. Keeping time helps them to keep moving, and their movement signals life. Disrupting the rhythm would mean what—a stumble? another injury? a step closer to the end of all movement? Through these gestural and vocal utterances dedicated to San Lázaro/Babalú Ayé, the pilgrims reinforce not only their aliveness, but their will to live.

WHEN IS AIDS ZERO DAY?[1]

Now that smallpox is no longer considered a threat in Cuba, *oricha* worshippers have come to associate Babalú Ayé with HIV/AIDS and its various stages of devastation. In particular, the skin lesions caused by the advanced stages of the disease are a stark reminder to friends and families of the afflicted that a pilgrimage to Rincón is necessary. The first cases of the HIV/AIDS virus were reported in the early 1980s, on the heels of the eradication of smallpox in the late 1970s. The eradication of the smallpox virus had taken a concerted, enduring, global effort, lasting ten years. Behbehani (1983) writes that there were three phases to the ten-year program for the global eradication of smallpox. During phase one (1967–1972), eradication was achieved in South America, Indonesia, and most of the African countries. During phase two (1973–1975), smallpox was eradicated from the Indian subcontinent. During phase three (1975–1977), smallpox was eradicated from the Horn of Africa. "The last case of naturally occurring smallpox in the world occurred in October 1977, in Somalia. The young man (a hospital cook) recovered uneventfully, and without transmitting the disease to anyone else" (Behbehani 1983, 499–500). The director general of the World Health Organization declared that October 26, 1979, was "Smallpox Zero Day" (Behbehani 1983, 498). With HIV/AIDS, the global response has been slower, piecemeal, "pockmarked," one might say. According to Hoffman (2004), Cuba's HIV/AIDS prevention program is one of the most successful in the world.

Even before the first case of HIV appeared in Cuba in 1986, the Cuban Ministry of Health took preventive measures, such as enacting Decree-Law 54, in April 1982, which mandated "the isolation of individuals suspected of suffering from a communicable disease, as well as the suspension or limitation of those individuals' activities" (Hoffman 2004), and destroying all foreign-derived blood products in 1983. Soon afterward, the Cuban Ministry of Health created the AIDS sanatorium in Santiago de las Vegas and quarantined permanently all HIV-positive Cubans between 1986 and 1994. After 1994, the quarantine was reduced to eight weeks. Hoffman (2004) states that .05 percent of the sexually active Cuban population has been infected with HIV/AIDS; compare this with a corresponding figure of infection rate of 0.3 percent in the United States. One wonders whether Cuba's long familiarity with Babalú Ayé and his scourge of smallpox helped persuade Cuban leaders to take the threat of HIV/AIDS seriously.

NAMING AND KNOWING

The naming of Babalú Ayé/San Lázaro points to a larger dynamic between naming and knowing in the study of *oricha* worship in the Americas. Until 2005 I used the term *Santería* in my research, primarily because the people with whom I studied and worked in Cuba referred to the religion in this way. Beginning at the end of the twentieth century, there has been a shift among scholars and practitioners toward calling this religious tradition Regla de Ochá. Of course, both the utterer and the listener construct the meaning of a term, and processes of constructing meaning are fluid and dynamic, responsive to particular historical contexts and individual requirements. For many practitioners of this religion, the term *Regla de Ochá* is an "insider's" term, partially because it refers to *orichas* (or deities) in its very name (*ochá* being another name for *oricha*). *Ochá* was the term used by the faithful to refer to their religion during the first half of the twentieth century, though many practitioners continue to refer to their deities as *santos*. *Santería,* which means "way of the saints," is a clear reference to the Catholic hagiographical overlay imposed on the West African polytheistic traditions that overlapped and interleaved during the almost four centuries of Cuba's participation in the Atlantic slave trade.

While Regla de Ochá points to the African roots of the people who worship *orichas,* Santería points to the Catholic faith of the slave owners who tried to eradicate *oricha* worship, especially during the nineteenth and twentieth centuries. *Oricha* worshippers from Nigeria, Benin, Togo, Ghana, and Cameroon, as well as polytheistic practitioners from central sub-Saharan Africa, were enslaved and forcibly landed in Cuba from the late fifteenth to the late nineteenth centuries. Cuba's participation in the Atlantic slave trade finally ended in 1886, and because most of the Africans who were brought to western Cuba during the nineteenth century came from southwestern Nigeria, it is the Yoruba speakers of Nigeria—many of them *oricha* worshippers—who have provided the outermost visual and aural layers of Cuba's West African influence. To persist in calling this religious tradition Santería would be to offer up what historian Edward Linenthal (2006) has called the "indigestible narratives" of contested histories. To jump to Regla de Ochá as a term of currency without interrogating it would be to engage in what Linenthal (2009) has termed "therapeutic history," erasing from language the painful realities of enslaved people in Cuba. The traditional form of greeting between junior and elder Ochá initiates is for the junior to request "Bendición," and for the elder to reply "Santo"—a clear echo of a Catholic practice, which conveys the exchange "May I have your blessing?" and "I give you my blessing." In fact, each *oricha* has at least one Catholic associate, which, in practice, begins to look less like historical imperialism and more like functionalist syncretism. There is room for translation and for various levels of religious engagement.

One of the primary performance practices of Regla de Ochá is the *tambor,* also known as the *toque de santo. Tambor* literally means "drum"; and in the context of Cuban Ochá, it refers not only to the instrument itself, but to everything that happens during a drumming ceremony. In Ochá, the doubleheaded, hourglass-shaped membranophones known as *batá* drums are the main instruments used during this ceremony. *Toque de santo* could be translated literally as "touch of the saint" and references the verb *tocar,* which means to touch or to play (the emphasis here is on the touching necessary to play musical instruments, especially drums). The word *toque* also evokes specific rhythmic patterns for particular *orichas.*

Because the main purpose of an Ochá drumming ceremony is to communicate with the *orichas* (also known as *santos*), a "touch of the saint" is always welcome. The drumming, singing, and dancing featured in a *tambor* are meant to summon the *orichas* to earth, so that these deities may interact with humans—providing counsel, revelations, and occasionally gossip. Rebukes, jokes, and other forms of ribald behavior are also manifested by *orichas* during *tambores,* depending on which *oricha* arrives. The arrival of an *oricha* during a drumming ceremony is usually manifested by a possession performance; that is, an adherent's physical and psychic self is temporarily inhabited by a divine entity. Each *oricha* owns certain songs, rhythmic patterns, and dance movements, and it is those gestures that are performed to invoke (and evoke) particular *orichas.*

THE POWER OF THE UTTERANCE

I am interested in how particular drum rhythms, songs, and dances performed by devotees of Regla de Ochá convey theological knowledge, in primarily non-semantic ways, through what I am calling "reinforced utterances." Within the context of folklore, utterances typically refer to performed language and imply semantic knowledge of the words themselves, which knowledge is compounded or emphasized by the way in which the words are "performed"—that is, the emotional effect or intent that informs the performance. In some cases, folklorists have included physical gestures within the realm of utterances, such as the gestured utterances of American Sign Language, which still implies semantic knowledge in that those gestures are understood to be representations of words and phrases. Other folklorists and psychologists have pinpointed gesture itself as a mode of communication, which may or may not rely on semantic knowledge (see, for example Adam Kendon's [2004] work on action and utterance, as well as Allanbrook's [1983] work on musical gesture and character development in Mozart).

I am expanding the definition of "utterances" to include not only performed words (sung or chanted), but percussed sound and danced gesture, as well as a rhythmic superstructure (the *clave*), which is always part of the performers' frame of reference. I include these expressive media within the realm of "utterance" because all of them function together to create a powerful performance complex within the context of an Ochá *tambor* aimed at communicating with the *orichas.* For participants in Ochá, this combination of performative events is not only powerful, it is "normal." Within the context of a *tambor,* all of these utterances produce a whole greater than the sum of its parts, a sonic and gestural outreach that is palpable in its evocation.

Performed speech is perhaps the most familiar of these categories, so I won't belabor it. Percussed sound is less often categorized as an utterance, and I include it for several reasons. First, the *batá* drums on which the Ochá rhythms are performed "speak" Lucumí, the Afro-Cuban liturgical language prevalent in Ochá ceremonies (Villepastour 2010). For example, a combined open-stroke/closed-stroke drummed phrase played on the larger head of the lead *batá* drum, *iyá,* is heard as "Di de, Di de, Di de," which is commonly understood to be Lucumí for "arise" or "get up" from the *moforibale* position, for which one lies on the floor to salute the *orichas*. Another reason to include *batá* drumming and other percussed sound within the concept of utterance is that these particular forms of sound are so closely associated with *oricha* worship at a *tambor*. The playing of consecrated *batá* drums is considered essential to the success of a *tambor* (the meaning of which, again, refers not only to "drum," but to everything that happens in this drumming ceremony). The *clave*, sometimes articulated and sometimes simply understood, functions as a percussed utterance in that it provides a rhythmic structure for other utterances at any given moment. I am including danced or otherwise physical gestures within this larger realm of utterance because, in many cases, the embodied movement emphasizes a sung syllable or a percussed phrase. Simply put, percussed sound reinforces vocalized sound, and danced gestures reinforce both the percussed and the vocalized phrase. The combination of these utterances conveys theological meaning quickly and palpably. The phrase "reinforced utterance" is used frequently in the scholarly literature on early language acquisition among young children. The phrase is also applicable here: in the same way that reinforced linguistic utterances help children create and retain semantic and syntactic meaning, the simultaneous performance of these gestural cues encourages practitioners to construct and remember theological knowledge.

DOES LIFE WITH THIS (G)OD NOT ENTAIL ANXIETY?

Yet a further gloss on "utterance" comes from exegetical analyses of the Old Testament, the Jewish Bible. Walter Brueggemann's classic text *Theology of the Old Testament* (1997) argues persuasively that it is the utterance that most fully characterizes YHWH (Yahweh):

> For the Old Testament faith, the utterance is everything. The utterance leads to the reality, the reality of God that relies on the reliability of the utterance. Presumably other utterances could have been accepted as true, but these particular utterances are the ones that have been preserved, trusted, treasured, and given to us . . . [A] student of Old Testament theology must pay close attention to the shape, character, and details of the utterance, for it is in, with, and under the utterance that we have the God of Israel, and nowhere else. (Brueggemann 1997, 122)

I invoke a biblical scholar deliberately here, to make clear my own positionality and that of my topic: *orichas* are deities, and as the humans who believe in them interact (willingly or not) with humans who believe in other deities, the similarities and differences between deities become both clear and blurry. In some contexts, Babalú Ayé begins to sound like the wrathful God of the Old Testament—"My God is an angry God." In some contexts, Babalú Ayé begins to sound like Jesus—"Come forth, my children, and I will heal you." If Babalú Ayé encompasses both of those extremes and everything in between, he is an unpredictable deity, requiring both vigilance and constancy on the part of his acolytes.

Brueggemann argues that the many utterances used to evoke Yahweh—as gardener, potter, shepherd, mother; as judge, warrior, king, father—indicate precisely that unpredictability, that Yahweh possesses a "vast repertoire of possible responses" (1997, 282), causing Israel to regard Yahweh with both awe and anxiety:

> While certain tendencies, propensities, and inclinations have some stability, being more or less constant, Israel and Israel's rhetoricians never know beforehand what will eventuate in the life of Yahweh. Thus it is not known whether: the judge will sentence or pardon, the warrior will fight for or against, the king will banish or invite to the table, the potter will work attentively or smash, the gardener will cultivate and protect or pluck up, the shepherd will lead and feed or judge between sheep and sheep, the doctor will heal or pronounce the patient terminally ill. . . . Does life with this God not entail anxiety? (Brueggemann 1997, 282)

THE LIFE AND DEATH (AND LIFE) OF BABALÚ AYÉ

Oggun: Un Eterno Presente (1990) is a film directed by Cuban filmmaker Gloria Rolando, which features a staged *tambor*. The singers and dancers in the film are members of Cuba's National Folkloric Ensemble (*El Conjunto Folklórico Nacional de Cuba*). One of the many interesting aspects of this performance of a *tambor* is that most of the musicians and dancers are not only members of this professional folkloric group, but they are also familiar with Ochá *tambores*, either from their own involvement as religious practitioners, or from living in neighborhoods where *tambores* occur several times a month. As a result, the performance not only sounds good, it looks and sounds like a religious drumming ceremony. Another component that makes this staged *tambor* seem as if it is happening in a religious context is that one of the performers appears to become possessed by an *oricha*. The staged possession performance shows how the singing, drumming, and dancing together form a critical mass of evocative energy aimed at bringing an *oricha* to earth. In this case, the *oricha* who comes to earth is Ogún, a warrior deity. Ogún lives in the forest and works at the iron forge with his anvil. He is also deeply associated with the hundreds of thousands of African slaves who were forced to work in Cuba's brutal sugar plantation industry (*ingenios*) during the eighteenth and nineteenth centuries. The dance gestures that represent him incorporate both the motions of cutting sugarcane and striking the forge with an anvil, all the while maintaining a syncopated clave rhythm with the feet. Many of the rhythms played in honor of Ogún are in duple meter, specifically 4/4 time, governed by a rhythmic structure known as "clave guaguancó" (dotted eighth, quarter, dotted eighth, eighth, quarter, with no rests; or "ka . . ka . . . ka . . ka . ka . . ." where "." is a rest). Ogún's possession performance gains meaning because we know something of his origins and his character. In this way, the sacred narrative (*patakí*) of an *oricha* acts as a resonating chamber for the elements of a possession performance.

Babalú Ayé/San Lázaro, like Ogún, has generated a plethora of origin stories within the Afro-Cuban sacred narratives known as *patakíes*. Each *oricha* has at least several *patakíes* that convey that deity's essential character, and Babalú Ayé's *patakíes* are particularly trenchant because they deal with lack of impulse control, humiliation, and rage. In the same way that we understand Ogún's possession performance more deeply because we were privy to his *patakíes*, so do Babalú Ayé's *patakíes* enlighten his sacred utterances.

One often told narrative begins with Babalú Ayé and the other *orichas* seated at the foot of Olodumare, the Supreme Being, asking for what they desire most. When it is Babalú's turn to make his request, he asks permission to have sex with each and every woman in the world. Olodumare accedes (the Spanish translation of the phrase uttered by Olodumare is: "Concedido"), but he attaches one condition: Babalú Ayé must not have sex on Thursdays. (Among Cuban Ochá priests, Thursday is the traditional day to pray to Babalú Ayé.) Babalú is able to honor this arrangement for one week, but then falls in love with a woman on a Thursday morning and has sex with her that evening. Olodumare's punishment is swift: Babalú is immediately afflicted with bleeding, oozing sores all over his body, and is condemned to wander the earth a homeless, suffering cripple (García Cortez 1980; Arce Burguera and Castro 1999).

Another popular Cuban *patakí* begins with all the *orichas* at a dance, drinking alcoholic beverages and making merry. The music is hot, and all the *orichas* are dancing except Babalú Ayé. Unbeknownst to his fellow deities, Babalú has a wooden leg; and he does not want his co-*orichas* to know that he is a cripple, even though they have seen him with his wooden staff. Conjuring up scenes of humiliating high school dances, the drunken *orichas* taunt and goad Babalú into dancing, at which point he falls down and loses his wooden leg. The other *orichas* start laughing at him, and no one helps Babalú regain his balance. Babalú becomes so infuriated that he begins hitting the other *orichas* with his staff, and as soon as his staff touches them, their skin erupts in painful and bleeding boils and blisters. (Think *Carrie* or any number of teenage horror/revenge flicks.) The *orichas* are terrified and flee the dance, leaving Babalú seething with fury. Olodumare hears about the incident and punishes Babalú by making him wander the world alone, crippled and friendless (García Cortez 1980; Ellis 1894; Buckley 1985).

Both of these narratives lead to various resolutions, which I will outline here. In one *pataki,* Babalú Ayé becomes so sick that he dies, and even his humiliated and abandoned wife (Ochún, in this version) feels sorry for him. She begs Olodumare to bring Babalú Ayé back to life, and with some hesitation, he does. Babalú Ayé then spends the rest of his life wandering the earth, spreading the scourge (smallpox, AIDS, leprosy, skin cancers, or any other infectious and epidemic disease especially associated with pervasive and long-lasting skin sores), wiping out entire communities (García Cortez 1980; González Wippler 1985).

In another story, Eleguá takes pity on Babalú Ayé and brings him to Orúnmila, the *oricha* of divination, for help. In this narrative, Orúnmila tells Babalú Ayé that if he goes to the land of Nupe, he will be king. Sure enough, as soon as Babalú Ayé arrives in Nupe, Olodumare sends down an effluvium of epic proportions, washing Babalú Ayé's wounds as well as all traces of the smallpox virus that caused them. The people of Nupe are impressed with his healing powers and crown him king (García Cortez 1980; Buckley 1985).

In yet another story, Babalú Ayé is cast out of his town by his own family, friends, and neighbors because he has smallpox; and so he wanders far from home, where he meets an *oricha* (Changó), who befriends him and gives him this advice: "Go to the land of the Nupe, where they are suffering the scourge. Heal them, and they will make you their king. All will be forgiven." Babalú Ayé takes Changó's advice and is able to return to his homeland a king (Arce Burguera and Castro 1999; Ellis 1894).

DÍA DEL MEDIO WITH BABALÚ

I remember sitting under my altar on the middle day of my *asiento.* This is the day when other *iyawos,* family, friends, and ritual relatives come by to celebrate the halfway point in the weeklong initiation process of Ochá. In the afternoon only a few people came by, and one was a recently made a child of Babalú Ayé. He came by himself. He was thin, perhaps twenty-five or thirty years old, with a tanned and slightly pockmarked face, wide cheekbones, and a thin-lipped mouth. He sat on the bench across from the *trono del asiento* and stared at me without speaking. I greeted him too enthusiastically, and then proceeded to babble into the silence. "Cómo estás? Cuanto tiempo tú tienes en santo? Yo no dormí muy bien anoche, por eso me dieron una almohada. Ahora estoy más cómoda. Te dieron una almohada? La mía tiene flores en el fondo." And on and on. The godchild of Babalú Ayé did not respond to my questions, nor did he make gestures of any kind. He stared at me and breathed quietly. And then he left.

In an iconic song for Babalú Ayé, the vocalized phrase "Mole yansa, mole ya . . . ba ke ba ke ba ke" is meant to represent the crippled, leprous, yet still dancing Babalú Ayé, and is reinforced and emphasized in the asymmetrical yet compelling rhythmic phrases (specifically on *iyá* and *itótele*), and also in the dance, in which the dancer steps lopsidedly on the "ba" of "ba ke"—dancing with a wooden leg, or with crutches, or with gnarled, hobbled limbs.

Another percussed utterance that informs musicians at a *tambor,* but which is not always articulated, is the organizing rhythmic principle of the clave. In most of Babalú Ayé's songs, the organizing rhythmic principle is a 12/8 clave, sometimes called *clave columbia* or *clave palo* in Cuba. It is derived from a ubiquitous sub-Saharan African bell pattern (quarter quarter eighth quarter quarter quarter eighth, with no rests; or "ka . ka . ka ka . ka . ka . ka," where "." is a rest). The clave orients all the other components of the performance complex, guiding dancers, singers, and drummers toward a musically consistent invocation.

The dynamic combination of singing, dancing, and drumming during a *tambor* is essential to *oricha* possession performance. The lead singer sings praise songs; a spontaneous chorus responds, which catalyzes drummers to play particular rhythms. The lead drum (*iyá*) plays a particular call for a specific *oricha,* which elicits the "correct responses" from the supporting *itótele* and *okónkolo* drums; dancers dance the "correct steps"—that is, embodying and reinforcing the rhythmic gestures of the drummers. The lead drummer then improvises, responding to the dancer's needs—that is, whether the person is on the verge of becoming possessed and needs to be pushed over the edge—and also improvises based on the "life" of the vocalized and percussed sound itself, shaping the intensity and the experience of the *tambor.*

A compelling connection exists between the power of words (chanted or sung utterances), drummed liturgy (percussed utterances), danced liturgy (danced utterances), and theological "truths." They happen simultaneously, and that simultaneity makes them that much more powerful. This idea is similar to Judith Becker's (1981) idea of the correlation between coincidences and nonarbitrary iconicity in Javanese gamelan. Becker argues that the coincidences of struck gongs in gamelan music are not only considered powerful, but also are valued as "beautiful sounds." Cubans might not characterize analogous coincidences in Afro-Cuban religious music as "beautiful," but they certainly understand them as powerful, in a particularly theological way. What's interesting here to me is that these coincidences or "reinforced utterances" do not happen regularly in Ochá performances. They do happen sometimes, with certain *orichas;* and from my research thus far, it seems that the *orichas* who are most often represented by this panoply of simultaneous utterances deal with death (and, one could say, "deal death")—Babalú Ayé, Oyá, and Ogún, for example. Indeed, they sometimes appear in one another's praise songs (Yansa is a recognized praise name for Oyá, and Mole, heard in the most emblematic of Babalú Ayé's praise songs, is often translated as "rainbow," another symbol of Oyá, mistress of whirlwinds and guardian of the cemetery). The phrase "*Bariba ogue de ma*" appears in one of Oyá's songs, according to Judith Gleason, and is translated to mean "searing medicine is on the way." When one considers "searing," one thinks of a sharply painful and burning sensation on the skin—Babalú's territory.

The *orichas* who are the most unpredictable and also powerful seem to "own" more of these reinforced utterances than other *orichas.* It is as if the "coincidence" of those utterances both reminds practitioners and players of the deity's power, and also brings that deity to earth (captures the essence?) for the duration of the "reinforced utterance." The theological knowledge of that deity—Babalú Ayé, *oricha* of healing and of smallpox (you can be healed, or you can die of an infectious disease)—is embodied in those reinforced utterances: an evocation and a reminder, a blessing and a curse.

These reinforced utterances—rhythmic patterns, sung prayers, and danced evocations—have become more defined in the years since the 1959 Cuban Revolution, primarily because of the *grupos folklóricos* that were founded in the 1960s and 1970s, many of which specialized in the "songs and dances of Santería." The standardization of repertoire, the theatricalization of the religious performance, and the externalization of the target audience (from religious practitioners, "insiders," to nonpractitioners and tourists, "outsiders") not only encouraged the creation of reinforced utterances, but made them more powerful as theological signifiers because these gestures had to convey quickly and in a kind of sonic shorthand the most essential information about the life-and-death (death-dealing) *orichas* to people with differing levels of familiarity with Ochá substance and practice.

The meaning of the utterance transforms as it is reinforced, which is essential for an audience that is not fully competent in either the Lucumí language, the drummed liturgy, or danced invocations of the divine. By itself, the sung phrase "*ba ke ba ke ba ke*" might not evoke much to those who don't understand Lucumí, and by themselves, the drummed patterns of that rhythmic phrase would not necessarily cue the listener to "expect" Babalú Ayé. It is the combination of these utterances, percussed and sung, with a dance step in which the feet stomp the same rhythmic phrase that makes a compelling case for Babalú Ayé. The heavy steps threaten to knock the dancer off balance, disrupting the flow of movement; and the asymmetry of the rhythm mimics the limp of a cripple.

In his book *Between Heaven and Earth: The Religious Worlds People Make and the Scholars Who Study Them* (2005), religious studies scholar Robert Orsi tells of a pious Catholic who sees the Virgin Mary in the Irish town of Knock, and thereafter refers to Knock as "the place where the transcendent broke into time." For Ochá worshippers, Babalú Ayé and the other life-and-death *orichas* always break into time, disorienting us, disrupting us. The murdering healer shows us the consequences of overindulgence, forcing us to pay attention as he wields his powerful staff, delivering blows of sacred and profane knowledge with each divine utterance.

NOTE

1. Each region, each demographic, has its neatly bounded response. June 8 has been declared Caribbean American HIV/AIDS Awareness Day. June 27 is National HIV Testing Day. September 18 is National HIV/AIDS and Aging Awareness Day. National Women and Girls HIV/AIDS Awareness Day is March 10. September 27 is National Gay Men's HIV/AIDS Awareness Day. National Black HIV/AIDS Awareness Day is February 7. March 20 is National Native HIV/AIDS Awareness Day. National Asian and Pacific Islander HIV/

AIDS Awareness Day is May 19. October 15 is National Latino AIDS Awareness Day. HIV Vaccine Awareness is May 18. The UN World AIDS Day is December 1.

REFERENCES

Allanbrook, Wye Jamison. *Rhythmic Gesture in Mozart: Le Nozze di Figaro and Don Giovanni.* Chicago: University of Chicago Press, 1983.

Altmann, Thomas. *Cantos Lucumí a los Orichas.* 3rd ed. Brooklyn, NY: Descarga, 1998.

Amira, John, and Steven Cornelius. *The Music of Santería: Traditional Rhythms of the Batá Drums.* Tempe, AZ: White Cliffs Media, 1991.

Arce Burguera, Arisel, and Armando Ferrer Castro. *El Mundo de Los Orichas.* Havana: Ediciones Union (UNEAC), 1999.

Baldwin, James. *Notes of a Native Son.* 1955. Reprint, New York: Beacon Press, 1984.

Becker, Judith, and Alton Becker. "A Music Icon: Power and Meaning in Javanese Gamelan Music." In *The Sign in Music and Literature,* edited by Wendy Steiner, 203–15. Austin: University of Texas Press, 1981.

Behbehani, Abbas M. "The Smallpox Story: Life and Death of an Old Disease." *Microbiological Reviews* 47, no. 4 (1983): 455–509.

Bolívar Aróstegui, Natalia. *Los Orishas en Cuba.* Havana: PM Ediciones, 1994.

Brown, David H. *Santería Enthroned: Art, Ritual and Innovation in an Afro-Cuban Religion.* Chicago: University of Chicago Press, 2003.

Browning, Barbara. *Infectious Rhythms: Metaphors of Contagion and the Spread of African Culture.* New York: Routledge, 1998.

Brueggemann, Walter. *Theology of the Old Testament: Testimony, Dispute, Advocacy.* Minneapolis: Fortress Press, 1997.

Buckley, Anthony D. "The God of Smallpox: Aspects of Yoruba Religious Knowledge." *Africa: Journal of the International African Institute* 55, no. 2 (1985): 187–200.

Cabrera, Lydia. *Anagó: Vocabulario Lucumí.* Miami: Ediciones Universal, 1986.

Drewal, Henry John, and John Mason, eds. *Beads, Body, and Soul: Art and Light in the Yorùbá Universe.* Los Angeles: University of California, Los Angeles, Fowler Museum of Cultural History, 1998.

Ellis, A. B. *The Yoruba-Speaking Peoples of the Slave Coast of West Africa: Their Religion, Manners, Customs, Laws, Language, etc.* London: Chapman and Hall, 1894.

García-Cortez, Julio. *Patakí: Leyendas y Misterios de los Orichas Africanos.* Miami: Ediciones Universal, 1980.

Gleason, Judith. *Oya: In Praise of an African Goddess.* 1987. Reprint, New York: HarperCollins, 1992.

González Wippler, Migene. *Tales of the Orichas.* New York: Original Publications, 1985.

Hagedorn, Katherine. *Divine Utterances: The Performance of Afro-Cuban Santería.* Washington, DC: Smithsonian Institution Press, 2001.

———. "Long Day's Journey to Rincón: From Suffering to Resistance in the Procession of San Lázaro/Babalú Ayé." *British Journal of Ethnomusicology* 11, no. 1 (2002): 43–69.

Hoffman, Sarah. "HIV/AIDS in Cuba: A Model for Care or an Ethical Dilemma?" *African Health Sciences* 4, no. 3 (Dec. 2004): 208–209.

Ìdòwú, E. Bolaji. *Olodumare: God in Yoruba Belief.* London: Longmans, Green, 1961.

Kendon, Adam. *Gesture: Visible Action as Utterance.* Cambridge: Cambridge University Press, 2004.

Linenthal, Edward T. "'Nothing Is Ever Escaped': Public History and the African American Historic Landscape." Lecture presented at the Center for the Study of World Religions, Harvard Divinity School. Cambridge, MA. April 11, 2006.

———. "Epilogue: Reflections." In *Slavery and Public History: The Tough Stuff of American Memory,* edited by James Oliver and Lois E. Horton, 213–24.. Chapel Hill: University of North Carolina Press, 2009.

Mason, Michael Atwood. *Living Santería: Rituals and Experiences in an Afro-Cuban Religion.* Washington, DC: Smithsonian Institution Press, 2002.

———. *Baba Who? Babalú!* (blog). 2009–2011. http://baba-who-babalu-santeria.blogspot.com.

Matory, J. Lorand. *Sex and the Empire That Is No More: Gender and the Politics of Metaphor in Oyo Yoruba Religion.* Minneapolis: University of Minnesota Press, 1994.

Oliver, James, and Lois E. Horton, eds. *Slavery and Public History: The Tough Stuff of American Memory.* Chapel Hill: University of North Carolina Press, 2009.

Orsi, Robert. *Between Heaven and Earth: The Religious Worlds People Make and the Scholars Who Study Them.* Princeton: Princeton University Press, 2005.

Thompson, Robert Farris. *Flash of the Spirit: African and Afro-American Art and Philosophy.* New York: Vintage Books, 1983.

———. *Face of the Gods: Art and Altars of Africa and the African Americas.* New York: Museum for African Art, 1993.

Villepastour, Amanda. *Ancient Text Messages of the Yorùbá Bàtá Drum: Cracking the Code.* SOAS Musicology Series. Burlington, VT: Ashgate Publishing, 2010.

Filmography

Carrie. Directed by Brian De Palma. Los Angeles: Culver Studios, United Artists, 1976. 35 mm film.

Oggún: Un Eterno Presente. Directed by Gloria Rolando. Havana, Cuba: Imagenes, S.A., 1991. VHS cassette.

Discography

Conjunto Folklórico Nacional de Cuba. *Música Yoruba.* Redway, CA: Bembe Records, 1996. BAMB 2010. Compact disc.

Milton Cardona and the Eya Aranla Ensemble. *Bembé.* Original release date 1987. Reston, VA: American Clavé, 1994. AMCL 1004. Compact disc; vinyl, LP.

ANA PAIS

10. Almost Imperceptible Rhythms and Stuff Like That

The Power of Affect in Live Performance

"Almost imperceptible rhythms and stuff like that," she said. For Portuguese choreographer Vera Mantero, this is what performers need to be listening to when attempting to maintain the interaction with the audience.

"These things are so minuscule that it is impossible to share among us [the performers] the same understanding, at each moment, of what is necessary to tighten that string, to keep hold of that thing," she admitted.

"That's a great image," I replied enthusiastically. She laughed like only children can.

"It's like there is a string connecting us to them, a string that we keep on pulling and stretching," she added.

"I will quote you!" I continued. Vera giggled.

"Feel free to do so because that's exactly what I feel in those performances. Really, really . . . We are there, they pick up one side of the string, we pick up the other, and there we go . . . ," she described. "We are doing the same work. We are all there, at the same time. If they let go of the string, well . . . we lose it," she concluded.

Like her laughter, Mantero's words are crystal clear. While the image of the string is imaginary, the activity of the audience is concrete: a negotiation of affect, tensions, and intensities that unfolds with the theatrical event, a point of tension permanently at risk of being lost. Mantero was referring to the type of engagement a production such as *Until the Moment When God Is Destroyed by the Extreme Exercise of Beauty (AQD)*[1] demands from the audience. Although spectators are seated in a traditional auditorium facing the performers, what is asked from them does not follow the conventions of Western theater, according to which the stage is the place for action and the spectator a passive beholder. *AQD* performs a critique both of action as something to be seen and of the voyeuristic and passive role it prescribes to the spectator: scarcely any action will be seen on stage. Instead, the bodies of *AQD* carry out a *chorus of activities,*[2] a choreography of words displaying their sounding materiality in playful rhythmic patterns. This *performative construction*[3] invites the audience to immerse itself in a cadence of sounds, challenging it to engage with the performance from an aural and, I will argue, an affective angle. *AQD* summons the audience to a particular kind of engagement with the performers on stage, an engagement that equates an exchange of affect with a practice of listening, rather than a production of effects. I will be claiming that this shift—from effects to affect—is a distinctive feature of contemporary performance that gestures toward a mode of intersubjectivity in the theater by which the performance lends itself to the affective impact of the audience.

AQD unfolds a practice of listening that challenges the audience to pick up and perhaps intensify patterns of rhythm initiated by the *choir of activities* performed on stage. Created by six guest dancers and Mantero herself, the production stages a situation of an apparent conversation with the spectators. Lined up at the front stage, the performers are almost as illuminated as the audience. Some of them smile; others seem to observe each spectator. They look happy, joyful. Their bodies are relaxed in their chairs, though attentive. Their costumes are extravagant, markers of individuality, whereas the words they say are the same. After a long silence, they lean forward and they ask, all at the same time: "Are we ready?" Pause. The way they speak is bizarre: they hold up each syllable (aaaare, weeeeee, readyyyyyy?) and pause heavily after each word. Breaking down the prosody of the English language, they make the familiar sound foreign. Despite its banal content, what they say doesn't sound like a conversation at all. At first hearing, words are pronounced at the same time, but a more careful listening will show how heterophony creates a specific sound texture. Like an unfamiliar choir, they speak in a repetitive cadence, deliberately disarticulating the common pace of speech and introducing variations in pitch and melody that widen the acoustic fabric of the show. Hence, this choreographic score is enunciated in a deliberately slow rhythm, rigorously scripted with a strong musical and choreographic sense.[4] It lays the foundations for the active and affective listening of the audience.

There is no theater without an audience.[5] However, not only does the way we conceive of the audience vary from culture to culture—ranging widely from voyeurism to participation—but it also varies within the Western paradigm throughout historical periods and according to sociocultural values. This means that perception and the modes of shaping it also change, making theater a privileged site to examine it. In this text, I will focus on the Western theater paradigm inherited from the nineteenth century, that is, marked by a passive gaze and subjecting the spectator to theatrical effects. These premises—passive gaze and theatrical effects—imply an understanding of looking as passive and of the spectator as a mere repository of those effects. Not surprisingly, in postindustrial societies measures of discipline and control in theatrical institutions as well as demands of silence and concentration from regnant aesthetic paradigms shaped the *habitus* of the bourgeois spectator, who was rendered silent in the gloomy auditorium. Since the late nineteenth century, in particular, after Wagner's revolutionary concept of the "total artwork" (*Gesamtkunstwerk*), the darkening of the auditorium has reinforced the separation between the spectator and the stage, improving strategies to optimize attention and produce effects in the audience. This became the norm for proscenium theater buildings and performances in the West and, not surprisingly, one of the targets of twentieth-century avant-garde provocations and aesthetic battles (both in the early decades and in the 1960s and 1970s). In addition, as these spatial and lighting technologies shaped the audience's perception, they reinforced an old idea: the audience as a single though collective entity that behaves, thinks, and feels the same. Eliding cultural, gendered, and individual differences, the conception of a unified audience has been critically addressed by authors who made clear that individual difference is key to understanding not only the implications of culture in reception (Bennett 1990), but also the processes of individual subjectivity within a collective entity or against an ideologically charged ideal of spectator (Dolan 1991; Auslander 2003; Rayner 2003). Acknowledging these critiques, I will therefore use the term *audience* in the sense of a collective made of singularities that by taking part in the performative event engage in a common process (Nancy 2002). Despite individual interpretations, thoughts, or feelings, I am interested in approaching here the background affective process that has an impact on the performance in which each spectator participates by the very singularity he or she brings to the theater room.

Theater is a privileged space in which to investigate hidden regions of individual and collective interactions through the relationship between performers and audience. Live performance happens mostly in the encounter between spectators and actors bringing forth a reciprocal dynamic that exceeds the logic of dramatic effects. This intangible dimension is often mystified as the *magic of theater,* or vaguely defined as a *flow of energy.* In a recent publication, theater academic Erika Fischer-Lichte (2008) suggests that the encounter between actors and spectators is, in various ways, a distinctive feature of the new performative paradigm initiated with performance art. According to Fischer-Lichte, the performative paradigm has restored the centrality of the reciprocity between actors and spectators to producing the theatrical encounter as interactivity unfolds in a *feedback loop* that produces the materiality of performance:

> In short, whatever the actors do elicits a response from the spectators, which impacts on the entire performance. In this sense, performances are generated and determined by a self-referential and ever-changing feedback loop. Hence, performance remains unpredictable and spontaneous to a certain degree. (Fischer-Lichte 2008, 38)

Despite her scientific purposes, Fischer-Lichte can hardly describe how that process happens in the concrete examples she gives without iterating the same mystifying vocabulary that pervades Western theater history. Contradicting her ambition of developing a vocabulary for the *aesthetics of the performative,* more often than not we are thrown back to the domain of emission, transference, and absorption of energy. The term itself remains intentionally unclear for, as the author reckons, *the immediacy of the perceptual experience* is insurmountable (Fischer-Lichte 2008, 211n11). Surely, what needs to be questioned is the method of thinking and writing about this specific perceptual experience. Such a concrete and vital feature of live performance demands a critical approach. This is where sound writing can provide an alternative pathway, a methodology to grasp and translate the experience of partaking in a live performance. I interrogate the dynamics of that relationship through the lens of affective listening. Claiming that affect, like listening, has a performative power that produces the ontological difference of live events, I will reassess the traditional conception of the audience as passive while finding words to name felt dimensions of performance. Affective listening is listening with the whole body to reverberations of the rhythms and intensities of performance, to a felt dimension where one can be touched (or not). This is what Deborah Kapchan defines in the introduction as "sound knowledge," a listening composed of felt echoes propagating within and without the skin. Writing affective listening—sound knowledge—is an attempt to get closer to the pressure, temperature, and vibrations of live performance's touchstone: touching, moving, resonating. Sound writing is the theoretical possibility of writing through such touch, making it reverberate in sound-words that echo sound-affect. As such, sound writing is an affective listening as well as a way of knowing how the performers and audience are touched. It performs the affective resonance of my experience in the performing arts.

My theoretical framework confronts contemporary theories of the transmission of affect with vocabulary used by performers to describe their encounters with audiences in order to rearticulate paradoxical aspects inherent to the theatrical event, especially those related to the sensorial experience it involves. Like the word *theory*, the Greek word for auditorium (*theatron)* is deeply rooted in the sense of vision that has overruled other sensorial layers of the theatrical experience. To see and to be seen is the hegemonic rule of theater in the Western canon, even though an emphasis on sound and the conditions of listening, rather than on vision, has long been key to theater architecture (Vitruvius n.d.). The privileged hierarchy of vision in relation to other senses in the theatrical experience mirrors the top position it occupies in Western culture, thought, and philosophy since its birth: seeing equals knowing and knowing equals consciousness and rationality. Yet, as many authors have argued, theatergoing is an embodied experience in which vision is just a part of a whole sensorial engagement (Bleeker 2011; Welton 2012; Di Benedetto 2010), and in which the whole sensorium is actively engaged. As Banes and Lepecki remind us, the senses are historically and culturally determined dimensions of experience that draw lines between *the perceptible and the imperceptible,* defining a *political economy of the senses*:

> The political economy of the senses subjacent to any system of presence, to any system of power, by casting a dividing line between the property perceptible and the imperceptible impacts on the ontological and political status of any perception by defining it as significant or as insignificant. (Banes and Lepecki 2007, 3)

What we need to realize when thinking about the spectator as an ontological condition is that, side by side with a politics of the senses, each performance as well as the bodies on stage engender a politics of affect that claims examination. Furthermore, perception in general, and looking in particular, cannot be easily dismissed today as passive. This conception has been radically revised in the past decades by the work of scientists such as Alain Berthoz or philosophers such as Alva Nöe, who advocate for perception as action—Berthoz (1997) sustains perception as simulated action in the brain, and Nöe (2004) argues that perceiving the work is already acting upon it and thinking it. Thus, science and arts scholarship seem to be reaching a conclusion that musicians, actors, or dancers intuitively know from experience: every audience participates in live performance events albeit in different degrees according to their own cultural, historical, and aesthetic conventions.

Yet, if the presence of the spectator is crucial to performance's ontology, his or her activity is rarely examined. In this chapter, I argue that the activity of the spectator involves an intensification and amplification of affect, enabling a moving together, a reciprocal movement between stage and audience. This movement, in turn, will be conceptualized as a *co-motion* that takes place through a specific kind of listening—an affective resonance. By influencing the quality of the event, that is, the charged, circulating, and fleeting affective quality of live performance, commotion produces the ontological difference of theater. I suggest that emotions, thoughts, or sensations carry affect, that is, sensitive charges or felt intensities that circulate in social spaces.

PATTERNS OF AFFECT TRANSMISSION

Fraught and slippery in meaning, these terms need further clarification. Indeed, we barely have words to refer to them because affect remains the underbelly of felt phenomena. Affects are concrete felt things that belong to our experience, such as feeling uncomfortable or suffocated when one enters a room. They are neither categorical emotions nor proprioceptive states of awareness of oneself. Since Darwin's research on human and animal emotions, they tend to be described as universals, categories of felt experience (joy, sadness, etc.) deeply entangled with the body's physiology. Despite its usefulness in understanding the intertwined processes of the body and the psyche, as Silvan Tomkins's work about emotion as a primary motivational drive suggests, inspiring the seminal work of Eve Sedgwick and Adam Frank (1995), these categories fail to give us instruments to think about more subtle and shifting qualities of experience. This is why affect, either as capacity of attachment to things, people, ideas, activities, or institutions free of constraints (Sedgwick 2003, 19) or as a flux, an intensity ungraspable by consciousness (that is not "captured" by the various systemic processing modes of the body) advanced by Massumi (1995) and other Deleuzians, has been granted such a rapturous reception in the academy, in particular, in the field of affect studies.

Subtle felt phenomena are more accurately described as affective impressions attached to emotions, thoughts, or sensations, hence, charging or intensifying social environments. Affective impressions can be conscious or unconscious in the sense that their meaning emerges through felt experience. One might not be rationally aware in the moment or even able to articulate it in words, but it still is a meaningful part of the experience. Making distinctions between affect, emotion, and feeling is challenging. As the editors of a groundbreaking publication bridging sound and affect put it, "The question, though, is never really what affect means but what it does" (Thompson and Biddle 2013, 18). Conceiving of affect as attached to emotions, thoughts, or sensations enables us to distinguish it from the latter and to enhance a description of its movement (and transmission) as circulating and performative particles that do things. For the purpose of this chapter, I will use the term *affect* to refer to sensitive charges that circulate in social spaces, intensifying them through the transmission *of patterns of rhythm.* Despite the common negative implications, charges are that which can be carried, transported, and set in circulation: "burdens," say those who feel charges as weight; "intensifiers," say those who feel charges as a potentiality for transmission. *To charge* means to act upon the surplus qualities of feeling, activating a movement that takes place in and heightens social spaces. This is clear if we think of this movement as the wind, the rain, or the sunshine that activates a certain kind of atmosphere in a social space. Affects of sadness can charge a funeral, as well as affects of enthusiasm intensify a soccer match. In the theater, this movement takes place between performers and audience members. Their reciprocal influence on the weather in the theater space affects the outcome of the performance. As Mantero states, this engagement is a permanent and subtle negotiation of the tension with which performers and spectators hold a string—this tension is the intensifier of the felt quality of the performance, of its movement.

Not surprisingly, the *Oxford English Dictionary* suggests that *affect* is also a "disposition toward mental or emotional states," thus, a possibility of being affected that comes together with assumptions about mobility or crystallization. As long as they are fluctuating and temporary, mental or emotional dispositions are a sign of health. On the contrary, if those dispositions become crystallized in more permanent bodily states, they indicate illness. In understanding affect as sensitive charges or felt intensities, I am, therefore, stressing the ideas of circulation and participation, and of how those processes allow us to highlight ontological aspects of theater in culturally charged scenarios. I will anchor this approach in three main authors. The theories of Teresa Brennan (2004) on the transmission of affect provide a broad framework for my argument. To further elaborate on the concept of affect and its processes, I will draw upon the connections between affect and sound, by means of vibration as a model for understanding transmission suggested by Julian Henriques (2010) and the concept of vitality affects as proposed by Daniel Stern (1985).

A WHOLE-BODY LISTENING

Live performance phenomena, in particular, those related to ways of connecting stage and audience, are historically grounded and culturally informed. Indebted to performance art's groundbreaking strategies to dismiss representation, postdramatic theater paved the way for intensified encounters between performers and audiences. According to the well-known concept elaborated by Hans Thies-Lehmann, postdramatic practices generated a shift in the mode of perception of live events (Thies-Lehmann 2006, 16). Instead of the linear narrative structure, based on the logic of the dramatic text, the spectator is confronted with simultaneous, fragmentary, and ambivalent discourses, ascribed to the audiovisual pervasiveness in globalized societies. Likewise, as opposed to traditional drama, postdramatic theater shifted the focus of dialogue and action from the stage—between characters performed by actors on stage—to a "theater situation" established with the audience (Lehmann 2006, 17). Self-reflexive and critical, this openness urges us to rethink the power of affect in performance. In other words, postdramatic theater's shift in perception reinforces the potential vulnerability of live performance to affect and be affected. But how can we assess this reciprocal movement?

Philosopher and social theorist Teresa Brennan has developed a theory that gives a provocative insight into the transmission of affect in the theater. Recuperating a philosophical tradition of passions as emotional states that circulate and visit us, Brennan claims that emotions are not ours. Rather, they result from an intersubjective exchange with the environment and the others. Social in nature, the transmission of affect impacts the biology of the body as, for Brennan, affect is *the physiological shift accompanying a judgment* (Brennan 2004, 5). The author emphasizes the materiality of affects and how they, on the one hand, differ from feelings because they cannot be captured in words and, subsequently, be discerned, and on the other hand, do not differ entirely from emotions (Brennan 2004, 6).[6] Contrary to the current positivist conception of emotions as expressions of a self-contained body, Brennan argues that we are open beings who receive signals from and emit signals to others and to the environment, perceived by the senses and therefore materialized in our physiology. The biological limits of the body do not contain our identity. Like the skin, the membranes of our existence are porous. Thus, Brennan's theory breaks through the limits of the body as the original site of emotions and container of identities, challenging the borders between the social and the biological as well as between the individual and the environment.

Interestingly, transmission is an equally pressing figure in describing sound behavior. In his historical approach to sound in the avant-garde, Douglas Kahn proposes a figure of transmission to account for new conceptual possibilities for understanding the relation between sound and space in the wake of technological innovations of the late nineteenth century. Transmission space, Kahn alleges, allows disembodied sounds to travel across the globe, enabling them to exist in two places at the same time, set apart by wired silence. Emitted and received throughout long distances, sound becomes a travelling signal (Kahn 1992, 20). Unlike the figure of vibration and inscription (recorded sound), transmission not only explains how invisible sounding phenomena can propagate through a medium (space, bodies), but also how it dissolves recurring issues of mysticism or religious spirituality in sound and music discourses in the West.

In a recent approach, however, Julian Henriques recuperates vibrations and their propagation process as a useful model to explain fleeting affective shifts occurring between bodies in social spaces (Henriques 2010; cf. Ridout 2008; Goodman 2010; Thompson and Biddle 2013). In his "rhythmanalysis" of a dancehall scene in Kingston (Jamaica), Henriques defines vibrations as an energetic or rhythmic pattern that propagates through mediums in different wave bands: corporeal (bodily kinetics), material (solids, liquids, and gas, including electromagnetic fields), and sociocultural (Henriques 2010, 59). Immersed in all these different wave bands, reciprocally contaminating each other, human beings relate and connect affectively in similar ways as vibrations flow and propagate rhythmic patterns. Both sound and affect are events that flow in a given rhythmic frequency and are felt haptically as intensities. They are, suggests the author, a "whole-body vibrotactile experience" (Henriques 2010, 78). In Henriques's account of affect transmission in the dancehall, he considers, however, that like sound, affect waves can be measured. His account proposes measuring rhythms as frequency, intensity as amplitude, and timbre as a distinctive quality of both sound and affect. The author further suggests that listening is a "connective relationship" (Henriques 2010, 76); listening with "all the senses"—a whole-body listening, one can say—is the adequate mode of approaching and grounding affective experience and transmission. Although equating sound and affect implies the puzzling proposition that affect can be measured, which is not my claim whatsoever, Henriques's insightful analysis can be helpful to understanding processes of affect transmission in live performance.

COMMOTION: WHEN THE SOCIAL IMPACTS THE AESTHETIC

To make sense of affect transmission in the theater, it is useful to think of this kind of listening as affective listening, a rhythmic resonance that enhances the amplification of affect in the relationship between stage and audience. According to Henriques's model, if amplification (of volume) equals intensification (of feeling or felt experience), then it is plausible to think that the audience's affective listening to a live performance, despite individual interpretations, expectations, and feelings, sets in motion and amplifies/intensifies rhythmic patterns or vibration frequencies initiated by the performance. This impacts the sensitive quality of the performance—its timbre—making each performance an affectively and aesthetically unique event. This sensitive quality or timbre expresses itself in a particular movement: commotion of resonant dynamic patterns, emitting and receiving material, corporeal, and sociocultural signals from the wave bands in which performers and spectators are immersed. Hence, as I will suggest below, the role of the audience in live performance is that of an intensifier of the sensitive quality of the performance, engaging in a co-motion of rhythms, a moving together like a vibrational flow. As in Brennan's theory, Henriques's model allows us to think beyond the self-contained individual. But unlike Brennan, it does not privilege physioneurological processes (such as entrainment in the propagation of hormones and pheromones in social spaces) but rhythmic patterns or frequencies as embodied cultural practices that are haptically felt. Although intensities in the theater space cannot be measured in the same way as sound vibrations in a dancehall, the vibration model seems to hint at good chances of dismissing the magic of live performance by showing the importance of listening to affective transmissions.

In the theater, the process of the transmission of affect has further implications. The ontological status of theatrical elements displayed on stage is paradoxical. Making the case for the dancer, Portuguese philosopher José Gil reminds us that the body on stage is paradoxical: bodies on stage are and they are not the bodies of actors and performers (2001, 57). Either representing characters or performing tasks in real time, they share a dual aesthetic materiality. According to Gil, as long as there is an affective investment in the body, it becomes paradoxical (Gil 2001, 58). It generates a space of intensities or what he identifies as a *space of the body*:

> Here, we would like to consider the body no longer as a "phenomenon," no longer as a visible and concrete perception moving in the objective Cartesian space, but rather, we would like to consider the body as a meta-phenomenon, simultaneously visible and virtual, a cluster of forces, a transformer of space and time, both emitter of signs and trans-semiotic, endowed by an organic interior ready to be dissolved as soon as it reaches the surface. (Gil 2006, 28, trans. André Lepecki)

Although I am not assuming the collapse of subject/object borders that such a Deleuzian-informed approach would imply, in an affective and poetic dimension, the audience is one with the work because of the paradoxical status of the body on stage. This is crucial to understanding how a theory of the transmission of affect can highlight the activity of the audience as an intensification or amplification of affect as sound knowledge. The audience is affected by the performance as much as it impacts the dual reality of the body, via its physiological shifts, states, and felt experience.

The audience gathered to attend a performance brings in an affective mood. Regardless of individual thoughts and feelings, a collective process of affective intensification takes place. Transmitting and receiving affect, the audience determines a social environment that has material consequences in physiological states, both in the body of the spectator and in the body of the performer. In this light, borders between biology and aesthetics are challenged. In many contemporary performances, such as Vera Mantero's, the logic of producing emotional effects on the audience recedes, cracking open the impact of the audience. In *AQD,* the choreographic and musical script creates patterns of rhythms and intensities, a sonic space that invites to hypnotic or trancelike states. It needs to be listened to, not seen. As meaning and narrative are suspended by means of a repetitive cadence, the emotional effects of its enunciation on the audience are not predetermined. One is not supposed to feel happy or sad. Instead, one is allowed to engage affectively with affects emerging during the performance. Thus, the circulation of those affects—the intensifying charges of spectators' felt experience—is left open by states of distraction and dispersion induced by the performance. What can they disclose? Agitation, annoyance, irritation, restlessness, impatience, and boredom as much as diversion, reverie, dreaminess, absorption, lightness, and laughter. These contradictory affects intensify the atmosphere in the theater, giving room both to individual responses and collective movements. We listen to the movement in *AQD* because we listen to its affective gesturing. In the social process of becoming an audience, spectators become whole-body listeners of these gestures, which impact the bodies of performers on stage, therefore influencing the outcome of the performance.

What I am claiming is that affect, like Kapchan's "listening act" (2016, this volume), is performative: it does something to the poetic encounter, to the bodies and to the sensitive qualities we experience in a live performance. Affect is the "stuff" commotion is made of. This performativity cannot be disentangled from the presence of the audience implicated in the affective materiality generated as the performance unfolds. To our great advantage, we can conceive of it as an affective resonance, listening to rhythms that can be felt through movement or by "movements of attention," as Martin Welton (2012) puts it in his recent volume *Feeling Theatre.* Welton suggests that, "In watching or performing theatre, we undertake practices of perception which are founded in certain kinds of movement—of visual or aural attention for example—and in doing so, we get a feel of how it goes" (Welton 2012, 3).

AFFECTIVE RESONANCE

I now focus on these movements of "aural attention." Rearticulating the engagement of the audience with the stage as an affective resonance, I claim that the movement of commotion intertwines listening and affect. In her essay "The Audience. Subjectivity, Community and the Ethics of Listening," Alice Rayner considers the audience as an *act of giving* itself to listening (Rayner 2003, 265), as in the linguistic expression "giving audience." Rayner suggests that the gift is the premise that distinguishes a judging audience from a giving audience. Brought forth by listening, the act of judging is grounded in authority, whereas the act of the giving audience is grounded in affects. The act of listening is defined as giving reception, as *an act of kindness* (265), for it opens itself to the flow of meanings between speaker and listener (264). Rayner emphasizes the affective nature of listening as a gift that grants an exchange of meaning in the theater. Yet there are no gifts without exchange, as Marcel Mauss (1967) famously argued. If we consider the gift of listening as an affective resonance that, like sound resonance, sounds again, amplifying felt phenomena, we can understand how the audience's attention can be *in tension* with the performers, thus moving with them. As a practice of listening, affective resonance can be thought of as the mechanism of affective mobilization that combines degrees of tension and attention, or of looseness and distraction, reaffecting the stage. This repetition does not entail feeling or thinking the same impressions, emotions, sensations, or thoughts, but sharing a common potentiality of individuals to engage with a resonant movement and be moved by it, through an (in)tense listening. Precisely because affect is a circulating charge and not a synonym for emotion or feeling, we are able to differentiate the performative potentiality of affect at play in an audience's activity.

Considering "affective resonance" as a mode of tension and attention, we can conceive of the audience as an active counterpart in live events. While allowing individual difference of feeling and interpretation, affective resonance is a collective state of tension that suspends the performance in a movement of affects as it lends itself to listening. Specifically, I am suggesting that this tension constitutes the means by which the audience heightens affective forces that sustain the delicate architecture of performance. Like geodesic domes, invented by American engineer Buckminster Fuller, performances need "tensigrity." *Tensigrity* consists of a systemic relation that describes a state of integrity resulting from an invisible tension that sustains it (Fuller 1975). Working together with forces of compression, tension guarantees the construction's flexibility and internal cohesion. Fuller's dome requires this systemic relation of opposing forces of compression and tension: its integrity depends on and results from the state of tension created by compression. Likewise, a performance requires an element of continuous tension created, at its inception, by its own movement. A collective atmosphere of affects, set into a reciprocal motion, is the conflicting force that grants the performance's integrity and dynamic, through affective resonance.

As I have suggested, thinking of the audience as a gift of listening and thinking of listening as an affective exchange might bring us to an interesting point of audition to understand how affects are crucial to performance. By means of what I call an "affective resonance," the audience sets affects in circulation and amplifies them, producing performance's constitutive difference or sensitive quality—commotion.

Considering that the average spectator attends a production once, whereas an actor or a dancer performs it repeatedly, it is the latter who is more likely to experience that difference. Performers, not the audience, have access to the affective nuances of a show. When Mantero envisages a string being stretched and connecting audience and performers, she is acknowledging a state of tension that is negotiated as a felt thing, an affect, an "imperceptible rhythm." As Daniel Stern reminds us, there is a specific quality of experience that has to do with the ways by which we experience abstract properties such as shape, intensity, motion, number, and rhythm. This experience involves "vitality affects that we experience as dynamic shifts or patterned changes within ourselves" (Stern 1985, 54). Stern sustains that they belong to the realm of affective experience, but since they do not fit emotional categories (such as joy or sadness), these elusive properties are better expressed through a kinetic vocabulary (a rush, a burst, a fleeting experience) (Stern 1985, 54).

DISCERNING AFFECT AS SOUND KNOWLEDGE

In the realm of my investigation on the power of affect in contemporary performance, I have been undertaking several conversations with performers, dancers, and actors. I wanted to understand how their perception of the audience influenced the way they perform since what happens in the encounter is commonly recognized as a concrete and undeniable imperative of live performance. At first, these conversations happened rather spontaneously. I talked mostly to friends or people I met during my research periods in Portugal and abroad. Yet they turned out to be a thrilling source of inspiration. Between 2011 and 2012, I have collected words and expressions from over fifty performers from mainly Portugal, Brazil, and the United States, as well as a few from other European countries. As subjective as this material can be, it nonetheless provided me with crucial insights about my topic.

From these conversations, I could observe four clear strategies of expressing such ineffable qualities of experience regarding the engagement with an audience: onomatopoeia, sensorial vocabulary, metaphors, and bodily gestures.[7] First, performers use onomatopoeia to signal a relation of potency, power, or weakness of the patterns of dynamic established in the affective relation with the audience. Mimetic reproduction of sounds to express ways of feeling shows how close intensities are to amplitudes of sound vibration and, therefore, to listening (as affective resonance) on the one hand, and on the other hand, how that affective resonance demands to break through the linguistic categories of signification to be expressed (cf. Weiss 2008). American dancer and choreographer Miguel

Gutierrez, for instance, perceives the gaze of the audience as bodily awareness, an "awakening of parts of the body" (background texture of the recording: cars, motorbikes, honking). He translates that intensity with an onomatopoeia: "It's like literally the actual side of my body that is facing you starts to have a kind of WINGWINGWING thing, that becomes awake if it's like an audience on one side situation." Words don't seem to accurately describe such felt experience as the quick rhythmic high sound of WINGWINGWING, as something that hits and uplifts you, as something that tickles your body as if with an invisible stick. Like many other performers, Gutierrez's use of onomatopoeia shows how it can break through limited word semantics by further highlighting the adequacy of sound to express affective experience.

Second, a sensorial vocabulary pervades the ways by which the audience makes itself present to performers. The feedback from the audience can be described as the "silence in the room," the feeling of the "temperature," of "smoothness" or "rigidity," a sense of proximity or distance, connection or disconnection, a sense of expansion or contraction. Like sound, the affective relationship between performers and spectators stands out as a whole-body experience. Australian dancer and actor Anton Skrzypiciel claims that there is an intensity that surrounds him: "When you feel like a show is going badly it's almost like somebody deflated a balloon, like all the air left . . . whereas when people are engaged, you feel like the air pressure is slightly more intense on you, it surrounds you [with] that intensity." This intensity, they argue, is a multidirectional or 360-degree perception, and it can be negotiated. German dancer and performer Eva Meyer-Keller describes her attitude in the solo performance *Death Is Certain*: "I don't look at them, I don't smile at them, but I can sense the presence in the room. I can sense their movement and how loud and silent it is. If it's too serious or too stiff, I try to shake it up. It's very subtle."[7]

Third, in line with these expressions, metaphors of rhythm are frequent: performers describe their connection with the audience as a wave that goes back and forth, a common breath, a pulsing heart. Theater actor Tony Torn uses the metaphor of the ocean to describe the energy flow (what I call here "circulation of affect") in live performance: "The energy flows off the stage into the audience, it recycles and comes surging back, so it's like the ocean. The wave goes crashing and then it is sucked back . . . so when it's happening like this you feel like there is this give and take, a suction and then a wave, a suction and then a wave. When you don't feel like the audience is with you is when this sucking, this undertoe feeling of the ocean is coming out that the wave is not coming back at you. You just feel a drain."[8] (I recall: morning light, people talking, smell of coffee, music.)

These metaphors describe vibrations as defined by Henriques, patterns of rhythm that propagate in various wave bands (corporeal, material, and sociocultural). Despite the subjectivity of each personal narrative, these strategies clearly indicate a common semantic ground: a sensual perception of rhythm that involves states of tension, in short, a movement of commotion.

Finally, commotion is inscribed in the bodies of the performers. When words fail them, bodies simulate movement. Rarely aware of those gestures, they magnify their felt experience by shaking their hands or swinging their torso back and forth while speaking. The rhythms of affect go under the skin of the performers. Since words cannot fully express the felt quality of the experience, performers embody the movement of commotion when recalling it from memory. Though "almost imperceptible," the ineffable rhythm enacted by the movement of affect sinks in the performer beyond the ephemeral experience of being onstage as "whole-body" listening, which stays with the performer as a resonating intensity.

CONCLUSION

A performance such as Vera Mantero's *Until the Moment* confronts the audience with a saturated visual image; when the only action and movement is performed by the voice, by the words spoken as a sort of hypnotic and distractive repetitive litany without a narrative or logic to them, the audience is challenged to suspend the need to understand and to simply let go, moving together with the affective rhythm underlying the aural materiality of speech. These are sounding words produced and *listened through* bodies onstage and in the audience. Writing such experience takes up the challenge of translating the layers of reverberation that mark the skin as traces of the affective felt dimension of performance. Sound writing proves to be particularly stimulating and adequate when thinking of performances such as *AQD* that, instead of aiming at affecting the audience, give room to being together with the spectators, allowing them to feel and think alongside it.

NOTES

1. The première was in Brest, France, in 2006.
2. Vera Mantero, in her project notes.
3. Ibid.

4. Vera Mantero's guest performers in this production are trained dancers. In an interview published in the program notes for the *Festival d'Automne,* Mantero describes the text as a "musical and choreographic score," rather than a conversation with the audience (Mantero and David 2006).

5. *Theater* is used here as a broad-spectrum term.

6. Although Brennan starts off by acknowledging this, she will use the term *affect* to designate negative ones. According to the author, negative affects need to be discerned by means of love as *living attention.* This is the bedrock of the paradigm of subjectivity she sees fit to cope with the increasingly violent and toxic global economies we live in (Brennan 2004, 22).

7. All of the quotes that follow are taken from conversations with the performers.

BIBLIOGRAPHY

Banes, Sally, and André Lepecki. *The Senses in Performance.* New York: Routledge, 2007.

Bennett, Susan. *Theatre Audiences: A Theory of Production and Reception.* London: Routledge, 1990.

Berthoz, Alain. *Le Sens du Mouvement.* Paris: Éditions Odile Jacob, 1997.

Bleeker, Maaike. *Visuality in the Theatre: The Locus of Looking.* Hampshire, UK: Palgrave, 2011.

Brennan, Teresa. *The Transmission of Affect.* Ithaca: Cornell University, 2004.

Di Benedetto, Stephen. *The Provocation of the Senses in Contemporary Theatre.* London: Routledge, 2010.

Dolan, Jill. *The Feminist Spectator as Critic.* Ann Arbor: University of Michigan Press, 1991.

Fischer-Lichte, Erika. *The Transformative Power of Performance: A New Aesthetics.* London: Routledge, 2008.

Fuller, Buckminster. *Synergetics: Explorations in the Geometry of Thinking.* New York: Macmillan, 1975.

Gil, J. "Paradoxical Body." *TDR/The Drama Review* 50, no. 4 (winter 2006): 21–35. Goodman, Steve. *Sonic Warfare: Sound, Affect and the Ecology of Fear.* Cambridge, MA: MIT Press, 2010.

Henriques, Julian. "The Vibrations of Affect and Their Propagation on a Night Out on Kingston's Dancehall Scene." *Body and Society* 16, no. 1 (2010): 57–89.

Kahn, Douglas. "Introduction: Histories of Sound Once Removed." In *Wireless Imagination: Sound, Radio and the Avant-Garde,* edited by George Kahn and Douglas Whitehead, 1–29. Cambridge, MA: MIT Press, 1992.

Lehmann, Hans-Thies. *Postdramatic Theatre.* London: Routledge, 2006.

Mantero, Vera, and Gwénola David. *Entretien avec Vera Mantero—Folha de Sala.* Paris: Festival d'Automne, 2006.

Massumi, Brian. “The Autonomy of Affect.” *Cultural Critique* 31 (1995): 83–109.

Mauss, Marcel. *The Gift: Forms and Functions of Exchange in Archaic Societies.* New York: Norton Library, 1967.

Nancy, Jean-Luc. *À L'écoute.* Paris: Galilé, 2002. Nöe, Alva. *Action in Perception.* Cambridge: MIT Press, 2004.

Rayner, Alice. “The Audience: Subjectivity, Community and the Ethics of Listening.” In *Performance: Critical Concepts in Literary and Cultural Studies,* edited by Philip Auslander, 249–68. London: Routledge, 2003.

Ridout, Nicholas. “Welcome to the Vibratorium.” *Senses and Society* 3, no. 2 (2008): 221–31.

Sedgwick, Eve Kosofsky. *Touching Feeling: Affect, Pedagogy, Performativity.* Durham, NC: Duke University Press, 2003.

———, and Adam Frank. “Shame in the Cybernetic Fold: Reading Silvan Tomkins.” *Critical Inquiry* 21, no. 2 (winter 1995): 496–522.

Stern, Daniel. *The Interpersonal World of the Infant.* New York: Basic Books, 1985.

Thompson, Marie, and Ian Biddle, eds. *Sound, Music, Affect: Theorizing Sonic Experience.* London: Bloomsbury, 2013.

Vitruvius. “De Architectura.” Perseus Project, Tufts University. http://perseus.uchicago.edu.

Weiss, Allen. *Varieties of Audio Mimesis: Musical Evocations of Landscape.* Berlin: Errant Bodies Press, 2008.

Welton, Martin. *Feeling Theatre.* Houndmills, UK: Palgrave, 2012.

PART FOUR

Listening and Witness

DEBORAH WONG

11. Deadly Soundscapes

Scripts of Lethal Force and Lo-Fi Death

On April 3, 2006, about a mile from where I live and teach, Lee Deante Brown was shot and killed by two Riverside Police Department officers, Paul Stucker and Terry Ellefson, in Riverside, California. I wasn't there when it happened, but word spread quickly: I received several e-mails and a phone call within an hour, and I drove to the seedy motel where it happened as soon as I could. The parking lot was full of yellow crime scene tape, scattered evidence markers with numbers, and stunned community members—mostly working-class African Americans and Latinos—still standing around looking and talking.

In this chapter, I address the pragmatics, proxemics, and performatives of police officers' belt recorders. Law enforcement officers in many US cities wear audio belt recorders that provide a record of their actions and interactions with the public. In Riverside, the audio recordings of "OIDs" ("officer-involved deaths") are transcribed and become essential data for after-the-fact assessments of what happened, why, and who was at fault when police officers kill a community member.

Addressing any aspect of law enforcement immediately catapults the writer into a world of bureaucracy and technicalities. In what follows, you will observe me actively working *against* the many ways that my thinking and writing are pulled centrifugally in that direction: qualifying, arguing, and "proving" are central to the logics of law enforcement, and my own location in it means that I don't have the scholarly luxury of writing about it in whatever way I want, simply in order to explore something that has seized my interest. Writing about the odd mobile devices called belt recorders has involved a self-conscious effort to reinsert myself as a thinker and writer, rather than the scholar-activist who is normally trying to engage with the terms of the edifice. Since 1999 I have pored over bureaucratic state and city documents, and have learned how to write memos full of short sentences and bullet points addressed to city officials. *That* reading and writing sometimes directly makes a difference. Helping to draft the language for a ballot measure focused on the citizens' police review commission was a kind of writing that *mattered,* though I had to let go of any sense of personal ownership, any humanities-driven poetics of persuasion. In this essay I draw together my experiences as an ethnomusicologist with an abiding interest in race, music, and performance, and as a grassroots community activist with over a decade of involvement with police oversight work. My research is situated in sound studies, a dynamic area of critical interdisciplinary work reaching across ethnomusicology, anthropology, sociology, and communication studies. If I seem to be taking a step away from "music," this shift has already taken place in humanities-based scholarship that relocates music as the cultural study of sound and (I hope) unmoors music studies from the positivist history of the art object. Anthropologist Steven Feld's well-known work on acoustemology posits that musicking is always part of broader sound worlds that are simultaneously real and metaphorical (Feld 1991; Feld 1996; Feld 2003; Feld 2012; Keil et al. 2002). It may seem strange for me as an ethnomusicologist to pursue research without any music in it, but it isn't. Rather, this is one among many ways music studies can break loose from its late Romantic baggage. Scholars of sound offer important perspectives on the moments when society has material effects on bodies.[1] It forces us into new ways of writing because the old ways aren't adequate.

The words *sound* and *audition* each have double meanings. Sound is the acoustic, the audio, the thing heard; it also means to be complete, in one piece, and fully functioning, for example, to be of sound mind. Audition is the act of hearing, the act of receiving sound and taking it into the body. It can also mean a test, a tryout, or an exercise in which one's skills are assessed. Any process that transforms sound into audition involves mediation. The audio recordings made by police officers of their interactions with "civilians" (as they are often called by law enforcement) are mediated in many different ways. Among other things, if they are used or needed—that is, if they must be revisited because of conflict, death, complaints, and so on—their rawness and supposed unmediated truth telling is foregrounded, but in fact it is assumed that they will be mediated. The audio must be "cleaned up," and even then it is simply assumed that the sounds will be transcribed. Sound writing is central to how law enforcement oversight and accountability is practiced. This kind of sound writing is interwoven with unmarked assumptions that are central to the power of the resulting thing inscribed.

I bring together here two of my permanent fascinations: the performative utterance, and the act of transcribing interactive talk. I love beautiful writing. The most sensuous ethnographic writing transducts experience. Sound writing should cross over from mere representation to generative critical creation. But while ethnomusicology is the deus ex machina of sound reproduction technology, I'm not sure we have done much more than decry the violence of schizophonia. I focus here on a culture of sound writing that renders sound into powerful data. Writing sound in that world is expected; the most potent theory drives it; and it thus challenges the ethnomusicologist's assumption that it is up to her to articulate a metadiscursive approach to written sound.

Earlier that afternoon, the Riverside Police Department (hereafter RPD) had received six 911 calls from different people, all reporting that a young African American man was walking up and down University Avenue screaming profanity, jumping on cars in traffic, lying in the street, kissing the pavement, stripping off his clothes and exposing himself, and generally exhibiting bizarre behavior. At 1:52 pm, Officer Paul Stucker drove past the Welcome Inn, a down-on-its-luck motel on University Avenue, and was flagged down by a local man who was living in the motel with his family. The man told the officer he thought the man, Lee Deante Brown, was on PCP.[2] Officer Stucker called for backup and got out of his patrol car. Brown was standing in the motel parking lot. By then he was wearing only Levis—no shirt, no shoes. When Brown saw Officer Stucker, he retreated to an inside corner of the motel parking lot near room no. 7. Officer Stucker got out his Taser, a form of "less-lethal" weaponry in the language of law enforcement, which delivers an electrical shock that disrupts voluntary control of the muscles, usually causing temporary paralysis. He followed Brown, issuing verbal commands that Brown ignored. Brown was talking incoherently, yelling for Jesus and "Mariah." It was later learned that Mariah is the name of the younger of his two daughters. He took a step toward Officer Stucker, who promptly tasered him, and Brown fell facedown to the ground.

All this happened in about two minutes' time. At 1:55 pm, Officer Ellefson arrived to assist. He got out of his patrol car with his Taser in his hand and approached Brown, who was still lying on the ground. Ellefson attempted to handcuff him, but Brown pushed him off. Chaos ensued. Officer Stucker struggled to remove the cartridge from his Taser so he could taser Brown again, but Brown grabbed Stucker's arm just as Officer Ellefson tasered him. Officer Stucker felt the electric shock and saw that he had a Taser probe stuck in his hand. He backed away, pulled out the probe, and wedged his Taser into his gun belt in the small of his back. Meanwhile, Officer Ellefson frantically removed and replaced his Taser cartridge and tried several times to taser Brown again, failing and then losing control of the Taser and dropping it. Half sitting, half squatting, Brown tried to stand up. Perhaps he tried to grab the Taser. Perhaps he actually did grab the Taser. Perhaps he did neither. Officer Stucker drew his baton and hit Brown. At the same time, Officer Ellefson drew his gun and fired, striking Brown in the left bicep, the right side of the chest, and the left side of the chest, tearing through Brown's heart. The officers called for medical assistance. The reports say that Brown died at the hospital, but he was probably dead before the paramedics got to him.

Twenty-four witnesses, most of them people living at the motel or cleaning staff, had seen the entire thing. Six had a clear line of sight and saw the shooting. None of them saw a Taser in Brown's hand. Only one later claimed that Brown was advancing toward the officers at the time he was shot. It all happened very quickly: Brown was shot two minutes and thirty-six seconds after Officer Stucker's arrival at the scene, and one minute and six seconds after Officer Ellefson's arrival. It turned out that Lee Deante Brown was a paranoid schizophrenic on a wide range of medications.

Sound writing always has an author, and usually more than one. Sound writing engages directly with the senses and with the warp and weft of aurality. I didn't witness what I have described. Everything I just wrote was drawn from other writing. The brief moments I described generated reams of writing, and my writing emerges from, is made possible by, and derives from the mountain of documentation and analysis that followed. The public report on "the officer-involved death of Lee Deante Brown" states,[3]

> Officer Stucker activated his belt recorder after making visual contact and giving verbal commands with which Brown failed to comply. The recorder ran for 8 minutes and 37 seconds. [. . .] Officer Ellefson activated his belt recorder as he approached Brown. The recorder ran for 13 minutes and 4 seconds.

Belt recorders are part of a movement that began in the 1970s in the United States and the United Kingdom to "police the police," at a point when the militarization of urban police forces had led to extreme distrust between communities of color and law enforcement. In the 1960s through the 1970s, the rise of criminal justice as a field offered new ways for addressing what is now a widespread awareness that law enforcement is unevenly asserted, and at its worst is a form of extreme social control. Urban communities began to articulate their relationship to law enforcement in terms of civil rights. The terms "police brutality" and "driving while black" were coined, though "DWB" was a phrase used knowingly in black communities for a long time before it became widespread, that is, before the ACLU began to use it.[4] The spectacularly brutal incidents between law enforcement officers and Rodney King, Amadou Diallo, and Abner Louima[5] have led to a broad awareness that lethal force is an extraordinary power granted to law enforcement officers, which requires community oversight (Walker 2001; Walker 2005).

Until recently, I regarded my ethnomusicological research differently from my work on police oversight.[6] I was drawn into police accountability work by the conditions of my community. I am not a trained expert in these matters, and this is the first time I have addressed it as a scholar rather than as a community worker and advocate. In 1998, a nineteen-year-old African American woman named Tyisha Miller was shot and killed by four Riverside Police Department officers as she sat in her car (either asleep, unconscious, or in medical distress—it was never clear). The community response was unprecedented for the working-class city of Riverside. My first reaction was that Tyisha Miller could have been any one of my students at the University of California, Riverside, a campus with a majority of students of color. I became a founding member of the Riverside Coalition for Police Accountability, a grassroots community organization; since 2004, I have been its cochair along with a local Quaker and peace activist. In 1999–2000, we successfully called for the creation of an oversight body, which was established in 2000 and named the Community Police Review Commission; it is now included in the city charter. As a result of the Tyisha Miller scandal, the Riverside Police Department was placed under a consent decree by the California state attorney general for five years, from 2001 to 2006, resulting in a number of reforms. Nonetheless, as is true in all cities that have instituted police oversight mechanisms, change is slow. Law enforcement culture is notorious for its insularity, secrecy, paranoia, and self-glorification, and for the ways those values support and sustain racism, sexism, homophobia, and machismo. The paramilitary structures central to virtually all law enforcement in the United States reinforce these patterns. Internal behaviors such as shunning, ridicule, and worse discourage officers from blowing the whistle on one another.

The popular media usually emphasizes ocularity as a key intervention into police brutality. George Holliday's now-infamous footage of Rodney King being beaten by LAPD officers in 1991 is emblematic of the ways that the visual is valorized as a means to reveal police brutality. Video makes visible that which has long been known by communities of color: it "proves" that police brutality is real. However, audio recording is pervasive in law enforcement (Drizin and Colgan 2001; Drizin and Reich 2004), and several points follow. First, many US police departments now require patrol officers to wear small digital recorders and to turn them on whenever they come into direct contact with suspects. Such patrol officers wear small digital recorders on their bodies while on duty, made especially for use by law enforcement but similar to the small solid-state handheld recorders widely available for private use. They attach the recorder to their belt or to their shirt pocket, and they decide when to turn it on, that is, it does not record continuously but has a large, easily accessed button that the officer pushes when she or he comes into contact with a "civilian" (in the parlance of law enforcement). The officer pushes it again to make it stop recording. Police officers must accept, allow, and submit to this form of quotidian surveillance: they must transform themselves into ambulatory audio recorders. Second, at the end of every shift, the officer downloads the recordings, which are archived (usually on the police department's server) and made inaccessible to the officer. The recorder's software automatically time-stamps each recording. Third, when the recordings are needed as evidence—if an officer is accused of misconduct or brutality, or if so-called lethal force is deployed—the audio recording of the incident is transcribed. A disinterested third party, usually a secretary or stenography service, listens to the recording and types it out, transforming it into text so that it can be read by supervising officers, attorneys, judges, grand juries, and more. The actual recording becomes evidence, but the resulting sound writing—the transcription—bursts into being and quickly acquires a life of its own. I would guess that transcriptions are read far more than recordings are ever listened to. As any ethnographer knows, transcribing the spoken word, whether an interview, conversation, storytelling, and so on, involves innumerable decisions about the nuances of inflection and emphasis. Transforming the sonic chaos of violent encounters between police officers and civilians into a transcript is thus a translative act that offers a fraught window on sound writing, by which I mean the ontological act of making sound into writing. While the powerful culture of law enforcement and the US legal system treat this as commonsensical, I consider it anything but. The transcribed sounds—which include who said what, and metadiscursive references to other sounds (e.g., the "sound of gunshots")—are a powerful form of sound writing with real-world effects. What sonic ways of knowing are suggested by both the low-fi recordings and their transcription? How do the recordings exceed the transcriptions? How does an exploration of either, or both, compel a new hearing without flattening the fidelity of lethal force? Sound writing is always schizophonic, whether playfully, violently, or both at once. The schizophonic act is doubled when officers' audio belt recordings are transcribed; or it is even tripled if forensic audio is needed, and it often is, since the low fidelity of the digital recordings and the chaotic circumstances under which they are made—fighting, running, and so on—mean that the act of recording is as utterly uncontrolled as can be imagined.

Prosthetic technologies are pervasive in law enforcement quotidian praxis and in training. The same tools and technologies formerly used *by* law enforcement for security and surveillance are now directed *toward* law enforcement, to police the police: recording devices are now widely integrated into police practice, often by fiat, to address officers' use of force, coercion, and more. The onus of proof has shifted to law enforcement. Extensive use of recording technology "proves" that policies and procedures were followed, or not. Interrogations, patrol, roll call, and more have become interactions that are automatically recorded and thus available for examination by anyone, from law enforcement superiors to attorneys and grand juries with subpoenas. The police have been redefined as objects of surveillance, and like all those surveilled, they have developed techniques for thinking about, talking about, and defeating it. Open surveillance is a preventative measure: it posits that problems won't occur if people know they are being watched, or in this case, heard. Wiretapping is now illegal precisely because it is covert—that is, the subjects don't know they are heard, overheard, or being recorded. Riverside Police Department officers are required to use small digital voice recorders. Of course, "voice recorder" is a misnomer; though the recorders are focused on voices and conversation, they record everything—not just voices. Sometimes they are referred to as "belt recorders" because officers often wear them on their belt in a holster. Indeed, officers wear a lot of gear on their belts. Some of it is regulation, but most police departments allow for a certain amount of individual choice. Officers' belts are big external carrying devices with an astonishing and often heavy assortment of weaponry and related technology. The RPD allows officers to decide for themselves whether to wear their recorder on their belt or in their front pocket. All patrol officers are issued a PUMA Digital Voice Recorder, which is not especially different from any small solid-state handheld recorder except that PUMA recorders are made "for" law enforcement: they have certain features that make them particularly useful for law enforcement. They have a large, easy on/off button, and they contain download options with foolproof time and date stamps. In short, the technology emphasizes ease of use and truthiness.

I use the word "truthiness" deliberately, taking it from comedian Stephen Colbert, who coined it to mean the truth we want to exist, a kind of truth in which facts matter less than felt-in-the-gut opinions. The American Dialect Society selected "truthiness" as its 2005 Word of the Year, writing that "truthiness refers to the quality of preferring concepts or facts one wishes or believes to be true, rather than concepts or facts known to be true." I argue that, in practice, belt recorders serve a truthiness purpose.

The audio recordings of the encounter reveal that the two officers and Lee Brown talked continuously during their brief encounter—talk that overlapped, talk that was supposed to make things happen, talk that was scripted and impelled by official policies, talk that came from two different realities, talk that created a wall of impossibility, talk that kept going even after Brown stopped talking because he was shot and dying—and the officers' belt recorders captured it all. The resulting audio artifacts are dense with sound. They are low fidelity, hard to understand, and full of the snap and crackle of bodies in movement.

Here is an excerpt from the official transcript of the audio from Officer Stucker's recorder.

Suspect Brown: (Inaudible.) No, I do believe in God.
Officer Stucker: Put your hands on the wall.
Suspect Brown: (Inaudible) fucking shoot and I'll (inaudible).
Officer Stucker: Put your hands on the wall.
Suspect Brown: No. I'm gonna see my—
Officer Stucker: Put your hands on the wall. (Sounds of Taser.) Put your hands on the wall.
Suspect Brown: Okay.
Officer Stucker: Now. Turn around. Turn around.
Suspect Brown: All right.
Officer Stucker: On the ground, now.
Suspect Brown: God. God. God.

Officer Stucker: Get on the ground, on the ground.

Suspect Brown: Okay. Okay.

Officer Stucker: Hands behind your back, now. Put your hands behind your back, now. Don't move, or I will shock you again.

Suspect Brown: Okay. Okay. Okay. Okay.

Officer Stucker: Don't move.

Suspect Brown: (Inaudible.)

Officer Stucker: Do not move.

Suspect Brown: (Inaudible.)

Officer Stucker: Don't you dare move.

Suspect Brown: Okay. I got to see my kids walk.

Officer Stucker: Don't move.

Suspect Brown: I'm a God.

Officer Stucker: Don't move.

Suspect Brown: I'm gonna kill you.

Officer Stucker: Don't move. Do not move.

Suspect Brown: I'll kill you. I'll kill you. I cannot die.

Officer Stucker: Don't move.

Suspect Brown: I'm not the devil. That's the devil.

Officer Stucker: Don't move.

Suspect Brown: That's the devil. Fuck the devil.

Officer Stucker: Don't move.

Suspect Brown: I am not a God. I'll kill you. Get away from me. (Inaudible.)

Officer Stucker: 235 Supervisor and Medical Aid. Don't move.

Suspect Brown: Mariah. I want to see Mariah. I'm God.

Officer Stucker: Don't move.

Suspect Brown: (Inaudible.) I've got to see Mariah.

Officer Stucker: Just stay there.

Suspect Brown: (Inaudible.)

Officer Stucker: (Inaudible.) Put your hands behind your back.

Suspect Brown: (Inaudible.)

Officer Stucker: Hands behind your back.

Officer Ellefson: Don't move.

Suspect Brown: (Inaudible.)

Officer Stucker: Don't move.

Suspect Brown: The devil will kill me. I've got to see Mariah.

Officer Stucker: Don't move. Put your hands behind your back, now.

Suspect Brown: Oh, my God, I've got to see Mariah.

Officer Stucker: Don't—put your hands behind your back, now.

Suspect Brown: I've got to see Mariah, Mariah.

Officer Stucker: Hands behind your back and don't move.

Suspect Brown: Mariah.

Officer Ellefson: (Inaudible.)

Officer Stucker: Hands behind your back.

Suspect Brown: Mariah. Help me. Help me. I need Mariah. Mariah. Mariah.

Officer Stucker: Hands behind your back, now.

Officer Ellefson: Put your hands behind your back.

Suspect Brown: (Inaudible.) God. God. God. God. God. God. God. God. God. God.

Officer Ellefson: Hands behind your back, now. (Sounds of Taser.)

Suspect Brown: (Inaudible.)

Officer Stucker: Get your hands behind your back.

Suspect Brown: (Inaudible.)

Officer Stucker: Get your hands behind your back.

Suspect Brown: God—Aztec warriors, rise up. Aztec warriors, rise up. Aztec—

Officer Stucker: Put your hands behind your back, now.

Suspect Brown: (Inaudible.)

Officer Stucker: Put your hands behind your back, now. (Sounds of Taser.)

Suspect Brown: Aztec warriors. Aztec warriors.

Officer Stucker: Put your hands behind your back, now. Get on the ground.

Suspect Brown: You can't hurt me.

Officer Stucker: Get on the ground. Get on the ground. Get on the ground. (Sounds of Taser.) Put your hands behind your back. Do it, now.

Watch that cuff. He's swinging that cuff. It's a weapon.

Officer Ellefson: I got it.

Officer Stucker: Put your hands behind your back, now.

Officer Ellefson: Hands behind your back.

Officer Stucker: Put your hands behind your back, now. Put your hands behind your back.

Officer Ellefson: Hands behind your back.

Suspect Brown: (Inaudible.)

Officer Ellefson: Hands behind your back. Pow. Pow. (Gunfire.)

Officer Stucker: Hands behind your back.

Suspect Brown: Uh—

Officer Ellefson: Stay down.
Officer Stucker: Get down.
Unidentified Speaker: (Screaming.)
Officer Stucker: 235 shots fired.
Unidentified Speaker: (Screaming.) Oh, my God.
Officer Stucker: Get your hands behind your back, now.
Unidentified Speaker: (Screaming.)
Officer Stucker: Get your hands behind your back.
Unidentified Speaker: (Screaming.)
(Sirens.)
Officer Stucker: Put your hands behind your back.
(Sirens.)
Officer Stucker: (Inaudible.) Put your hands behind your back.
Officer Ellefson: Stand by. Stand by.
Officer Stucker: He's got the Taser in his hand.
Sir, back to the office, please.
No. No. Stay.
Unidentified Speaker: (Inaudible.)
Officer Stucker: That's fine.
Hands behind your back, now.
Officer Ellefson: As soon as you stop fighting, we can get the ambulance in here.
Officer Stucker: Put your hands behind your back, now.
Officer Ellefson: Stay down, brother. Stay down.
Officer Stucker: Stay down.
Get your hands behind your back.
Officer Ellefson: Sir, put your hands behind your back, please.
Officer Stucker: We need to get medical aid up here for you. You need to put your hands behind your back.
Officer Ellefson: Hands behind your back.
(Sirens.) (Radio.)
Officer Ellefson: Put your hands behind your back, sir.
Officer Stucker: (Inaudible), bring some of—move these people back. Brandon, that lady that's screaming over there, we need her. She's a witness. And I believe she's got some relationship—she knew the guy's name. So let's get her in the back of the car. So you need to put her in the back of the car.
Unidentified Speaker: (Inaudible.) Mother fucker. (Inaudible.)
(Radio traffic.)

Officer Stucker: One victim. Let's bring Fire [i.e., fire department paramedics] in over here. I need to leave this unit where it is and that unit. So just bring Fire in that driveway over there, obviously.

(Radio traffic.) (Sirens.)

The transcription of Officer Stucker's belt recorder is a harrowing document. That Lee Deante Brown was out of his mind is immediately evident from the audio. Yet Officers Stucker and Ellefson don't sound terribly normal, either: they're verbally stuck—they repeat themselves endlessly—they sound more than a little crazy themselves. They're probably pumped full of adrenaline. Officer Stucker is trying to proceed by the book, but his endless reiteration of "Put your hands behind your back, now" makes him sound like he's a broken record. The officers could have backed off and could have called Brown in as a "5150"—the police code for someone in mental distress who is a danger to themselves or others—and could have waited and let paramedics take care of it. But they didn't. Brown was stuck in his own internal loop, and the officers were stuck in theirs: he wouldn't comply, therefore they had to make him comply.

Sound writing is always engaged with other sound writings. The official transcription of the recording is not equivalent to the sound of the recording. It is an interpretation and an extrapolation. But the sound of the recording is itself already a mediated object. Actually, two recordings were made of Lee Brown's last moments because Officers Stucker and Ellefson were each wearing belt recorders, and they both activated them. Recording 72–1298TE 04–03–2006, from Officer Terry Ellefson's recorder, is 13:06 minutes long, and recording 76–1320PS 04–03–2006, from Officer Paul Stucker, is 8:37 minutes long.[7] The previous transcription is from Officer Stucker's recorder. It begins jarringly in medias res, with Lee Brown's voice dominating: he wails continuously in a high, anguished, thready voice. He is so completely distraught that it's difficult to make out his exact words without the transcript. He is out of his head, and the high, hysterical tessitura of his voice is deeply unsettling. You then hear another high voice, shouting, overlapping with Brown's, tight with stress—it's Officer Stucker's voice, pitched to command, but the two voices are each so distorted with tension that they create a conjoined wall of busy, interlocking, hair-raising noise. Both voices are pushed to their limits. You can tell within seconds that neither is listening to the other, and you know this won't end well. Within sixty seconds, you give in to the distortion of both their voices and the limits of the recording technology itself, which emphasizes the high-end frequencies and cancels out the low end: you're just hearing a busy, weird, shrieking timbre that adds up to whines and howls—*both* men sound out of their minds. When Officer Ellefson suddenly, calmly, says "I got it," the normality of his voice—close by, from his chest voice rather than the disturbing head voices heard before, sounds even stranger, as if he's in a different narrative. The nearness of his dispassionate, matter-of-fact voice is oddly intimate precisely because it isn't from that world of chaotic, inchoate shouting. But it's gone as soon as you register it. The crackle of electricity—the Taser—sounds like a bad sound effect from a movie. The shouting immediately ratchets up again, though Brown's reedy howls have stopped; instead, it's the officers' voices and then, after the breathy *pow pow* of the gun, screams from—who? Other people. People we haven't heard before that moment, people we didn't know were even there.

It's a terrible recording in several different ways. Certainly it's full of dreadful, disturbing sounds. The recording quality is also quite bad, despite the fact that this recording is "enhanced," in the terminology of forensic audio. This enhancement was done professionally, by an audio forensic expert. I don't who was hired to work on these two recordings or what decisions that person made, but forensic enhancement generally removes "noise" and thus draws forward the sounds considered most significant or important: the expert may deploy equalization and volume increase or decrease as deemed necessary. A process of forensic listening *and* interpretation takes place before the recording is heard by anyone else, and its truthiness is mediated before it bursts onto the legal scene.

Listening to the voice of Lee Brown is hard in at least two ways. First, it is horrendously disturbing to hear his emotional pain, and hearing his silence is even worse—when he stops shouting and crying, it's for all the wrong reasons. Mark Anthony Neal writes that listening to the 911 tapes of Trayvon Martin's death[8] was rending because we are accustomed to *seeing* the black man (not hearing him), and further, we are conditioned to see him as menacing. "We have so little understanding of Black males as vulnerable, in pain, under duress, in terror and confronting death," Neal writes, "that those off-screen sounds are deeply unsettling" (Neal 2012). R. N. Bradley argues that the 911 calls (from Zimmerman and then from concerned neighbors) constitute a set of interrelated soundscapes, and she deliberately sound-writes a mixtape in which she hears the 911 recordings intercut with 50 Cent's "Many Men" in an attempt to hear the process of pathologizing black men. She explains, "I use the word 'mixtape' here to argue that the frequencies of trauma in which the (white) listener situates Trayvon Martin's death must be heard within a larger understanding of sound as a commodified and racialized space" (Bradley 2012). In sum, it is simply not possible to listen to the officers' belt recordings and hear what actually happened between them and Lee Brown. The lo-fi sound of Brown's distress and death is literally and figuratively (inaudible) (unintelligible) (already written).

Belt recorders nest in a thicket of peculiar practices that deserve attention for their oddness alone, but they speak in surprising ways when considered ethnographically. We must remind ourselves that audio recordings are needed because police officers won't inform on one another. Police officers' refusal to give one another up or to report on police misconduct is famously called "the blue wall of silence," and that silence has profound effects, from officers' strong resistance to either individual *or* systemic change, to the multiple ways that women or people of color are discouraged from becoming officers, or hit a glass ceiling for promotions within the ranks, to lives lost. That silence is what's *not* said, and what officers *refuse* to say. This principle of secrecy is a strong, effective, sustained, and pervasive perlocutionary act in law enforcement culture (Koepke 2000). Silence is thus part of police sound culture and is centrally part of what I want to write into existence: I am trying to hear that articulate silence. As Deborah Kapchan has written:

> What we do not have is a meta-discursive theory that puts musical style in conversation with styles of writing or other forms of representation. In other words, while ethnomusicologists have been scrupulous in their contextualization of musical style in the realms of class, gender, race, and culture, we have been less than attentive to the fact that styles of writing about these subjects create the very knowledge we intend to convey. (Kapchan this volume, 17n27)

I must consider not only *my* sound writing, but a sound culture with its own stringently codified forms of sound writing. My critical ethnographic sensibilities are focused on a sound writing culture that is not my own, yet has strong family resemblances with a practice I hold near and dear: the transcribed ethnographic interview. The script making of oral histories, interviews, conversations, and the talk between interlocutors is central to ethnographic work. It is sometimes valorized because we know that that talk is bigger than itself, offering essential testimony to the importance of the quotidian. The written representation of oral interviews is the most basic sound writing: we take sound and render it into the flatness of text using standardized practices.[9]

Law enforcement is stuffed full of transcribed interviews. The interview is central to police work, from interrogation of suspects to confessions to interviewing witnesses. Most such interviews are tape-recorded or videotaped, or both, and then transcribed. Coroners' criminal autopsy reports are often actually transcriptions of a spoken and recorded report created on the spot: during an autopsy, words are uttered over the remains of the deceased and then transformed into writing. Sound writing is thus central to police work. Most important, much of their work is sounded or uttered *for the purposes of recording,* and it then undergoes a transformation, a planned shift into the medium of the written word. This system of interlocking technologies is at the heart of sound writing in law enforcement work, and is based on a poetics of truthiness. It goes deeper than that: many utterances are performed with the *expectation* of that transformation; they are *designed for* that transformation and for specific kinds of sound writing. This poetics is very deeply rooted. If you have ever talked with a police officer, or listened to a TV news story featuring a law enforcement officer reporting on criminal events, you have seen the officer's ability to shift into the performance mode of "report speech," a compressed modality marked by fact talk, masking people as categories ("subjects," "witnesses," etc.), an unemotional demeanor, and even a very distinctive flattened monotone diction. They talk as if they are giving a report. No, they speak in anticipation of the report to come, the court testimony to come, the internal affairs interview to come. They rehearse the report.[10]

Such artifacts of law enforcement sound writing beg for further transformation. Documentary theater or "verbatim theater" is based on just such a conversion, literally taking real-life transcripts and reworking them for the proscenium stage, and often focused on traumatic events. Anna Deavere Smith is famous for a meticulous preparation process in which she records her interviews with subjects precisely so that she can then channel them in performances that address race riots and more (Kondo 1996). Performance studies scholar Stephen Bottoms has addressed the uptick in documentary stage drama following 9/11, suggesting that an "unmediated access to 'the real' is not something the theatre can ever honestly provide," and that it is "doubly illusory in presenting a 'realism' that purports to present us with the speech of 'actual' people involved in 'real' events" even while obviously and transparently (re)staged (Bottoms 2006, 57, 59).

Rickerby Hinds, a playwright, my colleague at the University of California, Riverside, and one of my closest interlocutors for this essay, has spent the last ten years writing and rewriting a play titled *Dreamscape,* which draws on documentary theater to address the death of Tyisha Miller,[11] the young African American woman I mentioned earlier who was killed in 1998 by four RPD officers (Hinds 2011). He embeds two transcripts into his play, a post-shooting interview by internal affairs officers with one of the involved officers and the autopsy report. The "official" story is thus told through their "actual" words, which are uttered onstage by a young African American actor who flips in and out of hip-hop delivery, thus disrupting their meaning and intent by inverting their source. But Tyisha Miller herself is the center of his play, and since she cannot speak for herself in the absence of any official transcript—she has literally been ex-scripted, one could say—Hinds renders her as vividly young and black, and all of her imagined talk is in response to the official transcripts. Whether she is asleep in the car moments before she is killed, or on the autopsy table, or going about her life before its end on December 28, 1998, all her words take flight from the transcripts. In a postshow Q&A session in 2011, Hinds jokingly said, "I didn't actually write any of this!"—but of course he was fully aware of the complexities of authorship in documentary theater. As Stephen Bottoms argues, "Stage realism purports to present a transparent representation of 'lifelike' behavior, while in fact providing a constructed authorial perspective on the real" (Bottoms 2006, 59). Further, as Carol Martin has written, contemporary documentary theater depends on a "the tripartite structure of technology, text, and body" (Martin 2006). That is, the very ability to present transcripts of the real emerges from the encounter between a body and various technologies of replication. Benjamin's aura is the animating spark that shapes and frames documentary theater: the technologies creating truthiness are primary to the form and not merely supporting detail. Martin continues,

> Those who make documentary theatre interrogate specific events, systems of belief, and political affiliations precisely through the creation of their own versions of events, beliefs, and politics by exploiting technology that enables replication; video, film, tape recorders, radio, copy machines, and computers are the sometimes visible, sometimes invisible, technological means of documentary theatre. While documentary theatre remains in the realm of handcraft—people assemble to create it, meet to write it, gather to see it—it is a form of theatre in which technology is a primary factor in the transmission of knowledge. (Martin 2006, 9)

Seen in this light, the transcribed law enforcement interview that must be created after a law enforcement officer has killed someone is an essential form of documentary theatre. It is wholly dependent on technologies that are prosthetic extensions of the officer's body, particularly his ears but also his voice.[12]

As Sarah Jain has noted, "'Prostheses' are discursive frameworks, as well as material artifacts"(Jain 1999, 32), and the belt recorder propels an elaborate set of discursive expectations into motion.

The craft of *not* using a recorder has emerged in tandem with the requirements that they must always be used: this is a soundscape that officers must know how to use and how *not* to use, so they learn how to accidently pause their devices or not turn them on. Knowing that the recordings can become sound writing, and knowing that the sound writing carries real power, means that some officers necessarily become expert in using and *not* using audio and video devices. If belt recorders transform police officers into active participants in their own surveillance, it should come as no surprise that they become expert users and misusers of the technology.

According to law enforcement logic, an officer-involved death can be fixed during the investigation by showing that the perlocutionary utterance ("Stop or I'll shoot! Put your hands behind your back!") was refused. If so, the officer's actions were "in policy" and the victim brought on the consequences, or the victim could have avoided the problem by complying. But the deeper problem is that the perlocutionary utterance failed: it was supposed to do something, but it didn't. This leaves everyone in impossible positions: the officer has no option except to keep repeating the key utterance, and anyone beyond the reach of such logic is in real danger.

So what do belt recorders "do"? Do they actively discourage officers from exerting the unnecessary use of force, or is their role simply to prove that none took place . . . or both at once? To what extent do the belt recorders shape officers' behaviors? Do officers now perform "for" the recorders and "for" the potential listener?

Jonathan Sterne has written about recordings of Osama bin Laden's voice, addressing the proliferation of anxieties over originals, copies, and forensic audio, including—most especially—the "anxiety of schizophonia" (Sterne 2008, 88) that has produced the need for voiceprint identification technologies—an entire industry unto itself. Sterne writes (90), "In the world of forensic audio, the voice is artifact, trace, and remnant." He argues (92) that forensic audio relies on a set of assumptions about the voice that are the exact opposite of Barthes's "body in the voice": voiceprint analysis posits the voice as already an artifact that can then be matched against other artifacts. Sterne then shows how tapes of bin Laden giving speeches were refuted by American politicians, who argued that the tapes weren't "really" bin Laden; they relied on technological proof that the voice had no grain or body, and that therefore the body politic he represented could be neither real nor effective.

Forensic audio analysis was done on Officer Stucker's and Officer Ellefson's belt recordings. Truthiness demanded that the sound writing be taken further, since it didn't clearly exonerate the officers, and DNA tests on the officers' Tasers didn't provide any clear evidence that Brown had been holding one when he was shot. So it came down to the officers' voices and the question of whether forensic audio "revealed" something that hadn't been heard before. The recordings and the resulting transcriptions raised as many questions as they seemed to answer, and their unintelligibility provided opportunities. Officer Ellefson claimed that Brown was holding his Taser, and the audio recordings will never quite tell us whether that was true or not, which is probably exactly why the claim was made. Here is an official transcription of a public session of Riverside's Community Police Review Commission on November 8, 2006—a final example of sound writing that transects and transforms the sound writing of the officers' belt recordings. The commission was deep into its review of Brown's death. "Vice-Chair Ward" is Jim Ward, an African American member of the commission with a keen analytical sense and the confidence to speak truth to power. "Mr. Warnberg" is Butch Warnberg, an independent investigator hired by the commission. Commissioner Ward asked some pointed questions about the recordings and truthiness.[13]

Vice-Chair Ward: Yeah . . . First of all, I'd like . . . um . . . you said something about some information that come [*sic*] to your attention as late as last night. Could you elaborate on that please?

Mr. Warnberg: Yes, sir. We had done an analysis of the belt recorders for Officer Ellefson and Officer Stucker and in a continued review of those belt recording statements, I'd issued the report, prepared the report, and included the analysis of those belt recorder statements. Last . . . last night, we found a statement on behalf of Officer Ellefson just prior to the shooting that we . . . that was inaudible prior to . . . in our prior listenings that changes the analysis significantly.

Vice-Chair Ward: What was the statement?

Mr. Warnberg: The statement by Officer Ellefson just prior to the shooting was, "Drop the guh . . ."

Vice-Chair Ward: What's a "guh?"

Mr. Warnberg: Well, we believe that it's pro . . . it was most likely the gun, the Taser gun. But there is still some evidence that is . . . that has not been submitted yet. We have an analysis of the fingerprint evidence on the Taser gun, which was inconclusive for Mr. Brown's fingerprints. However, the DNA evidence that was submitted by the Police Department has not been returned by DOJ for conclusive . . . finding. So . . . so we don't have the DNA evidence on the, uh . . . on the Taser gun. We had not previously heard that almost inaudible statement on the part of Mr. Elle . . . Officer Ellefson just prior to the shooting, so some of the analysis with regards to the statements as they pertain to the shooting are in error.

Vice-Chair Ward: Okay. One of my concerns is, in reading the report, I never heard any of the investigators or either one of the officers refer to the Taser as a gun. Every time they referred [to] it, they referred to it as the Taser. You might want to take a look at that. I did not review the reports with that in mind, but I don't . . . my recollection is that every time they made reference to a Taser, they called it a Taser, not a gun and um . . . So . . . And then, what I would like to know, in addition to that, if that were the fact that he said, "Drop the guh" or whatever, how does that comport with all of these other . . . all this other information that we have? You know, we have some people here, according to this diagram, we have three witnesses that's almost as close to the situation as the police is [*sic*] and none of those witnesses saw him with anything in his hands and, you know, it's kinda hard for me to put it together that none of the witnesses saw it, but all of a sudden, that's what happened.

In the end, the officers were cleared by the Community Police Review Commission. The many witnesses' accounts didn't exonerate the officers, and DNA tests on the officers' Tasers didn't provide any clear evidence that Brown had been holding one when he was shot, so forensic audio analysis was done on the officers' belt recordings because the RPD needed some kind of evidence to show they had done nothing wrong. So it came down to the officers' voices and the question of whether forensic audio "revealed" something that hadn't been heard before. The "guh" was enough: Brown might have been holding the Taser. The recording and the sound writing overran the witnesses' statements that no one had seen Brown holding the Taser. The shooting was pronounced within policy, and the officers were exonerated.

Who were those "unidentified speakers" in the transcription? In the seconds after Officer Ellefson shot Lee Brown, who was the "unidentified speaker" who said "motherfucker," and to whom was it directed? And finally, what about our act of reading the transcript from Officer Stucker's belt recorder, whether silently or aloud? As with all evidence of trauma, we are instantly part of a dynamic loop of witness and voyeurism, participants in spectacularized acts of looking . . . and hearing. We can't be immune to the deep ways that any act of violence is instantly fetishized as that-which-isn't-happening-to-me, that-which-is-consumed. We must try to bear witness in the ways that Diana Taylor has argued, where we are "caught in the spectacle" and acknowledge both the burden and the responsibility to pass on the insight (Taylor 1997, 25). Scholars and activists who work with testimony are terribly familiar with these dynamics and talk through the contradictions endlessly. When we reproduce the violence by watching the footage or playing the tape, do we carry that violence forward? Does the very passivity of witness transform the act of violence into that-which-is-consumed, a spectacularized thing? Isn't it better to watch and listen than *not* to do so? Most agree that it is better to witness than not to listen. Yet the terrible intimacy of reading or hearing Officer Ellefson shoot Lee Brown is profoundly unsettling and intrusive. This is the interzone that Deborah Kapchan has argued offers a new critical space for hearing and writing (Kapchan and Stanyek 2010, 3).

Put your hands behind your back.
Put your hands behind your back now.

This essay is an act of forensic audition, written so I can hear what should have happened.

ACKNOWLEDGMENTS

Many thanks to my colleague Rickerby Hinds for his stunning play *Dreamscape* and for helping me think through the ongoing effects of Tyisha Miller's death; to Jason Stanyek and Deborah Kapchan for modeling the power of sound writing; and to my colleague Jonathan Ritter for many long conversations about why it is challenging and necessary to write about music, trauma, and violence.

NOTES

1. I draw on a commanding body of scholarship on violence and sound for my ideas. Critical scholarly work on pain, violence, terror, and trauma has proliferated since the groundbreaking work of Scarry and many others in the 1980s–1990s (Scarry 1985; Caruth

1996). The anthropology of violence is now well established (Foucault 1979; Taussig 1987; Scheper-Hughes 1992; Das et al. 2000). The field of performance studies has addressed trauma and violence in consistently principled ways with far-reaching implications (Lawless and Carver 2009; Taylor 1997; Conquergood 2002). Dwight Conquergood argues that performance studies offers "its most radical intervention" by unsettling and collapsing the text versus performance distinction as a false divide that nonetheless gets played out as "epistemic violence" (Conquergood 2002, 148, 151). A growing number of music scholars address connections between sound and violence. Musicologist Suzanne Cusick's foundational articles on the use of music as torture by the US military offered essential interventions (Cusick 2006; Cusick 2008a; Cusick 2008b; Cusick 2013). Jonathan Pieslak's and Martin Daughtry's work on US soldiers serving in Iraq shows how central music was to their work as soldier/warriors (Pieslak 2007; Pieslak 2009; Daughtry 2012). Johnson and Cloonan have drawn together work that addresses the intersections of popular music with violence, whether viewed as causing, preventing, or emerging from it (Johnson and Cloonan 2008). Quite a lot of work broadly addresses music and political/ethnic conflict (O'Connell and Castelo-Branco 2010; Fast and Pegley 2012); a very small amount of work focuses on gendered violence and music (Pilzer 2012).

2. Phencyclidine, known as PCP, is a synthetic drug whose symptoms (delusions, hallucinations, disordered thinking, and extreme anxiety) mimic schizophrenia.

3. City of Riverside, Community Police Review Commission, *Officer-Involved Death, Lee Deante Brown: Public Report,* CPRC case no. 06–021, RPD case no. P3–06–093–205, November 28, 2007.

4. The American Civil Liberties Union, which has worked extensively for decades on police brutality, accountability, and oversight.

5. Rodney King was beaten by Los Angeles Police Department officers in 1991; Abner Louima was beaten and sodomized with the handle of a bathroom plunger by New York Police Department officers in 1997; Amadou Diallo, though unarmed, was shot and killed by New York Police Department officers in 1999. All were black men.

6. See Mina Yang's work on the Los Angeles Police Department and the jazz scene in South Central Los Angeles for the only work of which I am aware that offers critical attention to the relationship between music, communities of color, and law enforcement (Yang 2008).

7. I obtained both recordings from the Community Police Review Commission, as public documents.

8. Trayvon Martin was shot to death by George Zimmerman in Sanford, Florida, on February 26, 2012. Zimmerman was a neighborhood watch volunteer in a predominantly white gated community; Martin was an unarmed seventeen-year-old African American walking back to a relative's home after going to a convenience store. Zimmerman was acquitted of second-degree murder in a trial that ended in July 2013. The case received

nationwide attention, prompted numerous demonstrations, and reopened discussions on racial profiling.

9. Many folklorists, anthropologists, oral historians, and ethnomusicologists have struggled with both the praxis and the politics of interview transcription (Gumperz and Hymes 1962; Tedlock 1983; Behar 1993; Oliver, Serovich, and Mason 2005; Hamilton and Shopes 2008).

10. In related ethnographic research, Emily Colborn-Roxworthy has addressed the "performance paradigms" used in law enforcement training (Colborn-Roxworthy 2004).

11. I saw a staged version of the play at the University of California, Riverside, in 2007; a closed staging of the latest version on April 19, 2011, at the Culver Center for the Arts in Riverside, California; and subsequent full performances in March and July 2013 at the University of California, Riverside.

12. I am, of course, using the gendered pronoun deliberately.

13. City of Riverside, Community Police Review Commission, regular meeting minutes, November 8, 2006, doc. 06–63, Riverside, California.

REFERENCES CITED

Behar, Ruth. *Translated Woman: Crossing the Border with Esperanza's Story.* Boston: Beacon Press, 1993.

Bottoms, Stephen J. "Putting the Document into Documentary: An Unwelcome Corrective?" *TDR: The Drama Review* 50 (fall 2006): 56–68.

Bradley, R. N. "Death Wish Mixtape: Sounding Trayvon Martin's Death." *Sounding Out!* March 26, 2012. Accessed on March 1, 2016. http://soundstudiesblog.com/2012/03/26/death-wish-mixtape-sounding-trayvon-martins-death/.

Caruth, Cathy. *Unclaimed Experience: Trauma, Narrative, and History.* Baltimore: Johns Hopkins University Press, 1996.

Colborn-Roxworthy, Emily. "Role-Play Training at a 'Violent Disneyland': The FBI Academy's Performance Paradigms." *TDR: The Drama Review* 48, no. 4 (2004): 81–108.

Conquergood, D. "Performance Studies: Interventions and Radical Research 1." *TDR: The Drama Review* 46, no. 2 (2002): 145–56.

Cusick, Suzanne G. "Music as Torture/Music as Weapon." *TRANS-Revista Transcultural de Música* 10 (2006). Accessed on March 1, 2016. http://www.sibetrans.com/trans/a152/music-as-torture-music-as-weapon.

———. "'You Are in a Place That Is Out of the World . . . ': Music in the Detention Camps of the 'Global War on Terror.'" *Journal of the Society for American Music* 2, no. 1 (2008a): 1–26.

———. "Musicology, Torture, Repair." *Radical Musicology* 3 (2008b). Accessed on March

1, 2016. http://www.radical-musicology.org.uk/2008/Cusick.pdf.
———. "Towards an Acoustemology of Detention in the 'Global War on Terror.'" In *Music, Sound and Space: Transformations of Public and Private Experience,* edited by Georgina Born, 275–91. Cambridge: Cambridge University Press, 2013.
Das, Veena, Arthur Kleinman, Mamphela Ramphele, and Pamela Reynolds, eds. *Violence and Subjectivity.* Berkeley: University of California Press, 2000.
Daughtry, J. Martin. "Belliphonic Sounds and Indoctrinated Ears: The Dynamics of Military Listening in Wartime Iraq." In *Pop When the World Falls Apart: Music in the Shadow of Doubt,* edited by Eric Weisbard, 111–44. Durham, NC: Duke University Press, 2012.
Drizin, Steven A., and Beth A. Colgan. "Let the Cameras Roll: Mandatory Videotaping of Interrogations Is the Solution to Illinois' Problem of False Confessions." *Loyola University Chicago Law Journal* 32 (2001): 337–424.
———, and Marissa J. Reich. "Heeding the Lessons of History: The Need for Mandatory Recording of Police Interrogations to Accurately Assess the Reliability and Voluntariness of Confessions." *Drake Law Review* 52 (2004): 619–46.
Fast, Susan, and Kip Pegley, eds. *Music, Politics, and Violence.* Middletown, CT: Wesleyan University Press, 2012.
Foucault, Michel. *Discipline and Punish: The Birth of the Prison.* New York: Vintage Books, 1979.
Gumperz, John J., and Dell Hymes, eds. *The Ethnography of Communication.* Washington, DC: American Anthropological Association, 1964.
Hamilton, Paula, and Linda Shopes, eds. *Oral History and Public Memories.* Philadelphia: Temple University Press, 2008.
Hinds, Rickerby. "Dreamscape." In *Say Word!: Voices from Hip Hop Theater,* edited by Daniel Banks, 55–92. Ann Arbor: University of Michigan Press, 2011.
Jain, Sarah S. "The Prosthetic Imagination: Enabling and Disabling the Prosthesis Trope." *Science Technology Human Values* 24, no. 1 (1999): 31–54.
Johnson, Bruce, and Martin Cloonan. *Dark Side of the Tune: Popular Music and Violence.* Ashgate Popular and Folk Music Series. Aldershot, UK: Ashgate, 2008.
Kapchan, Deborah, "The Splash of Icarus: Theorizing Sound Writing/Writing Sound Theory." In *Theorizing Sound Writing*, edited by Deborah Kapchan. Middletown, CT: Wesleyan University Press, 2017.
Koepke, Jennifer E. "The Failure to Breach the Blue Wall of Silence: The Circling of the Wagons to Protect Police Perjury." *Washburn Law Journal* 39 (2000): 211–42.
Kondo, Dorinne. "Shades of Twilight: Anna Deavere Smith and Twilight: Los Angeles 1992." In *Connected: Engagements with Media,* edited by George E. Marcus, 313–46. Chicago: University of Chicago Press, 1996.

Lawless, Elaine, and M. Heather Carver. *Troubling Violence: A Performance Project.* Jackson: University Press of Mississippi, 2009.

Martin, Carol. "Bodies of Evidence." *TDR: The Drama Review* 50, no. 3 (2006): 8–15.

Neal, Mark Anthony. "Hearing Trayvon Die." *NewBlackMan (In Exile).* March 2012. Accessed on March 1, 2016. http://newblackman.blogspot.com/2012/03/hearing-trayvon-die.html.

O'Connell, John Morgan, and Salwa El-Shawan Castelo-Branco, eds. *Music and Conflict.* Urbana: University of Illinois Press, 2010.

Oliver, Daniel G., Julianne M. Serovich, and Tina L. Mason. "Constraints and Opportunities with Interview Transcription: Towards Reflection in Qualitative Research." *Social Forces* 84, no. 2 (2005): 1273–89.

Pieslak, Jonathan R. "Sound Targets: Music and the War in Iraq." *Journal of Musicological Research* 26, nos. 2–3 (April 1, 2007): 123–49.

———. *Sound Targets: American Soldiers and Music in the Iraq War.* Bloomington: Indiana University Press, 2009.

Pilzer, Joshua D. *Hearts of Pine: Songs in the Lives of Three Korean Survivors of the Japanese "Comfort Women."* New York: Oxford University Press, 2012.

Scarry, Elaine. *The Body in Pain: The Making and Unmaking of the World.* New York: Oxford University Press, 1985.

Scheper-Hughes, Nancy. *Death without Weeping: The Violence of Everyday Life in Brazil.* Berkeley: University of California Press, 1992.

Sterne, Jonathan. "Enemy Voice." *Social Text* 96, no. 26 (2008): 79–100.

Taussig, Michael T. *Shamanism, Colonialism, and the Wild Man: A Study in Terror and Healing.* Chicago: University of Chicago Press, 1987.

Taylor, Diana. *Disappearing Acts: Spectacles of Gender and Nationalism in Argentina's "Dirty War."* Durham, NC: Duke University Press, 1997.

Tedlock, Dennis. *The Spoken Word and the Work of Interpretation.* Philadelphia: University of Pennsylvania Press, 1983.

Walker, Samuel. *Police Accountability: The Role of Citizen Oversight.* Belmont, CA: Wadsworth, 2001.

———. *The New World of Police Accountability.* Thousand Oaks, CA: Sage Publications, 2005.

Yang, Mina. *California Polyphony: Ethnic Voices, Musical Crossroads.* Urbana: University of Illinois Press, 2008.

DEBORAH KAPCHAN

12. Listening Acts

Witnessing the Pain (and Praise) of Others

There are many ways to listen. Indeed, how we listen changes not only the perception of the listener, but what might be called, following Bourdieu, the social field of listening, that is, the aesthetic structure that constitutes a shared somatic environment or habitus (Bourdieu 1977). Just as one person looking at the sky will cause others to direct their gaze upward, one deep listener in a room will first change the vibrations of her own body and then affect the somatic attention of other bodies, sentient and non. Listening is an active conduit for the social transmission and transformation of affect.

What changes when ways of listening, like ways of speaking,[1] are recognized as social events? How does attention to listening change cultural analysis and perception? Following Austin's theory of speech acts, I define a "listening act" as listening that actively performs something in the world.[2] In this chapter, I evoke several listening acts that have emerged from my longitudinal research on Sufi Muslim rituals and festivals in Morocco and France to understand the performative power of listening: 1) in its role as *witness* to the pain and praise of others, 2) as a political *tactic*, and 3) as a *method* of sound knowledge transmission that often involves *lingering in the space of discomfort.* Listening acts are not just "objects" of the ethnographic ear, so to speak, but comprise a method of ethnographic translation. What's more, listening acts, when engaged with intention, restructure the aesthetic ground, thereby effecting what Rancière calls a "redistribution of the sensible" (Rancière 2010).

LISTENING ACT I: *IBTIHALAT*— LISTENING BETWEEN DARKNESS AND DAWN

Ibtihalat: these are Muslim prayers of supplication said at dawn in mosques and at home. As in many spiritual traditions, the act of rousing oneself from sleep in order to pray or to meditate when it is still dark outside is an act that accrues grace or blessing, either in this life or the next. In 1994 I lived down the street from the Hassan II mosque and mausoleum in Rabat. I rented a modest apartment on a street lined with statuesque palm trees extending all the way from the post office at one end to the marble plaza at the other, where the mosque stood overlooking the sea and the mouth of the Bougreg River. The first time I woke to the mournful sounds of the *ibtihalat,* they seemed to be drifting over the palm fronds in the chill of dawn. They were haunting, like sounds that carried one over the threshold from life to death. I thought I was still dreaming. But as they didn't dissipate, I began to listen more closely for their source. The voices were emanating from the mosque down the street.

Over the following months, these sounds became iconic of the neighborhood and my time in it. I remember standing on my balcony at 4 a.m. in a half-sleep, thinking of *maqamat*—literally, scales in Arabic music, but also the word for stages of initiation in Sufism, passages from one station to another, limens.[3] Recalling that listening act now, I hear those prayers, and the past returns, co-immanent with the present (Casey 1987).

Thresholds of sound: it is not accidental that Switzerland made the call to prayer illegal in the public sphere in 2009, or that many French people do not consider church bells an affront to the secular state but do object to the call to prayer from a minaret. Sounds bring us to our limits, our limens or thresholds, because sounds always exceed them—the limits of our body; the limits of secularism, of the private sphere, of property; the limits of our theorizing. Listening is a political act; who has the right to listen? Whose listening is curtailed?

LISTENING ACT II: LITERACIES OF LISTENING

I have been doing work in Sufi Muslim communities in Morocco since 1994, and in France since 2008. The Sufis with whom I work are in the Qadirriya Boutshishiyya order (QB), a Sunni lineage that traces its genealogy back to the prophet Mohammed. When I began doing research on Sufism in Morocco twenty-two years ago, I immersed myself in the practice of *sama'*—Sufi devotional singing—but also in relationships with a community of women, particularly in Casablanca.

In 2008, however, I began to do research with the same order in France. The QB order has been in France for at least twenty-five years, and their numbers are increasing yearly. Unlike Morocco, the majority of practitioners in France do *not* speak Arabic, necessitating the transliteration of the liturgy and the songs into a Latin alphabet. Despite the accessibility of the liturgical and song books, however, the women in France primarily learned the liturgy, as well as the songs and chants, by listening deeply to those around them.

In Morocco, the women in the QB order are native speakers of Arabic, many of whom grew up listening to the songs, chants, and prayers in the liturgy. Indeed, the sounds of Sufism writ large (Morocco has many Sufi orders) permeate Moroccan culture, from the public rituals of the Sufi brotherhoods, to the mediatized versions of the same, to say nothing of how Sufi aesthetics inhabit popular festivals, song, and dance. The Sufi women in France, however, are either second- or third-generation French North Africans or French Sufi Muslim converts. Most of them do not speak Arabic, nor have they grown up with the melodies of the praise songs. They learn the Arabic liturgy, song lyrics, and melodies by listening—closely, transitively—to sounds that are, for them, nonreferential. To hear them sing, however, one would not say so, as their pronunciation is flawless. This is because their initiation process takes place through the ear. Much like the process of second-language acquisition, or musical apprenticeship, the phonemic system of Arabic takes root in their being through intentional listening.

Sama' is both the genre of Sufi music as well as the verb "to listen" in Moroccan Arabic. *Sama'* contains both subject (listener) and object (sound) in its very meaning. Indeed, the performers of this music are not called "singers" (*mughaniyyin*) as in other musical genres, but are called "listeners" (*musama'yyin).* It is not an ordinary listening, however, but a *genre of listening* informed by the intention (*niya*) to find another way of being.

Doing research in France required that I listen to people listening—that I be an aural witness of *their* listening acts. Without knowing it at the time, I began to do an ethnography of listening. What's more, initiation into the order itself involved a restructuring of listening practices. I have referred to this phenomenon as "literacies of listening," that is, "the acquired ability to learn other cultures (specifically religious ones, though not exclusively these) through participating in their sound worlds"[4] (Kapchan 2009, 65). The women followed the transliteration of the liturgy, yes, but not being Arabic speakers, they would primarily *listen deeply* to their peers, rhythmically reiterating first the beginnings and the ends of phrases where the stress was most obvious, then incrementally weaving in more text. What's more, this intentional listening—particularly in the *dhikr,* or remembrance, part of the liturgy, where the names of God are chanted hundreds of times and quickly—often led to states of rapture. For Sufis, listening is a key activity in the production of the sublime (Kapchan 2012).

What does being an aural witness of such acts of listening effect?

LISTENING ACT III: WITNESSING LISTENING

We usually think of a witness as someone who has seen something. Yet the etymology of the word has nothing to do with vision, but rather is related to personal knowledge. From the Old English *witnes,* it means an "attestation of fact, event, etc., from *personal knowledge,*" and also "one who so testifies." Originally, it meant "knowledge, wit"[5] and was a literal translation of the Greek *martys* (see *martyr*), which, before it came to mean a sacrifice, was related to "care, trouble" and also to memory and mindfulness.[6] In short, to bear witness (an interesting idiom in itself, as it implies the ethical weightiness of such a task) is to testify from one's memory, from one's mindful experience and knowledge. To witness is not just to know, however; it is also somehow to transmit that knowledge and to do so publicly, that is, to testify. Witnessing in this configuration is a kind of social gnosis.

This became clear to me a few years ago when I gave a presentation on my research on Sufi listening in two different academic venues. Inquiring into the relation between listening practices and the spread of religion—in this case, the conversion or rededication of French and French North African women to Sufi Islam (Kapchan 2009)—I discussed how ways of listening, like styles of speaking, act to restructure perceptions that, in turn, create intersubjective feeling. My point was that not only are singing and other aspects of sacred aesthetics responsible for the spread of Sufism in France, but that listening itself—a particular kind of transitive listening (listening *to* the genre of *sama*ʿ, Sufi devotional music, as well as *dhikr,* the repetition of the names of God)—functions as a self-conscious pedagogy that transforms perception, enveloping the listening subject in new forms of affective, and in this case religious, imagination. Listening feels as if it is located in the discrete body, but is culturally learned and socially engaging. Initiates in the Sufi order acquired such “literacies”; but as an ethnographer, I also had to become literate in their ways of listening (Kapchan 2009, 65).

In these presentations I played an audio clip that I had recorded at a Sufi liturgy (*wadhifa*) in France, in which the women went into a kind of ecstatic trance, what is called *al-hal*, “the state.” Invoking the Prophet as well as the *shaykh* of their order, Sidi Hamza, these French women of North African descent began a sung weeping, praising and lamenting at once (Feld 1990).

The soloist in the recording began with a *muwal*—an improvisatory introduction, sailing into what we may not have trouble identifying as poetic invocation:

> My *shaykh* is like a white dove
> *shaykh-i ka hamama bayda*
> Living in my soul and satisfying me
> *sakina fi-ruh-i wa qnaʿ-ni*
> My love is in Madagh
> *hubbi-i fi madagh*
> Let’s go there and meet him
> *yalla bi-nah n-lqau-h*

The women in the circle responded to the beauty of her solo. Indeed, one woman in particular broke into a loud and tearful response. This is what is known as *al-hal*, a state where one is open to the dissolution of the normative subject. Sufis say it is a spontaneous and unintentional state inspired by God.

When the soloist finished the *muwal*, the group joined in. At first the women sang together. After the rhythm had been established and everyone was singing in unison, however, there was a *break*, a reorientation of the path as one person began a contrapuntal rhythm, intoning in another key as she transitioned into rapture. One state set off another, and soon what was a harmonious singing in unison became a dissonant mesh of sound that transformed the social field of listening, sending waves in other directions in perhaps a more troubling because irregular aesthetic. And all the while, the original chanting continued like an ostinato that carried the other riffs.

The aesthetic of this ritual has much in common with other genres of non-Sufi music that employ layering and improvisation. And although the regnant belief is that these states are spontaneous, it is clear that the women are listening closely to each other, as there is a subtle reiteration of new rhythms, a rich texture of tones, and a conversation that ensues through deep listening.[7]

When I played these sounds for academic audiences, they evoked interesting reactions. In Texas, one scholar was fairly shocked. "Do the Sufi women know that you are playing this in academic contexts?" she asked. For her, a respected scholar of the Muslim world (and one I respect), the clip was akin to an illicit unveiling. I had, it seemed, committed a particularly egregious form of schizophonia[8] by playing this clip outside of its context of origin for non-Muslim audiences. When I played this clip at a conference in Indiana, I had a different but equally thought-provoking response. Another colleague noted, "We can talk about trauma. We can even look at it. But somehow listening to it is unbearable," he said. Trauma. But this was a recording of rapture. Or was it?

What does it mean to be an aural witness to the pain and praise of others? This question is inspired by my reading of Susan Sontag's essay, *Regarding the Pain of Others.* In that book, Sontag asserts the basic democracy of the photographic image. Photography stands apart from the other arts, she asserts, in that almost anyone can take a good picture; indeed, much of what makes a really great photograph is a matter of chance and spontaneity. There are professional photographers, of course, but the cult of virtuosity is less evident in this domain than in literature or the performing arts. Yet however "accidental" the photo, it is ultimately positioned and framed and, as Sontag reminds us, "to frame is to choose." Intention inheres in the photographic act. If democracy characterizes photography, for Sontag the ethical problems emerge in the *viewing* of these photos, and in their interpretation. If we substitute sound recording for photography, then the ethics lie not in the viewing, but in the listening—listening to the pain and praise of others, listening to grief, listening to the sublime.

The sounds of pain are often indistinguishable from those of ecstasy. Hearing either one makes us uncomfortable, as if we were listening to something not meant for our ears, but that, upon the hearing, draws us into and implicates us in the experience, often as interlopers. Social listening has parameters that are often unrecognized and unspoken, but that come to light when transgressed. When such transgressions happen, they make conscious what is usually tacit and somatic, particularly the way in which categories of "private" and "public," as well as "animal" and "human," inhabit and overdetermine the body and its perceptions.[9] Unlike a visual witness, *listening* to the sounds of trauma is "unbearable," precisely because listening involves both subjects and objects in an interacoustic space. Indeed, in contradistinction to the self-owning body of the Enlightenment with its recognizable and legal boundaries (the "juridical body"), the parameters of what I call the "sound body" are malleable, expanding and shrinking according to the vibrations present in the social field of listening (Kapchan 2015). *Listening to the pain and praise of others forces an encounter between these two bodies and thereby transforms both.*

Academic audiences experienced these sounds as what Mary Douglas might categorize as "sounds out of place"; such sounds (of pain, of pleasure) do not belong in academic contexts, my colleagues implied, precisely because the non-Sufi witness can all too easily label them as dangerous or exotic (Douglas 1980). These sounds, however, demand an openness to experience that is deeply ethnographic. They invite us to let go of our habits, our preconceptions of subjectivity, and our prejudices against belief systems that may be associated with these experiences. As such, listening to these sounds, lingering in the discomfort that they may produce, is itself a *method* that takes us into otherness. Indeed, one audience member—an undergraduate music student—broke into tears when I played this recording. Hers was an open and empathic response.

Analyzing the meaning of these sounds takes us into an interpretive mode already related to our own culturally overdetermined positions as listeners. The question that arises is not, what do these sounds mean, but rather, *what does listening to these sounds, in all their vibrating materiality, do?*

LISTENING ACT IV: TACTICAL LISTENING AS ETHNOGRAPHIC ACTIVISM

How do we transform the *act* of intentional listening into an effective ethnographic *activism?* Is there a way to listen that can effect social change?

De Certeau has given us the vocabulary of the "tactic" to facilitate an understanding of how agency and energy are asserted in small acts that nonetheless subvert larger disciplining powers. Opposed to "a strategy," which relies on a notion of what he calls the "proper" (including property-in-the-person, a delineated and separate self, as well as the ability of that self to own private property and consume), a tactic is placeless. It is, he says,

> A calculus which cannot count on a "proper" (a spatial or institutional location), nor thus on a borderline distinguishing the other as a visible totality. The place of the tactic belongs to the other. A tactic insinuates itself into the other's place, fragmentarily, without taking over its entirety, without being able to keep it at a distance. It has at its disposal no base where it can capitalize on its advantages, prepare its expansions, and secure independence with respect to

> circumstances. The "proper" is a victory of space over time. On the contrary, because it does not have a place, a tactic depends on time—it is always on the watch for opportunities that must be seized "on the wing." (De Certeau [1984] 2011, xix)

De Certeau might be talking about sound, which also "belongs to the other . . . [insinuating] itself into the other's place . . . without taking over its entirety, [but] without being able to keep it at a distance"; or he might be talking about listening, which "does not have a [fixed] place . . . depends on time [and] . . . is always [ready] for opportunities that must be seized 'on the wing'" (ibid.). To listen tactically, then, is not to claim ownership of (sonic) territory, but rather *to attend to a vibration, to resonate that vibration within another environment (the body), to translate and thus transform the sound (to echo it, enlarge it, retune or remake it in similar or other media), and to circulate it.* Tactical listening, in other words, is listening with a motive. It is a self-conscious transmission and translation of perception.

In order to circumvent the law that prohibits loudspeakers without a permit, for example, Occupy Wall Street demonstrators developed a listening tactic, the human microphone: when one person spoke to the crowd, the assembly listened closely and repeated the message back, reiterating the words, but also disseminating them like a wave to the outermost reaches of the gathering (Cusick this volume). Since all listening transmits not only sound but the affect it carries as well, tactical listening has the potential to render all listeners ethnographers and translators. *Tactical listening listens for dissensus and thus becomes itself dissensual.*

The idea of listening in order to make a political intervention is not a new idea. What is called "compassionate listening" has been a technique of peace negotiations for some time now.[10] What's more, listening techniques are employed in truth and reconciliation commissions even when there is no transcript, or when the testimonies are anonymous (Feldman 2004). The very fact that people are listening to the narratives of victims changes the political and emotional resonance of the state. These are all acts of aural witness.

If tactical listening is about intentional attunement and transmission, however, there is also a negative side, a violent side—surreptitious listening, for example, listening in, or the opposite of tactical listening, which is nonelective listening, such as being bombarded with sound, as in the torture practices of Guantanamo Bay (Cusick 2008; Daughtry 2015). There are sonic tactics as well as listening tactics, and both have their shadows.

If tactics subvert the "proper," however, it is because they do not lay claim to a space. Rather they slip between and through spaces, infiltrating without owning, infusing without possessing, or possessing like a spirit possesses, rising up in another's body and disappearing at will. As such, tactical listening transforms the social field of listening subtly, magnifying sound knowledge while circumventing any visible threat to property and person.

LISTENING ACT V: THE FESTIVE SACRED—THE PROMISE AND PARADOX OF LISTENING

Sonic tactics rely on the basic paradox of sound—the ability to inhabit space without owning it—to effect transformation. Listening tactics rely on the same paradox, namely, that the listening subject is a listener while becoming as well what is listened *to.* These are the unique qualities of sound knowledge, being separate and together, singular and plural (Nancy 2000). But what promise do these tactics hold? Or in the words of political philosopher Jane Bennett, "How can humans learn to hear or enhance our receptivity for 'propositions' not expressed in words? How to translate between them?" (Bennett 2010, 104).

As noted above, the QB Sufi order is spreading throughout Europe and North America. One of the primary vehicles of this dissemination is sound. The QB order in France, for example, has practitioners in the metropoles as well as in the provinces. Because these groups meet in homes to worship and to sing, the performance of this religion remains in the private sphere, and invitations to participate must come from members. But there is a public forum for the performance of Sufi ritual, and that is on the stages of community centers throughout France,[11] where the QB Sufis regularly put on their own version of a sacred music concert (Kapchan 2013). These concerts are publicized and free. There is often a reception afterward, where audience members can meet the musicians, ask questions, and enjoy North African sweets and beverages made by the women in the order. Because of the regnant belief in the power of sacred sound to speak to the heart, the performances of these musicians are also a way of inhabiting the French public sphere differently; and it is an invitation for others to do so as well. Indeed, hospitality is at its core. For the Sufis, both sound and the example of deep, attentive listening, or *sama'*, are gifts offered to the French public. And as these are given to the public, so there exists an affective return.[12]

Such sacred music concerts in the QB order are largely inspired by the iconic Fes Festival of World Sacred Music, a model for the proliferation of sacred music festivals worldwide (Kapchan 2008). Indeed, even the Dalai Lama modeled his own sacred music festivals upon it. The Fes Festival was the idea of Faouzi Skali, author and anthropologist, recipient of a United Nations peace award, member of interfaith commissions, and a prominent Sufi in the QB order in Morocco. Indeed, Skali was instrumental in bringing these Sufi practices to France, giving lectures on Sufism and helping to set up groups of worship in French cosmopolitan areas. Skali's intention in founding the Fes Festival in 1993 was to introduce Western audiences to world sacred music, a large majority of which is Sufi music at the festival (Curtis 2007; Lynch 2000).[13] He is explicit that music transmits what words cannot. And while that may seem romantic, it is in fact no different from asking, with Jane Bennett, how humans can learn to "hear" or sense nonintellective meanings, and how they can translate between them (Bennett 2010, 104). Both Skali and Bennett are invoking sound knowledge, albeit in different ways.

The Fes Festival and other festivals like it rely on a promise—the promise of sonic translation, that is, "the trust in the ultimate translatability of aural (as opposed to textual) codes" (Kapchan 2008, 467). Like many musicians and activists, Skali believes that music can translate affect across linguistic and cultural divides. Of course, transparent translation is a virtual impossibility insofar as all translation requires new creation (Benjamin 1968; Derrida 1985; Venuti 1991). Yet as Derrida has convincingly argued, the will to translation relies on a promise of possibility, and it is this promise (and not its fulfillment) that carries the resonant charge that itself creates public intimacy. We could say that audience members come to the festival with the intent to listen tactically—that is, to attend to a vibration, to resonate that vibration within another environment (the body), to transform the sound (to echo it, enlarge it, retune or remake it in the same or other media), and to circulate it.

But if the promise of sonic translation animates the Fes Festival of World Sacred Music as well as other festivals (for example, the World Festival of Sufi Culture, also founded by Skali), it is active listening that actually performs the translation, thereby changing the social field of listening. It is telling that Sufi music at festivals and concerts rarely includes a performance of *al-hal*. Such sounds rankle, disturb, and question not only the line between grief and sublimity, but also that between subject and object, subject and subject.

LISTENING AS METHOD

If listening to the QB Sufi women made academic audiences uncomfortable, it is in part because certain sounds carry meanings associated with largely Western ideas of intimacy, privacy, and property-in-the-person. Auditors in Texas and Indiana reacted differently to the rhythms and vibrations of this sung weeping than did auditors in Morocco and in the North African cultural milieu in France. This is because public listening is not a passive activity. It requires participation as well as a willingness to share an ontology, even when what is sounded gestures toward the dissolution of being itself. When this intention is absent, what psychoanalyst Anzieu would call the sound envelope, or the skin ego, thickens, and we experience static in the social field of listening.

While social education teaches us when it is appropriate to use different speech genres, the rules for genres of listening are a less explicit part of socialization. Indeed, despite the fact that listening is a form of discipline ("Listen!" we instruct our children)[14] and is acknowledged as an activity ("to give ear" is to attend to a phenomenon), pedagogies of listening are pitifully underdeveloped in Western societies. We can listen for meaning, we can listen in order to be oriented in space or to create orientation, we can listen to a particular sound, or we can listen intransitively—that is, without an object—in either a "reduced" or a more "ubiquitous" mode of listening (Chion 2007; Kassabian 2013). However, when humans hear what social codes dictate is not meant for some ears, it produces particular forms of emotion in the listener—often shame, embarrassment, or pity, maybe anger or agitation. Sometimes—as in the case of the young student—it produces a mimetic, if subjectively inflected, emotional response; grief begets grief. Because sound touches us so intimately, in our very organs and viscera, questions of intentionality—who a sound is intended for or not—are literally moving issues.

It is the *hal,* the state of rapture or sublimity, that sounds like trauma, not the chants, not the songs. It is the appearance of the personal voice amid the sameness of other voices that evoked embarrassment or discomfort in some academic listeners. It is the assertion of difference that somehow makes us quake. This is what Rancière calls "dissensus"—that is, a repartitioning of the aesthetic norm that changes the parameters of what we consider public and normative.

Even more disturbing than the personality of the singular voice that breaks with the sonic field in *al-hal,* however, is its recklessness. When in this state, song transforms into cries, harmonies into dissonances, subjecthood as we know it dissolves. Listening to such a breaking apart is different from observing it. To listen to the explosion of subjectivity "brings us into intimacy, into coexistence with strangers" (Morton 2103, 194).[15] What's more, to witness this kind of sublimity is to testify to a genre of existence open to aesthetic transformation. For the women involved, such listening is itself a mode of knowing as well as a genre of being with other entities—musical modes, sound patterns, and for them, spiritual beings. To listen in this context is to be drawn into a public intimacy that requires participation in a shared sound knowledge, a nondiscursive form of affective transmission resulting from acts of listening (Kapchan 2015).

CONCLUSION

Ethnographers who do research on religion inhabit a vulnerable and thus a productive place. We are accused of being apologists, of going native, or of objectifying in an Orientalist way. We are in it, or we are out of it. It is very hard to be between. What listening does, however, is put us in the space of between, insisting that we ling there. At a moment when philosophy and theory announce the end of metalanguage and representation,[16] attuning ourselves to the materiality of the in-between, to the place of instability, to moment upon moment of openness, is a method that may be more politically viable than any theorization (Stoller 2009). Indeed, learning to listen—as a witness and as a pedagogue—is a *method* that changes the structures and hierarchies of a social field. Listening acts—both individual and collective—demand an openness to other worlds by obliging the listener to linger in an acoustic space of ambiguity and paradox, a shifting ground wherein preconceived ideas have not yet overdetermined either the subject or the interpretation. Listening to the pain and praise of others can be discomfiting, and yet the decision to intentionally inhabit those sounds is necessarily transformative—not only for the listener and the listened-to, but also for the social field of which they are a part.

I can't help but think that twelfth-century Sufi theologian and philosopher Ibn al-ʿArabi would have agreed. His focus was on ontology as much as epistemology. He acknowledged the materiality of the imagination, of the spiritual realm, of the corporeal realm, and of God, him- or herself. He acknowledged as well that paradox was the very portal into other forms of knowledge. It was necessary to embrace the paradox "God is/God isn't" (*huwa/laysa huwa*) in order to accede to other levels of gnosis. (For this he was often labeled a pantheist.) Ibn al-ʿArabi also stressed that humans could never fully understand God, who is only ascertained through symbols. These symbols—whether sonic, imagistic, or embodied—are not simulacra, however, but materializations of divine knowledge in the realm of human perception (Chittick 1989). In other words, *a symbol is not a representation for Ibn al-'Arabi, but a material reality.*[17] Insofar as he acknowledged that God is unknowable, Ibn al-'Arabi preceded the phenomenologists, who stress that objects are always in some sense withdrawn (that is, you can't see the other side of a coin). Lingering in the space of ambiguity and paradox requires another way of being—not rational understanding, but an attunement to objects on a vibrational level.

Does such intentional listening solve the political problems of power? Does it get rid of fanaticism? No. Listening to the pain and praise of others, however, is an ethnographic method that teaches us how to be in the world in beauty as well as in chaos and instability. It is an intervention in what I call "slow ethnography" as well as "slow activism"—an incremental transformation of the social field of listening whose effects are only felt in the *longue durée* (Kapchan 2016 and forthcoming).

Being an aural witness to the *ibtihalat* from my balcony in Rabat was a private listening act insofar as I stood there alone. The sounds that I heard, however, were in the public domain and ostensibly were perceived by others as well. They were material vibrations in the wet pre-dawn air of Rabat, tremors in the palm fronds that lined the street. As the ostinato that underlay the sounds of the waking city—calls from peddlers, cars beginning to move through the streets—these sounds affected not just everyone in the social field of listening, but everything. Consciously attending to these sounds (or any others) is a political tactic insofar as listening changes the body, which then resonates, translates, and transforms sound in other media. Listening is thus a method for the transmission of sound knowledge, for other ways of being in the world. While sound knowledge is not always pleasant to experience, lingering in the space of discomfort, in both the pain and praise of others, is an ethnographic and political imperative for social change. On this topic, the Sufis have a lot to say to those willing to listen.

NOTES

1. Dell Hymes, "Ways of Speaking," in *Explorations in the Ethnography of Speaking*, ed. Richard Bauman and Joel Sherzer (Philadelphia: University of Pennsylvania Press, 1974).

2. Like Austin's (1962) "locutionary acts," listening acts *en*act—that is, they are "performative"; they do not simply re-present sound, as waves reach the ears and are

relayed to the brain, but they *transduce* these sound waves, changing the waves, the body, and the environment in the process (Austin 1962; Helmreich 2015).

3. There is nothing but limens—*barzakh*—according to Islamic philosopher Ibn al-ʿArabi (Chittick 1989).

4. By *sound economy,* I simply mean an aesthetic system, bound by cultural norms and contextualized in a local and translocal economy, wherein it takes on different meanings and functions.

5. "Witness," *Online Etymology Dictionary,* accessed on February 28, 2016, http://www.etymonline.com/index.php?term=witness.

6. "Martyr," *Online Etymology Dictionary,* accessed on February 28, 2016, http://www.etymonline.com/index.php?allowed_in_frame=0&search=martyr&searchmode=none.

7. Think "lift-up-over-sounding" (Feld); think "participatory discrepancies" (Keil); think "deep listening" (Oliveros; Becker); think of the women "saying something" (Monson).

8. Steven Feld defines *schizophonia* as the separation of sounds from their source of origin (Feld and Keil 2004).

9. Elaine Scarry says that pain obliterates language and leaves only the cry, the moan. The infliction of pain, she says, reduces us to an animal state; or rather, the sound of pain makes us realize what we *share* with animals and plants. This would imply that the interpretation of pain takes place across species, that there are frequencies of sound that both cause and speak pain.

10. Inspired in part through the writings of Buddhist peace-activist Thich Nhat Hahn, listening to effect healing has now become a technique of conflict resolution. Compassionate Listening Project, accessed May 25, 2015, http://www.compassionatelistening.org/about/history.

11. Nonprofit organizations are called "associations" in France. They are incorporated and receive different forms of tax exemption.

12. It is important to note that no one ever goes into *al-hal* in these public contexts.

13. The festivals are also lucrative, bringing many tourist dollars and euros to Fes annually.

14. The relation of listening to obedience is present in the etymology of the verb—from the Latin *obeir* (to hear, to obey).

15. This forced intimacy, asserts theorist Timothy Morton, is not idiosyncratic, but rather characterizes what he calls "the age of asymmetry," in which the human is displaced from the center of an interpretable world to inhabit a multiverse of effects and objects that defy comprehension, but which demand our attunement to them in order for art to do anything at all—most important, to speak to the unconscious.

Furthermore, Brandon Labelle speaks of the intimacy of audition: "Auditory knowledge is non-dualistic. It is based on empathy *and* divergence . . . [it creates] shared spaces that belong to no single public and yet which impart a feeling for intimacy: sound is always already mine and not mine—I cannot hold it for long, nor can I arrest its itinerant energy" (Labelle 2010, xvii; emphasis the author's).

16. Morton 2013.

17. One that can conceivably be measured, though measurement was not Ibn al-'Arabi's preoccupation.

WORKS CITED

Austin, John Langshaw. *How to Do Things with Words: The William James Lectures Delivered at Harvard University.* Edited by J. O. Urmson and Marina Sbisà. 1955. Oxford, UK: Clarendon Press, 1962.

Barad, Karen. *Meeting the Universe Halfway: Quantum Physics and the Entanglement of Matter and Meaning.* Durham, NC: Duke University Press, 2007.

———. "Posthumanist Performativity: Toward an Understanding of How Matter Comes to Matter." *Signs: Journal of Women in Culture and Society* 28, no. 3 (2003): 801–31.

Barthes, Roland. *Image, Music, Text.* New York: Hill and Wang, 1977.

Benjamin, Walter. "The Task of the Translator." Introduction to a Baudelaire translation, 1923; translated by Harry Zohn, 1968. In *The Translation Studies Reader.* Edited by Lawrence Venuti. London: Routledge, 2000.

Bennett, Jane. *Vibrant Matter: A Political Economy of Things.* Durham, NC: Duke University Press, 2010.

Bourdieu, Pierre. *Outline of a Theory of Practice.* Cambridge Studies in Social and Cultural Anthropology. Edited by Ernest Gellner, Jack Goody, Stephen Gudemon, Michael Herzfeld, and Jonathan Parry. Translated by Richard Nice. New York: Cambridge University Press, 1977.

Chion, Michel. *Audio-Vision: Sound on Screen.* 1994. Edited and translated by Claudia Gorbman. Foreword by Walter Murch. New York: Columbia University Press, 2007.

Chittick, William. *The Sufi Path of Knowledge: Ibn al-'Arabi's Metaphysics of Imagination.* Albany: State University of New York Press, 1989.

Curtis, Maria. "Sound Faith: Nostalgia, Global Spirituality, and the Making of the Fes Festival of World Sacred Music." PhD diss., University of Texas at Austin, 2007.

Cusick, Suzanne. "Re-Soundings: Hearing Worlds from the Global War on Terror." Paper presented at the Sawyer Seminar, Harvard University, Cambridge, MA, November 2013.

———. "Music as Torture/Music as Weapon." *Journal of the Society for American Music* 2, no. 1 (2008): 1–26.

———. "'You Are in a Place That Is Out of the World . . .': Music in the Detention Camps of the Global War on Terror." *Journal of the Society for American Music* 2, no. 1 (2008): 1–26.

Daughtry, J. Martin. *Listening to War: Sound, Music, Trauma, and Survival in Wartime Iraq.* Oxford: Oxford University Press, 2015.

De Certeau, Michel. *The Practice of Everyday Life.* 1984. Berkeley: University of California Press, 2011.

Derrida, Jacques. *The Ear of the Other.* Translated by Peggy Kamuf. Lincoln: University of Nebraska Press, 1985.

Douglas, Mary. *Purity and Danger: An Analysis of Concepts of Pollution and Taboo.* New York: Routledge, 1980.

Feld, Steven. "Waterfalls of Songs: An Acoustemology of Place Resounding in Bosavi, Papua New Guinea." In *Senses of Place.* Edited by Steven Feld and Keith H. Basso. Santa Fe, NM: SAR Press, 1996.

———, and Charlie Keil. *Music Grooves.* Chicago: University of Chicago Press, 2004

Helmreich, Stefan. "Transduction." In *Keywords in Sound Studies.* Edited by David Novak and Matt Sakakeeny. Durham, NC: Duke University Press, 2015.

Hymes, Dell. "Ways of Speaking." In *Explorations in the Ethnography of Speaking.* Edited by Richard Bauman and Joel Sherzer. Philadelphia: University of Pennsylvania Press, 1974.

Kapchan, Deborah. "Slow Activism: Listening to the Pain and Praise of Others." *International Journal of Middle Eastern Studies 48* (2016: 115–119.

———. "Body." In *Keywords in Sound Studies.* Edited by David Novak and Matt Sakakeeny. Durham, NC: Duke University Press, 2015.

———. "The Aesthetics of the Invisible: Sacred Music in Secular (French) Places." *Theater Drama Review: The Journal of Performance Studies* 57, no. 3 (2013): 132–47.

———. "Reflecting on Encounters in Morocco: Meditations on Home, Genre, and the Performance of Everyday Life." In *Moroccan Encounters.* Edited by David Crawford and Rachel Newcomb. Bloomington: Indiana University Press, 2012.

———. "Learning to Listen: The Sound of Sufism in France." *World of Music* (special issue 2009).

———. 2009a. "Singing Community/Remembering in Common: Sufi Liturgy and North African Identity in Southern France." *International Journal of Community Music* (2009a).

———. "The Promise of Sonic Translation: Performing the Festive Sacred in Morocco." *American Anthropologist* 110, no. 4 (2008): 467–83.

Kassabian, Anahid. *Ubiquitous Listening: Affect, Attention and Distributed Subjectivity.* Berkeley: University of California Press, 2013.

Keil, Charlie. "Participatory Discrepancies." In *Music Grooves.* Edited by Steven Feld and Charlie Keil. Chicago: University of Chicago Press, 2004.

LaBelle, Brandon. *Acoustic Territories: Sound Culture and Everyday Life.* New York: Continuum Books, 2010.

Lynch, David. "Fes Festival of World Sacred Music." Master's thesis, University of Texas at Austin, 2000.

Monson, Ingrid. *Saying Something: Jazz Improvisation and Interaction.* Chicago Studies in Ethnomusicology. Chicago: University of Chicago Press, 1996.

Morton, Timothy. *Hyperobjects: Philosophy and Ecology after the End of the World.* Minneapolis: University of Minnesota Press, 2013.

Muller, Carol. *Rituals of Fertility and the Sacrifice of Desire: Nazarite Women's Performance in South Africa.* Chicago: University of Chicago Press, 1999.

Oliveros, Pauline. *Deep Listening: A Composer's Sound Practice.* Lincoln, NE: iUniverse Books, 2005.

Rancière, Jacques. *Dissensus: On Politics and Aesthetics.* Edited and translated by Steven Corcoran. New York: Continuum Books, 2010.

Scarry, Elaine. *The Body in Pain: The Making and Un-Making of the World.* Oxford, New York: Oxford University Press, 2004.

Sontag, Susan. *Regarding the Pain of Others.* London: Penguin Books, 2004.

Stoller, Paul. *The Power of the Between: An Anthropological Odyssey.* Chicago: University of Chicago Press, 2009.

Urban, Greg. "Urban Ritual Wailing in Amerindian Brazil." *American Anthropologist* 90, no. 2 (1988): 385–400.

Venuti, Lawrence. *The Translator's Invisibility.* New York: Routledge, 2008.

MICHAEL JACKSON

Afterword

Sound Properties of the Written Word

But we will analyze the metaphysical exchange,
the circular complicity of the metaphors of the eye and the ear.
Jacques Derrida, "Tympan," from Margins of Philosophy *(1984)*

In his childhood memoir, *Dreams in a Time of War,* the Gikuyu and Kenyan writer Ngugi Wa Thiong'o describes his first experiences of school at age nine and the Gikuyu primer with which he learned to read. At first he is attracted to the pictures that accompany the text, and only gradually does he learn to tackle long passages that lack any illustrations. One passage he reads over and over again until suddenly, one day, he begins to hear music in the words:

God has given the Agrikuyu a beautiful country
Abundant in water, food and luscious bush
The Ahikuyu should praise the Lord all the time
For he has ever been generous to them.

"Even when not reading it," Ngugi writes,

> I can hear the music. The choice and arrangements of the words, the cadences. I can't pick any one thing that makes it so beautiful and long-lived in my memory. I realize that even written words can carry the music I loved in stories, particularly the choric melody. And yet this is not a story; it is a descriptive statement. It does not carry an illustration. It is a picture in itself and yet more than a picture and a description. It is music. Written words can also sing.[1]

There is a long tradition in scholarship of seeing oral and literate technologies of communication as entailing radically different sensibilities and essentially different ontologies. It is argued that the transition from orality to literacy entails a dramatic transformation in consciousness in which words cease to sing,[2] intellectuality becomes divorced from feeling, the arts of memory atrophy, vision is privileged over all other senses, thought becomes independent of conventional wisdom, and the reader is alienated from his or her community.[3] These arguments are often informed by a romantic view that oral cultures enshrine a more ecologically balanced and socially attuned mode of existence in which the life of the community takes precedence over the life of the mind—as in Walter Benjamin's lament that modernity prefers information processing to storytelling, data to wisdom,[4] echoing Socrates's conviction that writing is a phantom, undermining memory, poisoning/drugging the mind, and leading us astray.[5]

I want to contest the assumption that orality and literacy are mutually antithetical and that writing necessarily entails a loss of authentic values, eclipsing oral modes of expression and undermining social bonds. I also want to argue against the view that we can characterize and contrast entire societies in terms of their dominant technology of communication—or for that matter, their dominant modes of government, economic life, or social organization. As George Devereux pointed out many years ago, a complete understanding of any social formation demands that we explore the ambivalence that arises from the copresence of manifest and latent patterns,[6] and hence the tension that exists between that which is publicly emphasized and that which is publicly suppressed, between dominant and subdominant leitmotifs, and between alternative ethical values and different modes of consciousness. No society exists or has ever existed that comprises individuals whose consciousness is wholly self-absorbed or entirely diffused into the collective, even though these polar positions may find expression in dominant ideologies. Just as persons exist both in their own right and in relation to others, so writing and orality imply both divergent and overlapping modes of communication. This undoubtedly explains the apparent contradictions in Walter Ong's celebrated work, where he claims a "vast difference" between literacy and orality, only to speak of this relationship as "complementary" and to assert that "writing can never dispense with orality."[7] In this vein, he writes that "in all the wonderful worlds that writing opens, the spoken word still resides and lives. Written texts all have to be related somehow, directly or indirectly, to the world of sound, the natural habitat of language, to yield their meanings."[8] Jacques Derrida takes this argument even further, arguing that writing is haunted by a sense of all that lies beyond its margins in the same way that philosophy is inevitably written in the shadows of the nonphilosophical. Derrida uses the image of the tympanum to capture this sense of sound, albeit muffled, that counters the apparent silence of a text, or the reader of a text, and is vital to the intelligibility of the written word.[9]

I have a tin ear. Cannot hold the simplest tune or learn a foreign language by listening alone. Much as I admire John Blacking's *How Musical Is Man,* his thesis that everyone has a capacity for music[10] does not apply to me. If deafness is a disability, so is tone deafness—the inability to discern, recall, or mimic sound. But it is said that people deficient in one area of the sensorium will compensate by developing skills and sensitivities in another, and Oliver Sacks describes how a person with expressive aphasia (speechlessness) may still be able to sing "very tunefully and with great feeling, but only getting two or three words of [a] song."[11] My eidetic memory is excellent. And since childhood I have depended on the written word to make good my aural-oral ineptitude. Yet writing has never been, for me, a substitute for speech any more than scholarly pursuits have been inimical to sociality. One mode of being or communicating does not necessarily preclude another. And so when I ask whether the oral is entirely absent when I read or write, I can confidently say no, since in composing this very sentence I am murmuring the words as I write them down, trying to get a feel for how they will sound in the sequence I am testing on my tongue, seeking a structural balance that will be easy on the ear. Fiction writers often confess a similar sense of hearing voices, of writing down dialogue they have heard and assessing its verisimilitude less against the standard of recorded speech than against an inner standard of what rings true. The idea is very old that thinking is a form of talking to oneself, which is why people who undergo surgery on their vocal chords are told not to read until the lesions heal. In brief, the distinctions we like to make between speech and writing, or speech and thought, are largely artificial; and there are greater phenomenological continuities between these conventionally contrasted activities than we are ordinarily aware of.

Consider, for example, the opening lines of Seamus Heaney's poem *Oysters:*

Our shells clacked on their plates.
My tongue was a filling estuary,
My palate hung with starlight:
As I tasted the salty Pleiades
Orion dipped his foot into the water.

Alive and violated
They lay on their beds of ice:
Bivalves: the split bulb
And philandering sigh of ocean.
Millions of them ripped and shucked and scattered.[12]

Is it not true that as one reads these lines one also hears them—and furthermore, that one sees and tastes the brine-slicked bivalves lying in their flaking, ice-caked shells on a pewter plate? Surely the written word not only conjures sound and sense, it is haunted by sound textures; it possesses metrical properties. And is this not true of both self-consciously rhythmic and tonal poetry *and* the less carefully composed, atonal prose of a novel, essay, or tract?

The inextinguishable presence of a voice in a written text may be a result of synesthesia[13]—a faculty that all human beings share to some degree, making it inevitable that one area of the sensorium will evoke others, including touch—which may explain why we speak of a piece of writing as a *text,* a term that derives, like texture, from the action of weaving. Whether written or spoken, language is always interwoven with threads of experience that are, strictly speaking, beyond words. Writing puts a spin on the ineffable, making it seem to be sayable, or subtly indicating what is outside its ability to signify.[14] We might therefore say that the *look* of a particular writer's prose, or our sense of his or her style, will evoke a memory of his or her voice—or, if we have never heard the writer speak, summon a voice that goes with the text, that makes it audible.

Despite these claims that literacy never entirely divorces itself from orality, the view is still held, particularly in the academy, that a logical, analytically coherent, and thoughtful disquisition on any subject requires the suppression of what Derrida, following Husserl, called "the sensory face of language."[15] Making experience intelligible requires the subjugation of its sensible properties, including sound. Yet we seem to have reached a moment in the history of the academy when this paradigm is giving ground to a new realism, where in-depth, detailed, direct recountings of experience are considered to be as illuminating, edifying, and thoughtful as the experience-distant jargon extolled by the rationalists of the Enlightenment. Arousing emotion, moving a reader, describing the living context in which one's thoughts unfold, and using artistic devices—narrative, imagery, idiomatic speech, montage—are valid ways of communicating a point of view, making an argument, or revealing a truth. It is becoming acceptable to stir or disturb one's audience in the same way that music and movies do. Rather than distrusting prose that evokes a slice of life, a lived event, or a personal experience, we are learning to distrust forms of discourse in which the assertion of authority requires an autocratic manner. We crave sincerity as much as scholarship, direct testimony as much as indirect speech. The world of thought is being brought back to life. The test of the soundness of philosophy—and by extension, the writing of philosophy—is whether, in the words of John Dewey, it ends "in conclusions which, when they are referred back to ordinary life-experiences and their predicaments, render them more significant, more luminous to us, and make our dealings with them more fruitful . . . does it yield the enrichment and increase of power of ordinary things?"[16] And so we ask, how may anthropology or philosophy become what Ivan Illich called "a tool for conviviality"?[17]

In addressing this question, my concern is less with the sound of writing than techniques of writing soundly—with writing that resonates with and remains in touch with the events, persons, and things being written about; writing that does justice to life, that makes sense, that rings true. This is not a call for reverting to old ideas of writing as mimesis or representation—mirroring the nature of the world or creating naturalistic images. Sound writing may capture or convey the spirit of lived experience by radical departures from naturalistic conventions, in the same way that literary dialogue can sound real without resembling actual conversation.

For me, the heart of the matter is what I have called elsewhere "writing intersubjectivity"[18]—developing a poetic and paratactic style that interleaves story and essay, and strikes a balance between the voice of the author and the voices of his or her interlocutors. One's writing thus preserves the oscillations in lived experience between moments of complete engagement and moments of detached reflection, while echoing the continual switching in everyday life between moments of self-absorption and moments of absorption in others. Ideally, one's writing shows how understandings emerge from the space between people—a space of conversation, negotiation, and encounter that switches unpredictably between accord and discord, attunement and disharmony. Indeed, the wealth of vernacular images derived from music and applied to both writing and sociality attests to the profound similarities between our relations with others and our sense of sound. Fieldwork is a way of sounding the other out—giving him or her a hearing, getting a sense of the world from his or her point of view. By extension, sound writing echoes the events, encounters, and conversations that make up our everyday life in another society, bringing them back to life on the printed page while at the same time offering our reflections on them.

I now explore in more detail the analogy I have drawn between the *technical* relationship of experience to writing and the *social* relationship of private to public life. I begin by spelling out some of the principles that have guided my own experiments in sound writing, and go on to provide an example of these principles in practice.

First, just as sound ethnographic writing is careful not to mute the voice of the ethnographer *or* his interlocutors, it does not exclude the reader. Rather, it invites the reader to enter into the text, to feel free to get his or her own sense of the scene or unfolding events, and to arrive at his or her interpretation of what the text conveys. This is what Eugenio Montale meant by "the second life of art."[19] While the author owns the process of authoring a text, painting a picture, or performing a role—he or she cannot lay claim to the work once it has been put into circulation in the public sphere. For the work is now not only available to readers or audiences, it belongs to them; it is theirs to interpret according to their own persuasions and predilections.

Second, sound writing reflects sound research. And the key to sound research is openness and inclusivity. This implies an observational alertness to what is happening in the field. But more important, perhaps, is one's *social* sensitivity to the people who have accepted one into their households and everyday lives. Sound research is, therefore, not simply a matter of suspending preconceptions and going with the flow; it is predicated on an awareness that the quality of what one may know is determined by the quality of one's relationships with those one comes to know in the course of fieldwork.

Third, it is imperative that one allows one's empirical material to determine any interpretative response. This means paying meticulous attention to vernacular expressions, local figures of speech, and ontological metaphors. These, rather than any theory one has acquired, provide the windows through which one may glimpse the inner workings of another lifeworld. In his fieldwork with ex-combatants in Guinea-Bissau, Henrik Vigh became familiar with the vernacular term *dubria*. Young men would use the word in describing their struggle for work, to make ends meet, or to find sources of enjoyment in an impoverished social environment. One informant conveyed the meaning of *dubria* to Henrik by moving his upper body in a disjointed yet rhythmical sway, looking somewhat as if he were shadow boxing: arms along his side, weaving and bobbing his torso back and forth as though dodging invisible pulls and pushes. "*Dubria!*" Pedro exclaimed. "You *dubria* . . . so that you can see your life." Henrik realized that *dubriagem* connoted the "use of shrewdness and craftiness to navigate dangerous or difficult terrain," and his concept of navigation as "motion within motion"—action in an unstable environment when you are yourself destabilized—was born of listening hard to what his informants were telling him.[20]

Fourth, one must entertain the possibility that every situation calls for a different response. Just as joking and avoidance are universal strategies for dealing with socially ambiguous or nonnegotiable relationships, so the ethnographer sometimes turns to contemplation, sometimes to writing, sometimes to speech, and sometimes to direct action in seeking the most appropriate way of responding to what others say or do, or demand. But even when one writes, there is always the question of what kind of writing is called for.

In early 2002, I returned to Sierra Leone after many years away. I took with me a book I had hastily bought at Gatwick airport, and I would read and reread this book during the following weeks, finding in its elegiac tone echoes of the devastated social landscape and tragic stories to which I would bear witness. When I came to write of that time, W. G. Sebald's *Austerlitz* haunted every phrase, every sentence, imparting to my narrative something of the sadness and resilience I experienced in Sierra Leone. In the following pages I describe an episode in my journey north, in the company of my old friend S. B. Marah, a few weeks before peace was officially declared. This was S. B.'s first visit to his political constituency in a long time, and a way of mending the political fabric torn apart by years of pillaging, violence, neglect, and scarcity. I hope this text will exemplify what I have been saying about sound writing—namely, that it is extraordinarily difficult, in a society of scarcity, to strike a balance between acquiring what one deems vital for one's own well-being and providing others with what is vital to theirs. How can there be social justice when the basic requirements of existence—food, shelter, and water—are insufficient to go around, so that one person's feast is always another's famine, one person's gain is inevitably another person's loss? The beef has, therefore, dual meanings: connoting an argument or point of ethical contention, as well as denoting a cattle beast, a source of life energy and power.

THE BEEF

For two days, a young steer had been tethered by a short rope to a mango tree at the edge of the compound. It was a gift to S. B., intended to be taken to Freetown, along with several goats. Constrained by the rope, the steer was unable to stretch its neck to the ground; all it could do was occasionally nose or lick dew from the long grass that was within its reach. When it defecated, it held its tail horizontal, its spine as straight as a spirit-level, and the tuft of hair by its penis twitched when it finished urinating. So forlorn did this animal seem, that I became convinced that it knew its imminent fate.

On the morning that we packed the vehicles, preparing to leave Kabala, it became obvious that there was not enough room in the back of the pickup for the steer. As the Big Men discussed their quandary, I sat some distance away, listening to an elderly man recount the history of Mande to a young newspaper reporter—passing from a description of Sundiata, who ruled the empire in the mid-fourteenth century, to an account of the first clans, the origins of the xylophone, and the birth of praise-singing. Old Musa's spectacle frames were tied upside-down to his cap, because this was the only way the one remaining lens could cover his one good eye. Earlier in the day, he had asked if I could send him some new glasses from Freetown—just as Leba had asked for a camera and the musicians had begged me to help them buy new guitars and amplifiers.

When I noticed that the Big Men and soldiers were gathering by the mango tree, I went down into the courtyard to talk with Leba, who said he had come to say good-bye. They are killing the beef, he observed. And as we watched from a distance, saying nothing, the steer was forced to the ground and its throat cut. The carcass was then cut into portions, and the head, neck, forequarters, rump, underbelly, entrails, hide, heart, and liver set out in separate piles on some banana leaves. Nearby, ten vultures stood their ground, occasionally flapping their ungainly wings and craning their necks toward the kill.

Suddenly, a young man standing next to Leba muttered something about how short life was. When I asked him what he meant, he said: "The way they slaughter these cows for these ministers. If we the young men wanted some of that beef, those Big Men would fight us, juju-way. They'd say, 'If any young man looks at the meat, let him beware.' So they make you afraid to go there. That is why we young people should not open our eyes too much on the meat. The Big Men could make us impotent. Or they could shoot us with their fetish guns."

I knew that many older men were similarly possessive of their young wives, but this was the first time I'd heard of possessiveness toward meat—though one heard rumors of Leopard societies that, in days gone by, committed ritual murders so that Big Men might augment their power by eating the vital organs of children. The logic ran as follows: Children, women, and cattle were wealth. A man's capacity to father children, to marry many times, and to acquire cattle were signs of power. And status and stature were intimately linked. It was not for nothing that one of S. B.'s praise names in the north was *simba*, elephant—an allusion to his physical bulk as much as his commanding presence, his social standing, and his political power. Still, it amused me that so many Big Men were immobilized by their own obesity—sluggish, unwell, and impotent. Was this why they were so preoccupied with the virility and appetite of young men? If so, the young men, denied meat and obliged to do the Big Men's bidding, seemed to find little consolation in the fact that what they lacked in status they made up for in strength and vitality.

When we drove off, I noticed that the vultures were clumsily quarreling around the spot where the steer had been butchered and picking at the blood-blackened earth.

The sun was hot. The summit of Albitaiya was lost in the haze of the harmattan. In the back seat of the 4Runner, I felt cramped and uncomfortable. Underfoot were several bags of meat, including the steer's severed head. Copies of the *Noble Qu'ran* in English, which Fasili had mysteriously acquired in Kabala, kept falling on my head. And our police escort again filled the landscape with its wailing sirens, as we drove over the rice and clothing that villagers had spread on the roadside to dry, or through smoke from burning elephant grass.

At Fadugu, the police Land Rover left us; and as if released from an obligation to behave itself, the 4Runner began to lose compression and suffer from brake failure. Yet even as we labored up the last hill toward Makeni, S. B. was pressing his nephew to overtake slower-moving *poda podas* (local minibuses), and urging us on. "Le' we go, le' we go," he said, as if his impatience and willpower would be instantly transmitted to the vehicle and it would obey. By the time we crawled the last few yards into a roadside repair shop, I realized it had taken us five hours to travel seventy miles. The hood of the 4Runner was quickly opened and propped up, and the engine exposed to the scrutiny of a dozen or so grease monkeys, while the Big Men issued advice, diagnoses, and orders from the makeshift seats that had been brought out for them. "This car na too slow," S. B. observed. "It don vex us too much," added his acolyte, Fasili. Watching the Big Men as they sat unmoving and unmoved in front of a rusty, wheelless vehicle that had been chocked up with driveshafts and a wooden mortar, I had a flashback to Gatwick Airport, when had I found myself with several hours to kill before my flight. The departure lounge had been almost deserted, though not far from where I was sitting a young businessman was talking on his mobile phone. As I listened to his conversation with diminishing interest, a woman started vacuum cleaning the walkway between us. As she drew near, I lifted my feet so she could reach under the seat. But when she moved on to where the man in the suit was talking on his mobile phone, he ignored her completely. It wasn't as if he could not see her; he simply did not want to acknowledge her. Nor, it appeared, did she expect anything of him. When he showed no sign of moving either his feet or his bag, the woman left the space around him as it was—littered with candy wrappers and used telephone cards. Trivial in itself, this incident had left me troubled. Not only did I want to know why certain people, as a matter of principle, will make absolutely no concession to those they consider their inferiors; it made me ask myself why I felt so acutely uncomfortable with status distinctions and sought, wherever possible, to avoid or nullify them. Recollecting this incident at Gatwick also reminded me of how awkward I sometimes felt at the hotel in Freetown, where I had lodged before traveling up-country. Where most people would readily accept being waited on—for after all, this is what waiters are paid to do—I felt embarrassed by the deferential or obsequious rigmarole, and could not abide having someone pour water into my glass, place a napkin over my lap, or call me sir. No one could be less suited for high office than myself. Indeed, so assiduous was my need to avoid the trappings of authority and privilege that I instinctively sought the margins and the shadows—the world of the underdog or the young.

I wandered away across the tamped, grease-and-oil-stained earth, past the decaying mud brick building that served as an office and the lean-tos under which old car seats, cylinder blocks, radiators, differentials, mufflers, and cannibalized engine parts had been stacked, to where I could sit alone, collect my thoughts, and scribble some notes. Then I strolled up the road to buy a bread roll and a tin of sardines from which to make a sandwich.

When I returned to the vehicle, S. B.'s nephew, who was known as Small S. B., explained that the brake fluid line to the rear wheels had been burned through by the broken muffler and needed to be replaced. The air filter also required cleaning. As one of the grease monkeys was dispatched into town to find a spare brake fluid line, food was brought for the Big Men—for the third time that day. But eating did not interrupt their critical commentary on the mechanics' efforts. "Why you no fix 'em before now?" the Alhaji asked testily. "Come on bo, le we go now," S. B. added, with a weariness that appeared to preclude any response. Dr. K. said nothing. He was too busy ordering one of the mechanic's boys to uncap two bottles of Heineken beer for him, as he tugged rubbery strands of meat from a boiled goat's head. "Kam eat," he said to me. When I explained I did not eat meat, he was incredulous. "Where do you get your protein?" he asked. "Where do you get your strength?"

"We Africans have tough stomachs," Fasili observed.

"It's not stomach," I said. "It's heart. I don't eat meat for health reasons."

When he had finished eating, Dr. K. removed his gray safari shirt and summoned a small boy to scratch his back. He was like a hippo, as dour as he was massive. And while he picked his teeth with a sliver of wood, the boy started to massage his enormous shoulders.

S. B. was being ear-bashed by two local men who had lost their businesses in the war.

Makeni, I knew, had been an RUF (Revolutionary United Front) stronghold. Even now there were billboards at the roundabouts in the center of the town with photos of Foday Sankoh and RUF political slogans.

Perhaps this was why S. B. showed so little sympathy for their plight. "No one went into exile here," he asserted. "You have only yourselves to blame for what happened here."

"We had nowhere to go," one of the Makeni men replied.

And then, as if to elicit my understanding, the second man described how well the RUF were organized. "They would send small boys to spy on prominent people," he said. "The kids would disguise themselves as cigarette sellers or petty traders. They would carry messages. We never knew who they were. They would get information about a place before they attacked it."

"You know," S. B said, half smiling, "one time the RUF entered a mosque and asked, 'Anyone here believe in God?' 'No, we don't,' everyone said. Even the imam. 'No, no,' he said, 'I do not believe!'"

The Makeni men both laughed.

"But seriously," S. B. said, "the SLPP [Sierra Leone People's Party] expects people to work for the country. Government is composed of people. You should not fear to speak the truth to your government. The government does not want to hurt you. As long as you are on the right side, you have nothing to fear."

As S. B. was talking, a truck had pulled in at the roadside. Intrigued by the slogan emblazoned on its side—"Fear Not the World but the People"—I walked over to the truck to see what it carried and was dismayed to find that twenty-five steers were crammed together in the back, their horns roped to wooden beams that were in turn lashed to a metal frame covering the vehicle's tray. The animals were unable to move. The flank of one had been so badly lacerated by the jolting of the truck over degraded roads that its hip bone was exposed. Like sardines in a can, they had been packed top to tail, in rows of five, to maximize space. Their muzzles were dry, foam flecked their mouths, their eyes were closed with pain and exhaustion, and their heads had been forced up over the rumps of the animals in front. From time to time an unbearable moan was released from the herd, and I was reminded instantly of the bobby calves I used to hear baying mournfully in the night when I was child, as they waited out the hours of darkness in a cramped railway wagon on a siding in my home town before going on to the slaughterhouse the next day.

The driver and his mate tilted the cab of the truck forward and began inspecting the engine, while a couple of other young men clambered up onto the back of truck and walked over the steers, checking the lashings.

"You should have bought your camera, Mr. Mike." It was Small S. B, who had sidled up to me unseen.

"I was thinking," I said, "that this is how Africans were once packed in the slave ships, head to foot, to save space."

But where I saw slaves, or imagined myself, Small S. B. saw only cows. And I did not feel inclined to share with him my ruminations on when, and under what circumstances, we might extend human rights to animals or, for that matter, deny these rights to our fellow human beings, treating them as if they were mere chattels or beasts. Yet it was suddenly very clear to me that my own notion of rights reflected the egalitarian ethos of the country in which I was raised. In tribal societies such as Kuranko, one's worth was ostensibly relative to one's patrimony, rank, and title, which is why, I guess, the Big Men always wore their status on their sleeves—honorable, doctor, paramount chief. In such a society, one's due was generally reckoned in terms of birth, not worth. A chief was due a retinue and tithes, not to mention praise and honor. A father was owed his children's respect. And a wife was duty bound to honor her husband and obey him without question. For the Kuranko, this calculus of social distinction was both categorical and unambiguous. People were superior to animals, firstborn were superior to secondborn, men were superior to women, adults were superior to children, the patriline was superior to the matriline, rulers were superior to commoners, and commoners were superior to praise singers, blacksmiths, and leather workers. At the bottom of the social scale, *finabas*—the bards and custodians of chiefly traditions—were superior to no one, except perhaps slaves. In practice, however, the worth of a person was far less fixed than this schema would suggest.

When Keti Ferenke explained this to me many years ago, he began by punning on the word *kina,* which, depending on a subtle difference in pronunciation, could mean either beehive or elder. His argument was that someone who is nominally elder could lose the right to be considered superior if he behaved unjustly or idiotically. A person could be an elder, a status superior, he said, but if he acted like a child he *was* a child. Superiority, he noted, derived not only from being born first or from being big and powerful; it also stemmed from the way one behaved. For Keti Ferenke, whose pride in his own intellectual adroitness was, at least in my company, undisguised, a person's true worth was defined by his or her social gumption, or *nous,* though other innate traits, such as temperament, bearing, and moral courage might also elevate a person beyond his given social position. Consider the myth of Saramba, for instance, a warrior chief of great renown, whose jealous half-brothers decided to waylay and murder him. When Saramba's humble *finaba,* Musa Kule, got wind of the plot, he devised a plan to save his master's life. After persuading the ruler to exchange clothes with him, Musa Kule rode the chief's horse ahead along the road where the ambush had been laid. As a result, Musa Kule was killed instead of the chief. In recognition of his sacrifice, Saramba declared that from that day hence their descendants should be considered equals, because the moral qualities of the lowborn *fina* had effectively eclipsed the status superiority of his master.

Subtle reciprocities are disclosed here: the relationship between respect paid and recognition returned, for example; or the implicit understanding that a chief will give his protection to those who submit to his authority and place themselves in his hands. But what if a chief or political leader turns into a tyrant—seizing people's property, taking advantage of his subjects, repaying tribute with obloquy? What if a husband abuses his dutiful and obedient wife? And should the young have regard for the ancestral order of things when it is evoked only to bolster the powers and prerogatives of an elite that is indifferent to their needs, contemptuous of their aspirations, and blind to their talents? For many young people in Sierra Leone, their patience with autocracy, traditional or modern, has worn thin. For them, their due was determined by need, and this is not delimited by their inferior station in life but by what they imagine might be theirs as citizens of the world. These questions, born of my Kuranko research, were, I realized, not unrelated to the RUF rebellion; but at that moment, as if to derail my train of thought, Small S. B. said that the 4Runner had been repaired and we could go on our way.

As I walked back to the 4Runner, I found the boss mechanic negotiating with S. B. for a little extra money. The mechanic's son was at his father's side. He was about the same age as my own son. As the father spoke to S. B., he cradled his son's head in his hand. Then he ran his hand over the boy's shoulders and back, pressing him to his side. And all the while, the boy was beaming with happiness.

NOTES

1. Ngugi Wa Thiong'o, *Dreams in a Time of War: A Childhood Memoir* (New York: Pantheon, 2010), 65.

2. David Howes speaks of this as "a crisis of intonation" and describes the "dwindling power" of traditional songs in the Trobriand Islands, where older people lament the passing of a "golden age of orality" when the measure of human greatness was the resounding quality of one's vocal presence. *Sensual Relations: Engaging the Senses in Culture and Social Theory* (Ann Arbor: University of Michigan Press, 2003), 64–67.

3. J. C. Carothers, "Culture, Psychiatry and the Written Word," *Psychiatry* 22 (Nov. 1959): 307–20; Jack Goody, ed., *Literacy in Traditional Societies* (Cambridge: Cambridge University Press, 1968); Marshall McLuhan, *The Gutenberg Galaxy* (London: Routledge and Kegan Paul, 1962); Walter J. Ong, *Orality and Literacy: The Technologizing of the Word* (London: Methuen, 1982); David Riesman, "The Oral and Written Traditions," in *Explorations in Communications,* ed. Edmund Carpenter and Marshall McLuhan (Boston: Beacon Press, 1960).

4. Walter Benjamin, "The Storyteller," in *Illuminations,* trans. Harry Zohn (New York: Schocken Books, 1968).

5. Plato, *Phaedrus,* trans. Christopher Rowe (Harmondsworth, UK: Penguin, 2005), 61–64, See also Jacques Derrida, "Plato's Pharmacy," in *Dissemination,* trans. Barbara Johnson (London: Athlone, 1981), 66–94.

6. "Each culture contains the negation of its manifest pattern and nuclear values, through a tacit affirmation of contrary latent patterns and marginal values. The complete real pattern of a culture is a product of a functional interplay between officially affirmed and officially negated patterns possessing mass." George Devereux, *From Anxiety to Method in the Behavioural Sciences* (The Hague: Mouton, 1967), 212.

7. Walter J. Ong, *Orality and Literacy* (New York: Routledge, 2002), 13, 5, 8.

8. Ibid., 8. This argument has also been made, eloquently and empirically, by William A. Graham in his study of the vocal and sensual character of scriptural texts; and he cites examples of how scripture is not only written but "recited, read aloud, chanted, sung, quoted in debate, memorized in childhood, meditated upon in murmur and full voice," its sacrality realized in the life of a vocal community. *Beyond the Written Word: Oral Aspects of Scripture in the History of Religion* (Cambridge: Cambridge University Press, 1987), ix, 7–8.

9. Jacques Derrida, *Margins of Philosophy,* trans. Alan Bass (Chicago: Chicago University Press, 1984), x–xii.

10. John Blacking argues that "the essential differences between music in one society and another may be social and not musical. If English music may seem to be more complex than Venda music and practiced by a smaller number of people, it is because

of the consequences of the division of labor in society, and not because the English are less musical or their music is cognitively more complex." *How Musical Is Man?* (Seattle: University of Washington Press, 1973), 102.

11. Oliver Sacks, *Musicophilia: Tales of Music and the Brain* (New York: Vintage, 2007), 232.

12. Seamus Heaney, *Field Work* (London: Faber and Faber, 1979), 11.

13. Oliver Sacks provides wonderful examples of musical synesthesia in which musical keys and chords are strongly associated with colors and tastes. "The Key of Clear Green: Synesthesia and Music," in Sacks, *Musicophilia,* ch. 14.

14. Cf. Jacques Derrida's comments on the textual metaphor of language. *Margins of Philosophy,* trans. Alan Bass (Chicago: University of Chicago Press, 1984), 160–61.

15. Derrida, *Margins of Philosophy,* 161.

16. John Dewey, *Experience and Nature* (New York: Dover, 1958), 7. More recently, Pierre Hadot has made a similar case for "philosophy as a way of life"—less a theoretical discourse than a "practice, an *askesis,* and a transformation of the self." *What Is Ancient Philosophy,* trans. Michael Chase (Cambridge, MA: Belknap Press of Harvard University Press, 2002), 275.

17. Ivan Illich, *Tools for Conviviality* (New York: Harper and Row, 1973).

18. Michael Jackson, *Minima Ethnographica: Intersubjectivity and the Anthropological Project* (Chicago: University of Chicago Press, 1998), 32–36.

19. Eugenio Montale, *The Second Life of Art: Selected Essays,* trans. Jonathan Galassi (New York: Ecco Press, 1982).

20. The term is no longer current in Portuguese, though it is a cognate with the French *se debrouiller,* meaning to fend for oneself, to get by in a murky situation in which one cannot see far ahead (*brouillard* = fog). Henrik Vigh, *Navigating Terrains of War: Youth and Soldiering in Guinea-Bissau* (New York: Berghahn, 2006), 128–30.

ABOUT THE CONTRIBUTORS

SUZANNE G. CUSICK, professor of music on the Faculty of Arts and Science at New York University and a recently elected honorary member of the American Musicological Society, has published extensively on gender and sexuality in relation to the musical cultures of early modern Italy and of contemporary North America. Her book *Francesca Caccini at the Medici Court: Music and the Circulation of Power* (University of Chicago Press, 2009) received the "Best Book" award for 2010 from the Society for the Study of Early Modern Women. More recently, she has studied the use of sound in the detention and interrogation of prisoners held during the twenty-first century's "war on terror," work for which she won the Philipp Brett Award of the American Musicological Society. She is currently working on a monograph that will explore gendered, eroticized, and politicized modes of hearing in Medicean Florence.

J. MARTIN DAUGHTRY is associate professor of ethnomusicology and sound studies at New York University. His work centers on acoustic violence, voice, listening, and musics of the Russian-speaking world. Daughtry is coeditor, with Jonathan Ritter, of *Music in the Post-9/11 World* (Routledge, 2007) and has published essays in *Social Text, Ethnomusicology, Music and Politics, Russian Literature, Poetics Today,* and a number of edited collections. His latest book, *The Amplitude of Violence: Sound, Music, Trauma, and Survival in Wartime Iraq* (Oxford University Press, 2015), won the Alan P. Merriam Prize awarded by the Society of Ethnomusicology.

KATHERINE JOHANNA HAGEDORN was professor of music and associate dean at Pomona College in Claremont, California, and published widely on Afro-Cuban ritual and folkloric music. Her book *Divine Utterances: The Performance of Afro-*

Cuban Santería (Smithsonian Books, 2001) won the Alan P. Merriam Prize for the best ethnography. Professor Hagedorn taught courses in the performance traditions of Latin America and the African diaspora, Roma performance, as well as ethnomusicology in theory and practice. In 2000, Professor Hagedorn was named California Professor of the Year by the Carnegie Foundation for the Advancement of Teaching. In 2002, Pomona College awarded her a Wig Teaching Award, and in 2005 she won a coveted Mellon New Directions Fellowship for her book project "Toward a Theology of Sound." Trained as a classical pianist, she performed Afro-Cuban, West African, and Indonesian percussive traditions for more than twenty years. A former member of the board of directors of the national Society for Ethnomusicology, Dr. Hagedorn taught at Pomona College from 1993 until her untimely death in 2013.

TOMIE HAHN is an artist and ethnomusicologist. She is a performer of *shakuhachi* (Japanese bamboo flute), *nihon buyo* (Japanese traditional dance), and experimental performance. Tomie's research spans a wide range of area studies and topics, including Japanese traditional performing arts; Deep Listening; monster truck rallies; issues of display, the senses, and transmission; and relationships of technology and culture. Her book *Sensational Knowledge: Embodying Culture through Japanese Dance* (Wesleyan University Press, 2007) was awarded the Alan P. Merriam Prize from the Society for Ethnomusicology for the most distinguished, published English-language monograph in the field of ethnomusicology. She is associate professor in the Department of the Arts and director of the Center for Deep Listening at Rensselaer Polytechnic Institute in Troy, New York.

DAVID HENDERSON began doing fieldwork in Nepal in 1987. He teaches music, film, and Asian Studies at St. Lawrence University in Canton, New York, where he is associate professor and chair of the Department of Music. His work appears in the collections *Global Pop, Local Language* (University of Mississippi Press, 2003), and *Theorizing the Local: Music, Practice, and Experience in South Asia and Beyond* (Oxford University Press, 2009), as well as in the journals *Ethnomusicology*, *Asian Music*, *Popular Music and Society*, and *World Literature Today.* He is coeditor, with Ron Emoff, of *Mementos, Artifacts, and Hallucinations from the Ethnographer's Tent* (Routledge, 2002).

MICHAEL JACKSON is internationally renowned for his work in the field of existential anthropology. He is a leading figure in contemporary philosophical anthropology and widely praised for his innovations in ethnographic writing. In New Zealand, he is best known for his poetry and creative nonfiction (*Latitudes of Exile* (Dunedin: McIndoe, 1976) was awarded the Commonwealth Poetry Prize in 1976, and *Wall* (Dunedin: McIndoe, 1980) won the New Zealand Book Award for poetry in 1981). Michael Jackson has done extensive fieldwork in Sierra Leone since 1969, and has carried out anthropological research in Aboriginal Australia, Europe, and New Zealand. He has taught in universities in New Zealand, Australia, the United States (where he was professor of anthropology at Indiana University, Bloomington, from 1988 to 1996), Denmark (as professor of anthropology at the University of Copenhagen), and at Harvard Divinity School, where he is currently distinguished professor of world religions. His most recent books include *Being of Two Minds, Road Markings: An Anthropologist in the Antipodes* (Dunedin: Rosa Mira Books, 2012), *The Other Shore: Essays on Writers and Writings* (Berkeley: University of California Press, 2013), and *Lifeworlds: Essays in Existential Anthropology* (Chicago: University of Chicago Press, 2013). His memoir, *The Accidental Anthropologist* (Dunedin: Longacre), was published to critical acclaim in 2006.

DEBORAH KAPCHAN is associate professor of Performance Studies at New York University. A Guggenheim fellow, she is the author of *Gender on the Market: Moroccan Women and the Revoicing of Tradition* (University of Pennsylvania Press, 1996), *Traveling Spirit Masters: Moroccan Music and Trance in the Global Marketplace* (Wesleyan University Press, 2007), as well as numerous articles on sound, narrative, and poetics. She is translating and editing a volume entitled *Poetic Justice: An Anthology of Moroccan Contemporary Poetry,* and is the editor of and contributor to *Cultural Heritage in Transit: Cultural Rights as Human Rights* (University of Pennsylvania Press, 2014).

MICHELLE KISLIUK, associate professor of music at the University of Virginia, received a doctorate in Performance Studies from New York University. Integrating performance theory, ethnography, and practice, since 1986 she has researched the music, dance, daily life, and cultural politics of forest people (BaAka) in the Central African Republic and has published on urban music and dance in the capital city, Bangui. Her work extends as well to the socioaesthetics of jam sessions at bluegrass festivals in the United States. Her essays have appeared in collections including *Shadows in the Field: New Perspectives for Fieldwork in Ethnomusicology* (Oxford University Press, 2008), *Teaching Performance Studies*

(University of Southern Illinois Press, 2002), *Performing Ethnomusicology* (University of California Press, 2004), and *Music and Gender* (University of Illinois Press, 2000). Her book *Seize the Dance! BaAka Musical Life and the Ethnography of Performance* (Oxford University Press, 1998) won the ASCAP Deems Taylor Special Recognition Award. She has been a Mellon postdoctoral fellow and a Laura Boulton senior fellow in ethnomusicology. Her current book project is a collection of theoretical essays and case studies that address performance theory and ethnography. Along with her academic teaching in "Music in Everyday Life" and "Field Research and Ethnography of Performance," she directs the University of Virginia African Music and Dance Ensemble.

CAROL MULLER is a professor of music (ethnomusicology), who has published widely on South African music, both at home and in exile. Her intellectual interests include the relationship between music, gender, and religious studies; migration and diaspora studies; and critical ethnography. Her publications include *Musical Echoes: South African Women Thinking in Jazz,* with Sathima Bea Benjamin (Duke University Press, 2011); *Shembe Hymns* (University of KwaZulu–Natal, 2010); *Focus: South African Music* (Routledge, 2008); and *Rituals of Fertility and the Sacrifice of Desire: Nazarite Women's Performance in South Africa* (University of Chicago Press, 1999). Muller has published on South African jazz and religious performance, as well as traditional and popular musics in a variety of journals that represent her interdisciplinary interests.

ANA PAIS holds a doctorate in theater studies, a master's degree in contemporary dramaturgies, and a bachelor of arts in literature from the University of Lisbon. She is currently working on revising her dissertation, entitled "Commotion: Affective Rhythms in the Theatrical Event," for publication. From 2011 to 2012, she was a visiting scholar at the Performance Studies Department, Tisch School of the Arts, New York University, and before that a visiting scholar at Departamento de Comunicação e Artes do Corpo, PUC–São Paulo. She has worked as a theater critic for the most distinguished Portuguese newspapers (*Público, Expresso,* and *Sol*) and has collaborated as a dramaturge and assistant director in both theater and dance projects in Portugal. She is the author of a study on dramaturgy entitled *Discourse of Complicité: Contemporary Dramaturgies* (Colibri, 2004), as well as several articles in national and international journals. From 2005 to 2010, she was assistant professor at the Escola Superior de Teatro e Cinema, and in

2009 was guest assistant professor at the University of Évora. Since 2003, she has been curating discursive practices talks, residencies, and events in theaters and cultural institutions in Portugal. Presently, she is an FCT postdoctoral fellow at CET (Centro de Estudos de Teatro da Universidade de Lisboa/McGill University).

ANNE K. RASMUSSEN is professor of music and ethnomusicology and the Bickers Professor of Middle Eastern Studies at the College of William and Mary, where she also directs the Middle Eastern Music Ensemble. Rasmussen's research interests include music of the Arab and Islamicate world; music and multiculturalism in the United States; music patronage and politics; and issues of orientalism, nationalism, and gender in music, fieldwork, music performance, and the ethnographic method. She is author of *Women, the Recited Qur'an and Islamic Music in Indonesia* (University of California Press, 2010); coeditor with David Harnish of *Divine Inspirations: Music and Islam in Indonesia* (Oxford, 2011), coeditor with Kip Lornell of *The Music of Multicultural America* ([Schirmer, 1997] University Press of Mississippi, 2015), and editor of a special issue of the journal *The World of Music* on "The Music of Oman" (2012). Rasmussen's interest in the Gulf region has been enhanced by her fieldwork, beginning in 2010–2011, in the Sultanate of Oman, when she was Sultan Qaboos Cultural Center Research Fellow. Rasmussen is president of the Society for Ethnomusicology (2015–2017).

ALEX WATERMAN is a composer, cellist, and scholar based in New York. He received his PhD in musicology from New York University. Together with Will Holder, he wrote and edited *Robert Ashley: Yes, But Is It Edible?* (New Documents, 2014). Waterman was an artist in the 2014 Whitney Biennial, where he built a television studio and installation space inside the museum in order to produce three operas by Robert Ashley. He has taught at Bard College (MFA program), New York University, Bloomfield College, and the Banff Centre for the Arts, and is visiting assistant professor of music at Wesleyan University in 2015–2016. His writings appear in *Dot Dot Dot, Artforum, Brooklyn Rail, BOMB,* and *The Third Rail.*

DEBORAH WONG is professor of music at the University of California, Riverside. She specializes in the musics of Asian America and Thailand and has written two books, *Speak It Louder: Asian Americans Making Music* (Routledge, 2004) and *Sounding the Center: History and Aesthetics in Thai Buddhist Ritual* (University of Chicago Press, 2001). She is a past president of the Society for Ethnomusicology and currently sits on the advisory council for the Smithsonian Institution's Center for Folklife and Cultural Heritage. She is a series editor for Wesleyan University Press's Music/Culture series and also serves on the editorial committee for the University of California Press. Her interests focus on sound, noise, and minoritarian location.

INDEX

MUSIC / CULTURE

A series from Wesleyan University Press
Edited by Deborah Wong, Sherrie Tucker, and Jeremy Wallach
Originating editors: George Lipsitz, Susan McClary, and Robert Walser

Frances Aparicio
Listening to Salsa: Gender, Latin Popular Music, and Puerto Rican Cultures

Paul Austerlitz
Jazz Consciousness: Music, Race, and Humanity

Harris M. Berger
Metal, Rock, and Jazz: Perception and the Phenomenology of Musical Experience

Harris M. Berger
Stance: Ideas about Emotion, Style, and Meaning for the Study of Expressive Culture

Harris M. Berger and Giovanna P. Del Negro
Identity and Everyday Life: Essays in the Study of Folklore, Music, and Popular Culture

Franya J. Berkman
Monument Eternal: The Music of Alice Coltrane

Dick Blau, Angeliki Vellou Keil and Charles Keil
Bright Balkan Morning: Romani Lives and the Power of Music in Greek Macedonia

Susan Boynton and Roe-Min Kok, editors
Musical Childhoods and the Cultures of Youth

James Buhler, Caryl Flinn and David Neumeyer, editors
Music and Cinema

Thomas Burkhalter, Kay Dickinson, and Benjamin J. Harbert, editors
The Arab Avant-Garde: Music, Politics, Modernity

Patrick Burkart
Music and Cyberliberties

Julia Byl
Antiphonal Histories: Resonant Pasts in the Toba Batak Musical Present

Daniel Cavicchi
Listening and Longing: Music Lovers in the Age of Barnum

Susan D. Crafts, Daniel Cavicchi, Charles Keil, and the Music in Daily Life Project
My Music: Explorations of Music in Daily Life

Jim Cullen
Born in the USA: Bruce Springsteen and the American Tradition

Anne Danielsen
Presence and Pleasure: The Funk Grooves of James Brown and Parliament

Peter Doyle
Echo and Reverb: Fabricating Space in Popular Music Recording, 1900–1960

Ron Emoff
Recollecting from the Past: Musical Practice and Spirit Possession on the East Coast of Madagascar

Yayoi Uno Everett and Frederick Lau, editors
Locating East Asia in Western Art Music

Susan Fast and Kip Pegley, editors
Music, Politics, and Violence

Heidi Feldman
Black Rhythms of Peru: Reviving African Musical Heritage in the Black Pacific

Kai Fikentscher
"You Better Work!" Underground Dance Music in New York City

Ruth Finnegan
The Hidden Musicians: Music-Making in an English Town

Daniel Fischlin and Ajay Heble, editors
The Other Side of Nowhere: Jazz, Improvisation, and Communities in Dialogue

Wendy Fonarow
Empire of Dirt: The Aesthetics and Rituals of British "Indie" Music

Murray Forman
The 'Hood Comes First: Race, Space, and Place in Rap and Hip-Hop

Lisa Gilman
My Music, My War: The Listening Habits of U.S. Troops in Iraq and Afghanistan

Paul D. Greene and Thomas Porcello, editors
Wired for Sound: Engineering and Technologies in Sonic Cultures

Tomie Hahn
Sensational Knowledge: Embodying Culture Through Japanese Dance

Edward Herbst
Voices in Bali: Energies and Perceptions in Vocal Music and Dance Theater

Deborah Kapchan
Traveling Spirit Masters: Moroccan Gnawa Trance and Music in the Global Marketplace

Deborah Kapchan, editor
Theorizing Sound Writing

Raymond Knapp
Symphonic Metamorphoses: Subjectivity and Alienation in Mahler's Re-Cycled Songs

Laura Lohman
Umm Kulthūm: Artistic Agency and the Shaping of an Arab Legend, 1967–2007

Preston Love
A Thousand Honey Creeks Later: My Life in Music from Basie to Motown—and Beyond

René T.A. Lysloff and Leslie C. Gay Jr., editors
Music and Technoculture

Allan Marett
Songs, Dreamings, and Ghosts: The Wangga of North Australia

Ian Maxwell
Phat Beats, Dope Rhymes: Hip Hop Down Under Comin' Upper

Kristin A. McGee
Some Liked It Hot: Jazz Women in Film and Television, 1928–1959

Rebecca S. Miller
Carriacou String Band Serenade: Performing Identity in the Eastern Caribbean

Tony Mitchell, editor
Global Noise: Rap and Hip-Hop Outside the USA

Keith Negus
Popular Music in Theory: An Introduction

Johnny Otis
Upside Your Head!: Rhythm and Blues on Central Avenue

Kip Pegley
Coming to You Wherever You Are: MuchMusic, MTV, and Youth Identities

Jonathan Pieslak
Radicalism and Music: An Introduction to the Music Cultures of al-Qa'ida, Racist Skinheads, Christian-Affiliated Radicals, and Eco-Animal Rights Militants

Matthew Rahaim
Musicking Bodies: Gesture and Voice in Hindustani Music

John Richardson
Singing Archaeology: Philip Glass's Akhnaten

Tricia Rose
Black Noise: Rap Music and Black Culture in Contemporary America

Nichole Rustin-Paschal
The Kind of Man I Am: Jazzmasculinity and the World of Charles Mingus Jr.

David Rothenberg and Marta Ulvaeus, editors
The Book of Music and Nature: An Anthology of Sounds, Words, Thoughts

Marta Elena Savigliano
Angora Matta: Fatal Acts of North-South Translation

Joseph G. Schloss
Making Beats: The Art of Sample-Based Hip-Hop

Barry Shank
Dissonant Identities: The Rock 'n' Roll Scene in Austin, Texas

Jonathan Holt Shannon
Among the Jasmine Trees: Music and Modernity in Contemporary Syria

Daniel B. Sharp
Between Nostalgia and Apocalypse: Popular Music and the Staging of Brazil

Helena Simonett
Banda: Mexican Musical Life across Borders

Mark Slobin
Subcultural Sounds: Micromusics of the West

Mark Slobin, editor
Global Soundtracks: Worlds of Film Music

Christopher Small
The Christopher Small Reader

Christopher Small
Music of the Common Tongue: Survival and Celebration in African American Music

Christopher Small
Music, Society, Education

Christopher Small
Musicking: The Meanings of Performing and Listening

Regina M. Sweeney
Singing Our Way to Victory: French Cultural Politics and Music During the Great War

Colin Symes
Setting the Record Straight: A Material History of Classical Recording

Steven Taylor
False Prophet: Fieldnotes from the Punk Underground

Paul Théberge
Any Sound You Can Imagine: Making Music/Consuming Technology

Sarah Thornton
Club Cultures: Music, Media and Sub-cultural Capital

Michael E. Veal
Dub: Songscape and Shattered Songs in Jamaican Reggae

Michael E. Veal and E. Tammy Kim, editors
Punk Ethnography: The Sublime Frequencies Companion

Robert Walser
Running with the Devil: Power, Gender, and Madness in Heavy Metal Music

Dennis Waring
Manufacturing the Muse: Estey Organs and Consumer Culture in Victorian America

Lise A. Waxer
The City of Musical Memory: Salsa, Record Grooves, and Popular Culture in Cali, Colombia

Mina Yang
Planet Beethoven: Classical Music at the Turn of the Millennium